The Countryside in the Age of the Modern State

The Countryside in the Age of the Modern State

Political Histories of Rural America

Edited by
CATHERINE McNICOL STOCK
and
ROBERT D. JOHNSTON

CORNELL UNIVERSITY PRESS

Ithaca and London

First published 2001 by Cornell University Press
First printing, Cornell Paperbacks, 2001

Printed in the United States of America

Library of Congress Cataloging-in-Publication data

The countryside in the age of the modern state : political histories of rural America / edited by Catherine McNicol Stock and Robert D. Johnston.
     p.cm.
     Includes bibliographical references and index.
     ISBN 0-8014-3850-0 (cloth : alk. paper)—ISBN 0-8014-8771-4 (pbk. : alk. paper)
     1. United States—Rural conditions.   2. Agricultural laborers—United States—History.   3. Populism—United States—History.   I. Stock, Catherine McNicol.   II. Johnston, Robert D.

     HN57 .C69 2001
     307.72'0973—dc21   2001003485

Cloth printing   10   9   8   7   6   5   4   3   2   1
Paperback printing   10   9   8   7   6   5   4   3   2   1

For our own rural families:
four generations of townsfolk in the Dakotas and
four generations of farmers in Pine Grove, Oregon

Contents

Foreword

James C. Scott

If, as I assume, you are looking for farmers in this volume, you are unlikely to find narratives and analyses that will remind you much of Grant Wood, Thomas Hart Benton, Carl Sandburg, or Hamlin Garland. There are, of course, farmers galore between these covers and, for that matter, farmers who seem to match the stereotypical white, Anglo-Saxon, midwestern, grain-farming nuclear family. But as with most stereotypes, while they actually do exist, they tend to occlude one's view of a far more diverse, unruly, and interesting rural population. It is especially these populations and their resolute failure to play their assigned role of invisibility or conformity in the standard narrative that have caught the attention of the contributors to this volume.

Thus we encounter Native Americans and their white Populist allies fighting the allotment that stripped away much of their common-property land; smallholding African American farmers in Texas politically organizing against crop liens and barriers to credit; small farmers in California persisting and thriving amidst corporate agriculture; rural southerners taking over a program of birth control that had partly eugenic intentions and putting it to their own gendered purposes; Caribbean and Mexican farmworkers struggling to organize and shape their work, their compensation, and the legislation governing their lives; Appalachian mountaineers resisting the resettlement policies of the liberal welfare state; and Amish women going their own unique way and, occasionally, attracting the admiration of federal policymakers.

On this basis alone, *The Countryside in the Age of the Modern State* goes a long way toward redressing a "central tendency" predilection in rural history, a tendency that fails to see how the enormous variety of agrarian experience in America has shaped cities, public policy, and state formation. Agrarian radicalism, by the same token, has taken many forms, some of which have, contrary to our image of the angry and reflexively antistatist farmer, provoked the creation and shaping of national institutions.

This book, however, has even larger purposes, as I see it, than rewriting revisionist histories and enlarging our sense of populism—those of doing justice to the breadth and diversity of rural history, and of making it abundantly clear that state-making in America can only be understood in the context of agrarian struggles.

One bright thread that holds the fine individual pieces together and makes of this book more than the sum of its parts is what might be called "an argument against flatness." The "flatness" in question can be a monotonic historical or political narrative on the one hand or a "real-project-in-the-world" on the other. Take, for example, the International Monetary Fund or the World Trade Organization: each a real project in the world if there ever was one. Their job is the production of flatness, uniformity, synchronization, standardization. Their utopian project in the world, one that cannot in the nature of things be realized, is to fashion an international economy in which each political jurisdiction—or country—will have the same legal code, the same business regulations, the same intellectual property rights, political institutions, bureaucratic apparatuses, and will permit and encourage the free flow of capital and goods (but not people!) across borders. To the degree they succeed, it will not make much difference where a businessman or woman wakes up; the business will follow more or less the same drill and, given the hegemony of English, perhaps be conducted in the same language as well. The demonstrations in Seattle against the WTO, invoked by the editors in the volume's introduction, were, to a considerable extent, a forceful argument against this flatness and its consequences for people and their environments.

In an analogous fashion, the aggregate effect of these essays is a powerful argument against flatness in American agrarian history. There is no stock Populist movement here, no stock account of the triumph of industrialism and the disappearance of agriculturalists, no normative family farm, no simplified account of interest group politics and the triumph of corporate farming, no easy narrative of how the Department of Agriculture is always promoting large industrial farms.

Instead, what the authors and editors have offered us is a subtle, detailed, and carefully positioned analysis of agrarian change that is always conscious of existing interpretations and always reminding us that they will not do. *The Countryside in the Age of the Modern State* recovers a larger and more contingent past, a present that is less cut-and-dried and more alive with possibilities, and, hence, a future that is, in part, ours and that of our fellow citizens to remake in their own image.

Acknowledgments

The editors owe their greatest debt of thanks for the quality of the volume to its contributors. Rather than working in isolation, each with a single editor, the essayists created a unique and very real scholarly collaborative. They collectively read several drafts of the volume, commented on all aspects of it, and helped revise each other's work by communicating directly with one another. This process created a meaningful scholarly community for all participants and greatly enriched and deepened the quality of the volume as a whole. The contributors were also more than patient with their editors' quirks, delays, and misunderstandings. This anthology is much greater than the sum of its parts, thanks entirely to the quality of mind and spirit shown by its talented essayists.

The volume also benefited from the suggestions, criticisms, and recommendations of senior scholars in rural history, including Edward Ayers, Hal Barron, David Danbom, Pete Daniel, Tom Dublin, John Mack Faragher, Glenda Gilmore, Steven Hahn, David Oshinsky, Nancy Grey Osterud, Jonathan Prude, and James Scott. Valuable comments were also provided by Jeanette Keith and Frieda Knobloch. Parts of the volume were presented at two conferences—the annual meeting of the Western History Association in Portland, Oregon, in October 1999 and the annual meeting of the Organization of American Historians in St. Louis, Missouri, in April 2000— as well as at a meeting of Yale University's Agrarian Studies Program. Individual essays and the volume as a whole benefited from the insights of panel participants and audience members at all three events.

The editors and staff at Cornell University Press showed both enthusiasm and fortitude in the task of shepherding the volume toward publication.

Initially, Peter Agree encouraged the editors to go through with a project that they had long considered but not yet undertaken. Along the way the comments of the anonymous reader commissioned by Cornell helped the editors bring a group of diverse essays into a coherent whole. In the end Roger Haydon saw to it that the "book in a box" became a book on the shelf, and Teresa Jesionowski and Gavin Lewis provided superb production and copyediting work. For this we are truly grateful.

Funding for much of this collaborative work was provided by the Provost and Dean of the Faculty at Connecticut College, and by the R. F. Johnson Faculty Development Fund at Connecticut College. Special thanks to Molly Battistelli for her work on all aspects of the project, particularly for coordinating the contributors' conference on December 7, 1999. We are also thankful for the assistance of Regina Foster at Connecticut College, Essie Lucky-Barros at Yale University, and Conor M. Reardon.

Finally, all the authors of the volume would like to thank their families. Writing takes much time away from family activities, of which there is precious little in twenty-first-century America to begin with. All told, the fifteen members of the writing group are the parents of twenty-two children, an astounding thirteen of whom are under six years old. There is no doubt that the care of children is more important than any other work and we recognize this even more in the light of the tragic death of Rachel Anne Gaschott Ritchie, the daughter of agrarian activists Mark Ritchie and Nancy Gaschott. We want to acknowledge and thank those children for their love and all of our partners for their willingness to care for them so well when we could not—above all Peter Lefeber and Anne Johnston.

C. M. S.

R. D. J.

The Countryside in the Age of the Modern State

Introduction

CATHERINE McNICOL STOCK
AND ROBERT D. JOHNSTON

For most of the 1990s, the great debate that framed the Cold War world—the role of the modern state in regulating economic, social, and political culture—appeared to be over. Globalization, privatization, and free trade were no longer buzzwords of a hopeful future, but resolute realities upon which the prosperity of the present depended. If large-scale alternatives in the East—Marxism, Leninism, Maoism—were discredited, so were most small-scale ones in the West. Environmentalists, labor unionists, feminists, and other activists were portrayed as extremists, kooks, cranks, sixties throwbacks, or card-carrying liberals. The defeat of communism and the triumph of global capital in the form of multinational corporations like Microsoft, Nike, and Archer Daniels Midland proved not only that history was over, but that so too was the power and relevance of the modern state.

Even in the most remote corners of the world—and certainly in the rural communities of the United States—the consensus that less government was better government seemed to have triumphed. The 1996 "Freedom to Farm Act," for example, which was supported by many Farm Belt politicians and farm organizations, promised farmers the "right" to pursue economic gain unfettered, without the farm subsidies—and the attendant red tape—that had arguably been the most essential part of federal agricultural policy since the New Deal. Likewise the Immigration Reform Act of 1986 increased government oversight of immigration in all economic areas except two of the most important to the rural economy—traditional migrant farm laborers and the new temporary workers allowed to fill in labor shortages in huge southern and midwestern hog- and poultry-breeding facilities. In nonagricultural rural areas, the government was also farther from view than it had been for decades. Few new building regulations hindered the vast development of the Sunbelt and Rocky Mountain states, where in the 1990s the population grew by more than 20 percent. Relatively laissez-faire policies meant that housing, recreational facilities, and tourist destinations came to dot a landscape that had recently been desert, mountaintop, and fragile grassland.

Moreover, rural people seemed not just to disdain the government, its programs, regulations, and representatives, but actually to despise them. The best-known rural Americans of the 1990s were militiamen, Freemen, survivalists, members of the Posse Comitatus and the Aryan Nation, and assorted bombers of federal facilities, abortion clinics, and high-technology corporations. Of course, rural folks who advocated violence against the government were the exception rather than the rule in every community. Nevertheless, even more family-friendly rural folks like Juanita and Darrell Buschkoetter of the unexpectedly popular 1998 PBS documentary, "The Farmer's Wife," did not appear to embrace an activist politics that engages the democratic state. As this couple struggled (on camera) to save their Nebraska farm from bankruptcy and their marriage from divorce, they instead sought private therapies of counseling, education, and religious faith. No liberal farm organizations, no federal farm programs, no marches, rallies, concerts, or strikes made public the family's private agonies. Privatization, it seemed, had conquered the hearts as well as the minds of rural men and women.[1]

And then—at the very end of the twentieth century—came an opportunity for people around the world to think again about the role of the state in their own and their nations' futures. In December 1999, the World Trade Organization (WTO), the Geneva-based multinational association that regulates trade and promotes economic growth, held a week-long meeting in Seattle. For eighteen months prior to the meeting, activist groups prepared for protests and tried to spread their view that what was essentially a private association of corporate executives with only a veneer of public accountability had no business determining important national and international policy. The confrontation that ensued shocked millions out of the complacency that prosperity had engendered. While police outfitted in riot gear shot tear gas, pepper spray and rubber pellets at protesters, the meeting's activities ground to a halt. At a time when Americans were said to hate politics, the "battle in Seattle" opened a distinctly public debate about the future of citizenship in the global village. If the alternative was an economy run by unelected rich elites, "several removes from

[1] Ironically, despite the almost complete neglect of politics in the six-hour series, one learns on "The Farmer's Wife" Web site that the Buschkoetters have become involved in a number of agrarian causes, ranging from Farm Aid to the Nebraska Farmers' Union. See www.pbs.org/wgbh/pages/frontline/shows/farmerswife/letters/.

popular sovereignty," then active engagement with the democratic state might be worth pursuing after all.[2]

Rural people were among the leaders of this new movement to reconsider and reconceptualize the role of the state in world affairs. Indeed, rural folk from the United States and elsewhere went to Seattle—and then to other protests in Washington, D.C., and at the summer's presidential nominating conventions in Philadelphia and Los Angeles—to make it clear that a fully globalized, privatized, and politics-free rural trade zone was not what they envisioned for their children's futures. To do so, they built alliances with unlikely partners—including environmentalists and labor activists—to protest the WTO's plan to remove government funding from agriculture worldwide. According to the WTO, government subsidies of small-scale farming substantially raise the cost of living for consumers. The expense of subsidizing just dairy cows, proclaimed the organization, would pay for those same cows—41 million of them—to fly first class around the world. But, according to WTO critics, the ending of farm subsidies worldwide would bring about the final industrialization of the countryside, the end of regional agricultural diversity, and the unrestrained development of genetically engineered foods. Most of all, by pitting farmers from one country against those from other countries, it would assure that all farmers would receive the lowest possible price for their crops—prices that would make the crisis prices of the last three years of the twentieth century seem generous by comparison.[3]

It is fortunate that we have the protests in Seattle and elsewhere, if only to remind us of the complex, very public, and strikingly political relationship between rural people and the modern state in the twentieth century. It is less fortunate that most historians have failed to recognize this connection between the countryside and the state. For many years rural history, like rural people themselves, was largely invisible, written as a subdivision of something else—colonial history, frontier history, or southern history, for example—or devoted merely to "demonstrat[ing] the transcendent worth of country life." Especially since 1985, with the publication of *The Countryside in the Age of Capitalist Transformation,* new rural historians have proven that rural history is an important field of its own, in part because, as the editors of that volume put it, rural people themselves have "shaped American history" in "complex and powerful ways" not fully appreciated by historians. In particular, the new rural historians have shown that the countryside served as a staging ground for the industrialization of American economic life which eventually transformed all of American society. They have also taught us about, among other subjects,

[2] Robert Kuttner, "The End of Citizenship?" *American Prospect* 11 (December 1999): 99.
[3] For the cost of cows, see http://www.wto.org/wto/10ben/10ben04.htm; for a reprise of WTO criticism, see Kuttner, "End of Citizenship."

the communal exchanges that constituted a distinctive agrarian moral economy, as well as the gendered division of labor in nineteenth-century farms that often served to empower women.[4]

Most new rural historians, however, leave off the story of the country-side at the close of the 1800s. By the beginning of the twentieth century, they implicitly ask us to believe, the story of industrialization was complete, and from then on, rural folks increasingly lost the power to influence and shape social, cultural, and economic change. After the defeat of the Populist party in 1896 and the ascent of urban culture in the United States, the particulars of country life became increasingly irrelevant—an exotic backdrop, perhaps, to the main story of modern America. This has meant that developments in American history in our time that had been critical, indeed transformative, episodes in the countryside—including the Great Depression, the civil rights movement, and the modern labor movement, among others—have been by and large left to urban and social historians. Without the attention of focused scholarship in rural history, rural people and their stories have moved, as one prominent historian has put it, "from majority, to minority, to curiosity."[5]

This volume seeks to begin where much of the work of the new rural historians has ended, thus continuing the process of revitalizing the history of rural America. However urban the nation has become, twenty percent of its citizens still live outside major metropolitan areas. Moreover, rural economic activity—agricultural, extractive, recreational, and industrial—has a significant impact on the nation's overall economic well-being. And the stories of contemporary rural people—whether told in film, fiction, journalism, or popular music—still have the power to move us. They do at least in part because they reflect the values, dreams, and ideals at the core of the economically, racially, and ethnically diverse American experience. Today one typical American rural family may be the Buschkoetters,

[4] Steven Hahn and Jonathan Prude, eds., *The Countryside in the Age of Capitalist Transformation: Essays in the Social History of Rural America* (Chapel Hill: University of North Carolina Press, 1985), 7, 17. Other examples of important scholarship in the new rural history, with its strong anchoring in social history, include: Christopher Clark, *The Roots of Rural Capitalism: Western Massachusetts, 1780–1860* (Ithaca: Cornell University Press, 1990); Allan Kulikoff, *The Agrarian Origins of American Capitalism* (Charlottesville: University of Virginia Press, 1992); John Mack Faragher, *Sugar Creek: Life on the Illinois Prairie* (New Haven, Conn.: Yale University Press, 1986); Nancy Grey Osterud, *Bonds of Community: The Lives of Farm Women in Nineteenth-Century New York* (Ithaca: Cornell University Press, 1991); and for work that brings these concerns into the twentieth century, Mary Neth, *Preserving the Family Farm: Women, Community, and the Foundations of Agribusiness in the Midwest, 1900–1940* (Baltimore: Johns Hopkins University Press, 1995); Deborah Fink, *Agrarian Women: Wives and Mothers in Rural Nebraska, 1880–1940* (Chapel Hill; University of North Carolina Press, 1992); and Hal S. Barron, *Mixed Harvest: The Second Great Transformation in the Rural North, 1870–1930* (Chapel Hill: University of North Carolina Press, 1997). For an important overview, see David B. Danbom, *Born in the Country: A History of Rural America* (Baltimore: Johns Hopkins University Press, 1995).

[5] Danbom, *Born in the Country*, 266.

indebted but would-be independent landowners in Nebraska. But another may live in a trailer park and commute an hour to clean condominiums at an expensive Colorado ski resort, while another may live on an Indian reservation in Oklahoma or in a migrant workers' camp in Florida. Rich, diverse, complex, and still central to American life after all: this is the story of the countryside in the twentieth century.[6]

This anthology also consciously adds a critical element to the story of rural America that the new rural historians, the national media, most popular writers, filmmakers, and songwriters have left out, but that the protests in Seattle remind us still remains. If the transformation of the economy was the central and defining feature of rural life in the eighteenth and nineteenth centuries, the transformation of the state played that central role in the twentieth. Beginning in the mid- to late nineteenth century and lasting until the recent postliberal dismantling began, rural America served as one of the most important locations for the construction of the modern American state. Nowhere else in the United States did people experience the power and control of the modern, centralized state as early or as directly as did people in the countryside. We have come to know that this was particularly true in the trans-Mississippi West, where rural people encountered the United States Army, the Bureau of Land Management, the Bureau of Indian Affairs, the Fish and Wildlife Service, and other agencies devoted to the development of public lands. But in settled areas as well—in the Jeffersonian Midwest, the plantation South, the uplands of Appalachia, and increasingly industrialized New England—agencies of the Department of Agriculture, the Internal Revenue Service, and the Department of Interior (along with multiple governmental units at the state and local levels) worked to bring supposedly backward people and regions into the heart of the modern bureaucratic complex of power relations.[7]

However much the countryside served as a "kindergarten for the American state," in historian Richard White's phrase, country people rarely behaved like timid children on their first day of school. Instead they took

---

[6] For the continued fascination with American rural culture see, for example, the twin revivals of agrarianism and anti-agrarianism as best symbolized in the work of Wendell Berry and Jane Smiley. For an introduction to the prolific Berry, see *The Unsettling of America: Culture and Agriculture,* 3rd ed. (San Francisco: Sierra Club Books, 1996); Jane Smiley, *A Thousand Acres* (New York: Knopf, 1991).

[7] For the valuable insistence of new western historians on the importance of the federal government, see Richard White, *"It's Your Misfortune and None of My Own": A New History of the American West* (Norman: University of Oklahoma Press, 1991), especially 57–59, and Patricia Nelson Limerick, *The Legacy of Conquest: The Unbroken History of the American West* (New York: Norton, 1987); for critiques see Robert D. Johnston, "Beyond 'The West': Regionalism, Liberalism, and the Evasion of Politics in the New Western History," *Rethinking History* 2 (summer 1998): 239–77, and Karen R. Merrill, "In Search of the 'Federal Presence' in the American West," *Western Historical Quarterly* 30 (winter 1999): 449–73.

active roles both in resisting and in constructing the state and the role of its agencies in their lives. On the one hand, rural folks have a long and hallowed tradition of staging protests against the power of the state, whether through resistance to taxation, farm strikes, or explicitly antigovernment organizations. On the other hand, citizens of the countryside have worked with and for the state, inviting extension agents into their homes, seeking the intervention of high-level federal authorities in the workings of the market, creating farmer-labor political parties, and designing policy in times of rural crisis. The dual nature of the relationship between rural Americans and the state is, in fact, one of the most intriguing aspects of twentieth-century American history, and the variety of rural politics defies easy categorization. Some rural folk have spoken for an easily defined political Left, many others for the Right. Some have embraced nonviolence and transformed American history forever; others have wielded a firebrand or a noose. Yet the complexities of twentieth-century rural political history generally belie easy labels or simple interpretations.[8]

By emphasizing the politics of rural history, we follow the lead of several disciplines that have carefully documented a new American political history. In focusing on the state, we hope to contribute to one of today's most important lines of academic inquiry. After the nearly two-decades-long hegemony of a social history that neglected, and indeed often opposed, the study of governmental institutions, many scholars have finally begun to return to that most traditional of viewpoints: that politics is central to our study of the past. Political scientists and sociologists, upon finding in the 1980s that historians had largely abandoned issues of power, began to argue most forcefully for (in the famous words of one scholarly manifesto) "bringing the state back in." These seekers of theoretical generalization did pioneering analysis of the critical role of state institutions and long-term ideologies in American political development. Then, once historians began to understand the importance of what their colleagues on the other side of campus were accomplishing, they too caught the politics bug, albeit in a significantly different way. Historians were above all able to bring people back in, with their hopes and dreams, constraints and struggles. Throughout the 1990s historians—despite the increasing strength of a cultural studies whose practitioners often expressed hostility to the political—produced pathbreaking works that showed not only that politics was central to the national past but that public matters were truly fundamental to the lives of ordinary people. In other words, humanists and social

---

[8]White, "It's Your Misfortune," 58. For a more complete discussion of the contradictory politics of rural America see Catherine McNicol Stock, *Rural Radicals: Righteous Rage in the American Grain* (Ithaca: Cornell University Press, 1996).

scientists were able to begin to write, in some ways for the first time, a truly democratic past for a democratic nation.[9]

Our desire to uncover the full spectrum of rural politics is necessary not only for intellectual reasons, but for civic purposes as well. One recent book about rural politics shows just how high the stakes are in this dramatic reconstruction of our past. Elizabeth Sanders, in her brilliant *Roots of Reform*, argues that the central force in American history seeking to tame an inegalitarian and exploitative capitalism has been a radical agrarianism. Farmers, especially in the South and to some extent in the Midwest, drew on their Jeffersonian heritage to fight for institutions such as the Interstate Commerce and Federal Trade Commissions that helped to render economic competition more fair and political power more equitably distributed. Even the Federal Reserve System was, in large part, initially an agrarian institution, the purpose of which was to bring banking and the currency under full popular control; only later did it become an agency that populists targeted as betraying the democratic interest. Farmers were able to become the primary builders of the American state not only by mo-

---

[9] Peter B. Evans, Dietrich Rueschemeyer, and Theda Skocpol, eds., *Bringing the State Back In* (New York: Cambridge University Press, 1985). For historicized political science, see especially the journal *Studies in American Political Development;* for the reinvigoration of political history through its integration of social history, see the overview by Mark Leff, "Revisioning United States Political History," *American Historical Review* 100 (June 1995): 829–53; and the masterworks of Lizabeth Cohen, *Making a New Deal: Industrial Workers in Chicago, 1919–1939* (New York: Cambridge University Press, 1990); Glenda Elizabeth Gilmore, *Gender and Jim Crow: Women and the Politics of White Supremacy in North Carolina, 1896–1920* (Chapel Hill: University of North Carolina Press, 1996); and Thomas J. Sugrue, *The Origins of the Urban Crisis: Race and Inequality in Postwar Detroit* (Princeton: Princeton University Press, 1996).

For a sampling of the increasing strength of politics within the literature of twentieth-century rural history, see Kitty Calavita, *Inside the State: The Bracero Program, Immigration, and the I.N.S.* (New York: Routledge, 1992); Pete Daniel, *Lost Revolutions: The South in the 1950s* (Chapel Hill and Washington, D.C.: University of North Carolina Press and Smithsonian National Museum of American History, 2000); Cindy Hahamovitch, *The Fruits of Their Labor: Atlantic Coast Farmworkers and the Making of Migrant Poverty, 1870–1945* (Chapel Hill: University of North Carolina Press, 1997); David E. Hamilton, *From New Day to New Deal: American Farm Policy from Hoover to Roosevelt, 1928–1933* (Chapel Hill: University of North Carolina Press, 1991); Jeanette Keith, *Country People in the New South: Tennessee's Upper Cumberland* (Chapel Hill: University of North Carolina Press, 1995); Paula M. Nelson, *The Prairie Winnows Out Its Own: The West River Country of South Dakota in the Years of the Depression and Dust* (Iowa City: University of Iowa Press, 1996); Catherine McNicol Stock, *Main Street in Crisis: The Great Depression and the Old Middle Class on the Northern Plains* (Chapel Hill: University of North Carolina Press, 1992); Jeannie M. Whayne, *A New Plantation South: Land, Labor, and Federal Favor in Twentieth-Century Arkansas* (Charlottesville: University Press of Virginia, 1996). These works follow in the scholarly path of such important works as David B. Danbom, *The Resisted Revolution: Urban America and the Industrialization of Agriculture, 1900–1930* (Ames: Iowa State University Press, 1979); Richard Stewart Kirkendall, *Social Scientists and Farm Politics in the Age of Roosevelt* (Columbia: University of Missouri Press, 1966); Howard Robert Lamar, *The Far Southwest, 1846–1912: A Territorial History* (New York: Norton, 1970); and Richard Lowitt, *The New Deal and the West* (Bloomington: Indiana University Press, 1984).

bilizing in insurgencies such as populism but even more by capturing the Democratic party and using it as an effective vehicle of political power.[10]

Sanders's book contains huge quantities of evidence on voting data and economic relations that scholars will be processing and debating for years. Yet *Roots of Reform* is fundamentally a civic testament, a plea for a more humane and democratic politics and a book whose power resides in many ways simply in its revealing of the strength of the American heritage of humane and democratic politics. And by moving the politics of the countryside from periphery to center, Sanders proves that we can be neither good citizens nor creative scholars unless we fully engage the rural political tradition.

The essays in *The Countryside in the Age of the Modern State* also all confront the possibilities of American democracy, although several authors are considerably less confident than Sanders of the decency of the rural political legacy. Despite the common theme of the essays, they propose no unified argument; indeed the essays at times disagree with each other in exciting ways. Some authors see the agrarian agencies of the modern American state as the most democratic of all American political institutions; others are much more wary of the hierarchical vision of the experts staffing these organizations. Some contributors are convinced that agrarianism is a political ideology that has once, and could again, inspire a multicultural political movement of workers and small-propertied people; others point to the dismal record of the state in defending labor rights as a warning about what we might realistically expect from the government. Beyond their creative disagreements, all of the essays attempt to open new perspectives and illustrate imaginative approaches to the study of twentieth-century rural political history. In the end, they help us reconceive how we might envision the political itself, since *The Countryside in the Age of the Modern State* takes the politics of skiing, poaching, and birth control as seriously as it does the politics of subsidies, populism, and crop control.

The Countryside in the Age of the Modern State begins with a reconsideration of one of the grand questions in American history: what are the democratic possibilities of our agrarian legacy? The easy (and all too common) answers to this question, at least for the twentieth century, are that agrarianism has either almost completely lost its influence or that it has turned sour, spawning a harvest of hate in the heartland. Yet Benjamin Heber Johnson, Debra Ann Reid, and Victoria Saker Woeste have a much more complex, and a much more hopeful, set of responses in their wrestlings with the agrarian legacy.

---

[10] Elizabeth Sanders, *Roots of Reform: Farmers, Workers, and the American State, 1877–1917* (Chicago: University of Chicago Press, 1999); Robert D. Johnston, "Peasants, Pitchforks, and the (Found) Promise of Progressivism," *Reviews in American History* 28 (September 2000): 393–98.

Benjamin Johnson opens the volume with a reconsideration of the most powerful agrarian political tradition—populism—through the figure of T. A. Bland. Despite his name, Bland was a fiery radical Indian reformer who used the contrast between Native American and European property relations to throw into question the racial domination of whites over Indians and to form political alliances with Native Americans. Johnson's essay reminds us that the ideas of populism were not reserved for agricultural policy for white farmers, and, moreover, that all agrarians (much less all country people) were not themselves white. Debra Reid amplifies this theme with a study of five African American agrarians in Texas who built a surprisingly strong set of political institutions during the height of Jim Crow, between populism and the New Deal. Well into the twentieth century, then, the agrarian legacy remained powerful among groups that historians have barely ever recognized as part of that tradition. In turn, the standard agrarian icon, the white small-propertied family farmer, was supposed to have been rendered economically and politically powerless in the course of the twentieth century. Victoria Saker Woeste effectively challenges that standard trope of agrarian declension, showing through an innovative use of census records that family farms remained robust and family farmers remained politically powerful even in that homeland of industrialized agriculture, California, in the decades leading up to World War II.

Despite the significance of the agrarian state-building tradition, a hoary part of populist rhetoric has involved celebrating virtuous rural folk holding off the corrupting forces of the modern state. The next group of essays examines the uses of the state and the politics of the dispossessed. Karl Jacoby, Johanna Schoen, Cindy Hahamovitch, and Stephen Pitti explore the tense and complicated relationships between a wide variety of rural residents and a wide array of governmental bodies. It is clear that the modern state was constructed not just *by* but *through* the lives of ordinary, often quite powerless people. Not just agribusiness profits but also national parks were the direct result of deliberate dispossession on the part of governments, working in tandem with elites. Yet poor and subaltern folks also could wrest power, and at times a modicum of justice, from the modern state, whether by working actively to obtain diaphragms from public health officials or by resisting attempts to impose racial segregation in transnational labor markets.

Karl Jacoby looks at the creation and early years of Yellowstone Park to explore the many conflicts between park officials and local inhabitants in and around this wilderness. Building on the literature of global insurgency, he posits a rural moral economy among poor whites that both sanctioned and limited poaching of wild game, and in the process he reveals our need to be attentive to the class conflict—as well as the dispossession of Indians—that was present at the birth of one of our national treasures. Yet Johanna Schoen reminds us that poor people did not just resist, but also imaginatively used, the modern state. The record of twentieth-century American reproductive policy is full of attempts to control the reproduction of the poor, but Schoen insists that we reconsider models of victimization by exploring the creative ways in which black and white rural North Carolinians embraced elite-originated birth control policies for their own benefit.

In an age of increasing transnational labor migration, though, it was not just American citizens who made use of, and experienced the limitations of, the American state. Cindy Hahamovitch shows how Jamaican farm laborers, recruited to work in the United States during World War II, demanded fair treatment in the fields. In vigorous attempts to gain their rights, they challenged not only local employers and federal agencies in the United States, but their own government as well. In turn, Stephen Pitti extends the insights of Hahamovitch and joins with her in urging us to recognize that the twentieth century was the age of modern *states*. Pitti focuses on the political vision of Ernesto Galarza, the most powerful Mexican American labor leader of the postwar years, to show how the most effective political organizing of Mexican and Mexican American agricultural workers in the age of the bracero migrant labor program consciously used Mexican nationalism to criticize not just the United States government but the supposedly revolutionary government of Mexico as well. In the end, though, growers in both contexts were far more successful than farmworkers in shaping federal immigration policies in ways that suited their own purposes.

The third group of essays looks at a more traditional subject, federal policy. Deborah Fitzgerald, Jess Gilbert, Katherine Jellison, and Robert Weise take us through the New Deal and beyond in order to come to grips with the legacy of national state actions in matters of class, gender, bureaucracy, and local control. Their essays together show the enduring relevance of what we might call high politics—the visions of policymakers, the bureaucratic infighting between agencies, the making and implementation of laws—at a time when the bulk of scholarly attention has moved away from such a direct engagement with the inner workings of the state. These articles also show the enduring promise of vigorous intellectual debate, as crucial civic questions receive attention while the authors argue the fine points of the historical literature.

Deborah Fitzgerald begins the conversation by making a forceful argument that the intellectuals and policymakers reshaping American rural life during the 1920s are *not* the place to look if we hope to recover a democratic rural political tradition. Rather, the dominant powers in interwar agriculture were scientific and technological elites who wished to impose what Fitzgerald, following James Scott, characterizes as a "high modernist" ideology upon the countryside. Jess Gilbert, in contrast, contends that most high-level agricultural officials in the New Deal U.S. Department of Agriculture were not elites in the sense of being from the ruling class but rather came from, and represented, a powerful class of midwestern family farmers. In an attempt to significantly democratize the American government, these New Deal policymakers envisioned a third, or "intended," New Deal that would have greatly empowered rural citizens.

Katherine Jellison is more ambivalent as she explores how Old Order Amish women fascinated certain New Dealers. A powerful minority of government officials saw in the Amish an alternative to the destructive tendencies of modern industrialized farming and mass consumption and recognized the significant productive contributions that women made to Amish farms, although they did not fully probe the impact of patriarchy on these women's lives. Finally, Robert Weise takes us beyond the 1930s to see the New Deal rural order playing itself out in Great Society programs in what seems now like a forgotten place in the age of urban riots—rural Appalachia. During the 1960s, Weise reveals, the commitment of federal and foundation planners to an urban and cosmopolitan version of modern America led them to associate poverty with rural isolation. The best route out of poverty, therefore, was the integration of supposedly backward relics into the national economy. These planners failed, both because of the narrowness of their ideas and because of the reluctance of local people to abandon their rural lives. Yet in the long run their vision prevailed; Weise closes his essay by asking us to recognize that the WTO's dream of a unified global economy brings Walmarts to the mountains of Kentucky in the same way that it encourages sweatshops in Indonesia. Dissident voices from both the Right and the Left, however, still speak of a genuine revitalization of rural communities.

Finally, Annie Gilbert Coleman and Mary Summers examine the ways in which the contemporary countryside is the location of new, as well as traditional, forms of politics. Coleman explores the political conflicts engendered by the development of the skiing industry in Colorado as promoters, skiers, environmental activists, and local residents all have attempted to advance their vision of the good life by acting on different conceptions of the landscape. Her essay helps us to understand how much the politics of today's countryside has become both less dependent on state action and much more a contest over the meaning of "rural." Indeed, a rural place today is as likely to have mobile homes as grain silos, just as likely to be a site for backpackers trekking through a national park as an area for ranchers herding their sheep on land leased from the Forest Service. Yet at the same time, Mary Summers convincingly demonstrates how even in the midst of what we might call a postmodern countryside, old-fashioned agrarian politics still retains its power both to influence the state and to shape our democratic dreams. Through a study of the family farm crusade of the 1980s and its historical roots, Summers makes it clear that we need to move beyond the myth, permeating scholarship and journalism, that all contemporary farmers care about is their own crude material self-interest. Activists continue to be able to rekindle a populist vision of political economy—one firmly anchored in the family farm tradition. And this vision still retains a claim on our democratic ideals as much at the dawn of the twenty-first century as it did at the end of the nineteenth century.

"Born in the country," American history has long been shaped in powerful ways by the actions and ideals of country folks. While most Americans today live in cities, the importance of the rural experience has changed many times but, in many crucial ways, has not diminished. We certainly hope that in presenting this collection of innovative essays by newer scholars we stimulate further research on the many areas of twentieth-century rural life that we were not able to investigate here. Even more, though, we trust that by insisting on the significance of rural people's encounters with the modern state that we help to make more complex and powerful the story of American democracy, and in that small way restore some of the democratic faith that is one of the noble qualities of the American rural past.

PART 1

AGRARIAN LEGACIES

Red Populism? T. A. Bland, Agrarian Radicalism, and the Debate over the Dawes Act

BENJAMIN HEBER JOHNSON

The last two decades of the nineteenth century were a critical turning point for both American Indians and the nation as a whole. With the military defeat of the last independent Indian nations on the Great Plains, American Indians entered the era in which they would live, and struggle to maintain a measure of freedom and autonomy, within the boundaries of the nation's political and economic system. At the same time, an explosive transformation altered America's economic and political fabric. The rise of railroads, large industrial corporations, and finance capital shifted the heart of the economy from smaller, owner-operated enterprises to a corporate form of capitalism. An increasingly integrated national market and its corresponding calculus encroached upon more and more local markets and subsistence networks.[1] This encroachment prompted enormous political and economic tumult, culminating in Populism, the most powerful challenge to modern capitalism and the two-party system in American history.

What were the connections between this wrenching economic transformation, the central national dynamic of the period, and the central Indian event of this time, the allotment of Indian lands? In 1887, eastern "Friends of the Indian" secured the passage of the Dawes Act, which provided for the eventual elimination of all Indian reservations and the dispersal of their communal lands into individualized Indian possession. Their support for allot-

---

[1] T. J. Jackson Lears, *No Place of Grace: Antimodernism and the Transformation of American Culture, 1880–1920* (Chicago: University of Chicago Press, 1994 [1981]); Nick Salvatore, *Eugene V. Debs: Citizen and Socialist* (Urbana: University of Illinois Press, 1982); Lawrence Goodwyn, *Democratic Promise: The Populist Moment in America* (New York: Oxford University Press, 1976); Gerald Berk, *Alternative Tracks: The Constitution of American Industrial Order* (Baltimore: Johns Hopkins University Press, 1994); and Martin Sklar, *The Corporate Reconstruction of American Capitalism, 1890–1916: The Market, the Law, and Politics* (New York: Cambridge University Press, 1988).

ment rested on a faith that the broader economic transformation was both so beneficial that Indians could not in good conscience be prevented from participating in it by their tradition of communal landholding, and so powerful that resisting it was a path to certain extinction.

Neither allotment nor its justification, however, proceeded without opposition, although historians have rarely noted it. This essay explores the National Indian Defence Association (NIDA), which included both whites and Indians, and its arguments for the maintenance of Indian landholding. NIDA's leaders argued that reservations should be preserved as the collective property of tribes, which could use their resources to integrate into American life on terms of their own choosing. NIDA used the political language of agrarianism—so often used as a justification for dispossessing Indians—to attack both allotment and the economic ideology behind it. Because his fear that allotment would wreak havoc on Indian peoples was so deeply bound up with a much broader opposition to the rise of corporate capitalism, NIDA head Thomas Bland was able to assemble an influential though ultimately unsuccessful coalition to oppose allotment. Where the champions of allotment viewed the Indians as passive and rather pathetic recipients of white largesse, NIDA became a cultural meeting ground where some Indians and whites found a way to defend similarly besieged ways of life. Agrarian radicalism, and the hostility toward concentrated economic power that lay at its heart, thus played as critical role in the debate over allotment as it did in the late nineteenth century United States as a whole.[2] Exploring the role of NIDA in these debates, then, also allows us to rethink the power, the limitations, and the legacy of agrarianism for the modern political history of the rural United States.

Allotment and the Whig History of U.S.–Indian Relations

At least among the articulate leaders of the majority culture, there was a uniform conviction that economic expansion, political freedom, and the widening influence of institutions such as the home, the school, and the churches would hold the country's social fabric together.

—Frederick Hoxie, *The Final Promise* (1984)

Except for the conquest of independent Indian nations, allotment is arguably the single most important event in the history of U.S.–Indian relations. The Dawes Act granted the executive branch the authority to break

[2] I follow Christopher Lasch's lead in the use of term "agrarian" to denote a "part of a movement that appealed to small producers of all kinds." See Christopher Lasch, *The True and Only Heaven: Progress and Its Critics* (New York: Norton, 1991), 217.

up Indian reservations into individual allotments (generally 160 for heads of household and 80 for single adults), mandated that leftover lands be sold to white settlers, and provided that allotted Indians could become citizens. In abrogation of many treaties with Indian peoples and over NIDA's vigorous protest, there was no provision requiring tribal consent for allotment of their remaining lands. In contradiction to the public statements and best intentions of the reformers who had proposed and agitated for its passage, the act was an unmitigated disaster. Between its passage in 1887 and repeal in 1934, it underwent substantial revisions, but the dispossession of Indian lands remained constant. Indians held slightly over 150 million acres before the act; that estate shrank to 104 million acres by 1890, to 77 million by 1900, and to 48 million by 1934. R. Douglas Hurt concludes that by 1906 "the ability of Indians to alienate their lands with ease... [had] eroded any possibility that they would become self-sufficient agriculturists." By 1934, about two-thirds of the Indian population was "either completely landless or did not own enough land to make a subsistence living."[3]

About 250,000 Indians, living under widely disparate environmental conditions, shared the 150 million pre-allotment acres. In some places this landholding was enough to sustain an independent agropastoral existence. Indeed, Hurt argues that "had severalty not deprived the Indians of their commonly-held open-range lands they might have been able to become self-sufficient cattlemen." Some tribes and bands did in fact maintain a surprising degree of economic independence well into the twentieth century.[4] Had the allotment drive been defeated, many more Indians would have had a much larger resource base to draw upon in their efforts to make reservations viable and even semiautonomous homelands rather than the concentrations of abject poverty that most soon became.

The idea of Indian allotment had been around long before the 1880s. Prominent Euro-Americans such as John Winthrop and Thomas Jefferson noted with distress that Indians lacked the private landownership that was so essential for their cultural assimilation. The federal government allotted

[3] Arrell Morgan Gibson, "The Centennial Legacy of the General Allotment Act," *Chronicles of Oklahoma* 65 (1987): 244; Francis Paul Prucha, *The Great Father: The United States and the American Indians* (Lincoln: University of Nebraska Press, 1986), 227; Janet A. McDonnell, *The Dispossession of the American Indian, 1887–1934* (Bloomington: Indiana University Press, 1991), 8, 121; R. Douglas Hurt, *Indian Agriculture in America: Prehistory to the Present* (Lawrence: University Press of Kansas, 1987), 147, 151.

[4] Hurt, *Indian Agriculture in America*, 152. See Richard White's study of the Navajo in *The Roots of Dependency: Subsistence, Environment, and Social Changes among the Choctaws, Pawnees and Navajos* (Lincoln: University of Nebraska Press, 1983), for a case where a large and powerful tribe managed to maintain its economic independence well into the twentieth century. Peter Iverson, *When Indians Became Cowboys: Native Peoples and Cattle Ranching in the American West* (Norman: University of Oklahoma Press, 1994); David Rich Lewis, *Neither Wolf nor Dog: American Indians, Environment, and Agrarian Change* (New York: Oxford University Press, 1994).

the lands of several eastern tribes in the 1820s and 1830s, resulting in the loss of 80 to 90 percent of their lands, and federal officials made similar proposals for wider allotment programs. By the 1880's there had been a subtle yet important shift in the role that allotment played in the overall project of Indian acculturation. Reformers continued to argue that Indians needed to convert to Christianity, give up war, adopt bourgeois family structures, become literate in English, and acknowledge the supremacy of Anglo-American legal practices. Yet the reformers had come to place allotment at the center of their agenda out of the belief that the maintenance of tribal landholding was the principal force allowing Indians to resist their integration into the mainstream of American political and cultural life.[5] This emphasis reflected the reformers' optimism about the direction of the American polity and the extent to which a commitment to economic modernization had come to dominate their own political ideology.

Scholars have documented the connections between capitalist expansion and Indian dispossession. However, students of Indian policy have failed to recognize the deeply anticapitalist strains of American politics, let alone to trace the connection between these strains and Indian policy. John Moore, for example, argues that "the important fact about the invasion of North America is not so much that the invaders were European foreigners, but that they were *capitalist* foreigners." Such views, often shared by historians of the West and other fields of U.S. history, mistakenly assume that capitalism has been virtually unchallenged as the dominant force in modern American history.[6]

Historians of Indian policy in the allotment period have either misunderstood or altogether ignored Bland and NIDA because they also assume that a monolithically capitalist white America wielded irresistible power in its quest to destroy Indian landholding. For example, in his authoritative study of late nineteenth-century Indian policy, Francis Paul Prucha

[5]See William Cronon, *Changes in the Land* (New York: Hill and Wang, 1983), 56; Hurt, *Indian Agriculture in America*, 86, 89, 94; House, *Memorial of the Creek Nation on the Subject of Lands in Severalty among the Several Indian Tribes, with Accompanying Papers*, 47th Cong., 2d sess., 1883, H. Misc. Doc. 18; Robert Berkhofer, *The White Man's Indian: Images of the American Indian from Columbus to the Present* (New York: Random House, 1979), 172; Francis Paul Prucha, *The Great Father* (Lincoln: University of Nebraska Press, 1984), 659.

[6]See, among others, White, *Roots of Dependency*; Angie Debo, *And Still the Waters Run: The Betrayal of the Five Civilized Tribes* (Princeton, N.J.: Princeton University Press, 1940); James H. Merreil, *The Indian's New World* (New York: Norton, 1989); Albert Hurtado, *Indian Survival on the California Frontier* (New Haven, Conn.: Yale University Press, 1988); H. Craig Miner, *The Corporation and the Indian* (Columbia: University of Missouri Press, 1976); John H. Moore, ed., *The Political Economy of North American Indians* (Norman: University of Oklahoma Press, 1993), 15; Karen Ordahl Kuppermann, *Settling with the Indians: The Meeting of English and Indian Cultures in America, 1580–1640* (New York: Rowan and Littlefield, 1980); Edmund S. Morgan, *American Slavery, American Freedom* (New York: Norton, 1975); Robert D. Johnston, "Beyond 'The West': Liberalism, Regionalism, and the Evasion of Politics in the New Western History," *Rethinking History* 2 (summer 1998): 239–77.

accurately portrays the sense of inevitability that the mainstream reformers brought to their assimilationist mission, but makes their determinist assumption a premise of his own work. For Prucha, as for almost all other scholars of Indian policy during this period, the only real debate in white society was between the assimilationists like Dawes and the nearly psychopathic extremists willing to resort to genocide to acquire Indian lands and resources. Similarly, William Hagan, in his study of the Indian Rights Association (IRA)—the most important pro-allotment group—assumes that it "was only a matter of time until some sort of severalty bill would be enacted into law." This prevents him from exploring the basis of Bland and NIDA's quarrels with pro-allotment groups.[7]

The most sophisticated study of white efforts to assimilate Indians, Frederick Hoxie's *A Final Promise: The Campaign to Assimilate the Indians, 1880–1920*, likewise fails to avoid the pitfalls of consensus history. Hoxie explicitly argues that "a study of the Indian assimilation campaign should look beyond specific government programs...to consider their relationship to broader changes in the United States' political culture." Yet his depiction of America in the last two decades of the nineteenth century has no place for the massive strikes of the 1880s and 1890s, or the political upheaval and violent suppression of Populism in the 1890s. His account of Indian policy, in turn, does not mention Bland or NIDA.[8] Hoxie thus echoes other scholars in his assumption that the economic optimism behind allotment was an accepted and unchallenged conviction.

Even those historians who study Bland and NIDA accept the inevitability of allotment and overlook the role that agrarianism played for its opponents. Jo Lea Wetherilt Behrens's account of NIDA's role in defending the Great Sioux Reservation from reduction casually terms the reservation's reduction "inevitable." Thomas Cowger, despite his vivid reconstruction of Bland's efforts to stop allotment and the reprisals that they provoked, remarks that "his fight to allow the tribes freedom from interference was hopeless." Heavily relying on Bland's early writings on Indian policy and paying little attention to his agrarian tracts, Cowger mistakenly assumes that "Bland largely accepted the goal of Indian assimilation as outlined by humanitarian reformers of his generation."[9]

---

[7]Francis Paul Prucha, *American Indian Policy in Crisis: Christian Reformers and the Indian, 1865–1900* (Norman: University of Oklahoma Press, 1976), 168, 167; William Thomas Hagan, *The Indian Rights Association: The Herbert Welsh Years, 1882–1904* (Tucson: University of Arizona Press, 1985), 37, 66.

[8] Frederick Hoxie, *The Final Promise: The Campaign to Assimilate the Indians, 1880–1920* (Lincoln: University of Nebraska Press, 1984), 38–39.

[9]Jo Lea Wetherilt Behrens, "In Defense of 'Poor Lo': National Indian Defense Association and Council Fire's Advocacy for Sioux Land Rights," *South Dakota History* 24 (fall/winter 1994): 156; Thomas Cowger, "Dr. Thomas A. Bland, Critic of Forced Assimilation," *American Indian Culture and Research Journal* 16 (March 1992): 90, 77; see especially 91 n. 2. Other scholars have also noted Bland and NIDA's distinctiveness, but have not connected them to

We can find, however, a more sophisticated approach to white-Indian relations in the works of historians of Indian peoples in earlier times. These stress the importance of the cultural, diplomatic, and political meeting ground—the "middle ground" in Richard White's memorable work—of Europeans and natives. In these accounts, both Indian and colonial societies are complicated entities with diverse factions, goals, and understandings of themselves and the world around them. Capitalism is a powerful but contingent force that competes with other ways of understanding economic life. Unfortunately, the modern nation-state all too often comes into these studies like a gigantic wrecking ball, demolishing future possibilities for even small measures of indigenous autonomy and commonality. In Richard White's work, for example, the end of formal autonomy for Indian nations is accompanied by a seamless, monolithic, and devastating onslaught of government-sponsored acculturation. Indians never become passive victims in White's account, but American society and its increasingly powerful state present a single face to them.[10]

A full incorporation of Bland and NIDA into the history of the allotment debate should lead scholars to recognize the continuation of important aspects of the middle ground into the era after United States conquest. It is true that, for example, the Sioux had fewer viable options in 1885 than in 1820, but there was more fluidity, contingency, and common ground between whites and Indians in the late nineteenth century than we have previously recognized. Indian leaders could be sophisticated political actors, attuned to divisions within American society and able to exploit them for any advantages they might offer. Although Indian peoples were culturally distinct from Americans—as Americans were often culturally distinct from one another—there was nevertheless enough common ground for true understanding and sympathy. American society itself was not a unified whole, offering only one narrow set of options to Indians. In particular, the rise of agrarian radicalism, so often associated with extreme paranoia and

agrarian radicalism or restructured their accounts to allow them any place other than that of a noble curiosity. See Debo, *And Still the Waters Run*, 22; and Robert Wiston Mardock, *The Reformers and the American Indian* (Columbia: University of Missouri Press, 1971), 221; Arrell Morgan Gibson, *The American Indian: Prehistory to Present* (New York: D.C. Heath, 1980), 459, 491.

[10]See especially Richard White, *The Middle Ground: Indians, Empires, and Republics in the Great Lakes Region, 1650–1815* (New York: Cambridge University Press, 1991); Daniel K. Richter, *The Ordeal of the Longhouse: The Peoples of the Iroquois League in the Era of European Colonization* (Chapel Hill: University of North Carolina Press, 1992); James H. Merrell, *The Indians' New World: Catawbas and Their Neighbors from European Contact through the Era of Removal* (New York: Norton, 1989); John Demos, *The Unredeemed Captive: A Family Story from Early America* (New York: Knopf, 1994). See the chapter "The Federal Government and the Indians" in Richard White, *"It's Your Misfortune and None of My Own": A History of the American West* (Norman: University of Oklahoma Press, 1991).

racism, actually offered Indians their best chance of holding on to what remained of their estate.[11]

The National Indian Defence Association, Thomas Bland, and Agrarian Democracy

The desire to become rich has become a mania, a species of insanity, which is both epidemic and contagious.

—Thomas A. Bland, *How to Grow Rich* (1881)

Thomas Augustus Bland was born in 1830 to Quaker parents who had migrated to southern Indiana from North Carolina in 1817. He attended the Eclectic Medical Institute in Cincinnati, and after a stint as a surgeon in the Union army became a prolific writer and supporter of medical reform, the Greenback Party, and eventually the Populist movement and Progressive era political reforms. Living in Boston, Bland and his wife and co-worker Dr. Mary Cora Bland met former Indian Superintendent Alfred Meacham in 1875. Meacham, despite his near death at the hands of Modoc Indians several years before, had turned to the lecture circuit to plead for the defense of Indians from further territorial encroachment. The Blands became both Meacham's personal physicians and his collaborators in Indian reform. Meacham returned to the East in 1877 and with the Blands' encouragement began to publish *The Council Fire,* a monthly journal concerned with Indians and Indian policy. Shortly before his death in Washington, D.C., in 1882, Meacham convinced the Blands to continue publishing the magazine, which they did until its demise in 1889.[12]

By 1882 eastern philanthropists had already organized three major Indian reform groups—the Boston Indian Citizenship Committee, the Women's National Indian Association, and the Indian Rights Association (IRA). These groups' emphasis on forcibly acculturating Indians through allotment and other territorial cessions soon caused a split in the ranks of white easterners concerned with Indian affairs. Bland's disputes with Senator Dawes and the IRA prompted him to join with like-minded whites in founding the National Indian Defence Association (NIDA) in 1885. NIDA's early membership

---

[11]For a discussion of the depth of opposition to Indian removal in the 1830s, see Mary Hershberger, "Mobilizing Women, Anticipating Abolition: The Struggle Against Indian Removal in the 1830s," *Journal of American History* 86, no. 1 (June 1999): 15–40.

[12]Cowger, "Dr. Thomas A. Bland," 78–80, Wetherilt Behrens, "In Defense of 'Poor Lo,'" 155. For the history of the "eclectic school" of medicine, see John S. Haller, Jr., *Medical Protestants: The Eclectics in American Medicine, 1825–1939* (Carbondale: Southern Illinois University Press, 1994). For Bland's egalitarian views of gender roles and family life, see T. A. Bland, *Pioneers of Progress* (Chicago: T. A. Bland & Co., 1906): 46–53, 157.

included numerous prominent and powerful whites. James Denver, the former governor of Kansas Territory, became the organization's first president. Judge A. J. Willard, former chief justice of the South Carolina Supreme Court, was a founding member and eventually the group's legal counsel. Other prominent members included former Indian Affairs commissioners Francis Walker and George Manypenny, former assistant commissioner Alonzo Bell, anthropologist James Owen Dorsey, superintendent of Indian schools James Oberly, Washington, D.C., minister Alexander Kent, and former Senate chaplain and abolitionist Byron Sunderland, who was President Grover Cleveland's pastor as well as NIDA's vice president. Shortly after its founding, NIDA was as large and prominent as any of the other Indian reform groups that have received the bulk of scholarly attention.[13]

Indians occupied a position in NIDA quite different from the ones they did in any of the other reform groups. Whereas other groups treated Indians as the passive recipients of their charity, NIDA's leadership welcomed Indians as members, regularly consulted them about the course of Indian policy, and printed their often lengthy speeches and letters. It is impossible to ascertain what proportion of NIDA's membership was Indian, but of the 425 members signed up between May 1886 and February 1887, Bland proudly claimed that "not less than 200 are members of various Indian tribes." In his capacity as NIDA's corresponding secretary and editor of *The Council Fire,* Bland directly consulted with the Sioux about whether or not they would agree to the allotment of their reservation, and if so upon what terms. He frequently printed speeches and reports of lobbying efforts of Indians against allotment proposals and sharply criticized Dawes for removing a provision requiring Indian assent to allot their lands.[14]

[13]Hoxie, *The Final Promise,* 7–11; Cowger, "Dr. Thomas A. Bland," 77–78; *The Council Fire* 5 (May 1882): 144. See also H. W. Thomas's introduction to Bland, *Pioneers of Progress,* 10–12; Behrens, "In Defense of 'Poor Lo,'" 154. Before the 1885 split, Bland's views on allotment and the other Indian reform groups were much more ambiguous, perhaps because he wanted to work with the other reform groups, or had not yet concluded that his own agrarian radicalism required the defense of the Indian commons. See Prucha, *The Great Father,* 629, for a description of Bland and NIDA's split with other reform groups.

[14]See T. A. Bland, ed., *A Brief History of the Late Military Invasion of the Home of the Sioux* (Washington, D.C.: National Indian Defence Association, 1891), 12, 20; *The Council Fire* 10 (February 1887), 18; *A History of the Sioux Agreement: Some Facts Which Should Not Be Forgotten* (Washington, D.C.: National Indian Defence Association, [1889?]), 20; *The Council Fire* 10 (February 1887): 22, 34–35. Since NIDA left no records, it is impossible to determine its active or dues-paying membership. If Bland was honest in his printed claim of over 400 new members in less than a year, then NIDA was about the same size as IRA, which had 250 members in 1885 and about 1,200 in 1889 (Hagan, *The Indian Rights Association,* 45–47).

For examples of Indian letters and NIDA consultation with Indians, see especially *The Council Fire* 1 (March 1877): 44; 2 (July 1828): 108; 6 (May 1883): 79; 6 (June 1883): 95; 7 (January 1884): 15; 7 (June 1884): 101; 7 (August 1884): 98; 7 (December 1884): 166; 8 (July 1885): 114; 10 (February 1887): 26, 35; 10 (March 1887): 48; 10 (May 1887): 67; 10 (November 1887): 78.

In NIDA the radical democracy envisioned by Populists easily extended to Indians. The leadership of NIDA consistently maintained that forced allotment was illegitimate simply because it allowed the Indians no choice in their own destiny. Once the Dawes Act had passed, NIDA President Alexander Kent asserted that any "legislation of this sort, not asked for by the Indians, is an impertinence even if beneficial" and further stated that "all legislation protested against by them is an outrage, whatever its character."[15]

Bland was committed to having Indians participate in the debates about their future as equals. In early 1887, while attending a meeting sponsored by the Board of Indian Commissioners, he insisted that he be replaced on a committee by the Creek leader Pleasant Porter, who proceeded to make his case against allotment. He often hosted Indians visiting Washington on lobbying trips, whether or not the visiting Indian peoples agreed with his opposition to allotment.[16]

Bland's 1884 visit to the Great Sioux Reservation reveals the often extraordinary relations between some Indians and NIDA. With a letter of permission from the interior secretary, Bland came in order to meet with NIDA member Red Cloud about Congressional proposals to drastically reduce the reservation's size. Despite his formal invitation, shortly after Bland's arrival the Pine Ridge Agent Valentine McGillycuddy called Bland into his office, threatened him, conspicuously issued his officers several rounds of ammunition, and ordered Bland to leave the reservation. Red Cloud, who at first thought that Bland had been murdered, offered to send a large armed escort to bring him back onto the reservation. Bland, fearing that such an action would provoke a violent government response, declined the offer. Red Cloud and over a hundred members of his band instead rode to a nearby ranch where Bland was staying, in order to discuss the reduction of the reservation and the possibility of replacing Agent McGillycuddy.[17]

The reverberations of the conflict provoked by Bland's visit continued long after his return to Washington. Allotment's leading advocate, Senator Henry Dawes, publicly attacked Bland as "a very strange man, having some notions about Indians which seem kind, but on the contrary making trouble and mischief with everybody who is trying to help that people." The IRA distributed nearly three thousand copies of Dawes's denunciation to eastern philanthropists. Back on the Great Sioux Reservation, Valentine McGillycuddy found his efforts to gain control over Red Cloud hampered

[15]Ibid., 10 (March 1887): 38; (January 1887), 20.

[16]Ibid., 10 (January 1887): 20.

[17]Ibid., 7, no. 7–8 (July–August 1884), 99–100; James C. Olson, *Red Cloud and the Sioux Problem* (Lincoln: Nebraska University Press, 1965), 295; Cowger, "Dr. Thomas A. Bland," 81; Robert Larson, *Red Cloud* (Norman: University of Oklahoma Press, 1997), 240–44. See William T. Hagan, *United States–Comanche Relations: The Reservation Years* (New Haven, Conn.: Yale University Press, 1976), 201, for a description of how one of Bland's visits to Indian territory helped spur Kiowa leader Lone Wolf to oppose allotment.

by Bland's visit with the Sioux leader. He wrote to the Commissioner of Indian Affairs of his concerns. He said of allotment that "I have been scattering the Indians with that end in view." Noting that Red Cloud and his allies were opposed to his plans, he told the commissioner that "I had almost succeeded in scattering Red Cloud's village near the agency and the least progressive of all of the villages when this man Bland came along and now they are huddled more than ever dancing, feasting, and counciling day and night."[18]

Bland used his ejection from Pine Ridge to argue that the U.S.'s treatment of Indians was a violation of its true principles:

> When agent McGillycuddy ... said to me, "*I will let you know that you are not in the United States now you are on an Indian reservation where I am in supreme command,*" he spoke advisedly. He uttered a truth which should cause a blush to mantle every American cheek. An Indian reservation is an absolute despotism. There are thirty-eight independent republics (states) in this country, and sixty-five absolute despotisms (Indian reservations).... An Indian policy that puts it in the power of a commissioner, who is a religious bigot, to order the Indians punished for worshipping God in their own way, and to enforce that infamous order, is out of harmony with the political and religious spirit of this age and country.... The system that enables an Indian agent... to arbitrarily arrest and forcibly remove from an Indian reservation a white man or Indian who is not guilty of crime is an infamously despotic, and therefore anti-republican and un-American system.[19]

As Bland's relationship with Red Cloud suggests, NIDA largely ignored the distinctions that other reformers made between "progressive" and "backward" Indians. For example, the IRA's founder Herbert Welsh, discussing the Ghost Dance movement and subsequent Wounded Knee massacre, emphasized that there were two parties "among the Sioux Indians to-day." One was "the old pagan and non-progressive party" whose "delight is in the past" and whose "dream is that the past shall come back again." The other was a "new, progressive, and what may properly be termed Christian party," whose members were "among the most peaceable and industrious Indians to be found in the country" and who held their lands in severalty. Bland was on good terms with members of the "non-progressive party." Where Welsh identified Sitting Bull and Red Cloud—both of whom NIDA claimed as members—as backward leaders of the party of the past,

---

[18]House Select Committee, *Investigation of Expenditures of Appropriations for Indian Service and Yellowstone Park; Part I: Report*, 49th Cong., 1st sess., H. Rept. 1076, 47–48; Hagan, *The Indian Rights Association*, 37; McGillycuddy to Hon H. Price, Commissioner of Indian Affairs, July 13, 1884. Pine Ridge Records, box 36, vol. 5., RG 75, Federal Records Center of Kansas City. Special thanks to Jeff Ostler for providing me with this information.
[19]*The Council Fire* 7 (September 1884): 121.

Bland published letters from Red Cloud and lauded Sitting Bull, who was assassinated in 1890 on the Pine Ridge reservation, as "the last great prophet of the Dakota's [*sic*]." Another NIDA member praised Sitting Bull for having "held tenaciously to the traditions of his people as a sacred legacy. He distrusted the innovations sought to be forced upon the Indians.... for this he was denounced as an obstructionist, a foe to progress."[20]

Bland and his cohorts paid so little attention to whether or not individual Indians were "progressive" because their own political ideology deeply questioned the entire notion of capitalist progress. An agrarian suspicion of the emerging American political economy lay at the heart of NIDA's relationship with Indians, its support for their political autonomy, and its opposition to allotment. Above all, deep fear of the moral and social effects of concentrated economic power was the common element in NIDA's and Bland's numerous quarrels with the mainstream reformers.

Whereas the proponents of allotment were clearly optimistic about the course of white civilization, the body of Bland's writings told a populist tale of how economic power continually undermined individual morality and social harmony. His first work, *Farming as a Profession; or, How Charles Loring Made It Pay*, distinguished between healthy and unhealthy economic activities. Meant to inspire young couples to chose farming as a career, the didactic novel contrasted two promising Harvard graduates. Charley, from a hardworking but economically modest household, returns to his home county to take up farming; Fred, from a family of inherited wealth, takes up lawyering in Boston. Fred berates Charley and proclaims that "that idle whim of yours" will "bury your brilliant talents in a corn-field, or compost heap." He tells his friend that "you would make a capital lawyer; and if you will join me in the study of that profession, I'll insure you a seat in Congress inside of ten years." Five years later, when the two have agreed to reunite, Fred is miserable, just barely making ends meet, and unmarried. Charley, though, has wedded his high school sweetheart, made a reasonable return on his investment in land and agricultural implements, and become a respected pillar of his community. By the book's end, Fred sees the light and agrees to follow in Charley's footsteps and become a tiller of the soil. Charley's ancestral community provided the framework to bind together family and work, personal happiness and communal stability. Living outside such a

[20]Welsh, "The Meaning of the Dakota Outbreak," *Scribner's Magazine*, April 1891, 443–44; Bland, *A Brief History of the Late Military Invasion of the Home of the Sioux*, 20, 25, 28. For a response, see *The Indian Problem—Secretary Welsh of the Indian Rights Association Reviews and Criticizes Dr. Bland's Recent Statements* (Philadelphia: Indian Rights Association, December 31, 1885; IRAP reel 102, A70), 6. Also see South Dakota Bishop William H. Hare's letter of December 16, 1890, Indian Rights Association Papers (IRAP) reel 102, A125.

context, on the other hand, was a recipe for personal and ultimately financial failure.[21]

When not writing heavy-handed novels, Bland often addressed specific political issues, as in his description of the Greenback party's 1879 Congressional delegation, his biography of Benjamin Butler, and his later Populist campaign literature. His 1879 work, *Life of Benjamin Butler,* spelled out most of his usual themes. Butler, a Union general during the Civil War, was a Greenback congressman from Massachusetts who became governor in 1882 and then the Presidential nominee of the Anti-Monopoly and National (Greenback) parties in 1884. Bland's glowing account of Butler stressed his supposed economic radicalism. The former general appealed to Bland as a challenger to the "foes of liberty, justice, and equality; the Tory element in American society; the men who believe in the aristocracy of wealth, and the right of the rich to ride and rob the poor," who had "intrenched themselves in the strongholds of the Government." He lauded Butler's conduct during the Civil War as the military governor of New Orleans, stressing his redistribution of property to the city's poor and his arming of black men. For Bland, the highlights of Butler's career were his support of legislation limiting work hours and regulating work conditions, attacks on railroads and government largesse to them, advocacy of fiat currency, and support for women's suffrage.[22] In his 1881 work *How to Grow Rich,* Bland returned to biography to address similar themes, this time through a series of contrasts between historical figures who grew rich at the expense of their neighbors and the people as a whole and those whose frugality and honesty earned them a comfortable if modest freeholding. The tone of the work was less hopeful than *Farming as a Profession,* for Bland's sketches made it clear that those who wished to do so could accumulate vast wealth. But Bland in the end affirmed moral limits to acquisitiveness. He argued that although acquisitiveness is a natural instinct, "a man whose life is spent in the service of acquisitiveness is simply an intellectual brute."[23]

In 1892, on the eve of widespread Populist electoral victories, Bland published *Esau; or, The Banker's Victim,* which brought a more ominous tone to his depiction of the corrosive effects of unrestrained acquisitiveness. The book follows Esau Lindley, an Indiana farm boy who goes off to fight for the Union in the Civil War, only to be betrayed by his evil brother Jacob. Jacob calls in Esau's house mortgage, which he is unable to pay because it is due only in gold or silver, and not greenbacks. Esau returns home in a vain ef-

---

[21] T. A. Bland, *Farming as a Profession; or, How Charles Loring Made It Pay* (Boston: Loring Publisher, 1870), 5, 66.

[22] T. A. Bland, *The Spartan Band* (Washington, D.C.: Rufus H. Darby, 1879); Bland, *People's Party Shot and Shell* (Chicago: Charles H. Kerr & Co., 1892); Bland, *Life of Benjamin Butler* (Boston: Lee and Shepard, 1879), 2, 95, 135, 14, 165, 177, 184.

[23] T. A. Bland, *How to Grow Rich* (Washington, D.C.: Rufus H. Darby, 1881), 3, 21.

fort to pay off the note, is therefore late in returning to his unit, and is arrested and promptly shot for desertion. Bland used this moralistic story to launch a populist diatribe against bankers and hard currency advocates, moralizing that "Esau Lindley fell victim to a financial conspiracy more far reaching and damnable than any that has cursed a civilized or barbarous nation since the eighteen hundred usurers of Rome strangled Liberty and became masters of that great empire."[24]

This was more than the story of one man's crucifixion on a cross of gold. Throughout the book Bland contrasted the world of small-town, personal networks with the ruthlessness of the world of big business and finance. He returned to this contrast near the end of the book, and in language very similar to his description of Indian landholding, made a broader criticism of unrestrained market rationality.

> Jacob Lindley justified his course by the same logic that had been and still is used by the business man of every community in relation to the money question not only, but in relation to business ethics in general. He held to the doctrine that a business man is justified in taking any advantage that the law gives him, and in this he was not peculiar....
>
> Had Esau been a stranger, Jacob's insistence that the note be paid in gold or silver, or their equivalent in currency, would have subjected him to no criticism. Yet is not humanity a brotherhood, and are not all men brothers?[25]

Bland's understanding of politics stretched beyond the formal legislative arena. In the 1890's, his concern for democratic self-governance led him to criticize the growing professionalization of American life. Professionals emphasized the possession of specialized knowledge as the basis for a claim to special legal standing. Bland criticized this development out of fear that the concentrations of power it created threatened the ability of people to control the circumstances of their own lives. Just as he maintained that Indian tribes had the authority to accept or reject legislation concerning them, so too did he argue that conventional medicine is destined to give way before the rising tide of popular intelligence, and to be replaced by a true science of healing, which the people can understand, by which they can cure themselves of the ail-

[24]T. A. Bland, *Esau; or, the Banker's Victim* (Boston: Arena Publishing Co., 1892), 88. For a discussion of the conspiracy theories of Populists and other nineteenth-century Americans, see Jeffrey Ostler, "The Rhetoric of Conspiracy and the Formation of Kansas Populism," *Agricultural History* 69 (winter 1995): 1–28.

[25]Bland, *Esau; or, the Banker's Victim*, 92. Bland's juxtaposition of local communities and hostile economic power has been a common theme for many American radicals. See Salvatore, *Eugene V. Debs*; Alan Brinkley, *Voices of Protest: Huey Long, Father Coughlin, and the Great Depression* (New York: Knopf, 1982); and David Thelen, *Paths of Resistance: Tradition and Dignity in Industrializing Missouri* (New York: Oxford University Press, 1986).

ments that arise from their errors and mistakes, their disobedience to the laws of health.

This medical crusade was part and parcel of Bland's general political perspective. He turned the language of republicanism against insulated professions, arguing somewhat hyperbolically that the establishment of a medical monopoly and licensing power was "an act of tyranny scarcely paralleled in the annals of Old World despotisms... an outrage upon the rights of the people and a disgrace to States professing to be Republican commonwealths."[26]

Bland's fear of concentrated economic power and emphasis on democratic self-determination infused NIDA's crusade against allotment. Both Indians and whites used agrarian language and assumptions to defend collective Indian landholding. The assumptions and arguments of allotment's ultimately victorious proponents could not have been more different.

The Debate over the Dawes General Allotment Act

> *The tacit admission, or rather the positive statement that "No power on earth can keep the whites from dispossessing the Indians," is the opinion, alone, of the foes of justice. It is the last argument of those who favor extermination of the Indians.... It is true that the Indians are, in most cases, surrounded by selfish, grasping and vicious whites.... it is not true that this government cannot protect them in their rights, if it will.*

—Thomas A. Bland in *The Council Fire* (1884)

In contrast to Bland's agrarian radicalism, the proponents of allotment saw nothing but blessings in the coming of America's modern economy. Hence they objected to tribal landholding because it blocked the healthy and inevitable economic advances that would benefit both whites and Indians. Herbert Welsh, founder and president of the Indian Rights Association, advanced this view when writing about a proposal to break up the Great Sioux Reservation—the same proposal that had brought Bland to Pine Ridge to meet Red Cloud. "For many years the whites of Dakota have sought to cut a great highway for civilization through the heart of the Sioux reserve," he wrote, "so that easy communication might be established through eastern and western Dakota, and Indian lands, practically unused, might be opened

---

[26]T. A. Bland, *How to Get Well and How to Keep Well* (Boston: Plymouth Publishing Co., 1896 [1894]), 194–95, 197. For the connections between economic populism and antiprofessionalism, see Thelen, *Paths of Resistance*, 189, and Robert D. Johnston, "Middle-Class Political Ideology in a Corporate Society: The Persistence of Small-Propertied Radicalism in Portland, Oregon, 1883–1926" (Ph.D. diss., Rutgers University, 1993).

to white settlement." Although he and other mainstream reformers objected to the specific terms of some proposals to break up the reservation, they understood that the "reservation could not be permitted permanently to block progress, and the Indian could not be allowed to rest in an isolation which kept him from contact with civilization, and nurtured savagery."[27]

Other mainstream reformers echoed Welsh's arguments. Carl Schurz, the secretary of the interior in the early 1890s, nearly equated civilization with individualized economics when he argued that whites had to "fit the Indians... for the habits and occupations of civilized life, by work and education; to individualize them in the possession and appreciation of property, by allotting to them lands in severalty." Elaine Goodale argued that boarding schools were not effective acculturation devices because the gulf between the schools and the savage life of the reservation to which the pupils returned would simply overwhelm them. She also stressed that a proper curriculum should "include a variety of industrial training—gardening, and whatever practicable elementary carpentry for the boys, cooking, sewing, laundry work, and general housework for the girls." Harvard law professor James Thayer, discussing the Dawes bill, seemed to equate civilization and certain economic practices when he wrote that "individual Indians should be allowed the immense stimulus towards civilized life which comes with the separate ownership of land."[28]

Reformers such as Welsh, Schurz, Goodale, and Thayer stressed civil service regulations—the application of managerial expertise and the principle of meritocracy—as an essential part of their Indian policy. This Progressive stance contrasted sharply with Bland's Populist concern for the undemocratic effects of professionalization. Where NIDA explicitly argued that Indian policy was bound up with issues of economic power and self-determination, its opponents assumed that Indian affairs were essentially a matter of technique and proper administration. The IRA's delegation to the 1886 meeting of the Lake Mohonk Conference, a gathering of elite reformers at an upstate New York mansion, stressed that "we want a business-like, non-partisan administration of Indian affairs." The delegation devoted almost all of its time to denouncing the patronage system and advocating civil service reform. A later IRA publication about United States Indian policy, *A Hideous System*, gave exclusive attention to the spoils system as the cause of poor Indian policymaking. After the passage of the Dawes Act, Herbert Welsh, satisfied that it had properly set the outlines for Indian policy, turned to civil service reform as his main crusade, arguing that it "is deeply and essentially related to the Indian question... The reform

---

[27]Herbert Welsh, "The Meaning of the Dakota Outbreak," *Scribner's Magazine* 9 (1891): 445.
[28]Carl Schurz, "Present Aspects of the Indian Problem," *North American Review* 133 (July 1891): 6–10; Elaine Goodale, "The Future Indian School System," *Chatauquan* 10 (1889): 53–54; James Thayer, "The Dawes Bill and the Indians," *Harper's*, March 1888, 317.

is essential to all sound executive government... and the Indian question is largely an executive question." Shortly after the Wounded Knee massacre, Welsh acknowledged that the hunger, poverty and dislocation on the Sioux lands that had followed the reduction of their reservations had helped to precipitate the unrest that led to the massacre. But even in the frozen corpses of Bigfoot's slaughtered band, Welsh's technocratic gaze could see only the need to bring the Indian Bureau more firmly under the regulation of civil service statutes.[29]

The comments of Lyman Abbott, perhaps the most vehement advocate of allotment, indicate most clearly that the arguments for allotment were starkly opposed to an agrarian political philosophy. In his remarks to the 1885 Lake Mohonk Conference, Abbot wove together the diverse melodies of allotment into a single triumphal chorus. Indians had no legitimate moral claim to any of this continent because they "did not occupy this land. A people do not occupy a country simply because they roam over it." He elaborated by pointing to the numerous ways in which Indian life did not correspond to modern industrial society: "They did not occupy the coal mines, nor the gold mines, into which they never struck a pick; nor the rivers which flow to the sea, and on which the music of a mill was never heard," he argued. For Abbot, the reservations simply perpetuated this barbarism. "The railroad goes to the edge of it and halts. The post-office goes to the edge of it and halts," he thundered. "There are mines there unopened, great wealth untouched by those who dwell there. The reservation system runs a fence around a great territory and says to civilization, 'Keep off!' "[30]

Many rejected the assumptions behind the arguments of Abbot and his circle. Bland and NIDA based their defense of Indian communal landholding on their opposition to America's emerging corporate order. NIDA prominently featured the leading institutions of corporate capitalism as the villains behind the allotment effort. NIDA publications on proposals to reduce the Sioux reservation pointed the finger at "the representatives of the Chicago, Milwaukee, and St. Paul railroad" and the "land syndicate connected with it." Writing in response to the Wounded Knee Massacre, Bland asserted that those opposed to reservations were supported "by certain persons who desired Indian territory thrown open

---

[29]*Address of Herbert Welsh, Delivered before the Mohonk Indian Conference* (Philadelphia: Indian Rights Association, October, 1886); Indian Rights Association, *A Hideous System* (Philadelphia: Indian Rights Association, December 1890); Herbert Welsh, "The Merit System a Necessity for the Indian Service," *Proceedings of the Eleventh Annual Meeting of the Lake Mohonk Conference of Friends of the Indian, Lake Mohonk Conference* (Philadelphia: Sherman & Co., 1893), 46. Welsh, "The Meaning of the Dakota Outbreak," 446, 452. See also Prucha, *American Indian Policy in Crisis*, 536.

[30]*Proceedings of the Third Annual Meeting of the Lake Mohonk Conference of the Friends of the Indian* (Philadelphia: Sherman & Co. Printers, 1886), 51, 52.

to the whites, and by railroad companies who desired land-grants therein."[31]

Bland and his associates not only accused individual whites of duplicity, they also consistently linked their critique of allotment to a broader condemnation of corporate power and plunder. Bland described Senator Dawes as "the author and most active champion of various bills and schemes to take the Indian lands from them" and added that "time would fail us to speak of his various railroad bills and other schemes which violate Indian treaties." In the heat of the legislative battle over the Dawes Act, Bland urged his readers to "[l]et no knee be bowed in submission to the great corporations, whose motto is that 'might makes right'."[32]

NIDA board member and Senate Chaplain Byron Sunderland echoed Bland's position when he argued that "the bill is chiefly in *the interest of white men*.... This, no doubt, is why so large a proportion of the public press, which is the mere tool of syndicates, charter companies, and stock-jobbing schemes of all sorts, are so loudly shouting for the passage of this bill." He asserted that the Dawes bill "has been pressed through by railroad men and other interested in breaking up Indian reservations. But these would not have been able to press their selfish scheme through if they had not had as active allies the officers of the Indian Rights Association." Enraged by the passage of the Dawes Act, Sunderland remarked that "'the *Indian Rights Association*' might now well change its title to the 'Land Shark's Rights Association'."[33]

Bland contrasted Indian landholding favorably to the white economic situation. Whereas wealthy white landowners could drive their impoverished tenants out of their homes, poorer Indians—whom Bland described in terms usually reserved for the white yeomanry—were far more secure. "The aristocratic Indian, who lives in a mansion and rides in his carriage," he wrote in late 1886, "owns not an acre more land than his neighbor, who

[31]Bland, *A History of the Sioux Agreement: Some Facts Which Should Not Be Forgotten*, 4, 17; Bland, *A Brief History of the Late Military Invasion of the Home of the Sioux*, 5. NIDA's attacks on railroads and land companies were not wishful conspiratorial thinking, for in fact railroads did play an instrumental role in opening up several Indian reservations. See Hagen, *United States–Comanche Relations*, 260; Arrell Morgan Gibson, *The Kickapoos: Lords of the Middle Border* (Norman: University of Oklahoma Press, 1963), 123; Melissa L. Meyer, *The White Earth Tragedy: Ethnicity and Dispossession at a Minnesota Anishinaabe Reservation, 1889–1920* (Lincoln: University of Nebraska Press, 1994), 158.

[32]*The Council Fire* 10 (January 1887): 2; 10 (February 1887): 18. NIDA's stance was similar in outline to the 1934 Indian Reorganization Act, which ended allotment, returned some lands to tribes, restored tribal political authority, and stressed the preservation rather than eradication of Indian culture. Its architect, Indian Commissioner John Collier, was a thorough primitivist and a self-conscious cultural relativist in a way that Bland was certainly not, but for both men protecting Indian landholding was a part of protecting values they felt were undermined by economic modernity. See Lawrence C. Kelly, *The Assault on Assimilation: John Collier and the Origins of Indian Policy Reform* (Albuquerque: University of New Mexico Press, 1983).

[33]Kelly, *The Assault on Assimilation*, 30; *The Council Fire* 10 (March 1887), 48.

lives in a log cabin and rides his Indian pony. He cannot demand rent from him and turn him and his family out of their home if they cannot pay."[34]

Many reformers—even the most jingoistic—would occasionally express doubts about white greed or materialism and make nostalgic statements about the passing of the different yet quaint Indian ways, much as they muttered platitudes about the yeoman farmer. But this should come as no surprise. As Christopher Lasch has argued, nostalgia in fact justifies radical socioeconomic transformations, because "it shares with the belief in progress, to which it is only superficially opposed, an eagerness to proclaim the death of the past and to deny history's hold over the present." For the nostalgic, the charm of the old agrarian order lay principally in the unlikelihood that any part of it would survive the onslaught of industrialization. In contrast, for Bland—although his public statements presented a bucolic, class-free, and naively untroubled view of white rural communities and Indian tribes alike—the praise of traditional landholding patterns was the basis for his advocacy of their preservation and renewal in the present. In the Indian commons Bland saw not a practice alien to the present or to his own culture, not something that he had to struggle to appreciate, but rather a living embodiment of some of his most cherished values. In one *Council Fire* article, he recounted a debate with an IRA member who asserted that "I don't sympathize with the policy which would allow a wild savage to monopolize twenty-five thousand acres of land, while civilized people need homes." Bland responded that "The Indian is not only just, but generous, in matters of property.... their land policy and tribal form of government [are] substantially like that prescribed by Moses." He sharpened this argument in an article written immediately after the passage of the Dawes Act, in which he held up Indian landholding as an antidote to the destructiveness of concentrated economic power. In his 1892 work *Esau; or, The Banker's Victim* he rhetorically asked: "is not all humanity a brotherhood, and are not all men brothers?" In this 1887 article, he used similar language when arguing that Indians hold their lands as a "common fund" and do so based on "the Christian idea that the bond between man and man is essentially fraternal, and that it is the largest interest of the whole that the means of successful industry should be placed at the disposal of each member of the community." This morality contrasted with the white economic order, in which "our practice is to allow the lands that constitute the means by which the coming generations are to be supplied with the means of industry, to be monopolized by the few" who thereby enrich themselves. Whites had failed where Indians had succeeded—in

[34] *The Council Fire* 9 (November–December 1886): 151. See Sherry Smith, *Reimaging Indians: Native Americans through Anglo Eyes, 1880–1940* (New York: Oxford University Press, 2000), for a discussion of later writers drawn to Indian cultures as alternatives to what they disliked about white culture.

controlling economic power.[35] As in the rhetoric of other reformers, Bland saw a contrast between Indian and white economic ways. But the contrast flattered Indians, not whites.

Occasionally Bland would specifically address the project of acculturating Indians to white norms, as in an article in which he satirized such efforts. He mentioned an offer made in the early eighteenth century by officials of the Colony of Virginia to educate some Indian youth to make them proper Virginia planters.

> The Indians... declined the offer with thanks, because... some of their youths had already been educated in northern colleges, and when returned to their tribes, they could not run well, nor build a tent, nor hunt successfully, nor were they good warriors; they were, in short, "no good" for the practical life of an Indian. They offered, however, to take half a dozen sons of the Virginians and educate them in the Indian methods, and pledged themselves to make men of them.[36]

There was no mention of their wrongheadedness or their need to adopt white ways.

Other NIDA members, both white and Indian, expressed similar hostility toward aspects of the U.S. political economy. Byron Sunderland directly addressed charges that Indian landholdings were "blocking the way of white settlements, white civilization, white transportation, white Christianity" and therefore had to be broken up. "Blocking civilization; blocking Christianity! Such civilization! Such Christianity!" he proclaimed. Moving far beyond reformers who criticized white greed but nevertheless saw it as inevitable, he proclaimed it "worse than the original barbarism. It ought to be blocked and be blocked forever! We have already had enough of it to cover the history of the Nation with disgrace... no Eastern idolatry was ever more merciless in its bloody rites than our modern Mammon worship." To leave no doubt as to where he and NIDA stood, he added that "We know that the policy we advocate is reactionary—not in line with progress."[37]

Indians themselves could also use agrarian language in opposing the onslaught of white acculturation. The Creek leader Pleasant Porter argued that whites "are all in competition with each other. The strong succeed, the weak fail. Then you build alms houses for the victims of your social and economic system of competition, and prisons for those who rebel against that

---

[35]Lasch, *The True and Only Heaven*, 118, 85; *The Council Fire* 10 (January 1887): 4–5; ibid., 10 (March 1887): 43. Bland himself did not buy into a nostalgic view of America before the coming of corporate capitalism. See Bland, *The Reign of Monopoly* (Washington, D.C: Rufus H. Darby, 1881), 7.

[36]Bland, *The Reign of Monopoly,* 49.

[37]In Bland, *A History of the Sioux Agreement: Some Facts Which Should Not Be Forgotten,* 15. Also see *The Council Fire* 10 (February 1887): 19, for a similar jeremiad against white greed.

system." The contrast with Indian ways was not favorable, for each tribe "is a harmonious brotherhood" with "no selfish competitions which affect injuriously the public interest" and "no land monopolists, hence no paupers." As a result, many "of the crimes of civilized society are unknown among us barbarians." Porter expressed his appreciation for some of "the advantages of education in literature, science and the industrial arts, which we get from the white man." But his gratitude was "greatly modified by the fact that these good things are accompanied by so much evil of which we knew nothing, and of which we would RATHER HAVE REMAINED IGNORANT."[38]

Several Indian tribes mounted their own lengthy and extensive campaigns against allotment proposals. The Cherokee were particularly active, sending repeated delegations, newspaper subscriptions, pamphlets, and holiday cards to congressmen. They continued to oppose allotment bills even when the Five Tribes were exempted in the final version of the Dawes Act. Indian memorials to Congress and pronouncements were of a piece with the major themes of NIDA's anti-allotment crusade. They argued that tribal landholding was the key to Indian prosperity, that its removal would lead to impoverishment, and that the intentions of those backing allotment were less than honorable. The Seneca Nation wrote that its own relative "condition of independence and prosperity is largely due to the system by which the lands are owned in common, controlled by the national councils, and are permanently inalienable." The memorial mirrored another of Bland's prominent themes, arguing that "Under this system, no Indian, however improvident and thriftless, can be deprived of a resort to the soil for his support and that of his family." The Cherokee protest to Congress upon the passage of the Dawes Act prominently featured charges that railroad companies and land speculators were the driving forces behind allotment. Indians continued to resist allotment even after the Dawes Act passed and was implemented. They often took their allotments adjacent to one another, thereby recreating their commons on a smaller scale. To the present day Indian nations have continued to insist that the United States honor the provisions of treaties guaranteeing the land and subsistence rights supplanted by the Dawes Act.[39]

---

[38] *The Council Fire* 10 (April–May 1887): 67; emphasis in original. Since the papers of the NIDA and Bland do not seem to have survived, there is no way of ascertaining if Bland heavily edited or even wrote some of the statements from Indians printed in *The Council Fire*. The romanticism of Porter's description of Creek society no doubt masked internal class dynamics and social tensions, one of the dangers of agrarianism's insistence that threats to communal harmony and justice were entirely external to those communities. See Brinkley, *Voice of Protest*, 159, on such communal rhetoric, and Jeffrey Ostler, "'They Regard Their Passing as Wakan': Interpreting Western Sioux Explanations for the Bison's Decline," *Western Historical Quarterly* 30, no.4 (2000): 475–98, for divisions among the Sioux.

[39] Tom Holm, "Indian Lobbyists: Cherokee Opposition to the Allotment of Tribal Lands," *American Indian Quarterly* 5 (spring 1979): 117; "Seneca Nation of New York Indians," December 21, 1881, resolution of the Council. Reprinted in *Message of President Transmitting*

Agrarianism and the American Political Imagination

Agrarian opposition was only one of the hurdles that the Dawes Act had to clear. A general allotment proposal was first introduced in 1881 and repeatedly failed to pass Congress, often never even getting out of committee. Despite the assumption that the act's passage was inevitable, as Francis Paul Prucha notes, "there was no concerted popular pressure, either western or eastern, for the bill." The fact that almost every vote on allotment was by voice precludes a full detailing of the Congressional coalitions for and against it, but significant Congressional forces opposed it. The arrogant belief that white culture was so much more advanced than Indian ways led many in Congress to doubt the efficacy of throwing Indians head first into the thick of American life. Indeed, the majority report of the Hollman Committee—established by the same Congress that later passed the Dawes Act—concluded that since "[t]he Indian, for the present at least, cannot compete with the whiteman in the struggle for life," allotment should be begun very slowly if at all, and be accompanied by a provision making "the power of alienation in any form . . . indefinitely suspended."[40]

Even after the act's passage, some politicians continued to make arguments similar to NIDA's. For example, Nebraska Populist Senator William Allen seemed to echo Bland's pragmatic doubts when he argued in 1894 that a rapacious absentee land company was behind the effort to allot the lands of the Omaha Indians. He concluded that "the entire fortune of these women and children is turned over to the tender mercies of the sharks who . . . are endeavoring to get their land from them as rapidly as possible."[41] Wider influence for agrarianism would have heightened such pragmatic doubts even among those who granted market forces a greater degree of latitude than did agrarian radicals. Moreover, because Populists sought to expand the authority of the state to check concentrated economic power, maintaining a distinct legal standing for Indian reservations would have been more plausible had agrarianism been more influential.

In the end, of course, neither NIDA's political lobbying nor active Indian resistance stopped the passage of the Dawes Act. The key role that agrarianism and agrarians played in opposing the act, however, requires an explanation. Unfortunately, much scholarship of Populism is of little help in understanding Bland and his circles. Despite a relative golden age

---

Memorial of Seneca Nation of New York Indians against Allotment of Lands in Severalty, 47th Cong., 1st sess., H. Exec. Doc. 83; Holm, "Indian Lobbyists," 123; Meyer, *The White Earth Tragedy,* 206.

[40]Hagan, *Indian Rights Association,* 66, Hoxie, *The Final Promise,* 71; Prucha, *The Great Father,* 669; House, *Investigation of Expenditures of Appropriations for Indian Service and Yellowstone Park, Part I: Report,* 49th Cong., 1st sess., H. Rept. 1076, xxxviii.

[41]*Congressional Record,* 53rd Cong, 2d sess., 1894, 26, pt. 8: 7680–81.

during the 1960s and 1970s in which Populists became "tolerant," the pendulum seems to have swung back to Richard Hofstadter's view that paranoia, status anxiety, and racism motivated the Populist critique of modern America. In Nancy MacLean's influential work on the 1920s Ku Klux Klan, for example, populism becomes a one-dimensional racist and patriarchal politics akin to an American version of fascism. Although Michael Kazin wants to reassert the centrality of "the populist impulse" to United States political history, he portrays—albeit in a much milder fashion than MacLean—populism and racial egalitarianism as competing and never fully reconcilable ideologies. Such views reflect the fact that Populists did sometimes succumb to virulent racism or sheer greed. For instance, Kansas Populist Senator William A. Peffer sounded indistinguishable from Lyman Abbot when he proclaimed that "[t]he time for bartering with the Indians for their land is passed... we need all the land in this country for homes." And certainly some southern Populists, often after the movement's overall defeat, embraced segregation and trumpeted white supremacy.[42]

A more important legacy of Populism, however, is the ability of many of its adherents to transcend racial and social divisions. Unlike contemporary multiculturalism, populist racial egalitarianism was based on an affirmation of shared humanity and underlying similarity across racial lines. The heart of agrarian radicalism, as Stephen Hahn argues, is the link of "freedom and independence with control over productive resources." The agrarians of Thomas Bland's circle had reason to see something of themselves in Indians intent on resisting allotment. The closure of the Indian commons came upon the heels of the closure of the commons of many white farmers—and, in the South, of rural blacks as well. In the South, the post–Civil War planter elite succeeded in closing the hunting and fishing commons and in passing stock laws that made owners of livestock liable for damage done even to unfenced crops. This enclosure, aimed at rationalizing staple production and securing a more reliable and disciplined supply of labor, helped lead some yeomen to develop the explicit and self-conscious critique of corporate capitalism that blossomed into southern Populism in the late 1880s and 1890s. Similarly, according to John Mack Faragher, midwestern farmers in communities like those of Thomas Bland's Orange County, Indiana, "utilized important rural productive resources in common with their neighbors," including common hunting and grazing areas.[43]

[42]Richard Hofstadter, *The Age of Reform: From Bryan to F.D.R.* (New York: Vintage, 1955); Walter Nugent, *The Tolerant Populists* (Chicago: University of Chicago Press, 1968); Nancy MacLean, *Behind the Mask of Chivalry: The Making of the Second Ku Klux Klan* (New York: Oxford University Press, 1994); Michael Kazin, *The Populist Persuasion: an American History* (New York: Basic Books, 1995); *Congressional Record*, 52nd Cong, 1st sess., 23, pt. 3: 2690; also see especially C. Vann Woodward, *The Strange Career of Jim Crow* (New York: Oxford University Press, 1955).

[43]See Stephen Hahn, *Roots of Southern Populism: Yeoman Farmers and the Transformation of the Georgia Upcountry, 1850–1890* (New York: Oxford University Press, 1983), 8; Stephen Hahn,

In the sense that they believed in private property and the importance of an individual work ethic, agrarians were squarely in the mainstream of American political thought. In as much as they believed that labor should not be a commodity and that in an ideal society, as Bruce Palmer puts it, "land or other resources on which to get a living are available to all," agrarians bound up economic activity within a dense thicket of social and moral relations and sanctions.[44] If, for agrarian thinkers such as Bland, the course of history was more complex than the rise of ever-growing economic might, then the future held more viable options—for both Indians and whites—than the stark choice of extinction or conforming with the exigencies of a modern capitalist society. A sober respect for human potential balanced a deep fear of concentrated power. Agrarianism was therefore uniquely suited not only to become the ideology of NIDA's defense of the Indian commons, but also to become the basis for the most sustained and organized opposition to corporate capitalism up to the present era. And the concerns and political language of agrarian radicals are still with us today, in a dramatically different America, for the same reason that agrarianism played a critical role in the debate over allotment: the assertion that the obligations of community life and the demands of morality outweigh the laws of an impersonal market.

"Hunting, Fishing, and Foraging: Common Rights and Class Relations in the Postbellum South," *Radical History Review* 26 (1982): 37–64; C. Vann Woodward, *Tom Watson: Agrarian Rebel* (New York: Macmillan, 1938); John Mack Faragher, *Sugar Creek: Life on the Illinois Prairie* (New Haven, Conn.: Yale University Press, 1986), 132.

[44]Bruce Palmer, *"Man Over Money": The Southern Populist Critique of American Capitalism* (Chapel Hill: University of North Carolina Press, 1980), 13.

African Americans, Community Building, and the Role of the State in Rural Reform in Texas, 1890s–1930s

DEBRA A. REID

Histories of African Americans in the postbellum rural South tend to depict sharecroppers and tenants as victims of the crop lien, racism, and the capitalization of agriculture. Few assess the activities of a small but influential group of African American agrarians who became spokespersons for private and public reform. These male and female reformers celebrated life in the country and believed that landownership, comfortable homes, better schools, and proper morality could offer security and freedom from economic and social bondage. Neither minority status nor incipient racism silenced these black agrarians. They formed private self-help groups to further their minority agendas. They influenced white politicians to pass legislation that supported their cause, and they sought public funding to further their goals of improving rural life. They became some of the first

The author wishes to thank several colleagues for commenting on earlier versions of this article, including Lynne E. Curry and Christopher Waldrep, Darren J. Pierson and Keith Volanto, and members of her Ph.D. dissertation committee: Robert A. Calvert (chair), Albert Broussard, Rebecca Sharpless, and David Vaught. In addition the author thanks Mary Summers for the ideas that helped move this article beyond a description of African American reform to an analysis of the interrelationship of private and public initiative in the struggle to correct societal inadequacies.

Funding from the Miss Ima Hogg Student Research Travel Award, Center for American History, University of Texas at Austin; and the Ottis Lock Endowment Award, East Texas Historical Association, made this research possible. Additional support from Texas A&M University included the 1999 Graduate Research Fellowship, Women's Studies Program; the 1999 College of Liberal Arts scholarship, Women's Faculty Network; and travel grants from the Department of History and the Office of Graduate Studies.

A version of this article appears as "African Americans and Progressive Reform," *Agricultural History* 74, no. 2 (spring 2000): 322–39.

African American employees of the federal and state government in the early twentieth century when state extension services and departments of agriculture throughout the South segregated their programs.[1]

Their activism generated only limited returns, however, as male and female reformers had to respond to local interests to remain effective. Those who became agents of the state served a white male bureaucracy that expected conformity regardless of race or gender. This reinforced racism and patriarchy and prevented the formation of a biracial coalition dedicated to saving the family farm. But black-owned and -operated farms still exist, and African Americans continue to recognize inequities and adopt a variety of approaches to secure fair treatment. The class-action suit launched by nearly five thousand southern black farmers against the U.S. Department of Agriculture (USDA) for discrimination between 1981 and 1996 illustrates this persistence. Their experiences as farmers in the United States, and their relationship with the welfare state, reflect a little-understood but distinctive agrarian tradition.[2]

Most rural African Americans were first and foremost southerners, and they adopted an agrarian ideology that reflected southern influences and prejudices, even if racism ultimately prevented white and black agrarians from allying politically or economically to bring profound change to southern agriculture. Thomas Jefferson's rhetoric provided inspiration for southern agrarians, black and white alike. Members of both races linked landownership to virtue and independence, but they adopted different political strategies. White southern Democrats defined their agenda by calling on Jeffersonian notions of state sovereignty, local authority, and herrenvolk democracy to maintain white hegemony in the rural South. African Americans, in contrast, tended to vote Republican prior to disfranchisement, respecting the authority of the federal government and the importance of interracial cooperation to further their citizenship goals. This difference in partisan affiliation, exacerbated by racism, made black agrarians formally powerless. Given their political situation, they countered by adopting fun-

---

[1] Studies of southern agriculture and the debilitating influence of the crop lien include Gilbert Fite, *Cotton Fields No More: Southern Agriculture, 1865–1980* (Lexington: University Press of Kentucky, 1984); Pete Daniel, *Breaking the Land: The Transformation of Cotton, Tobacco, and Rice Cultures since 1880* (Urbana: University of Illinois Press, 1985); and Jack Temple Kirby, *Rural Worlds Lost: The American South, 1920–1960* (Baton Rouge: Louisiana State University Press, 1987).

[2] "A New Season: Black Farmers in Texas Form Group to Take Control of Their Own Destinies," *Dallas Morning News*, April 6, 1999, D1, D14. Salim Muwakkil, "Grapes of Wrath," *In These Times* 21, no. 14 (May 26, 1997): 23–25; Salim Muwakkil, "Too Little, Too Late for Black Farmers," ibid., 23, no. 6 (February 21, 1999): 10–11. The consent decree of the district court case, *Timothy C. Pigford et al. v. Dan Glickman, Secretary, The United States Department of Agriculture*, appears at http://www.usda.gov/da/consent/htm. Thomas W. Mitchell, "From Reconstruction to Deconstruction: Undermining Black Landownership, Political Independence, and Community through Partition Sales of Tenancies in Common," *Northwestern University Law Review* 95 (winter: 2001): 501–80.

damentally economic goals, working to strengthen the family farm as a means to obtain land and independence. To further these "private" goals, they co-operated with white authority, and they sought and received support from federal programs that emphasized social welfare. In the process, they helped shape the growing state by insisting that rural African Americans deserved to participate.[3]

These black progressives undertook ambiguous reforms. They did not attempt a radical challenge to the crop lien system, a form of southern agriculture that created an impoverished and dependent class of farmers. Instead, black agrarians concentrated on those with the potential to succeed. As a result they provided information and inspiration to only a small percentage of the rural population, African Americans who either owned land or enough property to give them some control over their resources. Racial separatism complicated black reform also. Agrarians pursuing economic goals found themselves at odds with urban progressives who argued above all for political equality. Yet in the end it was the narrow attitudes held by white southerners about race and gender that most limited black agrarian effectiveness. Discrimination and underfunding reinforced the decision of African American reformers to focus on the deserving.[4]

After Reconstruction, black agrarians concentrated their efforts on improving rural life and developing strategies to mitigate poverty, illiteracy, injustice, and violence. Beginning in the 1890s, the self-help doctrine espoused by Booker T. Washington led many black southerners, men and women alike, to look for solutions internal to their own communities. They organized their rural peers into fraternal societies, built schools, supported black churches, and welcomed private philanthropy to accomplish their mission. Others were more convinced that the state could wield influence on their behalf despite the disappointments of Reconstruction, and they

[3] For an explanation of agrarianism see R. Douglas Hurt, *American Agriculture: A Brief History* (Ames: Iowa State University Press, 1994), 72–77.

[4] Dewey Grantham, *Southern Progressivism: The Reconciliation of Progress and Tradition* (Knoxville: University of Tennessee Press, 1983); Jack Temple Kirby, *Darkness at the Dawning: Race and Reform in the Progressive South* (Philadelphia: Lippincott, 1972). William A. Link explores the competing approaches to progressive reform in *The Paradox of Southern Progressivism* (Chapel Hill: University of North Carolina Press, 1992). For a survey of historiography on the Progressive Era in Texas see Larry D. Hill, "Texas Progressivism: A Search for Definition," in *Texas Through Time: Evolving Interpretations,* ed. Walter L. Buenger and Robert A. Calvert (College Station: Texas A&M University Press, 1991), 229–50.

African Americans operated one quarter of all Texas farms in 1890; 10.0 percent of these operators owned their farms. Bureau of the Census, *Negro Population in the United States, 1790–1915* (Washington, D.C.: Government Printing Office, 1918), 831–34. By 1910, nearly one-third (30.3 percent) of all African American farmers in Texas owned their farms, and these accounted for 10.8 percent of all farms in operation in the state. The percentage of black farmers who owned their land declined steadily to 29.9 percent in 1920 and 23.9 percent in 1930. *The Negro Farmer in the United States* (Washington: Government Printing Office, 1933), 39; *Thirteenth Census of the United States, 1910,* vol. 7, *Agriculture* (Washington: Government Printing Office, 1913), 655.

petitioned the government for appropriations for public agricultural colleges and experiment stations. Still, Washington's ideas gained influence at the same time that both the Republican party turned its back on its black members and the promise of involvement in third-party politics withered after 1896. It is quite difficult to document, at the height of white supremacy, competing African American rural ideologies regarding the relative merits of private or public reform. Going into the twentieth century, though, it was clear that the former held the upper hand—making the advocacy of even limited state action all the more historically significant.[5]

The activities of five self-conscious Texas reformers provide the means to assess black agrarian philosophy and strategy. These men and women pursued careers in politics, education, business, and philanthropy. They all believed those private initiatives could best inform rural families and help them attain economic solvency. Robert Lloyd Smith founded and operated the Farmers Improvement Society of Texas (FIS). He married twice, and both of his wives, Francis Isabella Isaacs and Ruby L. Cobb, held offices in the organization, worked as financial agents for the FIS school, and coordinated programs for women and junior members. Joseph Elward Clayton taught school and worked as a principal, eventually converting the private institute into a public school. His wife, Brittie White, assisted him in fund-raising and in other endeavors related to vocational education. Several factors including gender, age, and philosophy affected these reformers' decisions, and in some instances the reformers pursued competing goals. Generally, however, their similarities outweighed their differences. The men and women shared a middle-class identity, an interest in education for youth and adults, and the belief that scientific agriculture and household production could increase farm income. In addition, they cultivated racial harmony and encouraged prayer to attain economic solvency and contribute to society. The experiences of these men and women speak tellingly to the options that African Americans pursued to improve rural conditions in Texas between the 1890s and the 1930s.[6]

[5] Louis R. Harlan provides the most comprehensive study of Washington's ideology and influence in *Booker T. Washington: The Making of a Black Leader, 1856–1901* (New York: Oxford University Press, 1972) and *Booker T. Washington: The Wizard of Tuskegee 1901–1915* (New York: Oxford University Press, 1983). Glenda Elizabeth Gilmore documents the ways that black women used social and civic activism to engage more directly in political discourse in *Gender and Jim Crow: Women and the Politics of White Supremacy in North Carolina, 1896–1920* (Chapel Hill: University of North Carolina Press, 1996). Adolph Reed, Jr. explores the absence of political discourse in *Stirrings in the Jug: Black Politics in the Post-Segregation Era* (Minneapolis: University of Minnesota Press, 1999), 15–28.

[6] For biographical information on Robert Lloyd Smith, Isabella Isaacs, and Ruby Cobb, see Personal Materials, Smith-Cobb Family Papers, Texas Collection, Baylor University, Waco, Texas (hereafter SCFP); "Smith is Laid to Rest: Obsequies Held for Hon. Robt. L. Smith," *Waco Messenger,* July 17, 1942; "Hon. Robert L. Smith," in *The National Encyclopedia of the Colored Race,* ed. Clement Richardson (Montgomery, Ala.: National Publishing Company, Inc., 1919), 1:383; "Robert L. Smith," in *Who's Who in Colored America 1928–1929,* ed. Joseph J. Boris (New York: Who's Who in Colored America Corp., [1929]), 341–42; and Lawrence

Overall, only a small percentage of black property owners in Texas participated in the private reforms. Small memberships made it difficult for participants to endure white disapproval, economic depression limited the ability of poor black farm families to participate, and growing cities lured youth and talent away. Agribusiness made the small subsistence farms that reformers recommended increasingly difficult to maintain. And by the early 1900s, increased government funding for public education and extension work provided a stable income for qualified recipients, luring talent away from comparable private reform.

Agrarians modified their approach during this period of transition. They recognized that self-help strategies based on self-segregation isolated rural African Americans from mainstream white society, even though the black reformers had to nurture relations with white peers to ensure success. Booker T. Washington and other black agrarians believed that involvement with the state offered an opportunity to direct national attention toward black regional concerns. This led many agrarians to meld private with public support to accomplish their ends. Robert Smith and Joseph Clayton pursued this route. Smith became the first director of the segregated Texas Agricultural Extension Service in 1915, and Clayton became the first African American to organize farmers' institutes under the auspices of the Texas Department of Agriculture in 1917. Racism limited these efforts, however, as black agents remained dependent upon white patronage.

Gender bias also worked against black agrarians. Women assumed leadership roles in private as well as public offerings, thus legitimizing their quest for education by providing forums to apply their knowledge beyond the classroom. Women used their positions to focus attention on the household and make it a more productive and lucrative part of a farming operation. Their emphasis on canning and poultry production, however, challenged traditional fieldwork patterns practiced by black farm families, and many blacks remained generally skeptical about the benefits of book learning and scientific practices. Others resented the influence of educated women, particularly those who tried to train young and lower-class blacks to respect white authority. Progressive reformers believed that this strategy could help them mitigate white fears and preserve black male status, con-

---

D. Rice, "Robert Lloyd Smith," in *The New Handbook of Texas*, 6 vols. (Austin: Texas State Historical Association, 1996), 5:1108. For an interview with Smith see J. Mason Brewer, *Negro Legislators of Texas* (Dallas: Mathis Publishing Co., 1935), 101–4. For biographical information on Joseph Elward Clayton and Brittie White see "Joseph Elward Clayton," *Who's Who in Colored America, 1930–1932*, ed. Thomas Yenser (New York: Garrett and Massie, Inc., [1932]), 97; David L. Bearden, "Clayton Vocational Institute, A Superior School" (typescript), 11, Clayton Vocational Institute Papers, Austin History Center, Austin, Texas (hereafter AHC); and Kharen Monsho, "Joseph Elward Clayton," *The New Handbook of Texas*, 2:148.

sidered by some to be "the race's most important right." Their opponents believed it doomed them to second-class status.[7]

White government officials at the state and federal levels withheld adequate resources and authority but, ultimately, could not prevent rural blacks from participating. The segregated programs that resulted did not displace white authority in the countryside, but the black employees influenced decisions and this helped shape the emerging social welfare system. White administrators found themselves responding to demands from black agrarians to increase the number of black agents during World War I. Local funding rose steadily after the war, and the number of black public servants working in rural Texas increased as well, a trend that continued during the 1920s and into the New Deal era. Whites authorized these expenditures because, even at the height of Jim Crow, rural blacks exercised enough power to sway their opinions. But whites did not intend to give up their status within the hierarchy. Only with civil rights legislation in the 1960s were white officials forced to eliminate discrimination in the service based on race. Even then, though, they accomplished this by dismantling the black bureaucracy that extension agents had built over fifty years and marginalizing black farmers even more by reducing their direct access to government programs.

Robert Lloyd Smith (1861–1942), one of the most visible black agrarians in Texas between the 1890s and the 1930s, helped build the black bureaucracy. Smith was born in Charleston, South Carolina, to free parents who both taught school. He graduated from Avery Normal Institute, attended the University of South Carolina, and graduated from Atlanta University in 1880. In 1885 he moved to Oakland in south central Texas and worked with the newly organized Oakland Normal School. It became one of the best in the state. One-crop agriculture and dependence on the crop lien contributed to the depressed conditions in Oakland, but Smith did not see these as the causes of illiteracy and poverty. Instead, he believed that the institution of slavery, a condition he had never directly experienced, had engendered improvidence and thoughtlessness in the tenants he observed. In 1889, Smith gained inspiration from an article about self-help and improvement in New England that he read in the *Youth's Companion*. The article provided a model for him to use to satisfy his "'irresistible impulse' to improve... the 'common negro'" He attempted to persuade the poor tenants that emancipation did not mean freedom from

[7] Judith N. McArthur analyzes the involvement of women of both races in reform in Texas and the significance of public programs in *Creating the New Woman: The Rise of Southern Women's Progressive Culture in Texas, 1893–1918* (Urbana: University of Illinois Press, 1998), 5, 16–18, 38–39, 48–49, 143–49. For the quote, see Gilmore, *Gender and Jim Crow*, 104–5.

labor and that hard work, thrift, and morality could reduce their exploitation by white southerners. Smith wanted black farmers to learn the self-help philosophy by practicing it and paying their own way, and he criticized those who failed to follow his advice. In December 1889, Smith organized the Village Improvement Society with fourteen charter members to provide a structure to fulfill his goals.[8]

Smith's ideas to improve black communities revolved around the home. He urged members to purchase homes, to improve those that they already owned by furnishing them with items "necessary for the comfort of our families," and to plant shade trees and shrubbery—but to do all this within their financial means. He also cautioned Oakland residents to "set our faces against and unite our forces in fighting those evils which debase our character and destroy our homes, the principal of which are gambling, intemperance, and social impurity." He modified these goals in 1891 after six years of life in Texas. During this time Smith had broadened his perception of the debilitating effects of slavery to include the crop mortgage system. He recognized the significant third-party challenge brewing in the form of the Colored Farmers Alliance, founded in Texas in 1886, and the involvement of African Americans in the People's party in Texas in 1891. This prompted him to reorganize his society to provide farmers more support in their efforts to gain economic independence, and to distance his organization from Populism. White Republicans who elected Smith to two terms as their representative from Colorado County expected no less. Smith changed the organization's name to the Farmers' Improvement Society and focused on five objectives: to abolish the credit system, to improve methods of farming, to cooperate in purchasing, to aid members in sickness and in death, and to pursue home and community improvements.

[8] Smith had more than one reason to move to Texas. He had published a Republican newspaper in Charleston, but left following the overthrow of the Reconstruction government. He headed to Texas because he believed that it "offered the fairest field for the aspirant for distinction in the schoolroom," but a black politician recalled that Smith left South Carolina due to "social pressure placed upon him for marrying a dark-complexioned lady." See *National Encyclopedia of the Colored Race*, 383, and interview with William McDonald, April 16, 1945, in Douglas Geraldyne Perry, "Black Populism: The Negro in the People's Party in Texas" (M.A. thesis, Prairie View A&M College, 1945), 41, quoted in Merline Pitre, *Through Many Dangers, Toils and Snares: The Black Leadership of Texas, 1868–1900* (Austin, Tex.: Eakin Press, 1985), 180. Lawrence D. Rice comments on the status of Smith's normal school in *The Negro in Texas, 1874–1900* (Baton Rouge: Louisiana State University Press, 1971), 110–11. For an overview of the FIS see Robert Carroll, "Robert L. Smith and the Farmers' Improvement Society of Texas" (M.A. thesis, Baylor University, 1974). See also Purvis Carter, "Robert Lloyd Smith and the Farmers' Improvement Society, a Self-Help Movement in Texas," *Negro History Bulletin* 29 (1966): 175–91. Smith's criticism of poor Texas blacks appears in *Galveston Daily News*, 10 October 1902, SCFP, and in two articles by Smith, "Village Improvement Among the Negroes," *Outlook*, March 31, 1900, 734, and "An Uplifting Negro Cooperative Society," *The World's Work* 16 (July 1908): 10465.

In this way the organization combined civic and fraternal functions. It pursued self-help, a strategy that did not challenge the racial protocol of the time, and it offered practical solutions that individuals could implement within the support structure of an organization.[9]

Smith's larger objectives became evident in correspondence with Booker T. Washington. Smith thanked Washington for opening people's eyes to the value of industrial education as a means to attain "the profoundest statesmanship" so that the African American would not remain trapped as a "hewer of wood and drawer of water." Smith participated in the Tuskegee Institute's Negro Conference, an educational program suited to the needs of black farmers and their families, in 1896. The experience helped Smith realize how he could restructure the FIS to reach farmers beyond Colorado and neighboring counties. Smith wrote that "I should throw myself with all the energy of my being into the work of founding a Little Tuskegee at Oakland." Soon thereafter the FIS started an annual convocation and adopted a constitution and by-laws, a dues structure, and a method of forming local branches in order to sustain discussion of the issues that black farmers faced. Smith welcomed "all persons of good moral character of either sex that feel dissatisfied with their present condition" to join the society. He and other self-help proponents such as Booker T. Washington believed that blacks could earn their political rights by attaining economic independence. At the first annual FIS convocation in 1896, Smith called for a "second emancipation" based on "economic improvement through communal effort." Ultimately, Smith believed that if black men and women "possessed the qualities of true citizenship, the most intelligent and progressive white

[9] Carroll, "Smith and FIS," 20–28; 33. Alwyn Barr urges historians to undertake an in-depth study of black fraternal organizations in "African Americans in Texas: From Stereotypes to Diverse Roles," in *Texas Through Time: Evolving Interpretations,* ed. Walter L. Buenger and Robert A. Calvert (College Station: Texas A&M University Press, 1991), 63; Alwyn Barr, *Black Texans: A History of Negroes in Texas, 1528–1971* (Austin, Tex.: Jenkins Publishing Company, 1973), 106–7. Smith's political activities included participation in Republican conventions in Texas in 1896 and 1900. See Earnest William Winkler, ed., *Platforms of Political Parties in Texas,* Bulletin of the University of Texas, no. 53 (September 20, 1916), 359, 392–93, 433. Analyses of Smith's two terms in the Texas legislature (1894 and 1896) include Pitre, *Through Many Dangers, Toils and Snares,* especially 179–87; Merline Pitre, "Robert Lloyd Smith: A Black Lawmaker in the Shadow of Booker T. Washington," *Phylon* 46 (September 1985): 262–68; and Barry A. Crouch, "Hesitant Recognition: Texas Black Politicians, 1865–1900," *East Texas Historical Journal* 31, no. 1 (1993): 45. Booker T. Washington supported Smith's federal appointment as deputy United States marshall for the Northern District of Texas and prevailed over "lily-white" Republicans in Texas who attempted to discredit him. Smith retired from politics in 1904 following his loss in a bid to secure a post as delegate at large to the Republican convention. See Pitre, *Through Many Dangers, Toils, and Snares,* 202–4; Brewer, *Negro Legislators of Texas,* 101–4, 120–21; and Louis R. Harlan and Raymond W. Smock, eds., *The Booker T. Washington Papers,* 14 vols. (Urbana: University of Illinois Press, 1972–89), 4:295–97; 6:232, 346–47, 434–35, 488 (hereafter *BTW Papers*).

residents of the same community will recognize the fact" and extend full citizenship.[10]

Another quality of true citizenship, however, was whiteness. Neil Foley has explored this in the context of Texas cotton culture. He documents connections between whiteness, independence based on property acquisition, agricultural productivity, and citizenship. Those white males who could acquire real property attained manhood and status, while those poor whites who could not afford land, as well as African Americans and Mexicans, never gained status in rural southern society. Blacks who broke out of the limitations imposed by race or economics did so because whites actually conferred the status of "whiteness" upon them. Certainly, Robert Smith's political acumen helped him tailor the FIS message to suit the needs of different races. He described the FIS as a black-owned and -operated organization that advanced economic rather than political goals. This relieved some rural whites who opposed and feared social equality, and it helped a limited number of blacks acquire land and stabilize their farming operations. Foley's interpretation, however, fails to account for the efforts of blacks such as Smith and FIS members who used private and public reform to prompt change; in effect Foley's monolithic analytical concept of "whiteness" erases the agency of African American agrarians.[11]

Smith reported on the value of property owned by FIS members and their tax contributions, and newspaper editors responded with praise. White Texans also appreciated the economic boost that the gatherings of FIS members brought to their communities. In 1899 more than twelve hundred attended the annual state convocation in Columbus, the county seat of Colorado County. In 1902, newspapers commented on the significant financial resources controlled by landowning blacks attending the state convocation in Eagle Lake, and towns vied for the honor of holding the meeting.[12]

Smith used interracial cooperation to disarm white opposition. When he addressed FIS members at the convocation in Eagle Lake in 1902, a site of

[10] Carroll, "Smith and FIS," 37–8. For excerpts from the FIS Constitution of 1896 and the convocation see Carroll, "Smith and FIS," 40, 48. The Tuskegee Negro Conference began in 1892. Allen W. Jones, "The Role of Tuskegee Institute in the Education of Black Farmers," *Journal of Negro History* 60, no. 2 (April 1975), 254–56; and Earl W. Crosby, "The Roots of Black Agricultural Extension Work," *Historian* 39, no. 2 (February 1977), 229. Smith traveled with Washington to the North in 1899, encouraged Washington to speak to members of the FIS in 1900, and accompanied Washington during his tour of Texas in 1911. See *BTW Papers*, 5:3–4, 229–30; 11:332. *BTW Papers*, 4:290–92, 297; 5:100. Max Bennett Thrasher, "A Texas Experiment. A Revolution in Negro Life Under Way. An Institution from New England Planted in Texas—Robert Smith's Great Work Among the Colored Farmers—The Typical Freedman's Town," clipping [*Boston Evening Transcript*], 15 December [1899], SCFP.

[11] Neil Foley, *The White Scourge: Mexicans, Blacks, and Poor Whites in Texas Cotton Culture* (Berkeley: University of California Press, 1997).

[12] *Galveston Daily News*, October 10, 1902, SCFP. Carroll, "Smith and FIS," 49.

race violence during Reconstruction, he focused on an agricultural threat of grave concern, the boll weevil. He encouraged FIS members to "join hands with the whites in fighting the boll weevil and in any other matter which is made for the common welfare." Smith did not, however, advocate a cross-class coalition. Instead he expressed a bias that struck a chord with paternalistic Texans when he declared that "the best white and colored people" share "heavy burdens" and should protect their interests from the "low element"—that is, underdeveloped and ignorant whites and blacks. Other Progressive Era reformers criticized immorality, thriftlessness, and vagrancy. Black agrarians believed that these qualities could undermine the foundation of their ideology, one that linked independence with property ownership and virtue with family values. Robert Smith believed that members of both races had to take responsibility for their actions to avoid losing their savings to "King Credit." He apparently did not actively recruit whites, but his call for interracial cooperation to improve the rural economy accomplished at least his minimum objective. The editor of the *Weimar Mercury* wrote that "the white folks appreciated the racial harmony it generated."[13]

The rhetoric of acceptance by white residents made it possible for FIS members in local branches to undertake reform with some sense of protection. The society took additional precautions by maintaining a degree of secrecy. The constitution of 1896 designated mid-November through mid-December, plus the last two weeks of February, as the times devoted to cooperative endeavors. During these months local branches discussed member needs, identified wholesale markets, and made buying trips. They also explored the best means to sell their cotton. Only members participated during this critical period. Those who appeared as a security threat—anyone who seemed eager to discuss FIS business such as cooperative purchasing agreements with landlords, furnishing merchants, or other non-FIS members—were expelled.[14]

FIS attempts to mitigate racial tension arose from instances of intimidation and violence. More than five hundred blacks became victims of racial violence in Texas between 1870 and 1900, a figure unmatched by any other southern state. Texans passed an anti-lynching law in 1897, but it had little effect, as the state still ranked third in lynchings in the first decade of the

---

[13] *Annual Address of Hon. R. L. Smith, President Farmers' Improvement Society of Texas Delivered at Eagle Lake Texas, 8 October 1902 in the Seventh Convocation, Printed by order of the Society* ([Paris, Texas]: Farmers' Improvement Society of Texas, 1902), 16, FIS Records, SCFP. The FIS published a play by Smith's wife Ruby Cobb, *Trial of Old King Credit* (Waco, Texas: Juvenile Department, F.I.S., [c.1919]), 9, FIS Miscellaneous Pamphlets, SCFP. Characters included a "White Man" who explained how he lost respect for "darkies" and white farmers who "hasn't [sic] got sense enough to look out for himself." It is unknown if any whites joined the FIS. *Boston Evening Transcript* (1899), clipping, SCFP.

[14] Carroll, "Smith and FIS," 35, 47–48; *Constitution and By-Laws of the Farmers' Improvement Society of Texas* (n.p.: n.p. [c. 1909]), 17–18, FIS Miscellaneous Pamplets, SCFP.

twentieth century. FIS affiliates shared their brushes with violence in letters to Smith. R. S. Boone of Courtney, Texas noted the loss of two of his children, one of whom was murdered. Smith asked *The Helping Hand*'s readers to pray for Boone. In the same issue an FIS branch in Nettie, Texas, reported discussing questions such as "Will the Negro Be as Free as Other Races after the War?" Other Texans joined the National Association for the Advancement of Colored People in 1918 and 1919, but intimidation undermined this effort. Smith intended to protect the FIS from such a fate. He advised FIS members to practice prudence and patience in the post–World War I period because "the white people did not seem to be as cordial." He assured the members "after a period of unrest and adjustment that things would come out all right."[15]

Smith mitigated racial separatism among FIS members just as he assuaged white opposition to his society and its causes. Religion held the power to unite or divide communities, and the recognition of this prompted him to incorporate testimonials, sermons, scripture readings, prayers, and hymns into FIS meetings. As a result of Smith's imbuing FIS functions with religious fervor, the members, most of whom found comfort from their faith, felt more at home in the gatherings. Smith, a devout Methodist, de-emphasized congregational alliances "denominational affiliations" by avoiding the terms "convention" (Baptist) or "conference" (Methodist) in describing FIS gatherings. Instead he settled on "convocation," a neutral term borrowed from the Episcopalians. He also limited discussions of religion and politics at meetings. Smith's avoidance of topics that could potentially divide membership or upset white Texans helped the society grow and generated a sense of purpose among members.[16]

Smith needed a united FIS to accomplish some of his controversial goals. His efforts to keep the population in the country competed outright with other reforms. Urban elites believed that life in the cities offered the best opportunities for the race, and so did labor recruiters who relied on rural

[15] Robert A. Calvert and Arnoldo De León, *The History of Texas* (Arlington Heights, Ill.: Harlan Davidson, Inc., 1990), 166; 234. Steven A. Reich argues that the silence of state and federal government made private intimidation possible in "Soldiers of Democracy: Black Texans and the Fight for Citizenship, 1917–1921," *Journal of American History* 82, no. 4 (March 1996): 1490–92. *The Helping Hand* (18 August 1918), 3, 4. *The Helping Hand* (November 1919), 1. Smith later served as a member of the Texas Commission on Interracial Cooperation, organized in 1922 as part of the Atlanta-based Commission on Interracial Cooperation, and dedicated to eliminating extralegal violence against blacks. "Smith," *Who's Who in Colored America, 1928–1929*, 342. Program, Texas Commission on Interracial Cooperation meeting, November 6, 1925, and "Report of Texas Commission to General Commission on Interracial Cooperation, Tuskegee, Alabama, April 8, 1926," Texas Commission on Interracial Cooperation, University of Texas President's Office Records, Center for American History, University of Texas, Austin, Texas.

[16]Smith, "Uplifting Negro Cooperative Society," 10464, discussed in Carroll, "Smith and FIS," 8, 48–49.

southerners to operate urban factories. As the competition intensified, Thomas Campbell, an African American field agent for the USDA, commented that keeping blacks on the farm depended on who reached them first, the "Negro extension agent or the industrial labor agent." Smith believed that the FIS had to teach the farmer "where he can either sell to better advantage what he grows or grow to better advantage what he sells." Only then could blacks do better and improve their economic and social status. If this did not occur, Smith believed that black farmers would "lose [their] place in the industrial world." A fractured organization could not preserve the farmers' status, so Smith went to great pains to present a unified and vibrant FIS.[17]

Smith's efforts to involve women contributed significantly to the growth of the organization. Newspapers reported that "women have done almost as much as men" to further its objectives. Black women controlled farms, and they and their children used the information and programs of the FIS to their advantage. They held membership in local branches; male and female members elected them to office; and they undertook program development and fund-raising at the local, county, and state level. Female members coordinated the FIS Women's Barnyard Auxiliary, which organized local and state exhibitions of canned goods, garden produce, livestock, and items of handiwork such as quilts and clothes. These goods reflected both the valuable economic contributions that women made to African American farms and the culture of farm women.[18]

[17] August Meier discussed ideological divisions between rural and urban blacks thirty-five years ago in *Negro Thought in America, 1880–1915: Racial Ideologies in the Age of Booker T. Washington, with a New Introduction* (Ann Arbor: University of Michigan Press, 1988). Scholars working on racial separatism include Kevin K. Gaines, *Uplifting the Race: Black Leadership, Politics, and Culture in the Twentieth Century* (Chapel Hill: University of North Carolina Press, 1996); Amilcar Shabazz, "An Ideological Shootout in Texas: Separate Equality Versus Racial Integration, 1940–1950," paper presented at the Southern Historical Association annual meeting, Birmingham, Alabama, November 13, 1998; Ernest Obadele-Starks, "The Black Working and Middle Classes and the Politics of Racial Separatism along the Upper Texas Gulf Coast, 1883–1945," paper presented at the Southern Historical Association annual meeting, Birmingham, Alabama, November 13, 1998; and Obadele-Starks, *Black Unionism in the Industrial South* (College Station: Texas A&M University Press, 2000). T. M. Campbell to Dr. C. W. Warburton, June 21, 1924, General Correspondence, Negroes, box 2, USDA Record Group 16, quoted in Foley, *The White Scourge*, 52. For Smith's first quote see untitled and undated manuscript, Manuscript and Speech Drafts, FIS Records, SCFP; for the second see *The Farmers' Improvement Society... An Interesting Dialogue About its Objects and Methods* (Victoria, Tex.: n.p., [c1900]), 14, FIS Miscellaneous Pamphlets, SCFP.

[18] Smith, "Elevation of Negro Farm Life," *Independent*, August 30, 1900, 2103–6. Smith, "Village Improvement," 734, and Smith, "Uplifting Negro Cooperative Society," 10465. See also Smith, "An Effort to Improve Farmers in Texas," *Hampton Negro Conference, 1902* (Hampton, Va.: Hampton University Press, 1902), 40–41, quoted in Jack Abramowitz, "Accommodation and Militancy in Negro Life, 1876–1916" (Ph.D. diss., Columbia University, 1950), 134. For an analysis of the significance of household production to marginal farm economies see Sharon Ann Holt, "Making Freedom Pay: Freedpeople Working for Themselves, North Carolina, 1865–1900," *Journal of Southern History* 60, no. 2 (May 1994): 229–62.

Robert Smith welcomed women as members because he recognized the importance of the household economy to creating a self-sustaining farm. His recognition of their contributions, however, did not cause him to perceive women as equals to men. His goal to educate both sexes in vocational and moral training followed a strict gender division: boys gaining information on agricultural methods and animal husbandry and girls learning to sew, cook, can, and garden. This reflected the influence of Euro-American paternalism and progressive attitudes about gender roles in the household, not the reality of shared responsibilities that sustained poor black farm families in the plantation region of south central Texas. Yet the adoption of co-education and home economics instruction in black schools preceded their adoption by public white schools in Texas by several years. Thus, African American reformers provided more practical information to women—which they expected women to present—than did white reformers. Robert Smith's wives contributed substantially to the FIS's ability to involve women as members and in positions of influence. Robert married Francis Isabella Isaacs (c.1870–1918) in 1890, shortly after he founded the FIS, and she shared with him many organizational struggles. Together they developed a fiscally sound society before Belle died on February 22, 1918.[19]

Belle took an active role in developing educational programming for youth, a goal shared by other black agrarians. They believed that vocational education provided a means to reach those otherwise lost to poverty and illiteracy. Only 30.8 percent of the black school-age population in Texas (five to eighteen years) attended school regularly in 1900. Black landowners and tenants paid their share of the property taxes that funded public education, but the school terms and facilities proved woefully inadequate. Rural reformers founded secular schools and county and industrial institutes modeled on Tuskegee to improve conditions. These schools struggled to secure the funds necessary to operate, but they provided, in the eyes of agrarians, an alternative to inadequate public education. The Smiths believed that their FIS school would teach the value of rural life and farming to youth who would then become adults capable of "lead[ing]

[19] Belle was the daughter of Smith's principal associate and friend, William H. Isaacs, a blacksmith in Oakland, Texas, and one of the first black landowners in Colorado County. Isaacs and Smith traveled together on buying trips. When Smith left Oakland for Paris, Texas, in 1902, he left Isaacs in charge of the operation of the Oakland FIS branch. See Carroll, "Smith and FIS," 35–36, 54, 57. United States Bureau of the Census, Tenth Census of the United States, 1880, Schedule 1, Population, Colorado County, Texas, 359. Marriage record, R. L. Smith and Francis Isabella Isaacs, November 10, 1890, Book 1, p. 355, Colorado County Court House, Columbus, Texas. For a brief biography of the Isaacs family see "About Middleton's In-Laws," Nathaniel Hill Middleton File, Nesbitt Memorial Library, Columbus, Texas. Robert L. and Belle Smith raised two children, Roscoe Conkling Smith and Olive Belle Smith Hardeway. See "Smith Is Laid to Rest," *Waco Messenger*, July 17, 1942. *Boston Transcript*, 1899, clipping, SCFP. White women did not have access to industrial training until the state legislature established the Girls' Industrial College in 1901. McArthur, *Creating the New Woman*, 38.

the people out from the land of Bondage into the land of Independence." Smith administered the school, but the women of the FIS managed the finances and undertook the bulk of youth education.[20]

Booker T. Washington praised the Smiths' efforts to encourage tenants and youth to save their money, buy land, become farmers, and contribute to society. Yet his attitude about gender reinforced the secondary status of women. Washington praised Belle as Smith's "good wife," never crediting her with any individual accomplishments. Members of the society she helped run, however, recognized her contributions. FIS records documented her involvement in organizing activities particularly related to the Auxiliary, the FIS school that was established in 1906 and opened in 1908, and the Juvenile Branch, organized in 1907. Her photograph graced the frontispiece of published FIS constitutions and annual addresses. The caption identified her as "Financial Agent" for the "F. I. Society Agricultural College." In that capacity, she visited most FIS branches in southern and eastern Texas in 1906, soliciting funds for the new school. Belle's personal appearances in areas with black populations and the inclusion of her photograph in FIS publications ensured that society members recognized her.[21]

In 1918 the readership of *The Helping Hand,* the FIS newspaper, mourned Belle's death. Nevertheless, in May 1919, they welcomed the next Mrs. Smith, Ruby Cobb (1883–1966). Robert's marriage to Ruby provided a new administrator for the FIS. She assumed financial management of the school and leadership of the Juvenile Division in May 1919. In the process she revived juvenile branches after a dormant period and articulated FIS strategies through a play written for production by juvenile members. Ruby taught the children the evils of the crop lien system and how to avoid its debilitating effects in *Trial of Old King Credit.* Women took a secondary role in the play, which focused on male characters and had the ultimate goal of teaching positive traits of "Negro Manhood." Only one character presented the perspective of a woman, Mrs. Good Family, who described the ways that King Credit duped her hardworking tenant husband. Ruby's perceptions of women as supportive members of a farm family reflected Euro-American attitudes that she shared with her husband. Regardless, Belle Isaacs and Ruby Cobb assumed influential roles in an organization that relied on female as much as male members to survive. Women paid dues and served as officers of local branches, and they corresponded with the state FIS office, coordinated fairs and convocations, and served as state leaders. Their in-

---

[20] Calvert and De León, *History of Texas,* 239. *BTW Papers,* 4:296. Carroll, "Smith and FIS," 88–102. *Constitution and By-Laws of the Farmers' Improvement Society of Texas Organized December 20th 1890; Chartered July 8th 1901,* n.d., inside back cover ("General Educational Plan Adopted at the Third Annual Convocation, Held at Allyton, Texas, October 1898"), FIS Miscellaneous Pamphlets, SCFP.

[21] *BTW Papers,* 11:325. Carroll, "Smith and FIS," 8–102.

volvement with youth education and financial management gave them responsibilities and experiences in administration and public relations. In the end, the public participation of white women helped them achieve their quest for suffrage in the early twentieth century. Even though black women remained disfranchised, they, as much as their male cohorts, kept white southerners cognizant of the contributions that black farm families made to the local economy, and this helped influence local political decisions.[22]

Poor FIS members could not sustain FIS programs. By 1911, donations solicited from local branches to the FIS school fund proved inadequate to complete Smith's vision. Smith turned to politically active black men in an effort to increase visibility and garner more support from whites and blacks alike. He selected John B. Rayner, a prominent black Populist in the 1890s, as the new financial agent and charged him with increasing revenue. Rayner had experience in such matters, having served in 1904 as financial agent for the Conroe-Porter Industrial College, which had the goal of making it "to Texas what Tuskegee is to Alabama." Rayner's fund-raising strategies followed the Tuskegee model so closely that the white press dubbed Rayner "the Booker T. Washington of Texas." He sought the support of wealthy, white Texans and adopted a conciliatory stance with them that over time became increasingly unpalatable to his critics. One of his ideas, the Hall of Faithfulness, commemorated the loyalty of slaves to their masters during the Civil War. The Dallas minister A. S. Jackson, voiced his opposition to the scheme, declaring that "no kind of building and school was worth the sacrifice of manhood that Rayner was making," and warning that such activity would cause whites to expect more deference. Rayner continued the strategies he implemented in Conroe when he arrived at FIS, and he also requested funds from the John F. Slater Fund and the Anne T. Jeanes Fund. These proved inadequate and the FIS school struggled continually without the stability that public funding provided, dependent on the meager donations secured from FIS members or the larger donations given by paternalistic and philanthropic whites.[23]

[22] See Personal Materials, SCFP; "Smith Is Laid to Rest," *Waco Messenger,* July 17, 1942. Carroll, "Smith and FIS," 70. Ruby became involved in FIS finances after Roscoe Conkling Smith, the previous fiscal agent, nearly ruined FIS by overextending its resources in 1922, a problem she and Robert Smith discussed in their correspondence (October 24, 1922, October 28, 1922, and n.d. (November 1922), FIS Correspondence, SCFP; *National Encyclopedia of the Colored Race,* 383. She became financial agent for the FIS in October 1930. Carroll, "Smith and FIS," 77. Mrs. Smith, *Trial of Old King Credit,* 9. Debra Ann Reid, "Reaping a Greater Harvest: African Americans, Agrarian Reform, and the Texas Agricultural Extension Service" (Ph.D. diss., Texas A&M University, 2000), 102–3.

[23]Greg Cantrell, *Kenneth and John B. Rayner and the Limits of Southern Dissent* (Urbana: University of Illinois Press, 1993), 252; 253–58, 264; 267–70, 279. Carroll, "Smith and FIS," 5–7. John F. Slater donated money to develop educational facilities for African Americans in the

Robert L. Smith aged with the FIS, turning sixty in 1921, and he had trouble adapting his conciliatory tactics to the post–Booker T. Washington period of agrarian reform. He continued to tout economic reform undertaken by property-holding farmers and responsible tenants, and he remained mute on the ways racism limited black independence. By doing so, the FIS failed to serve the largest percentage of black farmers in Texas, share tenants and croppers, and this prevented the organization from making real progress against the credit system of agriculture, or challenging white paternalism and racism. Also, Smith's agrarianism failed to keep pace with the ideological changes wrought by cooperative demonstration work, begun in Texas in 1903, the growth of the Texas extension service, and the official involvement of blacks in these programs starting in 1915.

Smith's position with the FIS, and his connections with progressive farmers throughout the eastern half of Texas, paved the way for his appointment as the first state leader of the "Negro" division of the Texas Agricultural Extension Service (TAEX) in August 1915. Despite these new responsibilities, his priorities remained with the FIS. He maintained his TAEX office in Waco, which also served as the headquarters of the FIS. He used FIS meetings and the newspaper to convey educational material developed by the first two black extension agents in Texas, Mary Evelyn V. Hunter and Jacob "Jake" Ford. Smith's management style, though, did not fit the bureaucratic structure, and personal overextension made it difficult for him to administer effectively. Federal reviewers recommended a change in 1918. This, along with the emphasis that the TAEX placed on the involvement of public, not private, education led to Smith's eventual resignation and the designation of Prairie View Industrial and Vocational College (Prairie View A&M) as the headquarters of the segregated division of the TAEX.[24]

The regular, if inadequate, funding that Prairie View A&M secured from the state government created a more stable environment for a black agrarian reform effort to grow. Federally funded staff, instead of private volunteers, carried the messages into communities with FIS branches. Smith's FIS colleague and in-law, William Isaacs, served fifteen years as

South in 1882, with an emphasis on vocational training and summer teacher institutes. Darryl Stephens, "Reform without Change: The Motivation behind the Involvement of the General Education Board and the Southern Education Board in Black Southern Education, 1900–1915" (M.A. thesis, University of Houston–Clear Lake, 1992), 11, 14. Anna T. Jeanes began funding improvements to rural schools for blacks in the South in 1902. She never visited them but relied on educators such as Booker T. Washington and Robert Lloyd Smith to make informed decisions. Stephens, "Reform without Change," 13–14. Mary S. Hoffschwelle, *Rebuilding the Rural Southern Community: Reformers, Schools, and Homes in Tennessee, 1900–1930* (Knoxville: University of Tennessee Press, 1998), 28. "Smith is Laid to Rest," *Waco Messenger,* July 17, 1942.
[24]Reid, "Reaping a Greater Harvest," 66–73.

county agent in Colorado County; at least one FIS school student, Cleo Parish, secured an appointment as a home demonstration agent; and extension agents spoke at FIS functions regularly.[25]

These first agents concentrated their efforts in areas with the highest percentages of African Americans in the population, providing similar services for black farmers to those that white agents provided for white farmers and their families. They adopted the agrarian philosophy that stressed self-help and economic independence, but only for those who had the best chance at succeeding. Agents faced an uphill struggle. Parents lacked the resources to diversify or support children's involvement in the service. Agents had to gain acceptance from the clientele they served and funding from local agencies, county government, and other sources to match or exceed meager federal and state appropriations. Despite these obstacles, however, they were able to gain the approval of the extension administration by reporting the measurable accomplishments of the farmers they served. The state leader of the TAEX, Clarence Ousley, commented on the efficiency of the first agents and remarked on the receptivity of the rural black population. They recruited nearly four thousand members the first year and nearly thirty-one thousand by 1920. This was three times more than the number served by FIS, or 5.9 percent of the rural black population. Mary Evelyn Hunter reported that the total value of women's work undertaken under the auspices of TAEX agents contributed nearly $830,000 to black farm income in 1920.[26]

The success of the public program hurt the private one. The FIS reached its peak in the 1910s with eight hundred branches and twelve thousand members, an average of fifteen members per branch, by 1912. Yet growth in its remaining thirty years never matched the rise of the organization during its first twenty, and many branches faded into inactivity. Only two hundred additional branches began between 1912 and 1934, the last year a branch sought a charter. Many factors account for this decline. The segregated TAEX competed with the FIS for the time and resources of progressive black farmers. Other causes included unsound banking practices, increased deaths of elderly members, and vagaries in the cotton market and national economy that forced the FIS into financial trouble in the 1920s and again in the early 1930s. In October 1930, for example, the FIS had $40.30 in cash assets and $15,200 in outstanding burial claims and

[25] Texas Agricultural Extension Service Historical Files, Cushing Library, Texas A&M University, College Station, Texas (hereafter TAEX Historical Files).

[26] [Clarence Ousley], "Annual Report of the Director of Extension, Agricultural and Mechanical College of Texas, for the Calendar Year, 1915" (typescript), box 4, TAEX Historical Files. Reid, "Reaping a Greater Harvest," 65–67; 134. *Annual Report of the Extension Service, 1920* (College Station: Extension Service, A. and M. College of Texas and the U.S. Department of Agriculture Cooperating, 1921), 56.

other benefits. Members threatened to withdraw or to file suit against the FIS. The number of supporters dwindled, but Smith remained committed to his agrarian ideal to the end and the organization did not fold until Smith's death in 1942.[27]

۞

The activities of the independent FIS and the segregated TAEX prompted administrators of other Texas agencies to offer more services to rural African Americans. State's rights Democrats opposed the influence of the federal government in extension services, even if Democrats at the TAEX headquarters at Texas Agricultural & Mechanical College administered the funds. Staff of the Texas Department of Agriculture (TDA) thus welcomed Joseph E. Clayton (1879–1958) as an unpaid representative in 1917 and allocated funds for two positions to coordinate "Colored Farmers' Institutes" in 1919. Clayton was a young black agrarian and native Texan from the southern plantation county of Fort Bend. He received his education at Guadalupe College, a black-owned and black-operated Baptist school in Seguin. He was younger than Smith and more limited in his political activism by disfranchisement. He thus pursued a career in education and administration, became involved in grassroots activism, and advocated a vigorous self-help philosophy. He relied on white and black philanthropy, but he realized that government support could further his objectives.[28]

Clayton began his career as the newly appointed principal of the Manor Colored School in 1903. He administered a traditional public school in one building until 1911, when Booker T. Washington's tour of Texas inspired him to expand his institute. Between 1903 and the 1920s, Clayton enlarged the physical plant to include dormitories, additional structures to house classrooms, and land for a school farm. His dream depended on diversified funding from black residents, white philanthropists, and the government. Clayton's wife, Brittie (1880–?), played a central role in generating support. She had friends in the community because she grew up in the area, the daughter of a successful farmer from the neighboring black community of Littig.[29]

---

[27] Carroll, "Smith and FIS," 51, 77. Sister Sec. Annie Haynes, Columbus, Texas, to Mrs. R. L. Smith, December 8, 1931, and C. Matthews, vice president, Riverside, Texas to Bro. R. L. Smith, grand president, September 30, 1931, FIS Correspondence, Burial Benefits, 1931–1932, SCFP. For an overview of Robert Smith's later activities see Rice, "Robert Lloyd Smith."

[28]Reid, "Reaping a Greater Harvest," 90. Michael R. Heintze, *Private Black Colleges in Texas, 1865–1954* (College Station: Texas A&M University Press, 1985), 31.

[29]Ada Simond, "Looking Back," *American-Statesman Neighbor* (Austin, Tex.), January 27, 1983. J. E. Clayton, Chicago, to Dr. Gordon Worley, Austin, July 8, 1953, Clayton Vocational Institute Papers, AHC. Clayton married Brittie [McArthur] White in December 1899. Marriage Records of Travis County, transcribed, AHC; Bearden, "Clayton Vocational Institute,"

Clayton recalled that fund-raising took place "under the leadership of my wife." White friends and black students assisted in the struggle to secure funds for practical expenses such as desks. Clayton borrowed money from the Farmers' National Bank and "took the work of getting philanthropists interested in helping us to get an Industrial School there for our Race." He secured the support of George W. Brackenridge, a patron of Guadalupe College, Clayton's alma mater, to buy land, and over time the Claytons and community residents built and furnished a two-story building on the old school lot. Another building contained a cannery in which young men learned to preserve produce from their own farms to supplement family income. At this time, reformers and boosters considered canning a viable rural industry and encouraged men and women to engage in commercial production. Clayton secured the funding for this structure from an unidentified foundation in Washington. In another instance, Texas State Department of Education officials helped Clayton to locate a mover to relocate the schoolhouse, while the Rockefeller Foundation covered the expenses of the move. Important support also came when the Manor School became one of four Texas schools for African Americans designated to receive funds from the 1917 federal Smith-Hughes Act, designed to advance agricultural, home economics, and industrial education in public high schools.[30]

Also in 1917, Clayton became the first African American authorized by the TDA's Division of Farmers' Institutes to organize black farmers. Individuals in other states such as Georgia had developed institutes earlier to provide black farmers with participatory experiences and access to government publications describing scientific agriculture. By 1908 the farm director at Clark University, P. C. Parks, generated public support from white Georgians by arguing that illiterate black farm owners and tenants could not produce bountiful yields even from prime farmland; their illiteracy prevented them from learning the best methods. He urged white southerners to extend education to these "ignorant and unskilled" and "inefficient and shiftless" farm laborers as a means to improve conditions in the South generally. Black educators believed that public funds should be used to increase their knowledge, and that states should bear the burden. Two options existed. Each southern state could create either a special department of farmers' institutes or a separate extension division for black farmers. Parks believed that institutes provided a means to reach and influence

AHC. The Claytons had four children in the next seven years, so Brittie divided her time between child care and community fund-raising. *Who's Who in Colored America, 1930–1932*, 97.

[30]Clayton to Worley, AHC. For background on the Smith-Hughes Act see Elizabeth Sanders, *Roots of Reform: Farmers, Workers, and the American State, 1877–1917* (Chicago: University of Chicago Press, 1999), 338–39, 392. *Twenty-first Biennial Report, State Superintendent of Instruction, State of Texas. 1 September 1916–31 August 1918* (Austin: State Board of Education, [1918]), 258.

the farm workers most directly. State governments also funded black experiment stations to accomplish the goal. Ultimately extension work proved the most enduring.[31]

Clayton's appointment in Texas allows us to explore the nuances of publicly supported black agrarianism. He gained his position at substantial cost to his personal autonomy. First, he had to volunteer his services. White administrators likely assumed that this would undermine opposition to his appointment. Clayton also assured his white employers that he pursued only economic objectives. He told the white attendees at the state institute that they must "help train the negro how to intelligently and successfully till the soil, because we are getting them to more and more love the occupation of farming." At other times Clayton addressed state institute attendees obsequiously, explaining to them that black Texans would remain loyal to white Texans during the World War I years, as their slave ancestors had done during the Civil War. This approach frustrated reformers who favored confrontation with white authority, but rural southern blacks had few options if they hoped to participate in white southern institutions.[32]

Still, Joseph Clayton's achievements were considerable. He served as chairman of the Committee on Negro Farmers' Institutes, with William M. Cain acting as secretary. In those capacities they organized 289 colored institutes and spoke to 67,832 black men and women between July 1, 1918, and June 30, 1919. Clayton and his associates visited more than five hun-

[31] See P. C. Parks, "Conditions among Negro Farmers," *Southern Workman* 40 (February 1911): 100–104. Ed R. Kone, commissioner of agriculture (1908–14) began farmers' institutes in April or May 1909. Kone to Bradford Knapp, October 19, 1910, reel 1, USDA, Annual Narrative and Statistical Reports of the Cooperative Extension Work Demonstration Program, National Archives and Records Administration, Record Group 33, Microfilm Series (T-845 to T-895), Texas (1909–1944), T-890. The involvement of blacks in farmers' institutes needs more research, as does the development of black experiment stations. For the latter see Linda O. Hines, "George W. Carver and the Tuskegee Agricultural Experiment Station," *Agricultural History* 53, no. 1 (January 1979): 71–83; Irvin May, "Southern Agricultural Experiment Stations: Comment," ibid., 103; Reid, "Reaping a Greater Harvest," 44–45.

[32] Commissioner of Agriculture Fred W. Davis noted that Clayton was granted a commission by the state in 1917 but that it could not pay his salary or expenses. See *Proceedings of the Seventh Meeting, Texas State Farmers' Institute, 1917*, Texas Department of Agriculture Bulletin no. 57 (November/December 1917), 34. Clayton obviously accepted this arrangement, and he worked with the department from 1917 until it ceased operation after August 31, 1921. See *General Laws of The State of Texas, Thirty-seventh Legislature, First Called Session, 1921* (Austin: A. C. Baldwin & Sons, 1921), 197–98. For Clayton's first address to the Texas State Farmers' Institute see "The Negro and the South," *Proceedings Texas Farmers' Institute, 1917*, 34–35. For Clayton's assurance that black farmers would fight the Germans during World War I see J. E. Clayton, "The Work of the State Department of Agriculture Among the Negro Farmers of Texas," *Proceedings of the Eighth Annual Meeting Texas State Farmers' Institute 1918*, Texas Department of Agriculture Bulletin no. 63 (November/December 1918), 26–7. For Clayton's assurance that black farmers would remain as loyal as antebellum slaves see "Professor J. E. Clayton's Address," *Proceedings of a Joint Meeting of State Farmers' Institute (In Eleventh Annual Meeting) and Texas Pecan Growers' Association 1921*, State Department of Agriculture Bulletin no. 69 (July/August 1921), 98–9.

dred farms, organized 163 canning clubs, and demonstrated food preservation techniques to 5,418 men, women, and children. C. W. Rice, later a labor activist and newspaper editor in Houston, also organized institutes without expense to the state government other than transportation. After two years of sustained work with black families, the Division of Farmers' Institutes of the TDA requested and was granted salaries for two "colored field workers" at one thousand dollars each. In July 1921, Clayton reported that the number of black farmers' institutes had increased to 602 and canning clubs to 613. The poverty of those involved became obvious when Clayton noted that most farmers could not afford to purchase manufactured steam pressure canners but used lard cans and wash pots instead. In comparison, 26 black TAEX agents reported a 1920 membership of more than 37,000 adults and juniors who preserved nearly three hundred thousand cans of fruits and vegetables. Male and female agents garnered support for canning centers by cooperating with private residents interested in community building.[33]

The TDA and the TAEX competed in some areas, but in general they pursued different goals. Tenancy offered greater potential for large-scale production, a goal of the TDA more than the TAEX. As tenants, black farmers could expand production by renting more land; they were not restricted to the acreage they owned. With sound credit management, large-scale tenants had a better opportunity to participate in agribusiness than did those who owned small farms and worked to avoid credit, as the FIS and the TAEX urged. Clayton, as a result, sought solutions to issues that concerned black tenants as well as landlords. In 1919 Clayton and the committee on organizing black farmers' institutes recommended that landlords require and pay their tenants to plant cover crops to protect the soil from erosion and leeching over the winter months. In addition, he reported that the shift from tenancy to day labor placed a hardship on tenant farmers and that the Texas Farmers' Institute should use its influence to rent land to black tenants on the third and fourth shares. Under this arrangement, tenants would return to the landowner either one-third or one-fourth of the crop production as rent.[34]

[33] *General Laws of The State of Texas, Thirty-sixth Legislature, Second Called Session, 23 June 1919 to 22 July 1919* (Austin: A. C. Baldwin & Sons, 1919), 435. "Colored Division," *Proceedings of the Ninth Annual Meeting, Texas State Farmers' Institute, 1919,* Texas Department of Agriculture Bulletin no. 67 (July/August 1919), 8, 11. *Proceedings, Farmers' Institute and Texas Pecan Growers' Association 1921,* 96–97. *Annual Report of the Extension Service 1920* ([College Station]: Extension Service, A. and M. College of Texas and U.S. Department of Agriculture Cooperating, 1921), 53–55. Debra Ann Reid, "Locations of Black Identity: Community Canning Centers in Texas, 1915–1935," *Localités/Localities,* special issue of *Research and Review Series* 7 (May 2000): 36–51.

[34] *Proceedings Texas Farmers' Institute, 1919,* 109–10.

It remains unclear whether or not the TDA actually sponsored the scheme to rent land to tenants, but Clayton proceeded to undertake the settlement of families in counties with significant black populations. He reported in 1921 that "colored" institutes helped convince a group of black farmers in Brazoria County to buy a tract of twenty-two hundred acres near Sandy Point for colonization. Another group in Gregg County bought nineteen hundred acres at Easton. Both locations benefited from proximity to railroads. In addition, 309 families bought small farms at the encouragement of the agency. The TDA ceased offering farmers' institutes after August 1921, due to increased competition posed by the segregated TAEX, but Clayton remained active in rural resettlement and self-segregation. He continued to cooperate with railroad companies as he moved his activities outside Texas, working first in Louisiana, Arkansas, and Mississippi. Clayton's enthusiasm for these projects probably resulted from his interest in the work of Isaiah T. Montgomery and the all-black community Montgomery developed at Mound Bayou, Mississippi. Later Clayton expanded his reform zeal even further geographically and politically, dividing his time between Chicago, Houston, and Littig, Texas, and continuing to work with colonization efforts in Texas and Louisiana. He joined the National Association for the Advancement of Colored People and worked with the Southern Tenant Farmers' Union and community settlement in several states, all indicative of his growing support for cross-class reform. Joseph Clayton's awareness of the farm laborer, sharecropper, and tenant differed markedly from the Smiths' concentration on deserving property owners.[35]

The work of the Smiths and the Claytons indicates the way that African American agrarian ideology changed between the 1890s and the 1930s, with the 1910s marking the greatest period of transition. Private reform

[35] Residents of Manor who knew the Claytons recalled Joseph Clayton's preoccupation with the work of Isaiah Montgomery at Mound Bayou. Bearden, "Clayton Vocational Institute," AHC, 14. Janet Sharp Hermann focuses on Mound Bayou in *The Pursuit of A Dream* (New York: Oxford University Press, 1981). Adolph Reed describes Montgomery's commitment to interracial cooperation to further his all-black community in *Stirrings in the Jug*, 25–27. *Proceedings, Texas Farmers' Institute, 1921*, 97; Diana J. Kleiner, "Sandy Point, Texas," *The New Handbook of Texas*, 5:838. *Who's Who in Colored America, 1930–32*, 97, notes that Clayton organized the National Self-Help Association in 1924 and worked with the Phenix Aid and Development Association in Phenix, Arkansas, after 1930. See also Bearden, "Clayton Industrial Institute," 14–15, AHC; Clayton Vocational Institute Papers, AHC. Foley, *The White Scourge*, 190–91; and Harry Leland Mitchell, *Mean Things Happening in This Land: The Life and Times of H. L. Mitchell, Co-Founder of the Southern Tenant Farmers' Union* (Montclair, N.J.: Allanheld, Osmun, 1979), 183–85. Unfortunately, little is known of Brittie's life during these years except that she raised a daughter who became a lawyer. Bearden, "Clayton Industrial Institute," 14, AHC.

efforts, such as the FIS, lost influence as publicly supported programs, such as the TAEX and the TDA, gained funding and followings. This marked a departure from the agrarian activism as defined by rural blacks who became politically active during Reconstruction. At that time, blacks used their newfound political voice to influence local legislation to improve rural conditions. Some argued for more lenient crop lien laws and others for legislation that funded public institutions such as schools. Both protected the ability of black people to farm for a living and contributed to rural community development. Some even believed that blacks and whites could cooperate to bring about change more rapidly. The legacy of Reconstruction influenced Republican Robert Lloyd Smith and Populist John B. Rayner, and they cooperated with white southerners when their black peers could benefit. To this end, they avoided discussing white supremacy and discrimination. Instead they attributed illiteracy and poverty to the influence of outside forces such as slavery and the boll weevil, not racism. They held the poor responsible for their own misfortunes and criticized the intemperate and immoral. These middle-class activists dedicated their efforts toward farmers who could put their recommendations into practice. They believed that blacks could improve their status in agriculture if they practiced scientific farming, managed their debt more astutely, and lived within stable and supportive communities.

The agrarian radicalism that fostered interracial cooperation in the decades after the Civil War, however, no longer remained viable in the early decades of the twentieth century. White supremacy reappeared, and this severely limited the options available to black agrarians. Regardless of Jim Crow legislation, reformers still pursued political goals. African American agrarians used the persistence of black landownership to convince local and state officials to respond to their interests. Variations on the theme existed, most driven by the need to devise innovative means to protect the precarious hold many farm families had on their property and their way of life. For example, the private FIS functioned as a fraternal organization, and members recognized the benefits of insurance in providing a financial cushion to farm families whose deceased loved ones had made critical contributions to farm income. The segregated TAEX supported ownership as a means to economic independence, and black agents emphasized diversification and youth education to further this end. They could not threaten white landowners by being too aggressive in their campaign for land purchases, so they often discussed the economic contribution to counties that black property ownership generated. The TDA differed from the FIS and the TAEX in that it encouraged a back-to-the-land movement. Clayton spoke of developing responsible tenants and moving blacks from urban areas back to farms. This fulfilled an agrarian goal of nurturing rural life as much as it relieved white TDA officials of a concern over the loss of black labor. Clayton also urged farmers to devote themselves to scientific agriculture and cash crop production, goals of the more commercially oriented TDA.

The black agrarians did the best they could given the parameters in which they functioned. They had not only to respond to white authority and black poverty, but to compete with each other for limited funds. The structure of the programs also fueled the competition. The FIS convocations and fairs and TAEX congresses and institutes took farmers away from their work. Clayton believed that farmers lost valuable time in the field each year as they attended such meetings, encampments, and board meetings. He recommended that the Texas Farmers' Institute discourage the farmer from "the practice of running all over the State to attend so many conventions and boards and instead to put more time on his own crops."[36]

The most long-lasting contribution made by black agrarians related to their institutional legacy. These early reformers constructed a system that offered opportunities for those who believed that separatist, or private, initiatives could best help African Americans secure economic solvency and further their political goals as well as, increasingly, for those who favored involvement in the more expansive state. Their activism made it clear to rural southerners that agrarianism was not just a white political ideology but, rather, that it had multiracial applications. Most blacks lived in eighty-three counties in East Texas and accounted for one-quarter to three-quarters of all farmers in those counties. Almost all devoted more than one-third of their improved acreage to the production of "white gold," or cotton. Between 10 and 50 percent owned their farms, and some tenants owned stock and equipment with which they negotiated better crop contracts. This black property-owning group pressed for recognition and fairness.[37]

Involvement in publicly funded programs affected male and female agrarians differently. Robert Smith and Joseph Clayton both welcomed the recognition that the state appointments promised without realizing the consequences of their actions—the concentration of authority into one public program. They believed that by cooperating with the government they could reach many more African American farmers. They were able to generate public support for rural improvement, and they became members of an elite group of black government employees. Yet government officials soon realized that by favoring Smith and Clayton with appointments, they could expand new social programs to the underserved without committing substantive resources to the effort. Ultimately, the willingness of Smith and Clayton to serve the government helped defeat their own objectives. The expectations of white administrators forced black appointees

[36]*Proceedings, Texas Farmers' Institute, 1919,* 109–10.
[37]Reid, "Reaping a Greater Harvest," 10–11, 78–80.

to direct their efforts toward farmers who either controlled their own resources or depended on the government for aid, as in the case of the tenants whom Clayton helped settle. This did not, however, indicate defeat. In the following decades the growing welfare state made even greater allowances for the involvement of rural blacks. African Americans gained appointments at the local, state, and national levels, as county extension agents, state leaders of segregated extension services, and USDA field agents—arguably a crucial part of the agrarians' legacy.[38]

Women, too, benefited from their involvement in private and public reform, despite the limitations that patriarchy imposed. They gained visibility and used their positions to do race work by fighting the economic causes of social problems that affected black families. This paved the way for black involvement in home economics instruction, a new profession that conveyed new methods and standards into the rural home. Most who became involved gained their education at Prairie View A&M, the black land-grant institution in Texas, and used their positions with the TAEX to spread the book learning. The segregation of the TAEX in 1915 provided opportunities for these college-educated black women to express themselves, organize communities, and validate the importance of domestic production. They also gained entrance into an elite group. Only 2.5 percent of African American women in 1920 held professional positions, but those who did effectively attained middle-class status.[39]

By 1924 the TAEX's "Negro" division received more federal money than those in other southern states, and it employed more black agents than in most other states with significant black extension programs, a total of thirty-six employees. The Negro division continued as the largest in the nation through the New Deal era with the most staff, the largest geographic territory, and durable funding from federal, state, and local resources. During its first twenty-six years, agents reached tens of thousands of rural blacks in fifty-five counties in Texas with home and farm improvements, nutrition and health care, and the benefits of improved stock and cultivation practices and market involvement. The agents accomplished this by working within established rural networks based in community and family, and they reported remarkable things, economic and social. They praised men, women, and children who used the proceeds from scientific farm and home management to pay off mortgages, buy land, build houses, and go to high school and college. The agents recounted the numbers of

[38]Ibid., 48–60; 64–67; 70–77; 87–89; 106–7; 134.

[39] Ruby completed her B.A. degree at Prairie View State Normal and Industrial College in 1937, writing a thesis entitled "Teaching Reading to Retarded Children in East Waco Colored School," SCFP. McArthur, *Creating the New Woman*, 5, 48, 149; Julia Kirk Blackwelder, *Now Hiring: The Feminization of Work in the United States, 1900–1995* (College Station: Texas A&M University Press, 1997), 65–66; 84–85.

purebred pigs, cattle, chickens, and turkeys acquired; the number of jars canned; and the financial contribution that improved farm life. The positive reporting helped agents publicize their message to black farmers who had the freedom to participate. Yet naturally leaders had to cooperate with white administrators to sustain their reform. They did not overtly challenge the power structure that legitimized race and gender discrimination, but they did create a system that forced white officials to recognize their activism and allow their inclusion.[40]

The influence of black agrarians involved in public programming became more pronounced during the New Deal era. The few black farmers in Texas who benefited from relief, recovery, and reform were those who had a history of involvement with TAEX programs. By 1930, only 4.2 percent of all Texas farmers were land-owning African Americans; 13.2 percent were black tenants. By 1935, the percentage of owners remained steady but the percentage of black tenants declined to 10.2 percent. These blacks, accounting for 14.3 percent of all farmers, tilled only 2.8 percent of all Texas farmland. Yet, the black farmers who remained on the land and involved in publicly funded rural reform, namely the extension service, had direct access to New Deal relief, recovery, and reform. They participated in Agricultural Adjustment Administration programs such as the cotton plow-up campaigns, Farm Credit Administration offerings, and Farm Security Administration resettlement schemes. White administrators could have excluded black agrarians as they had poor whites, but instead white TAEX officials and agents involved their black peers, if reluctantly.[41]

World War II and the Cold War gave the segregated TAEX another boost, with black agents supporting patriotism, rural economic development, and civil defense. This sustained its growth into the 1960s. By 1964 the segregated TAEX employed 104 professional staff members working in sixty counties. This growth contrasted with the precipitous decline in the number of African American farmers who, by 1960, accounted for only 5.1 percent of farmers in Texas. The equality promised by the Civil Rights Act of 1964, however, worked against the black extension agents. Ultimately TAEX officials used civil rights legislation to eliminate, instead of strengthen, services to African Americans. Texas A&M University and TAEX officials recognized the professionalism of the black staff, but neither was willing to overcome racism

[40] O. B. Martin, *A Decade of Negro Extension Work, 1914–1924*, Miscellaneous Circular no. 72 (Washington, D.C.: U.S. Department of Agriculture, 1926), 12. Other states with significant programs included Alabama, Mississippi, Virginia, and Georgia. In Texas the black state leaders and state agents for home demonstration work submitted reports that appeared in published annual reports such as the *Annual Report of the Extension Service of the Agricultural and Mechanical College of Texas* (College Station, Texas: A. and M. College of Texas and U.S. Department of Agriculture Cooperating, 1918–1929). George R. Woolfolk, *Prairie View: A Study in Public Conscience, 1878–1946* (New York: Pageant Press, 1962), 248–54; 340–42.

[41] Reid, "Reaping a Greater Harvest," 205, 237–38.

in order to extend equal status to minority employees. Instead, on March 16, 1964, TAEX officials exchanged the designation "Negro" for "Associate." Then, to comply with Title VI of the Civil Rights Act, issued December 11, 1964, TAEX officials developed a single line of administration by eliminating the administrative authority of the segregated service housed at Prairie View A&M. They left black staff stationed at Prairie View A&M, however, justifying the decision by citing examples of white agents and supervisors who worked out of district offices. The TAEX administrators also conferred supervisory titles on the black agents, but the new position descriptions and lines of authority confirmed the subordinate status of the black employees. TAEX director John Hutchison believed that the strategy would "create fewer problems," and indeed most black agents accepted the change, with few accusing TAEX and Texas A&M University of discrimination.[42]

The needs of black farmers apparently fell by the wayside as black bureaucrats struggled to retain positions. Yet the minority agents knew that by securing their positions, they could preserve state and federal support for black farmers. Integrationists and self-segregationists alike realized gains in the process. Dempsey Seastrunk became one of the first black members of the TAEX headquarters staff and the most influential. On February 29, 1972, TAEX officials appointed him to the position of assistant director for special programs. In this capacity, Seastrunk implemented a new program that he had pursued while enrolled in the doctoral program in extension administration at the University of Wisconsin, Madison, one designed to provide special assistance to "marginal-income farm operators." The federal Agricultural Act of 1971 codified a similar initiative, but extension officials vested Prairie View A&M and 1890 land-grant institutions throughout the South with full authority for the new "Small Farm Program," thereby creating autonomous extension programs to serve economically disadvantaged and ethnically diverse populations throughout the South, separate from the "integrated" bureaucracies at white land-grant colleges. The TAEX selected extension agent Hoover Carden, Prairie View University–trained, to administer the new project on April 1, 1972.[43]

[42] John E. Hutchison, College Station, Texas, to Earl Rudder, College Station, December 30, 1964, box 79–16, Texas A&M University President's Office Records, Cushing Library, Texas A&M University, College Station, Texas (hereafter A&M President's Records). U.S. Department of Commerce, Bureau of the Census, *Eighteenth Decennial Census of the United States, Census of Population: 1960*, pt. 45: *Texas* (Washington, D.C.: U.S. Government Printing Office, 1963), xiii, 45–64.

[43] John E. Hutchison, College Station, Texas, to Earl Rudder, College Station, December 30, 1964, box 79–16, A&M President's Records. Dempsey H. Seastrunk file, Cushing Library, Texas A&M University, College Station, Texas. Douglas Helms, "Eroding the Color Line: The Soil Conservation Service and the Civil Rights Act of 1964," *Agricultural History* 65, no. 2 (spring 1991): 37; Dempsey Seastrunk, "Black Extension Service," *The New Handbook of Texas,*

Even with this new separatist extension service, and the alleged elimination of the racial employment barrier, blacks in Texas still realized that they did not reap the full benefits of participation in the TAEX. In the early 1970s Preston Poole, a county agricultural extension agent with more than thirty years experience, launched a class action suit that charged the TAEX with discrimination in employment. Poole believed that two groups of people suffered because of the chronic discrimination, the black employees of the TAEX and "those blacks who receive[d] the services provided... to the agricultural community." The resulting consent decree addressed the complaints of the first group, the black employees, because the TAEX voluntarily adjusted the pay scale to reflect merit and service, not race. The interests of the second group of persons, the blacks seeking services of the TAEX, were not addressed. The class action suit launched by black farmers against the USDA between 1981 and 1996, *Timothy C. Pigford et al. v. Dan Glickman, Secretary, The United States Department of Agriculture*, sought a solution to grievances similar to those not rectified in *Poole v. Williams*.[44]

The Cooperative Extension Program of Prairie View A&M University today serves Texans of diverse ethnic backgrounds and socio-economic levels in thirty-four counties, the result of Texans' ambiguous compliance with the Civil Rights Act of 1964 as well as a long heritage of proud service on the part of rural blacks. In some ways this reflects the philosophy of self-help and self-segregation that characterized the program since its beginnings in 1915. It also indicates the real, if limited, political power that black agrarians have wielded, and continue to wield, in the twentieth-century American South. Their insistence on public support for minority farmers has prevented the extinction of black farms, even at the same time that discrimination continues and black agrarians still struggle from their minority position to effect change.[45]

1:567. P.L. 92–73, August 10, 1971, U.S., *Statutes at Large, 1971*, vol. 85, 186; John E. Hutchinson, "The Texas Agricultural Extension Service: A Historical Overview," in *Southwestern Agriculture: Pre-Columbian to Modern*, ed. Henry C. Dethloff and Irvin M. May, Jr. (College Station: Texas A&M University Press, 1982), 132. For a discussion of changes in segregated extension programs and compliance with the Civil Rights Act in another state see Jeannie M. Whayne, "Black Farmers and the Agricultural Cooperative Extension Service: The Alabama Experience, 1945–1965," *Agricultural History* 72, no. 3 (summer 1998): 523–51. Unrecorded interview, Dr. Alfred Poindexter, Prairie View A&M University, conducted May 13, 1999, notes in author's possession. *Impact* 1, no. 1 (March 1984): 4 newsletter of the Cooperative Extension Program, Prairie View A&M University.

[44] *Poole* v. *Williams, Individually and as President of Texas A&M University System, et. al.*, No. 72-H-150, January 26, 1974, as corrected January 28, 1974, U.S. District Court, Southern District of Texas, in *Fair Employment Practice Cases*, vol. 7 (Washington, D.C.: Bureau of National Affairs, 1974), 102–4. For the *Pigford v. Glickman* decision, see http://www.usda.gov/da/consent.htm.

[45] George Ruble Woolfolk, "Extension: A Comment," Dethloff and May, *Southwestern Agriculture*, 146–47.

Land Monopoly, Agribusiness, and the State

Discovering the Family Farm in Twentieth-Century California

VICTORIA SAKER WOESTE

For decades, historians of California agriculture have focused on the causes and effects of the rise of agribusiness, an economic system best understood as the utilization of vertical integration in the "cultivation, harvesting, processing, distribution, and... sales promotion of crops." Scholars typically associate agribusiness with land monopoly, large farms, and disproportionate economic and political power. The conventional picture of agribusiness tells us that big interests reigned supreme, dominating politics at every level.[1]

Historians interested in characterizing the relationship between agribusiness and the modern state have often looked to California for incontrovertible evidence of the state's complicity in the evils of industrial agriculture. According to this line of scholarship, the historical record in California is replete with examples of how large landed interests dominated the outcome of every key regulatory controversy from the beginning of statehood. Water rights, the settlement of claims arising from the Mexican colonial era, irrigation, immigration and migrant labor, marketing and grading standards: the outcomes of all these important issues were apparently determined by the political influence that large, wealthy landholders wielded over the pu-

I am deeply indebted to Betsy Mendelsohn for her stellar research assistance, Barbara Leibhardt Wester for helpful comments on an earlier draft, and Keith Woeste for statistical consultation. I also wish to acknowledge the financial and intellectual support of the American Bar Foundation and its director, Bryant Garth, for this project. Finally, this article has been greatly improved by advice generously given by Jess Gilbert, Robert Johnston, and Catherine McNicol Stock.

[1] Sucheng Chan, *This Bittersweet Soil: The Chinese in California Agriculture* (Berkeley: University of California Press, 1986), 447 n. 55.

tatively democratic institutions of government. Implicitly the conventional picture has yielded the corollary view that the state served as passive hand-maiden to powerful economic interests. In short, this is a sorry tale of the American state's capitulation to the imperatives of capitalism.[2]

The view that large-scale, industrial agribusiness has always dominated California agriculture received its definitive statement during the Great Depression. The journalist Carey McWilliams captured the essence of agribusiness in a single compelling metaphor: the factory farm. In *Factories in the Field* (1939), McWilliams declared: "[The story of California agriculture] is a story of nearly seventy years' exploitation of minority, racial and other groups by a powerful clique of landowners whose power is based upon an anachronistic system of land ownership dating from the creation, during Spanish rule, of feudalistic patterns of ownership and control." For McWilliams, land monopoly was the ultimate cause of all that was wrong with California agriculture. It was evident in 1870, he argued, when one five-hundredth of the population in the state owned half of the land, and it continued unchecked into the twentieth, as the labor requirements of industrial agriculture created a permanent underclass of immigrants, migrant laborers, and tenants, to many of whom landownership was denied by law.[3]

The problem is not that McWilliams was wrong. There were factory farms aplenty. Hundreds of thousands of people went hungry during the Great Depression because California growers preferred their crops go to waste rather than be sold at a loss. Factory farm owners regularly resorted to violent, repressive measures against migrant laborers and union organizers. The environmental damage from decades of chemical-laden agricultural runoff will never be completely undone. The issue is whether, faced with this legacy and its intellectual and historical implications, scholars can nonetheless acknowledge the presence, persistence, and even growth of small-scale agricultural entrepreneurs and account for their contributions to and political power in California's agricultural economy and society.

This essay argues that it is possible to reconsider the conventional picture of California agribusiness and to begin to reformulate our understanding of the relationship between agriculture and the twentieth-century state. New analysis of data from the U.S. Census reveals the presence and persistence over time of a significant number of growers who owned and operated farms smaller than fifty acres. The analysis supports three

---

[2] For example, see Donald Worster, *Rivers of Empire: Water, Aridity, and the Growth of the American West* (New York: Pantheon Books, 1985); for more general works that share this view of the state's capture by economic interests, see, e.g., Gabriel Kolko, *Railroads and Regulation, 1877–1916* (Princeton, N.J.: Princeton University Press, 1963); Samuel Hays, *The Response to Industrialism* (Chicago: University of Chicago Press, 1957); Morton Keller, *Affairs of State: Public Life in Late Nineteenth-Century America* (Cambridge, Mass.: Harvard University Press, 1977).

[3] Carey McWilliams, *Factories in the Field: The Story of Migratory Farm Labor in California*, facsimile ed. (Hamden, Conn.: Archon Books, 1969), 7, 23, 146.

related claims: (1) there were many small farms in California; (2) their numbers increased over time rather than declined; and (3) small-scale agricultural entrepreneurs exerted significant influence over politics and the state in twentieth-century California. By recovering the relationship between these growers, the state's commercial horticultural industries, and the political issues surrounding the regulation of agricultural markets, we can begin to paint a new picture of agriculture, rural politics, and the state in the modern era. Small-scale growers made significant contributions to the state's agricultural development. In particular, they shaped the politics of the regulation of markets during the New Deal in crucial ways.[4]

For example, consider one of the parties in *Parker v. Brown*, a case decided by the U.S. Supreme Court in 1943. Porter L. Brown had been a Fresno County raisin grower all his life when he decided to challenge a California statute requiring him to participate in a New Deal marketing program. Brown owned 100 acres of raisin vines, a spread far below the statewide median farm size of 172 acres but well above the median farm size of about 25 acres in Fresno County. Still, his was a family farm—he was both owner and operator—and not atypical of the smaller-scale enterprise that anchored the fruit-growing industries of the state by the 1930s. His decision to attack the state law in federal court was not just a symbolic statement but an act that assumed that law offered him a remedy against a state regulatory structure he found oppressive.[5]

Acknowledging the presence in California agriculture of small-scale entrepreneurs such as Porter L. Brown does not require that we discount the cultural, economic, and political problems of agribusiness. It does, however, provide an opportunity for considering the possibility of economic, social, and political diversity in California agriculture. More than one kind of state—more than one level of governance—affected the California countryside; likewise, more than one kind of farmer interacted with these varying levels and structures of public institutions. The land barons were not the only group of agricultural producers with access to law and the state.[6]

---

[4] Most historians believe that almost no family farms were left in California by the early twentieth century. See, e.g., Gerald Nash, *State Government and Economic Development: A History of Administrative Policies in California, 1849–1933* (Berkeley: Institute of Governmental Studies, University of California, 1964); Donald J. Pisani, *From the Family Farm to Agribusiness: The Irrigation Crusade in California and the West, 1850–1931* (Berkeley: University of California Press, 1984); and Cletus Daniel, *Bitter Harvest: A History of California Farmworkers, 1870–1941* (Ithaca: Cornell University Press, 1981).

[5] For background on Porter L. Brown, see Complaint, Case No. 78, U.S. District Court, Southern District of California, in briefs filed in *Parker v. Brown*, No. 46, October Term 1942, microfilm version, Boalt Hall Law Library, University of California; and *Parker v. Brown*, 317 U.S. 341 (1943).

[6] My own study, *The Farmer's Benevolent Trust: Law and Agricultural Cooperation in Industrial America, 1865–1945* (Chapel Hill: University of North Carolina Press, 1998), analyzes the

My essay begins with a description of the origins of commercial horticulture in California, including a brief review of what historians have had
to say over the past sixty years about the influence of agribusiness in society and politics. I then present a statistical analysis of farm size between
1900 and 1940. Finally, to shed light on the historical significance of these
statistics, I tell an obscure yet important story about the political activity of
small growers during that time, activity related to the statute Porter L.
Brown attacked in court: the California Agricultural Prorate Act of 1933.
There may have been precious few yeoman agrarians in California, but
there have always been numerous small farmers who called upon the state
for aid just as effectively as the agents of agribusiness.[7]

The rise of commercial horticulture in California was directly linked to
the existence of small farms, which had their roots in the seventeenth-century Spanish missions—themselves a kind of land-grant experiment. When
the Spanish friars abandoned the missions in the first part of the nineteenth
century, they left behind varieties of locally adapted fruit crops for Euro-
American immigrants to find. Moving these plants from the temperate
coastline to the hot interior of the state posed the major challenge for the
new settlers. Microclimates, soil, and elevation all shaped the determination of what to plant and where. As growers learned which fruit crops could
grow in which parts of the state during the nineteenth century, their decisions began to establish direct relationships between geography and commodity and between commodity and farm size. Horticultural industries were
certainly driven by the profit motive, but the high value of fruit crops and
the economies of scale of horticulture made small, family-owned farms economically feasible.[8]

A bonanza in wheat first put California agriculture on the map during
the 1850s, but the decline of the wheat industry by 1870 forced large
landowning "wheat kings" to think about alternative ways to derive wealth

---

California raisin industry, arguing that the cooperatives formed by the raisin growers represent the formative example of the modern marketing cooperative, one that spurred substantial legal change at both the state and federal levels.

[7] In this essay, I use the term "commercial horticulture" to describe the production of fruit
and nut crops for off-farm sale. I do not include market gardens in this description, nor are
market gardens included in the statistical analysis of fruit farms. Likewise, the term "field crops"
includes such commodities as wheat but not vegetables. The census tracked market gardens
and commercial vegetable production separately and the variables reflect this separation.

[8] George W. Hendry, "The Source Literature of Early Plant Introduction into Spanish
America," *Agricultural History* 8 (1934): 64–71; Edward J. Wickson, "The History of California Fruit Growing," *Pacific Rural Press*, April 14, 1906, 228; James Blick; "Geography and Mission Agriculture," *Pacific Historian* 8 (February 1964): 3–38; Wickson, "California Mission
Fruits," *Overland Monthly*, 2d ser., 11 (1888): 501–5.

from the land. By subdividing their large tracts in the Central Valley, they hoped to make even more money by selling land to white prospective fruit growers from the eastern United States and Europe. Developers built irrigation works, secured water rights for their property, and advertised for buyers. The combination of land, water, and people was essential to horticulture. Without irrigation, most California farmland could support only dryland field crops. Without the capital that wheat farming infused into the state, the extensive irrigation works essential for a horticultural economy could not have been built. And without horticulture, no family could make a decent living off a family-sized farm in California. The shift from wheat to horticulture was not merely a reaction to the decline of the wheat industry; it funneled capital accumulated through the wheat trade back into land development, colonization plans, and irrigation companies.[9]

Differences in climate, soil conditions, and topography reinforced differences among farms. The mountainous areas in the east and north tended to be more suitable for ranching, while the flat lands in the San Joaquin and Sacramento valleys, the Santa Clara Valley, and southern California were easier to irrigate and improve for horticulture. Some counties lay across geographic regions, and some produced both fruit and field crops (cereals, grains, and hay) in large amounts. Still, as the analysis of the census data shows, we can differentiate the fruit-growing regions from field crop, mountain, and unimproved desert areas, bringing into sharp relief the importance of small farms in specific parts of the state.[10]

Small farms were ideal for horticulture. Or, to put it another way, the economy of scale of horticulture made small farms profitable to own. In fruit-growing industries, single families could and did run farms with their own labor most of the year, hiring migrant help only at harvest time. A 1913 pamphlet promoting Fresno agriculture did not exaggerate: "[T]he small raisin grower has advantages which are beyond the reach of the big grower. Where the owner does practically all the work, the profit per acre is higher, and one man can handle as many as forty acres without assistance except in the harvest period." In fact, at this time a family could support itself on a raisin farm of as few as fifteen acres. Although citrus fruit, dried apricots, peaches, prunes, raisins, and nuts were all luxuries to Gilded

[9] On the shift from wheat to specialized horticulture, see Robert G. Cleland and Osgood Harvey, *March of Industry* (Los Angeles: Powell, 1929); Lawrence J. Jelinek, *Harvest Empire: A History of California Agriculture*, 2d ed. (San Francisco: Boyd and Fraser, 1982); McWilliams, *Factories in the Field;* Rodman Paul, *The Far West and the Great Plains in Transition, 1859–1900* (New York: Harper & Row, 1988); Claude B. Hutchinson, ed., *California Agriculture* (Berkeley: University of California Press, 1946).

[10] On California geography, see Elna Bakker, *An Island Called California: An Ecological Introduction to Its Natural Communities*, 2d ed. (Berkeley: University of California Press, 1971); Robert W. Durrenberger with Robert B. Johnson, *California: Patterns on the Land*, 5th ed. (Palo Alto, Calif.: Mayfield, 1976); and Crane S. Miller and Richard Myslop, *California: The Geography of Diversity* (Pomona: California State Polytechnic University, 1983).

Age Americans, after 1900 California fruit growers invented new processing technologies and marketing methods to lower production costs and expand demand for their products.[11]

The rise of fruit growing in California was thus no accident. Promoters of settlement and colonization in the nineteenth century worked hard to show prospective buyers that fruit growing was both affordable and profitable. The subdivision of large holdings into many small parcels occurred at the same time as the accumulation of large tracts by a few owners. Subdivision was associated with fruit growing, large tracts with field crops and ranching. These areas tended not to overlap in some counties, but did in others; the more diverse spreads tended to be located in southern California, where there was less winter rainfall and more irrigation works. Many people believed that the state's progress depended on rapid settlement and aggressive economic development, and the critics of land monopoly saw settlement as essential to a more democratic society. In short, horticulture both introduced and perpetuated diversity in land ownership.[12]

This account of the origins of commercial horticulture contrasts sharply with the standard story of California agriculture. The accepted narrative is an evolutionary tale of small farms yielding inevitably to land monopoly. Taking Carey McWilliams as its touchstone, this story has guided the work of scholars principally concerned with defining agribusiness, tallying its social costs, and understanding the political, economic, and social reasons for its growth. Revisionism began in the early 1980s, spurred principally by a new interest in migrant laborers. Scholars in this vein criticized the earlier economic and historical studies for ignoring the voices of agricultural workers and treating them as if they lacked agency to order their own lives. The principal dynamic in this work, though, remained one of agribusiness versus labor, and as a result there has been little exploration of economic actors who fall into neither category.[13]

---

[11] M. B. Lerwick, *Fresno County California*, pamphlet (San Francisco: Sunset Magazine Homeseekers Bureau, for the Fresno County Board of Supervisors, n.d. [c. 1913]).

[12] California State Board of Agriculture, "Report of the State Statistician," in *Fifty-ninth Annual Report of the California State Board of Agriculture* (Sacramento: Friend W. Richardson, Superintendent of State Printing, 1913), 135. Representative examples of an emerging focus on small growers, in addition to my own work, include Victor W. Geraci, "The El Cajon, California, Raisin Industry: An Exercise in Gilded Age Capitalism," *Southern California Quarterly* 74 (winter 1992): 329–54; David Vaught, *Cultivating California: Growers, Specialty Crops, and Labor, 1875–1920* (Baltimore: Johns Hopkins University Press, 1999); Michael F. Magliari, "California Populism, a Case Study: The Farmers' Alliance and People's Party in San Luis Obispo County, 1885–1903" (Ph.D. diss., University of California at Davis, 1992); and Steven Stoll, *The Fruits of Natural Advantage: Making the Industrial Countryside in California* (Berkeley: University of California Press, 1998), 32–62. For these scholars, however, the overall story remains the same as that told by the agribusiness historians: the countryside becomes "industrial" regardless of the presence of smaller growers.

[13] See, e.g., Paul S. Taylor, "Foundations of California Rural Society," *California Historical Society Quarterly* 24 (1945): 193–228; Varden Fuller, "The Supply of Agricultural Labor as a Factor in the Evolution of Farm Organization in California," Senate Committee on Education

Understandably, historians sympathetic to the plight of exploited laborers and outraged at the environmental damage inflicted by industrial agriculture have drawn bold, broad conclusions about the effects of large farms and agribusiness. For the greater part of this century, historians have shown, powerful corporations and landowners swayed legislative actions to favor their interests in policy areas such as taxation, land use regulation, and perhaps most obviously, water policy. Other historians critical of agribusiness have focused on water law and irrigation policy as prime examples of how large landowners bent doctrine to serve their economic interests. Donald Worster, Donald Pisani, and Catherine Miller tell similar stories about the ability of large landowners and corporations to wield control over the state's dispensation of privilege and the right to appropriate natural resources. As wealthy interests used litigation to secure favorable changes in doctrine, smaller, undercapitalized growers supposedly lost ground. Cletus Daniel's *Bitter Harvest* (1981) explicitly implicated the state and federal governments in the creation of a caste of exploited laborers and an agricultural economy ruled by entrenched corporate interests.[14]

Recovering the history of small growers is thus not an easy task, not only because of the weight of historical opinion that they hardly existed but also because of the difficulty in finding reliable evidence. State statistical records

and Labor, *Hearings Pursuant to Senate Resolution 266, Exhibit 8762-A,* 76th Cong., 3d sess., 1940, 19777–898; Paul Gates, *Land and Law in California* (Ames: Iowa State University Press, 1992); Robert Cleland, *The Cattle on a Thousand Hills: Southern California, 1850–1880* (San Marino, Calif.: Huntington Library, 1951); Charles C. Teague, *Fifty Years a Rancher: Half a Century Devoted to the Citrus and Walnut Industries of California and to Furthering the Cooperative Movement in Agriculture* (Los Angeles: California Fruit Growers' Exchange, 1944); G. Harold Powell, *Letters from the Orange Empire,* ed. Richard G. Lillard (Los Angeles: Historical Society of Southern California, 1990); Murray Benedict, "The Economic and Social Structure of California Agriculture," in *California Agriculture,* ed. Claude Hutchinson (Berkeley: University of California Press, 1946), 395–435; Walter Goldschmidt, *As You Sow* (New York: Harcourt Brace, 1947); Richard Kirkendall, "Social Science in the Central Valley: A Rejoinder," *Agricultural History* 53 (1979): 494–505; Morton Rothstein, "West Coast Farmers and the Tyranny of Distance," ibid., 49 (1975): 272–80; Nash, *State Government and Economic Development,* 125–26; Clarke A. Chambers, *California Farm Organizations: A Historical Study of the Grange, the Farm Bureau, and the Associated Farmers, 1929–1941* (Berkeley: University of California Press, 1952), 1–4; Walton Bean and James J. Rawls, *California: An Interpretive History,* 3d ed. (New York: McGraw-Hill, 1978), 493; Marc Reisner, *Cadillac Desert: The American West and Its Disappearing Water* (New York: Penguin Books, 1993); Worster, *Rivers of Empire;* Pisani, *From the Family Farm to Agribusiness.* For examples of revisionist labor history, see Daniel, *Bitter Harvest;* Chan, *This Bittersweet Soil;* Devra Weber, *Dark Sweat, White Gold: California Farm Workers, Cotton, and the New Deal* (Berkeley: University of California Press, 1994); Vicki Ruiz, *Cannery Women/Cannery Lives: Mexican Women, Unionization and the California Food Processing Industry, 1930–1950* (Albuquerque: University of New Mexico Press, 1987); Patricia Zavella, *Women's Work and Chicano Families: Cannery Workers of the Santa Clara Valley* (Ithaca: Cornell University Press, 1987).

[14] Daniel, *Bitter Harvest.* See also Worster, *Rivers of Empire;* Pisani, *From the Family Farm to Agribusiness;* M. Catherine Miller, *Flooding the Courtrooms: Law and Water in the Far West* (Lincoln: University of Nebraska Press, 1993); Robert G. Dunbar, *Forging New Rights in Western Waters* (Lincoln: University of Nebraska Press, 1983); and Reisner, *Cadillac Desert.*

cover only the period from 1900 to 1920, and county-level data is not readily available. The manuscript schedules of the federal census—the handwritten reports of the census takers, recorded as they inventoried the rural population and economy—would have been the ideal source for this analysis. Unfortunately, these schedules are no longer extant. As a result, the kind of information about individuals, families, and farms that would allow for truly detailed analysis is lost forever. The best source for the period from 1900 to 1940 is the published census, now available in electronic form. Its county-level data on farm size, production, and crop values enable us to describe the diversity of California's farmers in new ways.[15]

Yet the census data limit what we can describe and what analyses we can undertake. Because of the loss of the manuscript schedules, we have no information about individual farms. We cannot determine the size of individual farms, nor can we know how much of what crops were grown or what each grower yielded in sales or net profits. The published census also is silent on the issue of labor, particularly how much help and at what rate of pay growers hired each year. Thus, for the purposes of my inquiry into the presence of small growers, I defined farm size by acreage rather than by gross sales or any other measure of production, because the constraints of the census made other definitions impractical.[16]

Limited as they may be, the published census data make it possible to cast new light on the diversity of farm size between 1900 and 1940. The census employed a wide variety of variables, collecting information about

[15] The federal agricultural manuscript schedules for 1890, 1900, and 1910 were destroyed in a 1921 fire at the Commerce Department in Washington, D.C. Telephone interview, Claire Prechtel-Kluskens, National Archives and Records Administration, Washington, D.C., August 25, 1994; Chan, *Bittersweet Soil*, 409.

For my analysis I used the published agricultural census schedules in both hard copy and electronic form. The electronic data were retrieved from computer files obtained from the Interuniversity Consortium for Political and Social Research at the University of Michigan (ICPSR). All tables in this article rely on ICPSR data and data culled from the published agricultural censuses. In a few cases, I generated variables using ICPSR data. The analysis was performed using SAS Statistical Software for the personal computer (SAS Institute, Cary, North Carolina) or by hand, as noted.

[16] Defining farm size according to gross sales might well be more revealing of the historical position of small growers than farm size in acreage. On the basis of his study of California dairy farms, Jess Gilbert has suggested to me that only those growers who did not hire any additional labor at any time during the year should be properly considered "small" or "family" farmers. Aside from the problems posed by the lack of sources, the issue of defining "small" or "family" farms according to their labor consumption (or lack thereof) is that it would simply exclude nearly every fruit farm save for the very smallest. Vineyards and orchards over five acres in size could not be maintained by a family's labor contributions alone; additional labor, whether in the form of neighbors or hired help, was essential to a timely harvest. I recognize that the labor issue is problematic for determining who was a family farmer in California, but I prefer to avoid measures that do not exclude all fruit growers by definition. For an example of work analyzing farm size in relation to wage labor, see Jess Gilbert and Raymond Akor, "Increasing Structural Divergence in U.S. Dairying: California and Wisconsin since 1950," *Rural Sociology* 53 (1988): 56–72.

the size of farms, the acreage in unimproved as well as improved land, and the amount and value of crops produced in each county. These data steer us away from preconceived conclusions about bigness and monopoly and toward more conclusive inferences about the existence of small farms and changes in the pattern of farm ownership over time.

There was a close and direct relationship between horticulture, geography, and the presence of small farms in California. Different crops were grown in distinct regions of the state for most of the first half of the twentieth century. For example, almonds were grown in the upper Sacramento River Valley; walnuts along the coast near Santa Barbara; table and wine grapes in Yolo, San Bernardino, and Sonoma counties. Prunes, plums, and other stone fruits thrived near the tiny town of San Jose, in Santa Clara County; citrus orchards spread across Los Angeles, Orange, and Riverside counties; and peaches, apricots, and raisin grapes grew in and around Fresno in the Central Valley. If we separate out the areas devoted primarily to fruit growing, we will be able to determine more conclusively the relationship between horticulture and farm size.[17]

Let us begin by noticing the difference between averages, or means, and medians for the purposes of describing countywide aggregations of farms. When historians look at farm size in California, what stands out is that there are more big farms there than anywhere else. The evidence for this impression tends to be the statistic of average, or mean, farm size. The pitfall of the average is that a few very large numbers skew the statistic, even if there are many small numbers in the sample. In contrast, the median represents the point at which half the numbers in a set are higher and half lower. Under certain circumstances, medians are a better measure of group characteristics than means, because unlike the mean, the median is not distorted by a few extreme values.[18]

---

[17] These commodities commanded prices high enough to make small farms profitable. Early studies by University of California agricultural economists demonstrated that fruit growing required far less land than field crop and livestock production. L. W. Fluharty and F. R. Wilcox, *Enterprise Efficiency Studies on California Farms: A Progress Report,* University of California Agricultural Extension Service Circular, no. 24 (Berkeley: University of California Printing Office, 1929); R. L. Adams, *Seasonal Labor Requirements for California Crops,* University of California Agricultural Experiment Station Bulletin, no. 623 (Berkeley: University of California, 1938). Of course, this kind of horticultural economy could not have prospered as it did without migrant workers to supply the seasonal labor demands of small farmers. For a map of California's early twentieth-century horticultural production regions, see Woeste, *The Farmer's Benevolent Trust,* 26–27.

[18] Paul W. Gates, "Adjudication of Spanish-Mexican Land Claims in California," *Huntington Library Quarterly* 21 (1958): 213–36. For studies that focus on the statistic of average farm size to argue for the dominance of large farms in California, see, e.g., McWilliams, *Factories in the Field,* 60–65; Pisani, *From the Family Farm to Agribusiness,* 14–15, 127, 284–85, 450–51; Daniel, *Bitter Harvest,* 17–24; Chan, *This Bittersweet Soil,* 144; Nash, *State Government and Economic Development,* 124–25. More general histories of California that take the large farm as normative include Kevin Starr, *Material Dreams: Southern California through the 1920s* (New

When applied to farms these descriptors produce significantly different results. Table 1 gives the figures for average and median farm sizes in California between 1860 and 1940, based on the census's report of total number of improved acres in farms. In 1860, the average farm in California was 622 acres. By 1940 it had dropped to 230 acres, still well above the 160-acre figure used in the federal homestead acts. Table 1 shows that median farm size was much smaller than statewide average farm size, dramatically in 1860, less so by 1940. In general, the median farm size was smaller than the average, by about seventy acres each decennial.[19]

An even more precise indicator of the presence of small farms is the census's breakdown of all farms by size. The published census reported farm size in range categories, giving the total numbers in each size category for each decennial. Table 2 shows that the number of smaller farms increased over the period to 1940. This increase began in the late nineteenth century and accelerated after 1900. Between 1880 and 1890, when the major horticultural industries were getting their footings, the number of farms of twenty to forty-nine acres more than doubled. The association between small farms and fruit growing began about that time; the number of farms between ten and nineteen acres grew fourfold by 1890 and doubled again by 1900. Between 1900 and 1930, most of the farms in the state belonged to the size category of twenty to forty-nine acres. In 1940, the bulk of farms fell into the next smaller category, ten to nineteen acres.

As a proportion of all farms, small farms made impressive gains over the first half of the century. In 1900, farms under fifty acres represented 39 percent of all farms in the state; this figure peaked at 63 percent in 1930 and dropped only slightly during the Depression to 59 percent in 1940. The number of farms smaller than one hundred acres and particularly smaller than fifty acres grew dramatically after 1900. That year, just under

---

York: Oxford University Press, 1990); Robert Kelley, *Battling the Inland Sea: American Political Culture, Public Policy, and the Sacramento Valley, 1850–1986* (Berkeley: University of California Press, 1989); Walton Bean and James J. Rawls, *California: An Interpretive History*, 3d ed. (New York: McGraw-Hill,1978); and Jelinek, *Harvest Empire.*

[19] On the homestead acts, see Paul W. Gates, *History of Public Land Law Development*, Report to the Public Lands Commission (Washington: Government Printing Office, 1968); reprint ed. (New York: Arno Press, 1978). Since the published census does not list the exact size of each individual farm, it is impossible to calculate median farm size with precision. I calculated it by taking the number of farms in each size range, multiplying by a number at the midpoint of each size range, and summing across both the number of farms and average number of acres in each size range. I checked the accuracy of this method against the published figures for total acres in farms in each census and found that my figure for total acres in farms more closely approximated the census's reported figure for *improved* land in farms than for *total acres in farms,* which includes unimproved land. The census's calculation of average farm size used total acres in farms, meaning that its reported figures emphasized large unimproved holdings rather than measuring what acreage was actually cultivated.

TABLE 3-1   AVERAGE AND
MEDIAN FARM SIZE IN CALIFORNIA, 1860–1940

	Total Number of Farms	Average Farm Size (in acres)	Median Farm Size (in acres)
1860	14,044	622	235
1870	23,724	482	284
1880	35,934	462	422
1890	52,894	405	389
1900	72,542	397	317
1910	88,197	317	260
1920	117,670	250	210
1930	135,676	224	180
1940	155,216	230	173

Source: ICPSR Data Sets, 1860–1940. Median farm size was calculated by hand from ICPSR data.

half of the farms in the state were smaller than one hundred acres; four decades later, over three-quarters were.[20]

Using data on the total value of crop production, we can identify the top counties in each agricultural sector. According to the standard historical story, counties with a high value of fruit and nut crop production presumably would have the largest farms, since agribusiness was dominated by large farms and horticulture was the wealthiest sector of the economy. So the first step is to identify which counties had the highest total value of horticultural production, and then draw the farm size profiles. During the period from 1900 to 1940, the top five horticultural counties were Los Angeles, San Bernardino, and Orange in southern California, Fresno in the Central Valley, and Santa Clara south of San Francisco. As table 3 shows, in each of these fruit-growing counties and in each decennial census, a definite majority of farms was smaller than one hundred acres. By 1920, in each county but Fresno, most of the farms were smaller than twenty acres, and that remained the case through 1940.[21]

The conventional story of the factory farm tells us to expect horticulture to be associated with large farms—fruit and vegetable growers were McWilliams's favorite foil—but the statistical correlations between fruit growing and farm size and between field crops and farm size belie that story. Correlations are mathematical expressions of the extent to which the amount of one factor predicts the amount of another. The statistic is expressed as a

[20] Figures calculated from data presented in table 2. In 1910, the percentage of farms under fifty acres was 49; in 1920, it was 56.

[21] Woeste, *The Farmer's Benevolent Trust,* 241. For a sorting and ranking of field crop–producing counties according to this method, see ibid., 242–43.

TABLE 3-2   NUMBERS OF FARMS
IN CALIFORNIA, BY SIZE (IN ACRES), 1860–1940

	<3	3–9	10–19	20–49	50–99	100–499	500–999	>1000
1860		829	1,102	2,344	2,428	6,541	538	262
1870	0	2,187	1,086	3,064	3,224	12,248	1,202	713
1880	143	1,064	1,430	3,475	3,969	20,214	3,108	2,531
1890	n/a[1]	2,827	4,010	7,691	5,796	24,531	4,367	3,672

	<3	3–9	10–19	20–49	50–99	100–174	175–259	260–499	500–999	>1000
1900	1,492	5,354	8,236	13,110	8,067	13,196	4,635	8,370	5,329	4,753
1910	1,269	9,324	11,932	20,614	10,680	12,015	4,689	7,862	5,119	4,693
1920	2,904	13,793	17,370	31,723	15,034	13,217	5,320	8,351	5,052	4,906
1930	8,527	20,365	22,037	34,948	16,378	11,561	4,976	6,969	4,861	5,054
1940	6,476	25,070	37,826	38,936	15,200	10,669	4,725	6,498	4,551	5,265

Source: ICPSR Data Sets, 1860–1940.
[1] In 1860, the smallest farm was "smaller than 10 acres"; in 1890, the category "smaller than 3 acres" was not used.

TABLE 3-3 SMALL FARMS AS A PERCENTAGE OF TOTAL FARMS IN FIVE FRUIT-GROWING COUNTIES, 1900, 1920, AND 1940 (FIGURES IN PARENTHESES ARE ABSOLUTE NUMBERS)

Size (acres)	Fresno	Los Angeles	Orange	San Bernardino	Santa Clara
1900					
1–19	11 (354)	44 (2,909)	33 (793)	50 (1,165)	39 (1,562)
20–99	51 (1,690)	36 (2,359)	53 (1,254)	35 (827)	37 (1,495)
100–499	26 (866)	16 (1,082)	10 (250)	13 (298)	19 (759)
500+	12 (380)	3 (227)	4 (91)	3 (60)	4 (179)
1920					
1–19	14 (1,229)	60 (7,505)	57 (2,385)	53 (2,123)	48 (2,408)
20–99	72 (6,439)	29 (3,401)	33 (1,388)	31 (1,247)	40 (1,982)
100–499	11 (967)	11 (1,309)	8 (322)	14 (569)	10 (508)
500+	3 (282)	2 (229)	2 (93)	2 (118)	2 (128)
1940					
1–19	42 (4,460)	66 (10,080)	64 (5,123)	65 (4,878)	52 (3,703)
20–99	44 (4,756)	28 (4,210)	32 (2,594)	29 (2,222)	40 (2,869)
100–499	10 (1,123)	5 (742)	3 (263)	5 (371)	7 (480)
500+	3 (365)	1 (170)	1 (69)	1 (79)	2 (122)

Source: ICPSR Data Sets, 1900, 1920, 1940.
Note: Percentages might not total 100 due to rounding error. Farms smaller than 100 acres are split into two groups for purposes of this analysis; since many fruit farms were as small as 20 acres, this table shows how many farms in theses counties fell into that category.

fraction, and as this fraction approaches one, the correlation becomes more significant. A correlation of one represents a perfect association between two phenomena. Table 4 gives these statistics for each decennial, correlating the value of horticultural production with each farm size category. What these numbers tell us is that fruit growing is highly correlated with farms between three and ninety-nine acres, and it is most highly correlated with farms that were between ten and nineteen acres in size. For farms above one hundred acres, the correlation statistic is lower and decreases as farm size increases. For present purposes, that observation means that farms between three and ninety-nine acres were mostly likely to have been fruit farms.[22]

---

[22] For fruit growing and farms between three and ninety-nine acres, the correlation statistic r was consistently greater than 0.8 (r 0.8), indicating a high degree of correlation. For farms greater than 100 acres, r values were around 0.6, a moderately high degree of correlation.

TABLE 3-4 CORRELATIONS BETWEEN FARM SIZE (IN ACRES) AND VALUE OF FRUIT CROP PRODUCTION IN CALIFORNIA COUNTIES, 1910–1940

	<3	3–9	10–19	20–49	50–99	100–174	175–259	260–499	500–999	>1000
1910	0.581	0.849	0.911	0.892	0.852	0.669	0.763	0.552	0.493	0.428
1920	0.69	0.833	0.900	0.872	0.8662	0.744	0.743	0.558	0.460**	0.429**
1930	0.749	0.860	0.916	0.898	0.859	0.786	0.734	0.568	0.375**	0.328**
1940	0.719	0.813	0.898	0.895	0.846	0.741	0.739	0.608	0.478**	0.304**

Source: ICPSR Data Sets, 1910–1940. Correlations performed using PROC CORR function of SAS.

Note: $N = 58$ (number of observations equals total counties), except in 1940, when $N = 48$. All Spearman correlation coefficients are significant at 0.001 probability level unless otherwise noted.

** Spearman correlation coefficient significant at 0.01 probability level.

TABLE 3-5   CORRELATIONS BETWEEN
FARM SIZE (IN ACRES) AND VALUE OF FIELD CROP
PRODUCTION IN CALIFORNIA COUNTIES, 1910–1940

	<3	3–9	10–19	20–49	50–99
1910	0.488	0.705	0.742	0.766	0.748
1920	0.133ˣ	0.220ˣ	0.336**	0.517	0.618
1930	0.537	0.615	0.667	0.741	0.769
1940	0.396*	0.477**	0.615	0.656	0.767

	100–174	175–259	260–499	500–999	>1000
1910	0.639	0.678	0.702	0.725	0.698
1920	0.591	0.629	0.605	0.581	0.468
1930	0.776	0.799	0.756	0.681	0.563
1940	0.722	0.799	0.760	0.666	0.550

Source: ICPSR Data Sets, 1910–1940. Correlations performed using PROC CORR function of SAS.
Note: N = 58 (number of observations equals total counties), except in 1940, when N = 48. All Spearman
   correlation coefficients are significant at 0.001 probability level unless
   otherwise noted.
** Spearman correlation coefficient significant at 0.01 probability level.
* Spearman correlation coefficient significant at 0.05 probability level.
ˣ Spearman correlation coefficient not significant.

Field crop production supplies a near-mirror image of this pattern.
Counties with the largest number of farms between 175 and 259 acres
tended to produce the most field crops. As reflected in table 5, field crops
were generally more highly correlated with larger farms than with smaller
farms. The correlation between rank for value of field crops and rank for
farm size is greatest for larger farms, although the association of field crops
with large farms is not as strong as the association of fruit growing with
small farms.[23]

The hallmark of Jeffersonian agrarianism, of course, was farm ownership. All these family farms in California are politically meaningless if ownership was beyond the reach of fruit farmers. In fact, fruit growing was
highly associated with farm ownership. Table 6 shows the mean number

[23] For field crops and farm size, *r* ranged between 0.4 and 0.7 for farms of three to ninety-
nine acres, but the pattern was not nearly so consistent as that for fruit farms. For farms of one
hundred acres and larger, *r* values were more concentrated between 0.6 and 0.8.

To determine whether the differences between fruit-growing and field crop counties were
statistically significant, I performed t-tests on the two sets of counties and found that counties producing most of the state's fruit had the most small farms; conversely, counties with
more large farms tended to produce more field crops and probably livestock too, though the
census failed to report livestock data consistently enough to include it in the analysis. For an
elaboration of these findings, see Woeste, *The Farmer's Benevolent Trust,* 245–51.

and percentage of owners, part owners, managers, and tenants in both fruit-growing and field crop counties. The fruit-growing counties had more of each kind of farm operator than the field crop counties. As a result, the proportion of owners to non-owner-operators was much higher in fruit counties than in nonfruit ones. While there were more tenants in fruit counties, tenants made up a higher percentage of the operators in non-fruit counties. Whatever the economic and legal disparities between independent owners and dependent operators, the small farms in the horticultural industries were not disproportionately populated by tenants, managers, or other stand-ins for absentee owners.

In sum, this analysis shows that farm size was directly correlated with commodity. The vast majority of California fruit farmers worked on farms of fewer than fifty acres, and for the most part they owned these farms and supplied most of their own year-round labor. The difference in farm size between fruit-growing counties and field crop counties was both substantial and statistically significant and lasted at least until 1940.

The existence of different modes of farm operation means that, among many important considerations, the dynamics of labor-capital relations in horticulture should not be reduced simply to a battle of large wealthy non-operators against exploited laborers. Rather, small owners and tenants constituted the bulk of operators in the horticultural regions and made small-holding a meaningful category of economic enterprise. Beneath the monolith of industrial farming lies unexpected complexity. In fruit-growing sectors, growers exhibited a wide diversity of economic interests, and farm ownership was surprisingly widespread among those people not disqualified as landowners by the state's Alien Land Laws.

These findings lay an essential foundation for understanding the existence and persistence of small farms in California from 1900 through 1940. They also make it possible to envision thousands of men and women like Porter L. Brown, supporting their families with the modest fruit farms they owned and worked. Finally, they make it imperative to explore the ramifications of small-scale agricultural enterprise for the politics of agribusiness and the state in twentieth-century California.

The Great Depression presented California growers with the worst economic crisis they had ever faced. Coming on top of agriculture's chronic overproduction during the 1920s, the nation's financial paralysis threw the marketing system into complete disarray. In 1933, the New Deal's federal program for agricultural recovery began under the Agricultural Adjustment Act. There was a state-level alternative as well: the California Agricultural Prorate Act, passed that same year. Under this law, growers sat on the agencies that wrote the marketing regulations, the committees that ran the marketing programs were locally situate, and nothing could happen until two-thirds of growers in an industry agreed to initiate public control

TABLE 3-6 LAND TENURE ON CALIFORNIA FARMS, BY FRUIT-GROWING AND NON-FRUIT-GROWING COUNTIES, 1910–1940

	N	Owners (mean) (%)	Part Owners (mean) (%)	Managers (mean) (%)	Tenants (mean) (%)
			1910		
Fruit	17	2,394 (78)	n/a	98 (3)	586 (19)
Nonfruit	41	632 (76)	n/a	10 (1)	200 (24)
			1920		
Fruit	15	2,997 (68)	379 (9)	213 (5)	838 (19)
Nonfruit	43	719 (60)	140 (12)	41 (3)	293 (25)
			1930		
Fruit	14	4,242 (70)	480 (8)	372 (6)	938 (16)
Nonfruit	44	704 (60)	146 (13)	58 (5)	256 (22)
			1940		
Fruit	18	3,544 (71)	460 (9)	143 (3)	862 (17)
Nonfruit	40	651 (61)	142 (13)	20 (2)	246 (23)

Source: ICPSR Data Sets, 1910–1940.
Note: All differences between fruit-growing and non–fruit-growing counties are significant at
0.001 probability using Student's T-statistics.

of markets. As a result, smaller growers had a voice in the regulation of markets during the 1930s, however messy and conflicted the regulatory process was under the statute.[24]

The state Prorate Law gave growers an administrative solution to the problem of oversupplied markets. In theory, whatever their economic sta-

[24] Only California passed a prorate law, because only in California were so many commodities produced within the state's boundaries, making it constitutionally permissible for the state to regulate production and prices. Donald L. Kieffer, "This Prorate Law—What is It?" *Pacific Rural Press,* July 16, 1938, 46.

tus, all growers stood to gain something from the law. Large growers, who lost millions during the Depression because cooperatives and other private organizations could not legally curtail agricultural production, gained the prospect of more stable profits. Small growers, who felt burned by the collapse of voluntary pools and the superior bargaining power of processors and packers, gained protection against both these problems. The state-run marketing system was called "proration" because it titrated the volume of commodities placed on the market over time, thus avoiding the usual pattern of the entire year's crop being sold right at harvest. Once the requisite two-thirds of the growers in an industry petitioned the state for a prorate program, everyone in the industry—growers, processors, and packers alike—had to participate. Mandatory participation no doubt curtailed the economic independence of some small growers, but it also meant that processors and packers could not hold growers hostage to low prices. Higher, stable prices for the producers benefited small growers, who could not hold out long after harvest before they had to sell their crops.[25]

The raisin industry was deeply divided over the issue of whether and how to regulate the market. A 1934 federal marketing order was canceled after only one year, when the commercial raisin packers and the cooperative Sun-Maid Raisin Growers could not agree on how to ensure that all growers and packers would participate. That left proration as the only alternative, but growers and packers could not agree for several years on the issue of how much of the crop should be designated as surplus and diverted to less valuable uses such as stock feed. The growers were divided not only against the packers but also among themselves, as the *Pacific Rural Press* commented: "[S]ome of the smaller growers [believe] that the larger producers are favored by the packers [who] buy more readily from the producers with large tonnages to sell." According to a contemporary economist, smaller growers naturally distrusted large growers and corporate vineyard owners, whom they believed acted in collusion to set prices: "[R]ich packers... tie up the farmer's crop in unfair contracts which leave the price to be determined later."[26]

When the industry finally voted in 1938 to establish a prorate program, it was largely because small growers united in a campaign to win the nec-

---

[25] California Prorate Act of 1933, *Cal. Stats.* (June 15, 1933), chap. 754, pp. 1969–70; Malcolm Watson, "An Analysis of Raisin Marketing Controls under the California Agricultural Prorate Act" (M.S. thesis, University of California, Berkeley, 1940), 11; Ellis A. Stokdyk, "Economic and Legal Aspects of Compulsory Proration in Agricultural Marketing," University of California Agricultural Experiment Station Bulletin, no. 565 (December 1933), 2–28. The statute's requirement of mandatory participation marked a stark departure from earlier attempts to control marketing by private cooperatives and the Federal Farm Board.

[26] "The Dried Fruit Growers Will Fight," *Pacific Rural Press*, August 21, 1937, 183; Watson, "Analysis of Raisin Marketing Controls," 23. Racial and ethnic divisions amplified the economic conflicts among the growers. See ibid.; Woeste, *The Farmer's Benevolent Trust*, 51–58, 173–88.

essary signatures despite the opposition of the packers and Sun-Maid. What the majority of growers wanted was to be able to sell all their raisins at the stabilized price rather than be obliged to divert any proportion of their crop to less valuable outlets. The more raisins that were diverted under the prorate, the less income growers made. Yet the stabilized price could and did collapse when growers resorted to unregulated selling in an oversupplied market. An economist pointed out: "[It] seems unreasonable for growers to complain and oppose the steps that had to be taken as a result of such a bad mistake as the drying of 290,000 tons of raisins" in 1938. The 1938 raisin prorate program committee diverted 80 percent of this huge crop to brandy making and stock feed, infuriating small growers who felt they had to bear the brunt of the costs of surplus management.[27]

If one problem with the prorate law was that it gave processors too much control over the administration of the industry program, another difficulty was that it gave growers just enough say in the matter to enable them to prevent surplus management entirely. Raisin growers were so frustrated at the handling of the 1938 crop that they refused to endorse a new prorate in 1939. The raisin growers were not alone in their dissatisfaction with the law: "I think the way the prorate act has been administered in California comes close to being Fascism," one olive grower told the *Pacific Rural Press*. A southern California citrus producer complained: "Proration holds back good fruit and tends to allow poor fruit to reach the market. It increases the cost of production and does not benefit growers." And a representative of the Fresno County Grange made it clear that growers did not trust the people running the programs: "The producers have little or no control over the acts of the program committees."[28]

The widespread discontent among small growers created a surge in grassroots support for changes in the Prorate Act. In 1939, the California legislature bowed to the growers' demands for more representation on the industry prorate committees. In addition, growers in the citrus, wine grape, and raisin industries began to recognize, after the heavy crops of 1938, that surplus control was necessary even if it meant they would not receive good prices for all they produced. Some citrus growers resorted to severe remedies and began pulling trees out of their orchards in order to cut their losses. In the raisin industry, one thousand growers convened at a mass meeting to demand new elections for the program committee under the new amendments. The growers agreed to withhold 20 percent of their crop from the market if the program committee ensured that the packers would not get to sell the surplus at higher

[27] Watson, "Analysis of Raisin Marketing Controls," 24–25, 44. Watson notes that the normal market for raisins during this time was approximately 205,000 tons per year. Ibid., 55.
[28] "Comments on Prorate By California Growers," *Pacific Rural Press*, April 8, 1939, 338.

prices than the growers received for it. The committee acceded to this demand.[29]

Still, some small growers opposed the idea of surplus control. They asserted their position in a variety of ways. They resorted to violence, protesting the shipment of raisins to the surplus pool. They obtained court orders barring the diversion of raisins to stock feed in 1938 and stopping the operation of the entire program in 1940. One of these actions was the lawsuit filed by Porter L. Brown. Still, by April 1940, according to the *Pacific Rural Press*, prices had sunk to such lows that outright opposition was becoming economically and politically untenable: "Most of the Fresno county growers seem now to favor amending the prorate program."[30]

In 1940, growers, government agricultural officials, and packers finally came to a common understanding of what constituted a successful proration program. For growers, especially small-scale operators who relied on one crop for their income, it was essential to have in place a mechanism that prevented packers—or anyone else—from disposing of surplus raisins. Until the 1940 prorate committee found a way to subsidize the losses growers took on these surpluses, by obtaining federal funds to underwrite the stabilization plan, growers refused to support proration. William B. Parker, California state director of marketing, brokered the arrangements between the federal Commodities Credit Corporation and the prorate committee, thereby bridging state and federal agricultural surplus management programs. Parker's direct involvement also helped lessen the tension created by growers who distrusted the packer representatives on the program committee.[31]

Once growers were assured of greater representation on the committee, and once federal financing of the surplus had been guaranteed, opposition to a control plan for 1940 dissipated quickly. During that summer, 2,656 growers, representing 73 percent of those voting, approved the implementation of a prorate for that year. In the raisin industry, the willing participation of small growers was essential to the success of any regulatory program that depended, as did the prorate, on the willingness of a democratic majority for its existence. In this sense the prorate program serves as

[29] Watson, "Analysis of Raisin Marketing Controls," 33–46; Donald L. Kieffer, "Market News and Comment," *Pacific Rural Press*, April 29, 1939, 406; ibid., May 27, 1939, 494; ibid., June 3, 1939, 510. On Sun-Maid's control over the prorate committee, see Kieffer, "Market News and Comment," ibid., August 28, 1937, 246.

[30] Kieffer, "Market News and Comment," *Pacific Rural Press*, September 23, 1939, 206; Watson, "Analysis of Raisin Marketing Controls," 53; Kieffer, "Market News and Comment," *Pacific Rural Press*, April 20, 1940, 326. Litigation was used by both supporters and opponents of the prorate law throughout the New Deal; the California state courts ruled in the law's favor (*Agricultural Prorate Commission et al. v. Superior Court*, 5 Cal. 2d 550 [1935]), but the federal district court in Los Angeles gave opponents their first victory (*Brown v. Parker*, 39 F. Supp. 895 [S.D.Cal. 1941]).

[31] Kieffer, "Market News and Comment," *Pacific Rural Press*, June 1, 1940, 430; ibid., July 27, 1940, 54.

a vivid example of the influence small growers could bring to bear on state and federal administrative regulation of agricultural markets. And the federal-state cooperation in financing the raisin prorate swayed the U.S. Supreme Court when it finally decided Porter L. Brown's case in 1943: the prorate law was upheld, and Brown lost.[32]

Growers and governments together struggled to stabilize agriculture during the 1930s. Raisin growers made it clear that no program of administrative regulation could succeed without them. Enmeshed in complicated local politics, California agriculture may ultimately be best understood as exemplifying what Gerald Berk has called the "constitutive politics" of the industrial era. Berk argues that local politics and political actors played significant roles in shaping law and reform during the late nineteenth and early twentieth centuries and that small-scale "republican" business firms were surprisingly powerful in the political arena. Focusing on local actors, public and private alike, permits him to argue for the importance of ideology and the contested nature of local political struggles in determining the outcome of economic and regulatory battles affecting the railroad industry.[33]

Similarly, the history of horticulture, the presence of small farmers as demonstrated by the analysis of the census, and the history of proration together bear out the importance of the local political context in California agriculture. The various economic and political actors and interests that constituted the state's rural sector all participated actively in state, local, and national politics, although that participation of course was often constrained by both law and the market. The prorate story demonstrates the significance of California agriculture's economic diversity and the economic and political power of small-scale producers.

Berk's insight, of reconceptualizing the Gilded Age and Progressive era in terms of "constitutive politics," may help us to transform the way we think about the culture of agricultural enterprise and its relationship to the modern state in twentieth-century California. If small growers had a significant impact on the direction and outcome of proration, which stands as a significant example of the political administration of markets, then they probably used similar methods to affect the dynamics of other central political issues. The politics of agribusiness in California, and indeed in the nation as a whole, therefore may well have

---

[32] Kieffer, "Market News and Comment," *Pacific Rural Press*, September 21, 1940, 190; *Parker v. Brown*, 317 U.S. 341 (1943).

[33] Gerald Berk, *Alternative Tracks: The Constitution of American Industrial Order, 1865–1917* (Baltimore: Johns Hopkins University Press, 1994), 1–11, 180–83. An example of an economic study that stresses the importance of local politics and regional categories of analysis is Sally H. Clarke, *Regulation and Revolution in United States Farm Productivity* (New York: Cambridge University Press, 1994).

been much more pluralistic than we have heretofore recognized. Not that corporate actors had no influence on the state, or that the state represented everyone equally well, but small growers found power in numbers and brought their perspective to bear on the public institutions that governed them even in the age of the powerful and bureaucratic modern state.

PART 2

The Uses of the State and the Politics of the Dispossessed

The State of Nature

Country Folk, Conservationists, and Criminals at Yellowstone National Park, 1872–1908

KARL JACOBY

Times is different now.... [I]n them days nobody said a word if a poor man wanted a little meat an' killed it, but now they're savin' it until the dudes get time to come up here an' kill it.... [and] they'd put me in jail ef I killed a deer when I needed meat. I dunno what we're a-comin' to in this free country.[1]

Thus did one aged inhabitant of the American countryside summarize what he considered to be the central transformation of rural life at the turn of the century. At first glance, such observations may seem to offer little more than an old man's highly idiosyncratic view of the past, one that neglects the grand trends of urbanization, industrialization, and immigration that have dominated most accounts of the Gilded Age, in favor of a parochial obsession with the chase. But the coming of game laws and other conservation measures did indeed mark the onset of "different times" in the United States, for conservation heralded the adoption of an unprecedented new role for the American state: manager of the environment. This shift loomed especially large in rural America, still the dwelling place of most Americans in the early 1900s, and the site where any effort by the state to oversee the use of natural resources would, of necessity, be concentrated.[2]

---

[1] *Boonville (N.Y.) Herald,* April 15, 1897. The quote comes from Alvah Dunning, a hunter and trapper who lived in what had become the Adirondack Forest Preserve.

[2] The literature on American conservation is extensive. Perhaps the most useful starting point remains Samuel Hays, *Conservation and the Gospel of Efficiency: The Progressive Conservation Movement, 1890–1920* (Cambridge, Mass.: Harvard University Press, 1959). In the last few

Prior to conservation's rise in the late nineteenth century, the American state had sought to exercise little oversight over environmental matters. Laws such as the Homestead Act of 1862 had focused not on preserving the ecological integrity of the public lands but rather on transforming them as quickly as possible into the yeoman farms so prized by republican ideology. Scarcely a decade after the Homestead Act's passage, however, members of the nascent conservation movement began to argue that state and federal governments should revise their efforts to privatize the public lands. Citing the need for expert, scientific oversight of environmentally sensitive areas, conservationists advocated that much of the public domain be withheld from sale and maintained as permanent state-owned holdings, managed by government-appointed technicians. In the words of *Garden and Forest,* one of the nineteenth century's leading conservation journals: "The state, with its continuous life, its comprehensive concern for the good of all, its ample capital, its purpose which can be held steady from generation to generation, can alone be trusted to administer this property [the public lands] to the highest advantage of the community."[3]

Convinced of the need for expert oversight and government intervention (both to become familiar elements of Progressive era reform), at the turn of the century Congress created an array of new institutions to manage the public lands. Suddenly, the federal government, which only a few years earlier had been a temporary caretaker of the rural landscape, eager to surrender its role to private property owners, was the owner of a growing mixture of national parks, forests, and monuments, making it one of the largest landholders in the American countryside. By 1910, for example, there were 150 national forests nationwide—a vast archipelago of some 200 million acres, embracing Florida, Arkansas, Kansas, and Puerto Rico as well as the territories of the rapidly developing American West. On the local level, these

---

years, a number of scholars have revitalized the study of the movement by examining it from "the bottom up," revealing early American conservation's social impact. Louis Warren studies poaching in *The Hunter's Game: Poachers and Conservationists in Twentieth-Century America* (New Haven, Conn.: Yale University Press, 1997); Mark Spence focuses on the effect that the park movement had on American Indians in *Dispossessing the Wilderness: The Preservationist Ideal, Indian Removal, and National Parks* (New York: Oxford University Press, 1999); Richard Judd attempts to place rural New Englanders at the forefront of the conservation movement in *Common Lands, Common People: The Origins of Conservation in Northern New England* (Cambridge, Mass.: Harvard University Press, 1997). See also Karl Jacoby, "Class and Environmental History: Lessons from 'The War in the Adirondacks,' " *Environmental History* 2 (July 1997): 324–42, and *Crimes Against Nature: Squatters, Poachers, Thieves, and the Hidden History of American Conservation* (Berkeley: University of California Press, 2001).

[3] "The Adirondack Reservation," *Garden and Forest* 4 (February 4, 1891): 49. Although this editorial focused on New York's efforts in the Adirondacks, many other articles in *Garden and Forest* extended similar arguments to the nation as a whole. See, for example, "A National Forest-Policy," *Garden and Forest* 5 (August 24, 1892): 397.

actions were paralleled by the growth of state forest commissions, charged with enforcing new state game laws and overseeing new state forests.[4]

Although these conservation sites varied remarkably in size and location, in few were the underlying tensions between conservationists and rural folk thrown into sharper relief than in Yellowstone, the nation's (and indeed the world's) first national park. Beginning in 1872, on the mountainous Yellowstone plateau bordering Montana, Idaho, and Wyoming territories, the United States launched its initial foray into conservation, originating many of the policies that it would later apply to national parks and forests elsewhere and establishing the park model that would in turn be exported by conservationists to the countrysides of Africa, Asia, and Latin America. The confrontations that took place in Yellowstone's two million acres thus serve as important precursors to the conflicts that have unfolded in countless locations around the world as country people have grappled with the coming of conservation and the rise of the managerial state.[5]

The Evolution of Park Policy

While conservation was marked by new systems of state control and administration, these systems did not take shape at all once. Indeed, at first Yellowstone possessed almost no control mechanisms at all: the congressmen who passed the Yellowstone Park Act in 1872 did not include any measures to staff the park or to enforce its rules. As a result, Yellowstone's first superintendent, Nathaniel Langford, received no salary and maintained a full-time job elsewhere as a bank examiner, not even visiting the park for years at a time. Because of this casual approach to park management, the rural folk living on Yellowstone's fringes initially paid little heed to park rules. Instead, they set fires to drive game or open up grazing areas; they cut trees for build-

---

[4] *Annual Report of the American Scenic and Historic Preservation Society, 1910* (Albany: J. B. Lyon, 1910), 130–33; *Annual Report of the Commissioner of the General Land Office, 1902* (Washington, D.C.: GPO, 1902), 81–83. The federal government remains the largest landholder in much of rural America, particularly in the Far West. See Richard H. Jackson, "Federal Lands in the Mountainous West," in *The Mountainous West: Explorations in Historical Geography*, ed. William Wyckoff and Lary M. Dilsaver (Lincoln: University of Nebraska Press, 1995), 255. The first forest commission and forest reserve were in New York. George H. Parsons, "Forest Administration—Federal or State?" *Proceedings of the American Forestry Association* 10 (March 1895): 125.

[5] For discussions of national parks in Africa, Asia, and elsewhere, see David Anderson and Richard Grove, eds., *Conservation in Africa: People, Policies and Practice* (New York: Cambridge University Press, 1987); Jonathan S. Adams and Thomas O. McShane, *The Myth of Wild Africa: Conservation Without Illusion* (Berkeley: University of California Press, 1996); Ramachandra Guha, *The Unquiet Woods: Ecological Change and Peasant Resistance in the Indian Himalaya* (Berkeley: University of California Press, 1990); and Patrick C. West and Steven R. Brechin, eds., *Resident Peoples and National Parks: Social Dilemmas and Strategies in International Conservation* (Tucson: University of Arizona Press, 1991).

ing supplies or firewood; they settled in the park, erecting everything from illegal hunting shanties to full-fledged ranches; and above all, they poached the park's animals—which included not only elk, deer, antelope, and mountain sheep but also one of the United States' last remaining buffalo herds. As Captain George S. Anderson, the U.S. Cavalry captain charged with overseeing Yellowstone for much of the 1890's, grumbled:

> Trouble with poachers continues to be one of the greatest annoyances the superintendent has to contend with. There is gradually settling about the park boundaries a population whose sole subsistence is derived from hunting and trapping.... In most civilized countries the occupation of such vandals as these is held in merited contempt. But it is not so in the [Yellowstone] region.[6]

In response to this persistent lawbreaking, the federal government was forced to revise its conservation program repeatedly, developing new and more efficient enforcement mechanisms and even placing the Army in charge of the park from 1886 to 1918.[7] Influenced by the complaints of Anderson and other park superintendents about local "vandals," these varied measures all shared a core assumption: that crimes such as poaching enjoyed widespread support in the communities surrounding Yellowstone. As we shall see, however, the truth was considerably more complicated. To be sure, the rural folk living near Yellowstone frequently saw little wrong with hunting in the park. But by grouping all hunting within Yellowstone into the simplified category of poaching and by assuming that all poachers enjoyed equal local favor, park officials failed to recognize the complex moral gradations that guided local inhabitants' interactions with the natural world. While these gradations ensured that the country people living near Yellowstone often disagreed with conservationists' policies, they also meant that the actual attitude of local residents to Yellowstone was far more nuanced than the unremitting opposition that the movement's supporters often described.[8]

---

[6] *Annual Report of the Superintendent of Yellowstone National Park, 1892* (Washington, D.C.: GPO, 1892), 3, 5, 9.

[7] For more on the army management of Yellowstone, see Duane Hampton, *How the U.S. Cavalry Saved Our National Parks* (Bloomington: Indiana University Press, 1971); and Karl Jacoby, "The Recreation of Nature: A Social and Environmental History of American Conservation, 1872–1919" (Ph.D. diss., Yale University, 1997), 196–212.

[8] The role that the state plays in (over)simplifying complex systems to make them more understable and manageable is brilliantly discussed in James Scott, *Seeing Like a State: How Certain Schemes to Improve the Human Condition Have Failed* (New Haven, Conn.: Yale University Press, 1998). For other conservationist accounts that stress the lawlessness of Yellowstone's rural neighbors, see William Hornaday, *Wildlife Conservation in Theory and Practice: Lectures Delivered before the Forest School of Yale University* (New Haven, Conn.: Yale University Press, 1914), 189–90; and Hornaday, *The Extermination of the American Bison with a Sketch of Its Discovery and Life History* (Washington, D.C.: U.S. National Museum, 1889), 520.

Among the earliest poachers Yellowstone authorities had to contend with were American Indians from the reservations that ringed the park: the Crow Reservation to the north, Fort Hall to the west, Lemhi to the south, and Wind River to the east. The inhabitants of these reservations, the Crows and the Bannock-Shoshones, had hunted in the Yellowstone region for generations, long before the park's creation. Indeed, early Euro-American travelers to Yellowstone stumbled across evidence of these peoples throughout the lands that would become part of the new park: trails carved by Indian ponies and travois; fires set by the Crows and Bannock-Shoshone to drive game or to create grazing areas for their horses; abandoned Indian shelters in "nearly all of the sheltered glens and valleys of the Park." Ironically, even as the U.S. government forced the Crow and Bannock-Shoshone onto reservations in the 1860s and 1870s, both tribes seem to have increased their use of Yellowstone. With their traditional quarry, the buffalo, virtually extinct and rations on their reservations limited, the Crow and Bannock-Shoshone had few alternatives but to intensify their seasonal hunts in the vicinity of the park. Explained the Indian agent on the Wind River Reservation in 1882: "The supplies furnished by the government are not sufficient alone for their maintenance. But they [the Bannock-Shoshone] are fortunately situated in a game country, and support themselves... in hunting during the winter season." Moreover, many local tribes, such as the Bannock-Shoshone, had the treaty right to hunt on "unoccupied public land." To hungry bands from nearby reservations, Yellowstone National Park, untouched by ranches or other Euro-American settlements, looked very much like unoccupied land, and they readily sought out its familiar terrain.[9]

These annual forays excited considerable concern among park authorities (as did a more spectacular excursion of the Nez Perce through the park in 1877, during which several tourists were killed or taken hostage). Refusing to recognize that native hunting expeditions were part of a seasonal cycle that predated the park's existence, Yellowstone officials labeled the Indian presence a new and unwelcome intrusion that needed to be contained as expeditiously as possible. Throughout the 1870s and 1880s, park superintendents experimented with various solutions to Yellowstone's "Indian problem"—more rigorous patrolling of park boundaries, tightening of reservation regulations, new treaties—but none proved entirely successful.[10]

---

[9] Descriptions of Indian traces inside the current park boundaries can be found in P. W. Norris, "Report of the Superintendent of Yellowstone National Park," in *Annual Report of the Secretary of the Interior, 1880* (Washington, D.C.: GPO, 1881), 605. For accounts of off-reservation hunting, see *Annual Report of the Commissioner of Indian Affairs, 1882* (Washington, D.C.: GPO, 1882), 499; *Annual Report of the Commissioner of Indian Affairs, 1883* (Washington, D.C.: GPO, 1883), 313–14; *Annual Report of the Commissioner of Indian Affairs, 1895* (Washington, D.C.: GPO, 1896), 65–66; and "Indian Hunting Rights," *Forest and Stream* 46 (May 30, 1896): 429.

[10] Firsthand descriptions of the Nez Perce incident can be found in Heister Dean Guie and Lucullus Virgil McWhorter, eds., *Adventures in Geyserland* (Caldwell, Idaho: Caxton Printers,

KARL JACOBY

Ultimately, it was not the park's limited enforcement efforts but changes going on outside Yellowstone that reduced native poaching. Each passing year, a growing number of Euro-Americans established ranches and farms on the park's periphery. Few of these newly arrived settlers looked kindly upon extended Indian hunts going on in their midst; many expressed outrage that native peoples were not bound by the new game laws that non-Indians were theoretically obliged to obey. Confrontations between Indian hunters and white settlers grew, peaking in 1895 when a self-proclaimed posse of twenty-seven men from Jackson Hole, trying to arrest several Bannock Indians "for wantonly killing game," shot six. As local Indians realized that the federal and state governments were unwilling to protect them from such violence—or to enforce their off-reservation hunting rights— many native hunters became reluctant to venture off their reservations.[11]

The collapse of Indian hunting did not mark the end of poaching in Yellowstone so much as a shift in its character. In place of large family bands of fifty or a hundred Bannock-Shoshones or Crows, hunting now took the form of small, surreptitious bands of white poachers. Yellowstone officials soon concluded that these new white intruders posed much the same threat to the park and its wildlife as had their Indian predecessors. Thus, rather than drawing a sharp racial distinction between Indians and whites, park officials often lumped the two into one uniformly dangerous class. In 1891, for example, *Forest and Stream* warned its readers that Yellowstone was fast becoming "a hunting ground both for whites and Indians, and the forests which cover its mountains are in constant danger of fire from these wandering and often careless invaders." Upon occasion, park authorities even claimed that whites and Indians were actively cooperating with one another to undermine Yellowstone. In 1886, the park's superintendent blamed "squaw-men" (white males married to Indian women) for a series of recent fires, asserting that the Indians troubling Yellowstone had been

<hr/>

1935). For a general summary of the Nez Perce "war," see Robert M. Utley, *The Indian Frontier of the American West, 1846–1890* (Albuquerque: University of New Mexico Press, 1984), 189–193. For more on early efforts to control Indians at Yellowstone, see Spence, 55–70, and Jacoby, "The Recreation of Nature," 156–83, 204–6.

[11] For descriptions of the shooting in Jackson Hole, see *Annual Report of the Commissioner of Indian Affairs, 1895,* 63–68; "Two Official Opinions" and "As to the Jackson Hole Outrage," *The Indian's Friend* 8 (October 1895): 6, 9–10, and the insightful discussion in Warren, *The Hunter's Game,* 1–20. A useful analysis of how the Bannocks lost their off-reservation hunting rights can be found in Brian Czech, "Ward vs. Racehorse—Supreme Court as Obviator?" *Journal of the West* 35 (July 1996): 61–69. Despite the Supreme Court ruling, many Indian communities maintained the legitimacy of their off-reservation hunting rights well into the twentieth century. An example of a later hunting foray into Yellowstone can be found in Hermann to Commissioner of Indian Affairs, November 5, 1898 (1898: Letter 50866), Bureau of Indian Affairs, Letters Received, RG 75, National Archives.

"incited to hunt in the Park by unscrupulous white men." Such formulations led to a peculiar blurring of the standard categories of race by many early conservationists. Discussions of lawbreaking in Yellowstone, for instance, contained frequent mentions of "Indians red and Indians white" or of "red or white Indians"—usages designed to suggest how the privilege of whiteness could be linked to one's environmental practices. As a Wyoming inhabitant put it in 1897: "We are aware that the laws are broken by white men. You can scarcely call them white men, but I mean by others than Indians."[12]

By the turn of the century, the Yellowstone landscape bore abundant evidence of these so-called "white Indians." Alongside the well-known system of tourist trails, hotels, campsites, and popular attractions that laced the park there existed a second, shadow landscape: surreptitiously erected footbridges; "unfrequented and little known trails," used by outlaws to move unseen through the park; hidden cabins or dugouts, where poachers could hide for the night or smoke the meat from the animals that they killed in the park.[13]

A transitory and secretive bunch, many of the denizens of this shadow landscape have permanently eluded the historical record. Scattered among court cases, newspaper reports, and park correspondence, however, there exist enough shards of evidence to construct portraits of two of Yellowstone's most (in)famous poachers, Ed Howell and William Binkley. While the portraits may be incomplete (and in some respects atypical, since Howell and Binkley were uncommonly bold and prolific poachers), they do allow us to glimpse the motivations that animated Yellowstone's poachers—and the limits of toleration that local communities possessed for the poachers in their midst.

[12] Accounts of Indian poaching can be found in the scouts' reports reprinted in *Annual Report of the Superintendent of Yellowstone National Park, 1889* (Washington, D.C.: GPO, 1889), 16–17; for comparisons between Indians and white poachers, see "Our National Parks," *Forest and Stream* 37 (December 3, 1891): 385; *Annual Report of the Superintendent of Yellowstone National Park, 1886* (Washington, D.C.: GPO, 1887), 7. S. N. L., letter to the editor, *Recreation* 6 (March 1897): 187. See also William L. Simpson, "The Game Question in Jackson's Hole," *Forest and Stream* 51 (December 10, 1898): 468; S. T. Davis, "Game in Jackson's Hole," ibid., 52 (January 21, 1899): 47. The fear that whites might revert to an Indian-like savagery was not unique to Yellowstone. See Richard Slotkin, *The Fatal Environment: The Myth of the Frontier in the Age of Industrialization, 1800–1890* (New York: Athenaeum, 1985), 480–84.
[13] References to this shadow landscape are scattered through a variety of documents. The quote about "unfrequented and little known trails" comes from House, *Report of the Committee on Expenditures for Indians and Yellowstone Park*, 49th Cong., 1st sess., H. Rept. 1076 (SS 2438), 248. See also: report of Peter Holte (scout), document no. 7095, Employees, January 1, 1904–December 31, 1908, item 27, Yellowstone National Park Archives [hereafter YNPA]; *Annual Report of the Superintendent of Yellowstone National Park, 1907* (Washington, D.C.: GPO, 1907), 23–24; Frank Calkins, *Jackson Hole* (New York: Alfred A. Knopf, 1973), 135; Elmer Lindsey, "A Winter Trip Through the Yellowstone Park," *Harper's Weekly* 42 (January 19, 1898): 107; and Verba Lawrence, "The Elk Tuskers' Cabin" (clipping), Tusk Hunters File, Jackson Hole Historical Society.

KARL JACOBY

The National Park Poacher

Howell's journey out of obscurity began near daybreak, March 14, 1894, when Yellowstone scout Felix Burgess located a set of ski tracks in the park's northeastern corner. For some time, local rumors had hinted that someone was in Yellowstone, killing buffalo for their hides and heads, worth one hundred to four hundred dollars at local trophy shops. In addition, the soldiers at one of the army posts along the park's eastern perimeter had recently found tracks indicating that a man pulling a toboggan had slipped by their station late one night in the middle of a blizzard. After efforts to locate this mysterious traveler failed, Captain Anderson had directed Burgess to make periodic patrols of the area where the tracks had been found. But even after several days of searching, the scout had not been able to find anything—until this particular morning.[14]

Together with Private Troike, one of the U.S. Army soldiers stationed at the park, Burgess followed these tracks a short distance. The two soon stumbled across a "teepee" and, bundled in gunny sacks and hoisted with a block and tackle into the trees to keep them away from the park's scavengers, the heads of six buffalo. Burgess and Troike also picked up a fresh set of ski tracks, which they followed to "a newly-erected lodge" where the poacher had obviously been staying. The next puzzle—figuring out where the poacher himself might be—solved itself shortly afterwards: the pair heard six rifle shots, coming in rapid succession. Upon going to investigate, Burgess and Troike spotted five dead buffalo several hundred yards away. The animals had been driven into the deep snow and then shot. Hunched over one of the carcasses was a man using a knife to remove the buffalo's hide.[15]

Despite the two hundred yards separating him from the poacher, Burgess decided that he needed to act before the wrongdoer detected the patrol's presence and slipped away yet again. The scout raced across an open field toward the poacher, a high wind helping to drown out the noise of his skis. Given the possibility of violence when arresting an armed poacher, this was a potentially reckless act, but, fortunately for Burgess, the man never looked up from his work. Not until he heard the words "Howell, throw up your hands!" did the hunter, a sometime sheepshearer from Cooke City named Ed Howell, know, in the words of one later account, that "he was not alone in the buffalo country."[16]

[14] Aubrey Haines, *The Yellowstone Story: A History of Our First National Park*, vol. 2 (Niwot: University Press of Colorado, 1977), 62; *Chicago Tribune*, December 23, 1894.

[15] Hiram Chittendon, *The Yellowstone National Park: Historical and Descriptive* (Cincinnati: Robert Clarke, 1895), 143–44; "The Capture of Howell," *Forest and Stream* 42 (March 31, 1894): 270; *Annual Report of the Superintendent of Yellowstone National Park, 1894* (Washington, D.C.: GPO, 1894), 9–10; *Livingstone Enterprise*, March 31, 1894.

[16] "The Yellowstone National Park Protection Act," in Theodore Roosevelt and George Bird Grinnell, eds., *Hunting in Many Lands: The Book of the Boone and Crockett Club* (New

Army officers posing at Yellowstone National Park at the turn of the century with buffalo heads confiscated from park poachers. (Photo courtesy of National Park Service, Yellowstone National Park)

Howell's capture rapidly became a national sensation. Not only was this the first instance of a poacher being caught in the park in the very act of killing and skinning an animal, but through a curious twist of fate, the arrest came at the same time that Emerson Hough, a correspondent for *Forest and Stream*, happened to be visiting Yellowstone, researching an article for the magazine. Hough telegraphed his editor, George Bird Grinnell, with the news of Howell's capture. With the help of the Boone and Crockett Club, the upper-class sport hunting and conservation group that he and Teddy Roosevelt had founded in 1887, Grinnell publicized Howell's arrest as incontrovertible evidence of the need for expanded protection of Yellowstone.[17]

For Grinnell and his supporters, Howell's arrest underscored the federal failure to include any measures to punish violators of the new park's regulations. In the case of Native American poachers, Yellowstone superintendents had been able to appeal to Indian agents to try to confine Indian hunters to their reservations. No such remedy existed, however, for white poachers, and so Yellowstone officials responded with a variety of ad hoc

---

York: Forest and Stream, 1895), 414; *Livingston Post,* April 12, 1894.

[17] Grinnell's efforts were not limited to the pages of *Forest and Stream.* See, for instance, "The Yellowstone National Park," *Garden and Forest* 7 (April 4, 1894): 131.

measures—expulsion from Yellowstone; confiscation of rifles, traps, horses, and other valuable goods; temporary detention in the army's guard-house—all of which had little effect. As Patrick Conger, Yellowstone's superintendent, lamented to his superiors in 1883: "Under the law as it now stands... I have not the legal right or power to arrest and detain any person charged with a violation of any of the rules governing the Park.... Now what am I to do?"[18]

Howell's well-publicized arrest created the perfect opening for conservationists to replace this improvised, legally questionable system with a far more powerful system of state control. Building on their network of well-placed allies in Congress, Grinnell and the Boone and Crockett Club sped through both houses "an Act to Protect the Birds and Animals in Yellowstone National Park, and to Punish Crimes in Said Park." Signed into law by Grover Cleveland "less than sixty days after Howell's rifle shots had rung out on the frosty air of the mountains," this measure declared all violations of the Department of the Interior's regulations at the park to be misdemeanors, punishable by a fine of up to one thousand dollars and two years in prison. The act also assigned a magistrate to the park with the power to try and punish offenders. Thus, "[i]n one sense it [Howell's killing of park buffalo] was the most fortunate thing that ever happened in the Park," enthused Captain Anderson in 1894, "for it was surely the means of securing a law so much needed and so long striven for."[19]

Those living on the park's perimeter, however, frequently drew a different set of lessons from Howell's arrest. A few inhabitants, in keeping with the common rural view that violations of the game law were forgivable when done to meet basic subsistence, expressed sympathy for the pressing human need that, they felt, must have pushed Howell, the former sheepshearer, to his "perilous" deed. Asked the *Livingston Post:* "Was he, like many another man in these times, out of employment and destitute of the means of securing clothing, a bed, or perhaps even food? Indeed, it would seem that he must have been surrounded by some such circumstances to induce him forward." While the *Post* did not think Howell's "slaughter of buffalo" should go unpunished, the newspaper did raise mitigating circumstances: "the plea of ministering to his own necessities ought certainly to have some weight in determining Howell's punishment."[20]

[18] Conger to Secretary of the Interior, November 27, 1883. *Correspondence on Yellowstone National Park.* 48th Cong., 1st sess., S. Ex. Doc. 47, 25. For an extended discussion of early attempts to control crime in Yellowstone, see Jacoby, "The Recreation of Nature," 188–91, 261–65.

[19] *Chicago Tribune*, December 23, 1894; *Annual Report of the Superintendent of Yellowstone Park, 1894,* 9–10. A discussion of the role played by both the Boone and Crockett Club and *Forest and Stream* in passing the Park Protection Act can be found in George Bird Grinnell, *Brief History of the Boone and Crockett Club* (New York: Forest and Stream Publishing, 1910), 18–20.

[20] *Livingston Post*, March 29, 1894.

Far more common, however, were expressions of local disgust at Howell's killing of a rare animal—by the 1890s, Yellowstone contained only two to three hundred buffalo—simply to sell their heads and hides on the trophy market. Howell "will find no apologists in this section... for his nefarious work," declared the *Livingston Enterprise*. "The sentiment here is universal that the small remnant of American bison still in the Park should be protected by rigid laws to prevent their extermination at the hands of poachers whose only object is to secure the valuable consideration offered for their scalps and hides." More often than one may suspect, such public declarations were supported by private gestures. Throughout the 1890s, park authorities received a steady trickle of notes from anonymous local sources, providing tips about threats to Yellowstone's wildlife, especially its buffalo. "I will drop you a few lines as a favor for the Buffaloes as they are about extinct," read one such letter which, bearing a postmark from Gardiner, Montana, told of the capture of several buffalo calves in the park and was signed "A Friend to the Buffalo." A similar missive told of a group of four men who, with several dogs and a sled, had gone into the park to kill buffalo. The writer urged the park authorities to capture the men, whom he or she dismissed as "scalp hunters and game slaughterers in general."[21]

In many respects, inhabitants' revulsion at Howell's wanton destruction of natural resources for personal gain differed little from the position of mainstream conservationists. Yet despite such congruences, locals and conservationists remained far apart on numerous park policies. In particular, conservationists' widespread support for the Army's management of Yellowstone sat poorly with many nearby residents. Sierra Club President John Muir, for instance, declared in 1901, "Uncle Sam's soldiers are the most effective forest police." But many locals felt that the military presence at the park was suspiciously akin to living under an "unAmerican" system of martial law. Indeed, several fretted that deeds such as Howell's provided a convenient justification for the Army's unwanted presence in their midst. As one inhabitant of Howell's hometown of Cooke City griped: "This place has a bad reputation as a roost for poachers... everybody living here is held responsible for the trespassing of a few men and the general opinion prevails that we are nothing else but a whole community of outlaws." "The residents of Park County do not desire to have odium cast upon them or any justification given for the obnoxious and unjust rules of the Park military authorities by the lawless acts of buffalo slayers," agreed the *Livingston Enterprise*. "They will stand upon their rights as citizens of Montana in the matter of killing game in this state in the open season, but very few if any will

---

[21] *Livingstone Enterprise*, March 31, 1894; anonymous, n.d., document no. 696. A–E, January 1, 1882–December 31, 1894, item 4, YNPA; anonymous, n.d., document no. 2553. F–K, January 1, 1895–December 31, 1899, item 11, YNPA.

be found to condone so open and flagrant a violation of the laws of Montana as the killing of the few remaining buffalo."[22]

Intriguingly, Howell, who was by no means silent in this debate, chose not to defend his actions in the economic terms employed by his defenders. Instead, in the chatty letters to the editor that he contributed to local papers, he attempted to defuse popular impressions of him as "a desperate, bad man" by focusing on the skill and daring that had enabled him to elude park patrols for so long and to survive a harsh Yellowstone winter over a hundred miles from the nearest settlement. As he stated in one letter, "I was doing what a great many more would do if they had my courage and ability." Delighting in his notoriety as the "National Park Poacher," Howell indulged a correspondent for *Forest and Stream* with a lengthy description of the techniques he and other poachers used to outwit Yellowstone's patrols when hunting elk:

> It is the simplest thing in the world. When the snow begins to fall in September and October, we wait until a nice snowstorm has set in, and then taking a saddle horse and two or more pack horses, we start for the Park and travel fast. After reaching the ground we have previously selected to hunt over, we make a long detour and cross our tracks perhaps ten miles from camp so as to ascertain whether the soldiers are following our trail or not. If no other tracks are seen we go back to camp feeling safe, for we know that the new snow will obliterate all tracks before dawn. We then secure enough elk to load our pack horses and are soon on our way out of the Park.

For Howell, then, poaching involved more than simply the killing of game. It was a test of his bravery, of his knowledge of the local landscape, of his skills as a hunter and tracker. Successful poaching, in sum, relied upon many of the qualities at the core of rural masculine identity. This connection between poaching and manliness may explain why poachers, despite the care they took to hide their lawbreaking from Yellowstone's authorities, so often bragged about their risk taking to fellow community members—an activity which frequently seems to have taken place in the male venue of the local saloon. Several of the anonymous notes received by park authorities tell of overhearing poachers in a barroom "mak[ing] their bosts [*sic*] of hunting in... the park" and "remark[ing] that he was 'too cute for any park policeman to take him in.'" Trial transcripts reveal that some poachers avidly displayed the results of their illegal hunting to bartenders

[22] John Muir, *Our National Parks* (Boston: Houghton Mifflin, 1901), 40, 188; Doyle to Pitcher, July 7, 1901, document no. 3759, Letters Received, A–E, January 1, 1900–December 31, 1902, item 15, YNPA; *Livingston Enterprise*, January 1, 1898. For local complaints about the Army presence at Yellowstone as being akin to martial law, see the *Livingston Post*, October 24, 1889; July 12, 1894; and the *Livingston Enterprise*, January 1, 1898; December 11, 1897; February 19, 1898.

and other saloon regulars. Such evidence suggests that poaching satisfied a number of masculine functions. Not only did it allow local men to fulfill their traditional male role as a provider of food and income; the risk that illegal hunting involved gave it—in certain circles, at least—a manly ca-chet. Poaching's many similarities (killing, the use of weapons, the risk of encounter with armed opponents) to the quintessential male activity—warfare—can only have heightened these connotations, especially once the Army assumed control of the park in 1886.[23]

Because of such factors, even those who decried poachers as outlaws were not immune to admiring their manly qualities. *Forest and Stream* might sniff that Howell was "a most ragged, dirty and unkempt looking citizen.... dressed in an outer covering of dirty, greasy overalls," but the magazine still expressed amazement at his skill in constructing his own skis and in hauling a heavily loaded, 180-pound toboggan across the frozen Yellow-stone landscape. Out of respect for the harsh winter conditions that Howell had endured during his surreptitious foray alone into the park, one correspondent for *Forest and Stream* termed Howell "in his brutal and mis-guided way a hero in self-reliance.... Howell, or any like him, I hate in-stinctively, but I salute him." The park's scouts, members of the local rural community who doubtless realized better than anyone the hazards involved in venturing into the park during its harsh winter months, also admitted to a certain grudging admiration for Yellowstone's poachers. As Thomas Hofer, a onetime scout for the park, later put it, "All these hunter[s] earned all they got on their trips. Hard work and exposure."[24]

Yet manliness was not the sole province of poachers, as the curious coda to Howell's experience reveals. In 1897, following a stagecoach robbery in Yellowstone, Colonel S. B. M. Young hired Howell, "who knew all the bad men and poachers around the park," as a scout. Howell's skillful tracking

---

[23] *Livingstone Post,* April 12, 1894; August 2, 1894; "Park Poachers and Their Ways," *Forest and Stream* 42 (May 26, 1894): 444; Sheffield to Anderson, November 19, 1895, document no. 1621, S–Z, January 1, 1894–December 31, 1895, item 7, YNPA; anonymous ["Quill"] to Wear, August 14, 1885, document 679, A–E, January 1, 1882–December 31, 1894, item no. 4, YNPA; *United States v. William Binkley, Charles Purdy, and Oscar Adams* (U.S. District Court, 9th Circuit, Southern District of California), 228(transcript), U.S. Commissioner Meldrum—Trial Records, item 82, YNPA.

For more on poaching as a "symbolic substitute for war," see Manning, *Hunters and Poach-ers: A Social and Cultural History of Unlawful Hunting in England, 1485–1640* (Oxford: Claren-don Press, 1993), 8, 35–56. A more general discussion of risk and daring as masculine at-tributes can be found in David Gilmore, *Manhood in the Making: Cultural Concepts of Masculinity* (New Haven, Conn.: Yale University Press, 1990), 56–77. For more on the linkage between saloons and manliness, see Michael Kaplan, "New York City Tavern Violence and the Crea-tion of a Working-Class Male Identity," *Journal of the Early Republic* 15 (winter 1995): 591–617; and Elliott Gorn, *The Manly Art: Bare-Knuckle Prize Fighting in America* (Ithaca: Cornell Uni-versity Press, 1985), 133–34.

[24] Hough, "The Account of Howell's Capture," 377–78; Hofer to Hill, February 5, 1927, Manuscript File 91-188, YNPA.

soon led park authorities to the robbers' trail, and after their capture, Howell received $150 in reward money (despite Theodore Roosevelt's objections to any sort of payment to the former poacher). During his employment as park scout, Howell also patrolled Yellowstone's western perimeter, reporting to Young that "I would like to locate all the buffalo I can on this trip that I may know where to go to protect them during the hunting season."[25]

On one level, Howell's apparent change of heart—from a poacher of buffalo to the animal's protector—may seem like an extraordinary transformation: a leap from one moral perspective to another, from one way of interacting with nature to another. On another level, though, there was an inescapable continuity between the two positions. Tracking and other outdoor skills, the competitive challenge of outwitting an opponent, toughness, and physical bravery: all were qualities that poachers and scouts alike called upon to perform their assigned roles. Paradoxically, many of the factors that animated those rural folk who attacked Yellowstone animated the park's local defenders as well.[26]

Tuskers and Workers

While Howell's arrest rid Yellowstone of what Anderson termed "a notorious poacher" and helped to establish a stricter enforcement policy, it did not signal the end of poaching at the park. As Anderson himself admitted the following year in his annual report, in spite of the "most healthy effect" that recent developments had had "upon the poachers who surround and prey upon the Park," local inhabitants continued to hunt illegally within the park's borders. One particularly troubling new development for Anderson and his successors was the rise of "tusking"—killing elk for their prominent upper canines or "tusks," which were popular in many forms of jewelry in the early twentieth century. In 1916 alone, park scouts reported finding "the bodies of 257 elk which had been killed for their teeth" by "certain lawless individuals" near Gardiner, the small Montana village on Yellowstone's northern border.[27]

Such tuskers proved even more difficult for park authorities to apprehend than poachers such as Howell. Since elk teeth were small, the fruits of one's lawbreaking could be hidden in a shirt pocket or tobacco sack, where they were safely out of view of any passing park official. Once outside Yellowstone,

[25] Haines, *The Yellowstone Story*, 2:205–7; Howell to Young, September 24, 1897, document no. 1504, Employees, etc., January 1, 1882–December 31, 1897, item 9, YNPA.

[26] For these same reasons, conservationists in Africa often hire former poachers as informers or park rangers. Nicholas Gordon, *Ivory Knights: Man, Magic, and Elephants* (London: Chapmans, 1991), 137–38.

[27] *Annual Report of the Superintendent of Yellowstone National Park, 1895* (Washington, D.C.: GPO, 1896), 12; *Annual Report of the Superintendent of National Parks, 1916* (Washington, D.C.: GPO, 1916), 37.

tusks could be easily concealed amid one's personal possessions. "It is a trick of such hunters," commented a knowledgeable observer, "to thrust a knife into the meat of the game they have, and so to make pockets in which to hide the teeth." Elk teeth's small size made selling them easy as well. Rather than smuggling a cumbersome hide or animal head to a nearby taxidermist, or preserving and marketing large cuts of meat, the tusker could simply mail a small package to any one of the dealers in elk teeth who advertised in local papers. And, because elk teeth did not spoil, they could be gathered year-round, whereas most other forms of hunting were concentrated in the winter months, when the cold weather ensured that animals' pelts were at their thickest and that whatever meat one killed would not rot.[28]

Experienced tuskers such as William Binkley supplemented these advantages with a number of additional tricks that made them all the more elusive. Like most inhabitants of the Yellowstone region, Binkley made a living through a variety of means. In addition to "prov[ing] up on a homestead," where he ran a few cows and "[r]aised some garden," he also worked from time to time as a butcher, a guide for visiting sports hunters, and according to the 1900 census, a teamster. But Binkley appears to have spent most of his time tusking, often with a number of compatriots from Jackson Hole. (Park authorities dubbed the group the "Binkley-Purdy-Isabel gang," in honor of its primary participants.) When poaching, Binkley favored a small-caliber rifle, a weapon that could seldom be heard from more than more than fifty yards away. Furthermore, after having killed an elk, Binkley seldom removed the teeth right away. Rather, as one game warden explained, the standard practice for Binkley and his compatriots was " shoot an elk, and probably not go to him for a week. His teeth wouldn't be hurt, at all. His teeth would be just as good in a week, and the elk would be partly ate up by animals, and then the man would be plumb safe to go back and get the teeth. There would be no evidence agin [*sic*] him." When it did come time to extract the elk's teeth, Binkley often took the added precaution of using a "skee"—"a flat piece of board and two mounted elk feet on it"—so that if he walked "where a band of elk had passed in the snow or mud... it resembled the track of the elk."[29]

The careers of Binkley and his compatriots offer not only a window on the strategies that poachers employed but also some tantalizing clues as to their motivations. One piece of evidence comes from a Wyoming saloon, where Binkley showed the bartender his finger, boasting that he had a cal-

[28] Elinore Pruitt Stewart, *Letters on an Elk Hunt: By a Woman Homesteader* (Boston: Houghton Mifflin, 1915), 127–28; Edward A. Preble, *Report on Condition of Elk in Jackson Hole, Wyoming, in 1911*. U.S. Biological Survey Bulletin no. 40. (Washington, D.C.: GPO, 1911), 21.
[29] 1900 Federal Manuscript Census, election district 13, Uinta County, Wyoming, roll 1827, T623, National Archives; *U.S. v. Binkley*, 69, 99, 291, 292; David Saylor, *Jackson Hole, Wyoming* (Norman: University of Oklahoma Press, 1970), 142; Calkins, *Jackson Hole*, 135;

lous from "pulling the trigger, shooting elk." Binkley proudly noted that this callous was the only one on his hand, because he "didn't work." A similar contrast between poaching and work was drawn by one of Binkley's partners in crime, Oscar Adams. Telling an acquaintance that "he was making more money [tusking] than by working on a ranch," Adams added that he believed it "was foolish to work for wages."[30]

Binkley and Adam's positioning of poaching and work as opposed categories may initially appear confusing. After all, to be successful, a poacher had to undertake considerable physical labor. He might spend days in the saddle or on snowshoes, making long, surreptitious journeys through rough terrain. To avoid encountering any of the scouts or soldiers patrolling Yellowstone, a poacher frequently operated at night or during snowstorms or other bad conditions. Moreover, neither Binkley or Adams were members of the one group for whom hunting truly was play: upper-class sport hunters, such as the members of the Boone and Crockett Club, who found the chase most glorious when it satisfied cultural rather than economic functions. For Binkley and Adams, poaching was no amusing pastime; it was the source of much of their annual income.[31]

Where tusking did diverge from the world of work was in the contrast that it posed to wage labor. When Adams remarked that he thought it "foolish to work for wages," he was no doubt celebrating poaching's freedom from the time discipline and dependency of wage labor. Despite the risk of arrest (apparently never overwhelming; Binkley and Adams, like many of Yellowstone's poachers, evaded capture for years), poaching allowed its practitioners to embrace many long-standing producerist ideals—to work at a rhythm and time of one's own choosing, to avoid subservience to bosses and employers—while also earning far more than the typical wage laborer.[32]

Because of such factors, poachers at Yellowstone tended to be drawn from the region's growing working class. Although the Army kept no precise data on the occupations of those it arrested, observers noted that most offenders were agricultural and industrial laborers, the latter typically from the coal and quartz mines that opened along the park's northern perimeter in the early 1900s. Explained one local informant to park authorities: "I know there is a great many people of the working class that will not hesi-

---

Stewart, *Letters on an Elk Hunt*, 127. A general recollection of tusking in Jackson Hole can be found in Sam Hicks, "Ivory Dollars," *High Country* 3 (winter 1967): 40–45.

[30] *U.S. v. Binkley*, 230; Palmer to Pitcher, April 9, 1907, U.S. Commissioner Meldrum—Trial Records, Miscellaneous Correspondence, item 83, YNPA.

[31] A compelling argument for valuing labor as a way of understanding the natural world is made in Richard White, "'Are You an Environmentalist or Do You Work for a Living?': Work and Nature," in *Uncommon Ground: Toward Reinventing Nature*, ed. William Cronon (New York: Norton, 1995), 172, and Richard White, *The Organic Machine* (New York: Hill and Wang, 1995).

[32] For more on the fear that wage work led to dependence, see Daniel T. Rodgers, *The Work Ethic in Industrial America, 1850–1920* (Chicago: University of Chicago Press, 1978), 30–40.

John Winegar, an accused poacher from Idaho, in a mug shot taken by the U.S. Army following Winegar's 1907 arrest for the illegal possession of firearms in Yellowstone National Park. (Photo courtesy of National Park Service, Yellowstone National Park.)

tate in going for game where ever they can find it up to a resonable [*sic*] distance in to the Park."[33] If some of these poachers, like Binkley and his compatriots, hoped to use poaching to avoid the workplace altogether, many others found illegal hunting a valuable supplement when unemployment hit during economic downturns. Historians of Great Britain, for example, have discovered that illegal hunting in nineteenth-century Eng-

[33] Sheffield to Brett, November 1, 1912. "Poaching, Reports of and Inquiries, 1909–1913," in "Protection, 1908–1914," item 105, YNPA; see also the letter to the editor in *Recreation* 6 (May 1897): 368, complaining about "coal diggers" from Aldridge, Montana, poaching Yellowstone's elk. Census information from 1900 indicates that many of the inhabitants of Horr, Aldridge, and Jardine, Montana, were coal or quartz miners. Federal Manuscript Census, 1900, Park County, Montana, roll 913, T623, National Archives.

land peaked during times of high joblessness and high food prices. The rate of poaching at Yellowstone appears to have moved in a similar rough accord with larger economic trends. Howell's poaching foray, for instance, occurred during a depression year. Similarly, following the panic of 1907, the number of arrests for illegal hunting in the park increased fivefold to ten from two the year before.[34]

Drawing upon long-standing republican traditions that equated hunting with independence and self-sufficiency (and game laws with European tyranny), many of those arrested for poaching in the park defended themselves by pointing to the debilitating circumstances that had impelled their illegal acts. Following his capture in 1914, for instance, Harry McDonald maintained that he had only hunted in the park because he was out of work and "broke all the time." McDonald took pride in noting that he had never poached for trophies; he "wanted no heads but wanted some meat whether it was a deer, elk or [mountain] sheep." Although unsympathetic to McDonald's plight, park authorities were not unaware that hunting often provided a legitimate subsistence cushion for local laborers. As Yellowstone's superintendent acknowledged in 1912, many of the elk killed after migrating out of the park went "to families that otherwise might have had a slim meat ration for the winter due to dull times for workingmen in this section of country."[35]

This use of poaching to distance oneself from the strictures of the workplace, however, left its practitioners vulnerable to charges of lacking the appropriate commitment to the work ethic and community improvement. Such concerns—and their connection to local class divisions—emerged sharply in the observations of one resident of Jackson Hole in 1898. "There are two classes of people living [here]," the man claimed.

> One is those who see in the country a future for themselves and families, and who are particularly anxious to protect the game within the borders of Uinta

[34] David Jones, *Crime, Protest, Community and Police in Nineteenth-Century Britain* (London: Routledge & Keegan Paul, 1982), 69; Record of Violations of Rules and Regulations, 1887–1921, item 145, YNPA; see also *Annual Report of the Superintendent of Yellowstone National Park, 1908* (Washington, D.C.: GPO, 1909), 12. Although it could be that this increase in arrests came as a result of heightened vigilance by the army, there were no changes in the park's administration until mid-May 1908, when Major H. C. Benson was appointed new acting superintendent and the number of troops at Yellowstone was increased to three hundred.

[35] Sacket to Lindsay, January 23, 1914, "Poaching, Reports of and Inquiries, 1909–1913," in Protection, 1908–1914, item 105, YNPA; L. M. Brett, *Annual Report of the Superintendent of Yellowstone National Park, 1912* (Washington, D.C.: GPO, 1912), 11. For thoughtful studies of the relationship between republicanism and the right to game, see Harry L. Watson, "'The Common Rights of Mankind': Subsistence, Shad, and Commerce in the Early Republican South," *Journal of American History* (June 1996): 13–43; James A. Tober, *Who Owns the Wildlife? The Political Economy of Conservation in Nineteenth-Century America* (Westport, Conn.: Greenwood Press, 1981), 18–20; and Alan Taylor, "The Unadilla Hunt Club: Nature, Class, and Power in Rural New York During the Early Republic," (unpublished paper, July 1996).

and Tremount counties. The other class is those who have no permanent interest, no property, nor anything to keep them, outside of being able to kill game for the meat, hides, heads and teeth; and in this manner they make a partial living without work.

A correspondent for the *Livingstone Enterprise* struck a similar note, asserting that those who supported themselves solely by poaching devalued other, more honorable forms of labor: "some men would rather spend a month or more time in trapping a beaver or two, or killing an elk at the risk of fine and imprisonment, than earn a few honest dollars by manual labor."[36]

For all of Binkley's success in eluding park authorities, he could not avoid the volatile emotions that poaching excited among the members of his own community. Jackson Holers' first effort to control the poachers in their midst came in 1899, when the town's inhabitants took up a collection to hire an additional game warden, primarily to prevent outsiders from hunting illegally in the area. Three years later, residents formed a Game Protective Association, designed, in the words of one participant, to "make it hot for the game hogs." Despite being early targets of the association, Binkley and his colleagues do not appear to have altered their behavior. By 1906, the wily tuskers' neighbors had had enough. Some twenty to twenty-five Jackson Holers formed a "citizens' committee" to bring the poachers to justice. After a brief debate over the merits of a summary lynching, the group decided to offer Binkley, Adams, and their compatriots an ultimatum: leave the area within the next forty-eight hours or they would be "left dead... for the scavengers to devour." Binkley and company fled within the appointed time, although not without sneaking out a wagonload of elk and moose heads and other trophies.[37]

Even after this close call, Binkley claimed he did not understand what he had done to anger his fellow residents. After all, he asked, had not members of the "citizens' committee" also killed game illegally? Therefore, "they are not any better than I am.... They have been doing just the same." While it was certainly true that many other Jackson Holers routinely ignored local game laws, Binkley, like Anderson before him, overlooked the distinctions that many rural folk drew between different modes of poaching. Viewing subsistence as a natural right, the residents

[36] William Simpson, "The Game Question in Jackson Hole," *Forest and Stream* 51 (December 10, 1898): 468; *Livingston Enterprise*, January 22, 1898.

[37] W. L. Simpson, "The Jackson Hole's Situation," *Forest and Stream* 51 (December 17, 1898): 485; Romey to Pitcher, May 16, 1902, document no. 4931, Employees, January 1, 1898–December 31, 1903, item 20, YNPA; *U.S. v. Binkley*, 289. Binkley's ultimatum is quoted in Robert Betts, *Along the Ramparts of the Tetons: The Saga of Jackson Hole, Wyoming* (Boulder: Colorado Associated University Press, 1978), 184. See also Elizabeth Hayden, "Driving Out the Tusk Hunters," *Teton Magazine* (winter/spring 1971): 36.

of Jackson's Hole rarely opposed poaching done for necessities such as meat, hides, or tallow. In fact, on an earlier occasion, Binkley himself had been a beneficiary of this local tolerance for subsistence poaching. A few years before his near-lynching, Binkley shot an elk out of season for an ill neighbor who needed meat, an act for which he was arrested not long afterward by the state game warden. Outraged at what they considered to be Binkley's unjust treatment, Jackson Holers took up a collection and paid his hundred-dollar fine.[38]

These same residents, however, were much less willing to extend a similar tolerance to Binkley's tusking. The town had long exercised an informal, extralegal control over the local resource base, most frequently by excluding (violently if necessary) those seen as outsiders: Indians such as the Bannock-Shoshone, hunters from other villages, migratory shepherds. Although attacks on fellow community members were much rarer, Binkley's relentless poaching eventually made him a target for the same sort of response, for his decimation of the elk herd threatened to undermine the game supply upon which all the town's inhabitants depended.[39]

Binkley's forced exile from Jackson Hole did not end his connection with Yellowstone. Not long after their flight from Wyoming, Binkley and Purdy were captured in Los Angeles and charged with having violated the 1900 Lacey Act, a federal measure forbidding the transportation of illegally killed game across state lines. The two men were fined $200 each, the maximum amount allowable, and were then shipped to Yellowstone, where they faced a second trial on charges of having poached game in the park. Found guilty of these counts as well, Binkley and his compatriot were fined $933 and confined to the Army's guardhouse for three months. Binkley's imprisonment did not last long, however; somehow, in October 1907, he managed to escape from his cell. Calling upon the considerable knowledge of Yellowstone's pathways and hiding places that he had acquired during his years as a poacher, he eluded all attempts to recapture him.[40]

---

[38] *U.S. v. Binkley,* 220. For accounts of other Jackson Holers poaching, see Betts, *Along the Ramparts of the Tetons,* 181. For the story of Binkley's arrest and fine, see Hayden, "Driving Out the Tusk Hunters," 23.

[39] Jackson Holers' treatment of outsiders reinforces E. P. Thompson's point that the management of common resources depends as much on exclusion as inclusion. E. P. Thompson, *Customs in Common: Studies in Traditional Popular Culture* (New York: The New Press, 1993), 147, 179. For a discussion of extralegal sanctions against migrant shepherds in Jackson Hole, see Betts, *Along the Ramparts of the Tetons,* 174.

[40] "Poaching in the Yellowstone Park," 255; *Annual Report of the Superintendent of Yellowstone National Park, 1907,* 24; "The Elk Cases," *Forest and Stream* 67 (December 22, 1906): 975. Popular legend has it that Binkley killed the two soldiers assigned to guard him and threw their bodies into one of Yellowstone's geysers. *Salt Lake Tribune,* March 13, 1955.

Having made good his escape, Binkley may—or may not—drop from the historical record. A number of clues—hair color, height, and a raspy voice—point toward Binkley as the masked man who, on the morning of August 24, 1908, undertook the most daring robbery in Yellowstone's history: the armed holdup of several of the park's tourist stagecoaches. Perhaps Binkley needed money to finance a final escape from the region. Or perhaps he wanted to "show" park authorities, as he had threatened during his confinement. But if the robber was indeed Binkley, his concern over the unfairness of the wage labor system and his belief in the political dimensions of crime apparently remained intact. When the first stagecoach pulled into view, the robber announced that he was only robbing tourists. "If you drivers have got anything," the man declared, "you keep it, for you have to work for your money."[41]

The Recreation of Nature

The tourists who stumbled into Binkley's holdup testify to a fundamental change sweeping the American countryside at the turn of the century: the rise of the tourist industry. When Yellowstone had been created in 1872, it was located several days' journey from the nearest railroad station. But by April 1903, the Northern Pacific Railroad's rails reached all the way to Gardiner, bringing the park into the full embrace of the West's rapidly expanding tourist economy. Already famous, Yellowstone National Park quickly became a standard stop for western travelers, a place dubbed "Wonderland" in honor of its vast herds of wild animals and its extraordinary geysers, mud pots, and springs. Many of these tourists pronounced a visit to Yellowstone akin to stepping back in time, a trip that enabled one see wild nature untouched by the modern era. Exclaimed the guide book author Thomas Murphy in 1913: "I rejoice that there is one spot still sacred to the old order of things, where . . . we may see the old-time Wild West something as our fathers saw it."[42]

If Yellowstone's image as a remnant of a long-lost western rural past appealed to visiting tourists, it also obscured a far more interesting reality. To the attentive viewer, Yellowstone offered as many insights on the nature of the state as it did on the state of nature. The park, after all, was a place patrolled and managed by the nascent administrative state, a site intimately bound up with many of the most pressing topics of the day, from Indian

---

[41] *Annual Report of the Superintendent of Yellowstone National Park, 1908*, 12–14; Haines, *The Yellowstone Story*, 2:149–53.

[42] Thomas D. Murphy, *Three Wonderlands of the American West* (Boston: L. C. Page, 1913), 1–2.

treaty rights to the fear of dependency that accompanied the rise of the wage labor system. Rather than preserving a vanishing "Wild West," it was a landscape that testified to the political and economic forces reshaping the modern twentieth-century rural landscape.

The richness of this human history surrounding Yellowstone serves as an important reminder that rural history need not confine itself to the familiar agrarian landscape of fields and fences. Certainly the inhabitants of the American countryside never did so. They regularly ventured into the woods beyond their farms, trapping, hunting, fishing, cutting timber, and gathering wild plants. Moreover, as such folk journeyed into the woods, the central issues of rural life accompanied them. In their often ambivalent relations with Yellowstone's poachers and conservation authorities, for instance, one can glimpse country people articulating many of the same concerns— the need to preserve economic independence and the dignity of work, to protect the interests of the rural community against self-interested individualism, and to attack the growing concentrations of political and economic power—that lay at the heart of American Populism. In subtle yet unmistakable ways, then, Yellowstone National Park was as much a monument to the human forces transforming rural life at the turn of the century as it was to the geothermal energies that powered its famous geysers.[43]

[43] For an overview of the People's Party in the states abutting Yellowstone, see Robert W. Larson, *Populism in the Mountain West* (Albuquerque: University of New Mexico Press, 1986). The main contours of American Populism are surveyed in Michael Kazin, *The Populist Persuasion: An American History* (New York: Basic Books, 1995); Lawrence Goodwyn, *The Populist Moment: A Short History of the Agrarian Revolt in America* (New York: Oxford University Press, 1978); and Robert C. McMath, Jr., *American Populism: A Social History, 1877–1898* (New York: Hill and Wang, 1993).

Fighting for Child Health

Race, Birth Control, and the State in the Jim Crow South

JOHANNA SCHOEN

In 1941, Josiah B. testified to his congregation, "The devil has been to my house and tempted me in my weakest spot."[1] The devil—in the person of public health nurse Lena Hillard—was touring Watauga County in the western part of North Carolina to offer condoms to all women of child-bearing age. Josiah, who was deeply torn between his moral objections to contraception and his wife's desire to accept the nurse's offer, sought spiritual help in his effort to solve this dilemma. He eventually acquiesced to his wife's wishes.

Throughout the early 1940s, Lena Hillard offered condoms and a contraceptive foam powder to every resident of Watauga County. As part of a study on the reliability of condoms, she kept careful records of the acceptance and effectiveness of the contraceptive devices she offered. Financed by entrepreneur and physician-philanthropist Clarence J. Gamble, heir of the soap firm Procter and Gamble, this so-called "condom project" was only one of several programs to bring birth control to North Carolina's rural poor population.

An earlier version of this essay was presented at the 1994 conference on Southern Women's History. The material discussed here presents a portion of my research on birth control, sterilization, and abortion in public health and welfare. For their practical assistance and thoughtful responses to ideas presented in this article I am grateful to Laura Briggs, Laurie Green, Jacquelyn D. Hall, Elizabeth Heineman, Molly Ladd-Taylor, Megan Seaholm, Susan L. Smith, Nancy A. White, and the anonymous reviewers of *Social Politics*. This work presents a portion of my book manuscript: Johanna Schoen, *A Great Thing for Poor Folks: Birth Control, Sterilization, and Abortion in Public Health and Welfare in the Twentieth Century* (forthcoming); it first appeared, in revised form, in *Social Politics* 4, no. 1 (spring 1997): 90–113.

[1] Sylvia Payne to Clarence J. Gamble, 17 November 1941. Clarence J. Gamble Papers [hereafter CJG-CML], file 442, box 25, Countway Medical Library, Boston.

During the 1930s, public health concerns sparked the establishment of southern birth control programs. With the registration of state mortality rates in the early twentieth century, awareness of infant and maternal mortality as a public health issue rose, and health professionals began to look at these rates as an index of regional achievement and pride.[2] To the embarrassment of health officials, North Carolina had one of the highest infant mortality rates in the nation. In this largely rural state, most women lacked access to the most basic health services. A study of health services across the country found that the physician-to-population ratios in extremely poor rural counties sometimes exceeded one in twenty thousand, and some counties had no practicing physician at all. Poor roads often made even a distance of ten miles insurmountable; medical and nursing care was usually unattainable for women living outside towns. As federal and state governments began to grapple with the massive economic collapse of the 1930s, health and welfare officials across the country looked to an extension of health care services to the rural poor. With the aid of Gamble, North Carolina health officials implemented a statewide birth control program to lower infant and maternal mortality rates and improve maternal and child health. Supporters of the birth control program saw contraceptives as an integral part of a public health service which, if offered along with pre- and postnatal care and increased supervision of the state's midwives, would improve the health of mothers and infants. Such a program, North Carolina health officials hoped, would put their state at the forefront of progressive health and welfare policies.[3]

---

[2] See Richard A. Meckel, *Save the Babies: American Public Health Reform and the Prevention of Infant Mortality, 1850–1929* (Baltimore: Johns Hopkins University Press, 1990), 26–32.

[3] For a discussion of rural health programs during the New Deal, see Michael R. Grey, *New Deal Medicine: The Rural Health Programs of the Farm Security Administration* (Baltimore: Johns Hopkins University Press, 1999). For more general information on rural health care, see Edward H. Beardsley, *A History of Neglect: Health Care for Blacks and Mill Workers in the Twentieth-Century South* (Knoxville: University of Tennessee Press, 1987); Susan L. Smith, *Sick and Tired of Being Sick and Tired: Black Women's Health Activism in America, 1890–1950* (Philadelphia: University of Pennsylvania Press, 1995); Sandra Lee Barney, *Authorized to Heal: Gender, Class, and the Transformation of Medicine in Appalachia, 1880–1930* (Chapel Hill: University of North Carolina Press, 2000). See also Committee on the Costs of Medical Care, *Medical Care for the American People: The Final Report of the Committee on the Costs of Medical Care*, publication no. 28 (Chicago: University of Chicago Press, 1932). Cooperation between northern philanthropies and southern state boards of health followed an established tradition. Northern philanthropies, often aided by the federal government, played a crucial role in the establishment of southern public health programs. During the early twentieth century, the Rockefeller Foundation launched a campaign to eradicate hookworm in the South and the United States Public Health Service (USPHS), aided by Joseph Goldberger, studied and fought pellagra. As

Feminists, civil rights advocates, and historians have debated the motivations of both proponents and recipients of birth control in the southern context. Some have held that birth control programs were motivated by racism and the desire to defend class distinctions, and that they met the resistance of many blacks and poor whites. Others have argued that the vulnerable position of black and poor white patients resulted in their exploitation as research subjects, and that the tentative professional status of African American health professionals led them to cooperate in public health programs even when these programs seemed to run counter to the interests of the black community.[4] Whether they emphasize resistance or cooperation, however, both of these analyses assume that the birth control program worked to the detriment of black and poor white interests.

A closer examination of North Carolina's birth control program reveals, however, that black health and social work professionals as well as black and poor white clients welcomed the services, participated in them, and helped shape the contraceptive programs offered by the state.[5] Both

---

historians have demonstrated, however, Southerners resented the stigma of poverty implied by theories marking hookworm and pellagra as endemic to the southern rural population and they were often hostile to the health and education campaigns by northern foundations. See, for example, John Ettling, *The Germ of Laziness: Rockefeller Philanthropy and Public Health in the New South* (Cambridge: Harvard University Press, 1981); Elizabeth Etheridge, *The Butterfly Caste: A Social History of Pellagra in the South* (Westport, Conn.: Greenwood Press, 1972); Margaret Humphreys, *Yellow Fever and the South* (Baltimore: Johns Hopkins University, 1992). By acknowledging poor maternal and child health as a public health problem that warranted aggressive action, North Carolina's public health officials hoped to break with the stereotype of Southern backwardness and sought to establish their state as a model of modern public health and welfare work.

[4] For a critical perspective on public health birth control programs, see Linda Gordon, *Woman's Body, Woman's Right: A Social History of Birth Control in America* (New York: Grossman, 1976), 330–35, 354; Angela Y. Davis, *Women, Race, and Class* (New York: Vintage Books, 1991); Simone Marie Caron, "Race, Class, and Reproduction: The Evolution of Reproductive Policy in the United States, 1880–1989," (Ph.D. diss., Clark University, 1989). Historians have explored the ethical implications of medical experiments on poor and minority populations and pondered the role that African American health professionals in particular played when participating in such programs. See: James H. Jones, *Bad Blood: The Tuskegee Syphilis Experiment* (New York: The Free Press, 1981); Ettling, *The Germ of Laziness;* Etheridge, *The Butterfly Caste*. But recently historians have begun to reexamine this interpretation. Susan Smith, for example, has pointed out that the black professionals associated with the infamous Tuskegee Syphilis Study supported the study in the belief that it would eventually increase black access to government resources. Smith, *Sick and Tired of Being Sick and Tired;* also: Vanessa N. Gamble, *Making a Place for Ourselves: The Black Hospital Movement, 1920–1945* (New York: Oxford University Press, 1995).

[5] African American health and welfare professionals often supported and participated in such public health programs because they saw them as a step on the way to better health programs for the black population. See Smith, *Sick and Tired of Being Sick and Tired,* 107–17. Black and white birth control advocates alike believed in having only as many children as one could afford. In addition, black birth control advocates saw birth control as an important tool for racial improvement. Black women were interested in controlling their fertility. They demanded birth control as part of the same struggle that sought to secure equal rights and

African American health professionals and clients repeatedly challenged the State Board of Health and influential whites to increase their outreach in black communities. If anything, they saw the denial of such services to be discriminatory. And both black and poor white women took advantage of the contraceptive services and quickly responded like educated consumers, making decisions about the continued use of birth control according to their satisfaction with the services provided. Clients and black health care professionals had their own interest in the services, often unanticipated by public health and public welfare officials.

The programs were nonetheless steeped in race and class prejudice, and this influenced both the delivery and reception of contraceptive services. Some health officials, hoping to attract the support of their colleagues for such a radical program, used the potential for population control as a sales pitch; others were so convinced of black and poor white women's inability to use contraceptives successfully that they failed to properly promote services and educate their clients appropriately. In addition, Gamble's research interests stood in stark contrast to the public health concerns of North Carolina officials, and they led to conflicts between Gamble, policymakers, local public health officials, and clients.

North Carolina was the first state in the nation to implement a state-supported birth control program. Because its state boards of Health and Public Welfare were among the first to establish county health and welfare departments, which were considered particularly efficient in public health and social work, North Carolina seemed exceptionally suitable for early contraceptive services. Other states, however, quickly joined North Carolina. Starting with South Carolina in 1938, they emulated North Carolina's example of offering birth control through their public health services. Florida, Alabama, Virginia, Georgia, and Mississippi eventually followed.[6] By focusing on North Carolina, this essay will thus illuminate a crucial chapter of race relations, public welfare, and reproductive health in the American South and throw light on the ways in which rural Americans negotiated potentially repressive state policies.

---

social justice for all black women and men. Carol McCann, *Birth Control Politics in the United States, 1916–1945* (Ithaca: Cornell University Press, 1994), 20, 135–38, 168–73; Jessie Rodrique, "The Afro-American Community and the Birth Control Movement, 1918–1942" (Ph.D. diss., University of Massachusetts, 1991).

[6] For early public health development in North Carolina, see "The North Carolina State Board of Health. Establishment—Development—Functions." State Board of Health (hereafter SBH-NCSA), 1924, 1925, Correspondence, box 20, North Carolina State Archives, Raleigh, N.C. On the establishment of other state-supported birth control programs, see Gordon, *Woman's Body, Woman's Right,* 330; Rodrique, "The Afro-American Community and the Birth Control Movement"; Patricia Evridge Hill, "'Go Tell It On the Mountain': Hilla Sheriff and Public Health in the South Carolina Piedmont, 1929–1940," *American Journal of Public Health* 85 (April 1995): 578–84.

As a poor and overwhelmingly rural state, North Carolina had one of the highest infant and maternal mortality rates in the nation. In 1919, the state's infant mortality rate stood at 104 infant deaths per 1,000 live births, a rate topped by only seven other states. The maternal mortality rate stood at 9.3 deaths per 1,000 live births, placing North Carolina third in the nation. In the state's urban areas mortality rates were even higher. A 1918 study in Winston-Salem recorded an infant mortality rate of 159.1. White babies died at a rate of 107.9 and black babies at a rate of 243.7.[7]

Alarmed by such conditions, officials of the United States Children's Bureau and the North Carolina State Board of Health sought to identify factors contributing to the high mortality rates and to formulate a plan to improve infant and maternal health. Physicians blamed the high rate of deliveries attended by midwives, a lack of pre- and postnatal care, and too frequent pregnancies. In the 1930s, approximately one-third of the deliveries in North Carolina were attended by midwives, 69 percent of births among African American women and 12 percent of the white births. So prevalent were midwife services that in 1933 there were nearly twice as many midwives as physicians in the state.[8] These midwives, public health officials charged, were untrained and of questionable competence. Describing deliveries unattended by physicians in bleakest terms, one physician warned, "the women [giving birth] pass through the valley of the shadow of death with no ray of the light of science to dispel the gloom and with only the flickering candle of the midwife to guide them through travail."[9]

---

[7] Only twenty-four states were included in the *Vital Statistics* of 1919. *Vital Statistics—Special Reports. Selected Studies,* vol. 16 (Washington, D.C.: U.S. Department of Health, Education, and Welfare, Public Health Service, National Office of Vital Statistics, 1944). "Report to the Honorable Mayor Correll, the City Alderman, the City Board of Health, Dr. H. L. Carlton, City Health Officer, the Delineator Survey Committees, and Other Citizens of Winston-Salem," [1918], SBH-NCSA, 1918, Correspondence, box 12, North Carolina State Archives.

[8] "Health Work for Negro Children," [1932], Social Services (hereafter SS-NCSA), Commissioner's Office, Subject Files, 1891–1952, Interracial Cooperation, 1919–1949, box 6, file: Rosenwald Study of Negro Child Welfare in North Carolina, 1932. Lynn Hudson, "Twentieth Century Midwives in North Carolina" (M.A. thesis, University of North Carolina, Chapel Hill, 1987), 2–3.

[9] W. S. Rankin, "The Mutual Interest of the Profession and the Public," n.d., 1. SBH-NCSA, 1922, box 17. For charges of incompetence, see "North Carolina State Wide Conference on Better Care for Mothers and Babies" (February 15, 1939), *The Child,* 3, no. 10 (April 1939): 222. Midwives' poor reputation has rightly been challenged as racist, and historians have noted that physicians' services did not always represent an improvement. Johanna Schoen, "A Great Thing for Poor Folks: Birth Control, Sterilization and Abortion in Public Health and Public Welfare," (Ph.D. diss., University of North Carolina, 1996), 49–59; Hudson, "Twentieth Century Midwives"; Frances E. Kobrin, "The American Midwife Controversy: A Crisis of Professionalization," in *Sickness and Health: Readings in the History of Medicine and Public Health,* ed. Judith Walzer Leavitt and Ronald L. Numbers (Madison: University of Wisconsin Press,

Poverty and lack of education made women hesitant to consult doctors. Although two-thirds of North Carolina's women consulted the services of a physician during delivery, half of those first saw a doctor with the onset of labor. Many of these women were overworked and poorly fed and thus in particular need of medical supervision during pregnancy. But they were frequently ignorant about the risks of pregnancy and childbirth, and they often did not recognize complications developing in their pregnancies. "Poverty and ignorance," one physician concluded, "make infant mortality a class disease."[10]

Public health officials followed a three-pronged approach for lowering mortality rates: educating mothers and midwives in the importance of pre- and postnatal care; licensing and regulating midwives; and offering birth control to allow women to space their children further apart. In 1920, the North Carolina State Board of Health began a systematic effort to instruct pregnant women and mothers throughout the state on the value of professional medical services. In addition, health officials instituted licensing requirements for midwives and began to offer formal midwifery instruction. Since they could not abolish midwifery, health officials hoped to train midwives and to exclude those whose skills they found unsatisfactory.[11]

With the 1922 passage of the Sheppard-Towner Act, which provided grants to the states to meet health needs of expectant mothers and newborns, the North Carolina State Board of Health began to organize maternal and infant health clinics for poor women. Twenty nurses were assigned to work in counties most needing such services. They conducted classes on prenatal care and infant hygiene, made home visits to pregnant women and women with infants, and offered midwifery classes. By 1926, the Bureau of Maternity and Infancy was able to employ three doctors and

---

1985), 197–205; Judy B. Litoff, *The American Midwife Debate, 1800 to the Present* (Westport, Conn.: Greenwood Press, 1978); Charlotte Borst, *Catching Babies: The Professionalization of Childbirth* (Cambridge, Mass.: Harvard University Press, 1995); Gertrude Jacinta Fraser, *African American Midwifery in the South: Dialogues of Birth, Race, and Memory* (Cambridge, Mass.: Harvard University Press, 1998).

[10] M. T. Foster, "Birth Control in the State and Local Maternal Infant Hygiene Program," n.d. [1939], 7. J. W. R. Norton Papers (hereafter JWRN-SHC) box 2, Misc. Papers, Southern Historical Collection, University of North Carolina–Chapel Hill. See also John Preston, "The Obstetric Problem in Rural Areas," *The Child*, 3, no. 10 (April 1939): 224.

[11] By 1926, one-fifth of the state's counties required midwives to visit a class for midwife instruction in order to qualify for a permit. In 1935, new legislation was enacted which made it illegal to practice midwifery in North Carolina without a permit issued by the State Board of Health. Hudson points out that these regulations severely limited midwives' practices, often discouraging midwives from practicing at all. In the half-century between the 1930s and the 1980s midwifery in North Carolina all but disappeared. See Hudson, "Twentieth Century Midwives"; Report of Committee of Regulation of Work of Midwives, n.d. [1920], SBH-NCSA, 1920, Correspondence, box 15; Rose M. Ehrenfeld to Anna E. Rude, January 20, 1921, Children's Bureau Papers, 1921–1924, 4-11-1-3(2) to 4-11-2-1 in box 195, files 4-11-1-3(225) Minn., to 4-11-1-3(40) Pa., National Archives, Washington, D.C.

four nurses. In 1929, however, funds from Washington were discontinued and only a skeleton of the services survived.[12] In the early 1930s, the North Carolina legislature made a permanent appropriation for maternal and child health work, and with the passage of the Social Security Act in 1935, officials developed a comprehensive statewide plan for maternity centers. County public health officials began to offer clinics for pre- and postnatal care. By 1939, the State Board of Health had established prenatal centers in forty-three of the state's one hundred counties and cared for about 16 percent of the state's pregnant women.[13]

Educating mothers and midwives and providing pre- and postnatal care, however, could not solve the whole problem. Too early and too frequent pregnancies—not just poorly handled pregnancies—also contributed to women's poor health and infants' high mortality rates. Young mothers were at particular risk, and the low age of marriages in rural districts of the southern states exacerbated the problem. "I find these young girls distressingly ignorant of the means to protect themselves against untimely childbirth," one physician lamented. "Many of them have diseases which would make childbirth almost certain death."[14] While the mortality rate for children born one year or less apart was 147 per 1,000 births, the rate sank to 98 or lower for children born more than twelve months apart.[15] There was only one solution to too frequent pregnancies: contraception. Birth control instruction, health officials concluded, had to be an integral part of a program for maternal and infant health.

The distribution of contraceptives was not entirely new to the North Carolina health officials who contemplated the establishment of public health birth control services in the mid-1930s. The first birth control clinic in North Carolina had opened in 1923 in connection with a maternity

[12] In 1925 alone, the North Carolina State Board of Health sent information on infant care to one-fourth of the state's pregnant mothers, including 18,843 brochures on infant care, and public health nurses made one or more home visits to about one-fifth of North Carolina's pregnant women (32,147 home conferences assuming that each mother was visited twice). Seventeen of the state's one hundred counties had a Maternity and Infancy unit, and in twenty counties health officials required midwives to receive instructions before issuing their license. See "Duties of the Visiting Infant Hygiene Nurse," n.d. [1919], SBH-NCSA, 1919, Correspondence, box 13; M. L. Townsend to Miss Jessie Eleanor Moore. August 19, 1926, SBH-NCSA, 1925, 1926, Correspondence, box 2; George M. Cooper, "Progress in Maternal and Child Health Work," *The Health Bulletin* (February 1937): 5–9. See also Molly Ladd-Taylor, *Mother Work: Women, Child Welfare, and the State, 1890–1930* (Urbana: University of Illinois Press, 1994), 167–96.

[13] G. M. Cooper to Mrs. V. R. Cooke, November 22, 1938. CJG-CML. box 23, file 412. "North Carolina's Program to Promote Maternal and Infant Welfare," SBH-NCSA, Administrative Services, Central Files, 1934–55, box 1, File: Reports of Irene Lassiter.

[14] The average age at marriage for girls in the rural areas of North Carolina was fifteen years, and mortality rates were highest below that age. "Medical Indications: Contraception," *Washington Herald,* February 19, 1938, JWRN-SHC, box 2, Misc. Papers, Associations... Societies.

[15] Clarence J. Gamble, "Contraception as a Public Health Measure," Medical Society of the State of North Carolina, *Transactions* (1938): 1–8.

center in Fayetteville. The clinic had been organized by a Red Cross nurse and sponsored by Fayetteville's citizens. In the early 1930s, the American Birth Control League (ABCL) had begun to send field workers to North Carolina to organize interested citizens. Encouraged by a 1932 endorsement of birth control by two of the state's social work organizations, field workers had discussed birth control services with residents of Raleigh, High Point, Winston-Salem, Durham, and Fayetteville; had established a clinic in Asheville; and had tried to interest officials at the State Board of Health in the establishment of state-supported birth control clinics.[16]

Despite the support the ABCL received from North Carolina's social workers, however, public health officials were wary of the national birth control organization and its representatives. As Dr. Cooper, state director for the Division of Maternity and Infancy, explained to the secretary of the Birth Control Clinical Research Bureau, "In the State of North Carolina, most people regard Margaret Sanger in the same light they do John L. Lewis. I have always had respect for Mrs. Sanger, so far as her convictions were concerned, but little respect for her methods."[17] The medical profession, Cooper explained, was a conservative group that feared any kind of sensation. The only way to establish a state-supported birth control program, he concluded, was to remain independent from national organizations.

The opportunity for this came in 1937, when Boston philanthropist Dr. Clarence J. Gamble became interested in North Carolina. Gamble was conducting private research on birth control methods and had developed a spermicidal powder, which, if applied to a moist sponge and inserted into the vagina before intercourse, promised to provide an easy birth control technique. Looking for a rural area in which to test his contraceptive, he offered to pay the salary of a nurse for birth control work if the North Carolina State Board of Health promised to promote the use of his foam powder through local public health centers. In March 1937, Gamble employed Frances R. Pratt as his nurse, and Pratt set out to organize birth control

[16] "The Birth Control Movement in North Carolina," n.d., JWRN-SHC, box 2, Misc. Papers, File: Associations, Societies, Birth Control Federation of America. Maternal Health Project, Second Quarterly Report, 15 November 1937; CJG-CML, box 23, file 405. In 1932, the North Carolina Association of Superintendents of Public Welfare and the North Carolina Conference for Social Services passed resolutions in favor of birth control. The ABCL's successful establishment of a clinic in Asheville was most likely due to the fact that the organization's president had a home there. Foster, "Birth Control in the State," 2, JWRN-SHC, box 2, Misc. Papers.

[17] George M. Cooper to Cecil A. Demon, January 25, 1938, CJG-CML, box 24, file 415. John L. Lewis was the head of the United Mine Workers and an aggressive organizer who was known for his outspoken and provocative manner. In an effort to "organize the unorganized" he broke with the more conservative American Federation of Labor (AFL) to form the Congress of Industrial Organizations. At the 1935 AFL convention he punched William L. Hutcheson of the carpenters' union in the jaw, after Hutcheson had called him a "bastard." It is likely that Cooper and members of the professional and middle class found him far too radical.

programs in North Carolina's public health clinics. "It was like manna from the sky," one social worker rejoiced.[18]

With Pratt responsible for the establishment of local birth control clinics, the program spread rapidly during the first two years. Clinics were held at public health departments, although clinic hours were different from those of prenatal clinics. By March 1938, the State Board of Health operated thirty-six birth control clinics in thirty-three counties and had reached 641 mothers. That year, more than half of all public birth control clinics in the country were located in North Carolina. One year later, the state had sixty-two centers in sixty counties, serving 2,000 patients, and by 1946 ninety-three of the state's one hundred counties offered contraceptive services.[19]

Despite official distrust toward Margaret Sanger and national birth control organizations, public health officials were proud to second Gamble's opinion that the North Carolina program was "the most progressive and

---

[18] Ella P. Waddill to [Hazel Moore], April 5, 1937, CJG-CML, box 23, file 408. Stiff competition between the national birth control organizations and leading birth control activists over the initiation of contraceptive clinics led to the ABCL's breaking with Clarence Gamble and the North Carolina State Board of Health. To the relief of the State Board of Health, the ABCL recalled its field worker from North Carolina as soon as it learned of Gamble's independent endeavor. Charging Gamble with obstruction of organized birth control work, the league called for Gamble's resignation from its board of directors of which he was a member. See Elsie Wulkop to Clarence J. Gamble, March 13, 1937, CJG-CML, box 198, file 3140. On Gamble's work, see also James Reed, *From Private Vice to Public Virtue: The Birth Control Movement and American Society* (New York: Basic Books, 1978; reprint ed., Princeton, N.J.: Princeton University Press, 1984), 225–77; Doone and Greer Williams, *Every Child a Wanted Child: Clarence James Gamble, M.D. and His Work in the Birth Control Movement* (Cambridge, Mass.: Harvard University Press, 1978), 159–73.

[19] North Carolina health officials feared the opposition of the Children's Bureau which was furnishing funds for prenatal work but was opposed to the establishment of birth control clinics. Officials of the Children's Bureau and the USPHS told Dr. Cooper "to keep his hands off birth control" as soon as the North Carolina program was inaugurated. While North Carolina officials received no direct warnings from Children's Bureau representatives, other states were threatened with the withdrawal of federal funds if they established a state-supported birth control program. See Schoen, "A Great Thing for Poor Folks," chap. 3. Katherine Lenroot, who headed the Children's Bureau during the 1930s, feared that any association between the birth control movement and the Children's Bureau would jeopardize her other programs of maternal and child welfare. Only in 1940 did Lenroot give begrudging support to the use of federal maternal health funds for state-supported birth control clinics. David Kennedy, *Birth Control in America: The Career of Margaret Sanger* (New Haven, Conn.: Yale University Press, 1970), 261–67; Reed, *From Private Vice to Public Virtue*, 267–68; McCann, *Birth Control Politics*, 198–200, 218. Of 478 birth control clinics reported in the United States in December 1938, 97 were public health department clinics. In December 1938, forty-three states were giving birth control advice in one or more clinics, with 71 clinics in New York, 56 in North Carolina, 37 in California, and 32 in Pennsylvania. Fifty-four of the 97 public health clinics and 55 of the 158 clinics receiving public funds were in North Carolina. Foster, "Birth Control in the State," 4, JWRN-SHC, box 2, Misc. Papers. For growth of the program in North Carolina, see Frances R. Pratt, "Outline Developed in North Carolina State Board of Health for Staff Education Programs for Public Health Nurses in Birth Control Work," October 18, 1939, CJG-CML, box 24, file 424; University News Bureau, "Ninety-three Counties Now Have Contraceptive Services," May 24, 1946, CJG-CML, box 26, file 463.

intelligent public health program yet attempted in any state."[20] Public health officials stressed the central role birth control should play in any infant and maternal health program. "The birth control program," Frances R. Pratt emphasized, "rounds out a program otherwise incomplete for the distressed mother desiring better health for herself, her family and future children."[21] In addition, officials understood the birth control program as a service offered to improve women's family lives. They offered contraceptives in the hope that mothers would control their reproduction and limit their families to a size that would allow them to provide financial and emotional security for all of their children. But despite their concern about births among the poor, health officials held that economic hardship alone should not disqualify parents from bearing and raising children. Thoughtful and responsible parents at any economic level, officials argued, should be able to plan for families of at least three or four children.[22]

Still, the internal contradictions between a progressive public health program and a conservative medical profession haunted the program throughout its existence and ultimately contributed to its demise. Despite the obvious need for and interest in state-supported birth control services, North Carolina's program failed to reach a significant number of women. Constantly worried about the possibility of opposition to his radical public health policies, Cooper refused to publicize the birth control program in any meaningful way. The lack of publicity had devastating consequences for the program. Potential clients never learned about the existence of clinics, so that contraceptive centers ran far below their capacity. This, in turn, frustrated Gamble, who ended his financial support in 1940, a decision that resulted in Pratt's resignation as a birth control nurse. The program continued to grow until the late 1940s, and then began to dwindle for lack of funds.[23]

[20] Clarence J. Gamble, "Birth Control in a State Public Health Program," *Journal of Contraception* (January 1938); see also Roy Norton, "Planned Parenthood in a General Health Program," *Southern Medicine and Surgery* 102, no. 3 (March 1940); Frances R. Pratt, "Programs for Public Health Nurses in Birth Control Work," *American Journal of Public Health* 30 (September 1940): 1096–98.

[21] Frances R. Pratt, "Outline Developed in North Carolina State Board of Health for Staff Education Programs for Public Health Nurses in Birth Control Work," October 18, 1939, CJG-CML, box 24, file 424.

[22] Gilbreth, "State Takes Lead"; Future [Press] Release, Science Service, January 19, 1940, JWRN-SHC, box 2, Misc. Papers, File: Associations... Societies. Birth Control Federation of America.

[23] Although health officials liked to boast about the large number of birth control clinics, a mere tally of clinics could be inconclusive and misleading. While the University News Bureau issued a statement in 1946 that ninety-three counties were carrying contraceptive services, a report on the history of family planning programs in North Carolina found for 1946 only fifty-two counties with birth control programs. Not only did reports on the number of clinics vary widely in a given year, but several clinics had few or no patients at all. See University News Bureau, "Ninety-three Counties Now Have Contraceptive Services," May 24, 1946, CJG-CML, box 26, file 463. If the number of patients served was one measure of the

During its relatively short life, however, this remarkably comprehensive program reached women all over the state—and it raised myriad issues concerning population control, public health work, class, and race. While infant and maternal health stood at the center of the program, those involved with the distribution of contraceptives often had goals that were only loosely connected to and occasionally contradicted the improvement of maternal and child health. George Cooper and Clarence Gamble were attracted by the potential of selective population control on eugenic grounds. Both hoped that the birth control program would also curb the high birth rate among dependent families. They were not alone. One local health officer who did not think his county needed contraception was asked to check his vital statistics. "When he discovered that Negroes were accounting for 85 percent of the births he quickly changed his mind."[24] "The South," one news reporter announced, "is teaching birth control on tobacco road and mill village alley."[25] If the birth control program was not directly targeting the African American community, this author suggested, it was at least targeting the poor and uneducated.

Assumptions about women's race and class background tainted health officials' approach to and interaction with clients and limited the effectiveness of the services provided. While health and welfare professionals considered birth control essential, they assumed that poor women lacked both the intelligence and motivation to use the diaphragm, the most effective contraceptive in the 1930s. Linda Gordon has pointed out that the diaphragm was a "rich-folks contraceptive," which was difficult to use without privacy, running water, and full explanation of fitting—luxuries not

---

quality of clinical services, a report on the impact of the birth control program concluded, the majority of clinic services were inadequate. "North Carolina Public Health Department Family Planning Program: Historical Background," n.d. [1968], 12, Ellen Black Winston Papers, box 9, file: Planned Parenthood—World Population, 1968–1973, University of North Carolina–Greensboro. In 1940, when Gamble ceased support, health officials reported 3,233 planned parenthood patients. The number rose to 4,441 patients in 1948 and then fell to almost half the number in the late 1950s. In 1957, after twenty-one years of service, state health officer Dr. Roy Norton confirmed to the American Public Health Association the array of problems birth control centers were facing. The county clinics, he reported, were dispersed among small and inadequate facilities throughout the counties. In addition, medical services in the clinics were inadequate. Most of the clinics were poorly housed and offered only limited physical, pelvic, and basic laboratory examinations. Williams, *Every Child a Wanted Child*, 137–45; J. W. R. Norton, James F. Donnelly, and Anne Lamb, "Twenty-One Years' Experience with a Public Health Contraceptive Service," *American Journal of Public Health* 49, no. 8 (August 1959): 997.

[24] Don Wharton, "Birth Control: The Case for the State," *Atlantic Monthly* (October 1939): 465. See also George M. Cooper, "Birth Control in the North Carolina Health Department," *North Carolina Medical Journal* 1, no. 9 (September 1940): 464.

[25] Frank B. Gilbreth, "State Takes Lead in Birth Control Clinic of South," *Raleigh News and Observer*, June 30, 1940.

available for many Americans.[26] As birth control nurse Doris Davidson explained to Mrs. Barclay, of the ABCL:

> We all know the ever-present need for a simpler method for unintelligent, illeterate [sic], lazy and poverty-stricken patients. Altho [sic] the diaphragm method may provide greater safety in the hands of the intellegent [sic] patient, it often acts in just the opposite way in the hands of the unintellegent [sic] patient, no matter how carefully she may have been instructed. This type of patient, (and I am referring to the low-intellegent [sic] strata found by the hundred in North Carolina, South Carolina, Tennessee and West Virginia) can learn a thing one moment and unlearn it the next with bewildering rapidity. Often by the time the poor creature has arrived back in her home, she is uncertain about technique and therefore hesitant in applying it.... If we are going to help this low-grade patient, do we not have to meet them [sic] on their own level?—give them something which is EASY for them to apply, and which they can readily understand?[27]

In order to reach the poor, health and welfare professionals advocated both the development of easy-to-use contraceptives and the distribution of birth control through public health channels. Researchers hoped to develop a birth control method so easy to employ that it could be used by patients who had neither the desire, the education, the privacy, nor the sanitary facilities to carry out more complicated procedures. Contraceptive foam powders and jellies met these conditions and had the additional advantage of making pelvic examinations, which were assumed to deter many women from using contraceptive methods, unnecessary. Although it was unclear whether these methods were as effective as the diaphragm, many researchers considered it more important to reach a large number of women than to provide the most reliable contraceptive. Clarence Gamble's financial support of the program came with considerable strings attached: the program had to promote a contraceptive foam powder, which he had recently developed and wanted to test. In addition, he hoped to test a number of other contraceptives to establish their reliability in comparison to each other.[28]

Still, despite the development of simpler contraceptives a belief that poor women were incapable of using contraceptives properly continued to pervade the program. Health professionals remarked repeatedly on patients' "shiftlessness," ignorance, and low mental capacity. One official warned Pratt that "some of these people, particularly the colored people,

[26] Gordon, *Woman's Body, Woman's Right*, 309.
[27] Emphasis in original. Doris Davidson to Mrs. Barclay, March 5, 1937, CJG-CML, box 190, file 2993.
[28] "North Carolina's Public Health Program in Birth Control," 3, n.d., CJG-CML, box 24, file 424.

are apt to misinterpret the procedure and conclude that the method used once becomes effective for all time."[29] In addition, health officials tended to blame patients for the failure of contraceptive methods rather than to question the effectiveness of the contraceptive, despite the experimental nature of the program. Although clients and county health officials repeatedly complained about a high rate of failure and unpleasant side effects of the foam powder, and the majority of clinics eventually switched to diaphragms, State Health Officer Roy Norton concluded in 1957 that the main cause of failure was neglect or carelessness by the patients.[30]

In spite of their classist and racist assumptions, however, most health officials were no more committed to preventing certain women from reproducing than they were to enabling women to choose not to reproduce. Rather, they wanted to help women to space their children in order to improve their and their children's health. Eligibility requirements for the program reflected the emphasis on infant and maternal health over selective population control. Patients had to be married and, if they were in basically good health, already have several children—usually three or four. Women with medical problems making pregnancy dangerous were considered ideal patients.[31]

In general, black women suffered from the same discrimination that African Americans experienced when seeking other health services: they had more difficulty gaining access to birth control services than did white women. Most health officers in counties with a large black population were uninterested in birth control and maternal and infant health work. While by November 1939 two-thirds of North Carolina's counties had one or more birth control centers, the counties with a high African American population had fewer centers than the rest of the state. In some county health departments it was left to the few black public health nurses—in 1950 less than 1 percent of North Carolina's nurses—to provide maternal and infant health services to black clients. Some officials cited white clients' refusal to attend the same facilities as blacks as an excuse for not extending services to African Americans. Others offered segregated services in the hope that

[29] Letter to Miss Pratt, n.d., JWRN-SHC, box 2. Also G. M. Cooper to Clarence J. Gamble, May 29, 1937. CJG-CML, box 23, file 406; Frances R. Pratt to Clarence J. Gamble, February 23, 1937, CJG-CML, box 23, file 403.

[30] Frances R. Pratt, "Eighteen Months of Health Department Contraceptive Work in North Carolina, 1 April 1937 to 1 October 1938," October 1, 1939, JWRN-SHC, box 2, Misc. Papers. For attributing blame to patients, see Norton "Twenty-One Years' Experience." Reports of cases where women got pregnant despite the use of contraceptives were common. A 1940 investigation of clinical success reported nine failures (9.54 percent) for 106 patients in Henderson and five failures (22.7 percent) for 22 patients in Elizabethtown. Although officials remarked that the diaphragm was considered the most satisfactory, all of the clinics, with the exception of Fayetteville, offered only foam powder. In Fayetteville patients could receive either foam powder or the diaphragm. Frances R. Pratt, Travel Narrative, February 1940, CJG-CML, box 25, file 432.

[31] Roy Norton, "Planned Parenthood," *The Living Age* (March 1940), 7; "Maternal Health Project. First Quarterly Report," 15 July 1937. CJG-CML, Box 23, File 405.

such accommodation to local customs would attract the largest number of both black and white clients.[32] In times of scarce resources, any allocation for African Americans was not only deemed unnecessary but feared as provoking opposition. When, in 1939, the Birth Control Federation of America offered North Carolina health officials funds to sponsor a birth control pilot project for the black community, Dr. Cooper declined. "A public health program limited to the Negro race will most certainly stimulate opposition to the entire project."[33] In other words, contraceptive programs were a valued service, and like all other valued services, they were reserved disproportionately for whites.

The program not only failed to provide black clients with their share of services, it provided often ineffective contraceptives to women lucky enough to have access—and its organizers were aware of this. Gamble's research interests put him at odds with public health nurses and officials. Seeking to improve maternal and child health, public health officials occasionally found that the contraceptive to be tested was not the one most suitable to prevent conception. When Lena Hillard discovered that four of her foam powder patients in Watauga county were pregnant, she complained to Gamble: "I am sick of attempting to persuade them to use the foam powder because I haven't the assurance that it is a very reliable method now. Why can't we start them on the Dreft? If it is more safe then it is very important that we do something now."[34] But even when Hillard suggested two weeks later that it was "very tragic for some mothers to get pregnant,"[35] Gamble remained unmoved and reminded Hillard of his interest in researching the effectiveness of contraceptives. "It is disappoint-

[32] Of the nine counties in which African Americans made up more than 50 percent of the population three had no birth control clinics; of the nine counties in which 45–50 percent of the population was black, five had no birth control program; and of the eighteen counties in which African Americans made up 35–45 percent of the population, seven had no birth control clinics. The population figures are taken from the 1940 census. John R. Larkins, *The Negro Population of North Carolina, 1945–1955* (North Carolina State Board of Public Welfare, August 1957); Virginia F. South to [Cecil] Damon, October 21, 1937, CJG-CML, box 14, folder 269. On the discrimination against African Americans in public health services see Beardsley, *A History of Neglect;* Smith, *Sick and Tired of Being Sick and Tired;* McCann, *Birth Control Politics,* esp. chap. 5.

[33] Roy Norton to Woodbridge E. Morris, November 17, 1939, JWRN-SHC, box 2, file: Associations… Societies, Birth Control Federation of America.

[34] Lena Hillard to Clarence J. Gamble, July 1, 1942, CJG-CML, box 25, file 44. Dreft was a laundry soap that Procter and Gamble produced in the 1940s. I assume that Gamble planned to test whether the application of Dreft—or some variation of the soap—to a sponge would kill sperms and prevent contraception. Hillard suggests using Dreft with the sponges she ordered for the Johnson and Johnson foam powder, indicating that Dreft might be a used like a foam powder. Soap solutions were one of many douching remedies touted in mid- to late nineteenth-century America. Even plant products with saponin compounds were considered of contraceptive value because they foamed like soap. And they may well have helped reduce the probability of conception.

[35] Lena Hillard to Clarence J. Gamble, July 14, 1942, CJG-CML, box 25, file 444.

ing to hear the pregnancies are developing in the group of mothers using foam powder," he responded to Hillard.

> I don't think, though, that the time has yet come to switch to another method.... It's very important to have enough mothers and enough time in your series. In previous tests it has never been possible to say whether the pregnancies were due to failure to use the method or failure of the method to protect.... If the foam powder is found to be an unsatisfactory method that will protect a lot of mothers from being given it. If it turns out reasonably well it may make it possible to furnish many mothers protection who otherwise wouldn't have any.[36]

While Hillard found the conflict between Gamble's research goals and the public health objectives so unbearable that she contemplated quitting her work, Gamble felt no such conflict and little responsibility for those women who had become pregnant while testing the foam powder.[37]

If Lena Hillard was so dissatisfied with the research aspect of the Watauga program that she considered her resignation as a public health nurse, how did female clients confront the issue? Which one of the multiple concerns behind the program—public health, research, or selective population control—most deeply affected clients, and how did they respond to aspects of the program they did not like?

Most women were eager for birth control information and often requested such information for friends and relatives. Indeed, a 1940 public opinion poll found that 77 percent of Americans approved the distribution of contraceptives through public health clinics. "In many cases it is not hard to sell a mother the value of preventing too frequent pregnancies," one of the nurses distributing condoms and foam powder in Watauga County found.[38] Interest rose even more with the American entry into World War II. "Since the rubber shortage," she reported a little later, "we can hardly keep Trojans! I wouldn't be surprised if our patients aren't hoarding them."[39]

Many became so committed to birth control that they were willing to sacrifice their meager income to obtain contraceptives themselves should the nurse stop free distribution. Lena Hillard reported one mother who had heard a false rumor that Hillard had stopped doing birth control work: "She told her husband that she would simply catch a hen and take it to the store and sell it in order to get money to buy some Trojans.... It is true that a lot of our mothers are not financially able to pay $.50 for three Trojans.

---

[36] Clarence J. Gamble to Lena Hillard, August 9, 1942, CJG-CML, box 25, file 444.

[37] Lena Hillard to Clarence J. Gamble, July 14, 1942, CJG-CML, box 25, file 444.

[38] Sylvia Payne to Clarence J. Gamble, January 19, 1942, CJG-CML, box 25, file 445. George Gallup, "Carolina Birth Control Clinic Plan Approved by Vast Majority in Poll," *Durham Morning Herald,* January 25, 1940. Gallup reported that in all the opinion polls conducted in the late 1930s between 70 and 80 percent of the population approved birth control.

[39] Sylvia Payne to Clarence J. Gamble, February 9, 1942, CJG-CML, box 25, file 445.

Yet, it is encouraging to see that some will be willing to sacrifice their chickens and eggs in order to stop babies from coming."[40]

Female clients sought birth control in order to improve their families' quality of life. In letters to the State Board of Health, one health official pointed out, women victimized by health hazards "pleaded for contraceptive advice." One mother described in a letter "13 pregnancies and only 4 living children." Another correspondent was twenty-six years old with "10th pregnancy and bedridden with cardiorenal disease."[41] Women's requests to the State Board of Health for birth control testified to the physical strain of constant childbearing. As one mother wrote:

> Since I married I've done nothing but have babies.... I do think there's a limit for it, for my health has begun to fail fast, I have congested ovaries and with my first baby my womb lacerated terribly bad. That is giving me lots of trouble now.... And too my legs and thighs hurt almost constantly. I don't know why unless it is caused from "coitus interruptus" as that method is used lots. We know it is dangerous, but I've tried suppositories, condoms, douche, a pessary, and everything I've heard of but none have kept me from conceiving. My husband and I are only normal beings.[42]

While this mother was unusual in that she had already tried a number of contraceptives, her description of the physical ailments which she attributed to constant pregnancies and childbearing is representative of women's requests for birth control.

Women emphasized the devastating social and economic consequences too many children could have. As the mother who had complained about her poor health continued,

> I have done nothing but... keep house and do the routine work that goes with that.... I'm completely shut in. I never go to the church, Sunday school, visiting, shopping, or anywhere except occasionally to see my mother and father who are very old and feeble.... I have never rebelled at motherhood and no one on earth is more devoted to their home and children than I am.... I feel like I've had enough children. My husband is 52 years old and his health is failing fast. He has no income except from the farm which is so uncertain and a failure some years. I do know that at my age I'll have several children yet unless a preventive is used.... We are not able financially to have more babies, as its a terrible time to make 'ends meet' as it is. In fact we haven't made them meet a year since we've been married.[43]

---

[40] Lena Hillard to Youngs Rubber Corporation, February 10, 1941, CJG-CML, box 25, file 442.

[41] Roy Norton, "A Health Department Birth Control Program," *American Journal of Public Health* 29 (March 1939): 253.

[42] Mrs. Edith Turner to Dr. Roy Norton, December 8, 1938, JWRN-SHC, box 2.

[43] Mrs. Edith Turner to Dr. Roy Norton, December 8, 1938, JWRN-SHC, box 2.

Women desired to limit their family size, then, for the same reasons public health officials wanted them to: so as to gain some control over the personal consequences of frequent childbearing. But while women complained about the burdens and isolation large families might bring, they made it clear that they could appreciate their children while desiring birth control. In fact, contraceptives would enhance their enjoyment of motherhood.

While women eagerly sought contraceptive advice, many felt they had to discuss the use of birth control with their husbands, neighbors, or friends first. Such discussions often took the form of neighborhood gossip. "There is nothing that goes so fast as gossip, good or bad," one physician acknowledged.[44] Some clients even felt the need to discuss the offer of birth control in a more public forum. Josiah B.'s church testimony is one such case. Since all Watauga County families with women of childbearing age were approached by Hillard, Josiah's testimony invited broad-ranging discussion in a congregation where others were likely to be facing exactly the same dilemma—and to know exactly what he was talking about. The reaction, or lack thereof, which his testimony received from the congregation may have contributed to his decision to accept the contraceptives offered.

To be sure, some remained adamant in their resistance to family planning. Occasionally patients opposed birth control on religious grounds, arguing that "they have had their number that God planned for them."[45] Husbands sometimes sabotaged their wives' efforts to prevent conception by forbidding them to use birth control, putting holes in diaphragms, or throwing the diaphragms out.[46]

But most women were eager for birth control information. To these women it mattered little that they had received contraceptives as part of a research study. They were glad to finally get *any* birth control information; their only concern was how to obtain contraceptives after the research project had ceased and the free distribution of birth control ended.[47]

This did not mean, however, that clients were passive, uncritical research subjects. Instead, they negotiated with their local public health officials over different birth control methods and acted as educated consumers on their own behalf. Women complained to their public health nurses and

[44] Preston, "The Obstetric Problem in Rural Areas," 225. Rumors on Lena Hillard's work ranged from criticism—"Mrs. Hillard is doing work for the devil"—to vague information about the nature of her work—"Mrs. Hillard is giving supplies to young people ... giving supplies to help ... signing up families for government, then, if any more babies come, the government can take them over." See "Weekly Report on Project in Watauga County, 29 November to 11 December 1939," CJG-CML, box 24, file 429.

[45] "Weekly Report on Project in Watauga County, 11 September to 15 December 1939." CJG-CML, Box 24, File 429.

[46] Grace Woodward Welch, "Planned Parenthood Services in Four North Carolina Health Departments" (M.A. thesis, University of North Carolina, Chapel Hill, 1946), 146–47.

[47] Lena Hillard to Youngs Rubber Corporation, February 10, 1941, CJG-CML, box 25, file 442.

physicians about the high rate of failure and unpleasant side effects of the foam powder that Gamble distributed as part of his testing series. They also kept each other informed about their experiences with certain contraceptives and listened to the recommendations of friends and family members. If a method had proved unsatisfactory to some women, public health officials could find it difficult to interest other women in the contraceptive. As Hillard explained to Gamble, "If news gets about that foam powder fails, I am going to find it very hard to get them to accept Dreft when I do start using it." [48] Indeed, women who became confident about one method were usually hesitant or unwilling to switch to another when the research project asked for it. While women's complaints and preferences might have fallen on deaf ears with Gamble and public health officials in the state capital, local health officials often responded to their clients' wishes. They ignored the requirements of the research program and instead offered women the contraceptives they demanded.[49]

Clients and their health advocates also ignored larger issues of discrimination if they felt that the benefits of the birth control program outweighed its problems. Despite the racist attitude of Gamble and many health officials and the overtones of selective population control, black as well as white doctors, nurses, and social workers emphatically spoke out about the need for better pre- and postnatal care and contraceptive services. African American health and welfare professionals supported the distribution of contraceptives wherever they could. Educators promised to include birth control information in their speeches to PTAs and women's clubs. And when the Planned Parenthood Federation of America (PPFA) established a special Division on Negro Work in the 1940s, many of the state's African American educators, social workers, physicians, and ministers supported and endorsed its work.[50]

[48] Lena Hillard to Clarence J. Gamble, July 1, 1942, CJG-CML, box 25, file 44.

[49] For women's unwillingness to switch contraceptives, see Lena Hillard to Claire E. Folsome, April 8, 1942, CJG-CML, box 25, file 445. For responses by public health nurses, see Frances R. Pratt, "Eighteen Months of Health Department Contraceptive Work in North Carolina, 1 April 1937 to 1 October 1938," October 1, 1939, JWRN-SHC, box 2, Misc. Papers; Sylvia Payne to Clarence J. Gamble, November 17, 1941, CJG-CML, box 25, file 442.

[50] North Carolina members included: F. D. Bluford, president of A&T College; Dr. Charlotte Hawkins Brown, president of Palmer Memorial Institute; Rev. T. H. Dwelle of Fayetteville; H. A. Parris, M.D., of Rich Square; and Rev. G. J. Thomas, Wentz Memorial Congregational Church at Winston-Salem. See "National Sponsoring Committee, Division of Negro Service, Planned Parenthood Federation of America," April 1, 1945, SS-NCSA, Work Among Negroes, box 236, file: Birth Control Federation of America, Inc. The PPFA held special educational meetings to interest black citizens in planned parenthood. At one such meeting, held in Cumberland County in 1944, about two hundred African Americans attended and expressed their interest in planned parenthood. See "Minutes of the North Carolina Maternal Health League," December 8, 1944, SS-NCSA, Public Assistance Division, General Correspondence, 1938–1955, American Red Cross—Maternal Health League, box 1, file: Maternal Health League, Minutes and Correspondence, 1944. Also Clarence J. Gamble, Memo on

Expecting cooperation from the State Board of Health, African American physicians demanded help if they felt health officials were delinquent in their responsibilities. One black physician in Oxford, frustrated by his patients' inability to obtain contraceptives, carried a box of contraceptives to the office of the county health officer. He presented the box to the health officer and indicated that he was, right then and there, going to give the contraceptives to a patient whom he had brought along. The health officer took the hint. He promised henceforth to keep a supply of contraceptives for local doctors and he immediately wrote to the State Board of Health to request an adequate supply and to ask for the help of Frances Pratt in organizing a clinic.[51]

Some clinics reported that black women were overrepresented among clients. Black women thus overcame tremendous odds to gain access to services they desired. Black patients, public health officials found, tended to maintain better contact with the clinics than did white patients. As one physician pointed out, the greatest problem was not to attract black women, but to reach "white mothers who are not among the poorest yet who will not have a doctor until delivery."[52] Women's continuing interest in the birth control program depended largely on their experiences with clinic staff. "It is our duty," one official emphasized, "to get these women into clinics for prenatal and postnatal care, to bring to them newer methods in scientific care, to educate and hold them after we get them. But we cannot hold them unless the members of the clinic staff have sympathy, understanding, and kindness."[53] It was these characteristics, one physician testified in 1939, that led to the success of the program in overwhelmingly black Northampton county.

> There are several maternity and infancy centers [in Northampton county], and these centers are visited not by one, five, or seven women, but by crowds. They come from far and near; a few in cars, others in carts drawn by mules and many on foot. They keep coming, bringing their friends. Why do they come? Because the clinics are presided over by sympathetic physicians, assisted by indefatigable and enthusiastic nurses who give the clinic a wholesome and cheerful atmosphere. It is evident by the large attendance at these clinics throughout the county that these mothers are wholeheartedly accepting the facilities that have been provided for the safeguarding of their health.[54]

Negro Birth Control Education, February 15, 1939, CJG-CML, box 24, file 421; McCann, *Birth Control Politics*, 160–68. Charges by some black leaders that the state's birth control program was a veiled form of genocide, aimed at reducing the black population, did not surface until the late 1960s. See "Birth Control Seen As Aimed at Negroes," *Raleigh News and Observer*, November 20, 1968, 26; Schoen, "A Great Thing for Poor Folks," chap. 3.

[51] J. A. Morris to Dr. Cooper, May 23, 1938, CJG-CML, box 24, file 415.

[52] Mrs. Wilbur H. Currie, "The Moore County Committee," *The Child* 3, no. 10 (April 1939): 228.

[53] Walter J. Hughes, "The Particular Needs of Negroes," ibid., 229. Also Frances R. Pratt, "Outline Developed in North Carolina State Board of Health for Staff Education Programs for Public Health Nurses in Birth Control Work," October 18, 1939, CJG-CML, box 24, file 424.

[54] Hughes, "The Particular Needs of Negroes," 229–30.

While public health concerns provided the impetus for the establishment of a state-supported birth control program in North Carolina, the birth control program also depended on interests that ran counter to those of the clients. Financial support depended on Clarence Gamble, whose aim it was to test a variety of contraceptives in rural public health clinics. Public health officials used the promise of selective population control as a sales pitch in advertising the program to health and welfare officials throughout the state.

To evaluate the effect the birth control program had on its clients, however, we need to look at the grassroots level of birth control clinics, beyond the goals of those who sponsored and established state-supported birth control in North Carolina. Local public health workers and recipients pounded out a contraceptive program that did not necessarily resemble the interests of those higher up. Rather than seeing their duty in testing contraceptives or controlling the growth of certain sections of the population, local public health officials often saw themselves as women's advocates. They thus listened to women's complaints and adapted the services to their clients' demands, knowing full well that women's participation hinged on their satisfaction with the services. Seeking not to lose clients, they negotiated and lobbied in women's interest.

To be sure, rural women's lack of access to decent health and contraceptive services, their poverty, their race, and gender significantly influenced their decision to participate in contraceptive field trials or take advantage of public health birth control programs. Their choice was conditioned by their lack of other alternatives. They took advantage of the services in a social and economic context that denied them access to safe, effective, convenient and affordable methods of birth control and equitable social, political, and economic conditions under which to make choices.[55]

Despite these constraints, however, black and poor white women used the state's public birth control services to improve their quality of life. They took advantage of contraceptive information and supplies whenever they could, and they recommended the services to friends and relatives. Al-

---

[55] See Sonia Correa and Rosalind P. Petchesky, "Reproductive and Sexual Rights: A Feminist Perspective," in *Population Policies Reconsidered: Health, Empowerment, and Rights,* ed. Gita Sen, Adrienne Germain, and Lincoln Chen (Cambridge, Mass.: Harvard University Press, 1994), 107–23. While one could correctly argue that most decisions are conditioned by outside factors, Iris Lopez points out that some people have more social space to make decisions than others. Iris Lopez, "Agency and Constraint: Sterilization and Reproductive Freedom Among Puerto Rican Women in New York City," in *Situated Lives: Gender and Culture in Everyday Life,* ed. Louise Lamphere, Helena Ragone, and Patricia Zavella (New York: Routledge, 1997), 157–71.

though North Carolina's birth control program was tainted by the deep race and class bias of health officials, women continued to seek contraceptive advice. However, they were not blind to the program's problems, and they bargained with local officials over the conditions of contraceptive advice. Analysis of the North Carolina birth control program indicates how clients of such programs were constricted by the policy goals behind the services in question. It also, however, demonstrates that, despite such programs' limitations, clients not only were able to benefit from the services but could also shape them and, indeed, set the conditions under which they would participate. Rural people once again proved to be active shapers of the state as they helped construct one of the government's most intimate forms of outreach to its poor and dispossessed citizens.

"In America Life Is Given Away"

Jamaican Farmworkers
and the Making of Agricultural Immigration Policy

CINDY HAHAMOVITCH

Even as the United States extended its economic and political reach across the globe in the twentieth century, its officials exerted an ever-increasing amount of energy in an effort to secure their control over the nation's borders. This was a new function for the nation's bureaucrats and law enforcement officials. The Constitution had given Congress the right to determine which immigrants could become citizens of the United States, a power Congressional representatives used in 1790 to limit the right of naturalization to whites only. But all other immigration questions had been left to the individual states, which meant, in practice, that the nation's borders were effectively open for much of the country's history. As in Canada, Argentina, and Australia, immigrants seeking work, land, or asylum in the United States could enter freely and stay permanently. Federal officials only began screening immigrants for infectious diseases late in the nineteenth century, and no one policed the nation's land borders. This laissez-faire immigration policy only began to change in the nineteenth century as Congress first barred the importation of slaves, and then, in the latter half of the century, banned employers from contracting workers abroad, prohibited the immigration of prostitutes, and excluded Chinese immigrants. But, with the notable exception of the slave trade ban, these laws had little effect on the scale of immigration to the United States, which increased dramatically over the course of the century. Even the 1885 law banning employers from contracting labor overseas failed to prevent private labor contractors from advancing the fares of foreign workers and then renting them out to the highest bidder.

In contrast, the twentieth-century timeline is dotted with legislative and executive actions designed to limit immigration, such as literacy tests, quota acts, the rejection of Jewish refugees in the Nazi era, the mass expulsions of Mexicans during the Depression, and the creation of border patrols. We could almost say that the nineteenth century was a period during which immigrants (with the significant exception of Asians) were welcomed, while in the twentieth century immigration was discouraged.

Almost, but not quite. The problem with this formulation is that the countless examples of twentieth-century efforts to restrict immigration have rarely been applied to agriculture. While industrial employers lost their ability to hire whom they pleased, the small percentage of agricultural employers who hired migrant laborers continued to demand and get workers from abroad. Industrial employers were starved for labor during the First World War, but only farm employers were allowed to drive to the Mexican and Canadian borders and contract with foreign farmworkers. When unemployment during the Depression inspired the U.S. secretary of labor to order the mass expulsions of Mexicans living in the United States, growers were able to convince local officials to ease up on repatriating farm laborers (except those involved in strikes). Agriculture has long been the exception to the twentieth-century history of federal efforts to restrict immigration, and immigration policy continues to be shaped by the demands of the nation's largest agricultural employers.[1]

Up to the Second World War, federal immigration policy in agriculture was basically permissive. Rules that applied to industry were simply not applied to agriculture. During the Second World War, however, the federal government embraced a much more activist immigration policy. Beginning in 1942, the governments of the United States, Mexico, and the British West Indies agreed to a plan whereby the U.S. government would transport, house, and feed tens of thousands of Caribbean and Mexican farmworkers who would labor in the United States under no-strike, fixed-term contracts. The U.S. government became, in a sense, a *padrone* or crew leader, supplying foreign workers to the owners and managers of the nation's farms. The workers would not be immigrants but temporary labor migrants or agricultural "guestworkers," required by the terms of their contracts to leave when they were no longer needed.[2]

The author would like to thank Raymond B. Craib, Rohan D'Souza, Judith Ewell, Leon Fink, Rhys Isaac, Robert Johnston, Kay Mansfield, Scott R. Nelson, Richard Price, Jim Scott, Michael Simoncelli, Catherine McNicol Stock, the College of William & Mary's Faculty Summer Grant Program, the Breakfast Club, and the Program in Agrarian Studies at Yale University.

[1] On U.S. immigration policy during the First World War, see Camille Guerin-Gonzales, *Mexican Workers and American Dreams: Immigration, Repatriation, and California Farm Labor, 1900–1939* (New Brunswick, N.J.: Rutgers University Press, 1994), 114–16.

[2] This argument and those made over the next few pages are made in greater detail in my book, *The Fruits of Their Labor: Atlantic Coast Farmworkers and the Making of Migrant Poverty,*

We could write off this new direction as a wartime anomaly, except that the "Emergency Labor Importation Program" did not end when the war did. Though American legislators renewed restrictive immigration policies in the two decades after the war, they allowed employers of farmworkers to import some 4.5 million Mexican "braceros" and Caribbean "offshores," as the workers were called. The 1952 McCarren-Walter Act closed the door tightly to permanent immigrants, but section H-2 of the act institutionalized Caribbean farm labor migration (which became known from that year forward as the H-2 program). Likewise, the western "Bracero Program" brought ten times more workers to western farms in the 1950s than it had a decade earlier.[3]

Why growers were able to play such a major role in shaping immigration policy is an open question. Certainly the effectiveness of the agricultural lobby is a large part of the answer. U.S. agricultural capital became highly concentrated in the years following the war, with a shrinking number of "agribusinesses" dominating markets at home and abroad. At the same time, the nation's biggest agricultural producers became better organized as a group, in no small part because only large producers and associations of producers could obtain guestworkers. Farmers' organizations could not promise to deliver votes—the number of Americans living on farms plummeted in the twentieth century—but they could deliver dollars into the campaign coffers of strategically influential politicians. Moreover, although agribusinesses increasingly produced farm products much in the way General Motors produced cars—with machines, engineers, chemicals, and shrinking workforces—they were nonetheless very effective in promulgating the hallowed notion that farming is a "way of life" necessary to the preservation of the American republic. Ironically, the power of the agrarian myth helped undermine what little remained of its reality.[4]

1870–1945 (Chapel Hill: University of North Carolina Press, 1997). See also Wayne D. Rasmussen, *A History of the Emergency Farm Labor Supply Program, 1943–47*, Agricultural Monograph no. 13 (Washington, D.C.: U.S. Department of Agriculture, Bureau of Agricultural Economics, 1951).

[3] The best recent book on the Bracero Program published in English is Kitty Calavita, *Inside the State: The Bracero Program, Immigration, and the INS* (New York: Routledge, 1992). See also Ernesto Galarza's classics, *Merchants of Labor: The Mexican Bracero Story: An Account of the Managed Migration of Mexican Farmworkers in California, 1942–1960* (Charlotte, S.C.: McNally and Loftin, 1964) and *Spiders in the House and Workers in the Field* (Notre Dame, Ind.: University of Notre Dame Press, 1976).

[4] For example, the Florida Fruit and Vegetable Association grew out of the Fruit and Vegetable Committee of the Florida Farm Bureau, which lobbied vigorously for foreign workers during the Second World War. When Congress granted Florida growers access to Caribbean workers in 1943, the "committee" became an association, which could sign the international labor agreement and share imported workers. For an interesting discussion of the power of the sugar lobby, see Nancy Watzman, *The Politics of Sugar* (Washington, D.C.: The Center for Responsive Politics, 1995).

Another part of the answer to the mystery of agricultural exceptionalism, certainly, is that agricultural employers have different needs than other employers. Like industrial employers, agricultural producers have mechanized to a degree unimaginable fifty years ago, but there has always been (at least thus far) a limit to what can be done to crops by machines. And the turn to machines has not eliminated the need for harvest labor in many cases; it has merely reduced the days of work being offered, making farm jobs even less attractive than before. Thus mechanization has both solved and exacerbated agricultural labor shortages. Similarly, while industrial employers can cut costs by moving plants to lower-wage labor markets, farmers seeking to cut costs have to bring lower wage workers to their plants. Agricultural capital can be mobile—agribusinesses were, after all, some of the first multinationals—but once a field is planted here or elsewhere, the workers must come. None of this should be taken to mean that agricultural employers have faced a dearth of labor in the last half-century. Farm employers might have drawn from the enormous numbers of poor people who immigrated to the United States after the liberalization of immigration laws in 1965. But legal, permanent immigrants were not nearly as attractive to employers as guestworkers were precisely because, as residents, they would have had the freedom to negotiate, to quit before the end of the season, and to protest. And, most importantly, they would not have been susceptible to the threat of deportation.

Had the guestworker programs remained small and had the guestworkers always left at the end of their contracts as promised, both programs might have continued with little controversy. Instead the Bracero Program grew and many guestworkers chose to overstay their official welcome. Public alarm over the Bracero Program's expansion resulted in its cancellation in 1964. But by then west coast growers were unwilling or unable to wean themselves from foreign labor and they turned increasingly to undocumented workers. Always much smaller and more isolated from surrounding communities, the H-2 program continued with only occasional bursts of controversy. In both cases, growers' learned dependence on foreign workers resulted in the rapid internationalization of the agricultural labor market and the persistence of migrant poverty. In no part of American life, then, have the effects of state-driven immigration policies been more profoundly felt than in agriculture.[5]

[5] On the tendency of guestworkers to become permanent workers, with or without state sanction, see Philip L. Martin, *Guestworker Programs: Lessons from Europe*, U.S. Department of Labor, Bureau of International Labor Affairs, Monograph no. 5, (Washington, D.C.: GPO, 1980). According to Richard Mines, Susan Gabbard, and Anne Steirman, "A Profile of U.S. Farm Workers: Demographics, Household Composition, Income and Use of Services" (U.S. Department of Labor, Office of the Assistant Secretary for Policy, unpublished report prepared for the Commission on Immigration Reform, April 1997) (in the author's possession), iii, some 70 percent of the agricultural workforce in 1997 was foreign-born.

This essay examines the roots of U.S. immigration policies in agriculture by focusing on one group of wartime migrants. Jamaican war workers were not the first to arrive—Bahamians and Mexicans came first—but the Jamaican program, which expanded into the British West Indian program, has operated continuously since its start in 1943. Moreover, the Jamaican experience reveals in stark detail the rapid decline of immigrant farmworkers' condition in the United States. Jamaicans came eagerly to northern farms in the United States, and they were welcomed as war workers. As black men with what sounded to American ears like British accents, who behaved as the equals of whites, the press treated them as curiosities. Though they encountered inadequate conditions in some regions, they demanded respect and by and large got it. Yet, as Jamaicans ventured reluctantly into the Jim Crow South, taking jobs as cotton pickers, vegetable harvesters, and sugarcane cutters, they found themselves to be no better off and no more highly regarded than the African American farmworkers who labored alongside them. Which of these norms would prevail would depend to some extent on the struggles of Jamaican migrants themselves, but even more on the intervention of U.S. and Jamaican officials—that is on the intervention of the state in the affairs of farm labor migration.

The Politics of Labor Scarcity

It would be several years after the outbreak of war in Europe in 1939 before employers of migrant farmworkers had cause to worry about any reduction in their labor supply. After twenty years of agricultural depression, the nation's fields were glutted with labor. In Belle Glade, Florida, the southern source of the east coast migrant stream, growers could pick from among thousands of black farmworkers who would gather at dawn for the daily "shape-up." With many more people looking for work than there was space to stand upright in the back of growers' trucks, employers enlisted the help of local police to beat off the workers who clung to the outsides of their vehicles.[6]

Although nearly 10 percent of African Americans left the South during the war to take war jobs or enlist in the military, and a similar number shifted within the South from farm to city, many of these wartime migrants abandoned the fields, not because they saw better opportunities beckoning them, but because they had been supplanted by agricultural machinery. Indeed, officials of the departments of Agriculture and Labor, who were given the responsibility of estimating farm labor needs in early 1941, insisted that, despite pockets of labor scarcity, the overall supply of labor

---

[6] Lawrence E. Will, *Swamp to Sugar Bowl: Pioneer Days in Belle Glade* (St. Petersburg, Fla.: Great Outdoors): 189–93; Hahamovitch, *The Fruits of Their Labor,* 3–4, 113–37.

was still more than adequate to meet farm employers' needs.[7] Even after Pearl Harbor, as growers started to predict disaster if their accustomed workforce abandoned them, federal officials pointed out that the growers who complained most vociferously about labor scarcity and spiraling wages were the growers who paid the least. The problem, according to federal officials, was not labor scarcity, but a maldistribution of labor, made worse by many growers'—particularly white southern growers'—unwillingness to recruit workers by paying attractive wages.[8]

Federal officials could not address the problem by trying to ensure that farmers paid the minimum wage established by Fair Labor Standards Act in 1938, because the act had specifically excluded farmworkers from its provisions. The problem of labor maldistribution seemed more tractable. The Farm Security Administration (FSA), which had been created during the Depression to address the most stubborn forms of rural poverty, quickly stepped into the breach, transforming the migrant labor camps it had built to house homeless farmworkers into a labor redistribution system. Rather than encouraging farmworkers to abandon the migrant life for more sedentary work as the labor camps had been designed to do, the FSA shuttled domestic workers from job to job, transferred large groups from areas of surplus to areas of need, and provided them with meals, shelter, and sanitation facilities in Quonset huts and orderly tent camps.[9]

Many small farmers were content with this arrangement—happy to be spared the expense and effort of securing harvest labor themselves—but large growers were often outraged when federal officials stepped in to remove men and women deemed "surplus." Southern growers became particularly angry when African American farmworkers, who made up the vast majority of the eastern migratory workforce, used federal labor

[7] Memorandum, "The Impact of War and the Defense Program on Agriculture: Report No. II," transmitted by J. A. Fleming, chairman, Subcommittee of Inter-bureau Coordinating Committee, to the Secretary of Agriculture, February 17, 1941, cited in Rasmussen, *History of the Emergency Farm Labor Supply Program*, 14–15; Report of the Interbureau Planning Committee on Farm Labor, "Review of the Farm Labor Situation in 1941," December 31, 1941, National Archives and Records Administration (hereafter NARA), RG 16, Records of the Office of the Secretary of Agriculture, no.17, General Correspondence of the Office of the Secretary, 1906–1970, subject: Employment, file: "1. Labor Oct 4 to" [1941?].

[8] In 1941 average hourly wages were thirty-one cents in the eastern states from New Jersey to Maine. Wages in Delaware, Maryland, and Virginia averaged twenty-two cents an hour, and in the coastal states from North Carolina to Florida, wages were among the lowest in the nation at twelve cents an hour. Wages climbed slightly between October 1, 1942, and January 1, 1943, but farmworkers still made only 39 percent of what unskilled factory workers earned. N. Gregory Silvermaster's report to Wayne H. Darrow, director, Agricultural Labor Administration, March 20, 1943, NARA, RG 244, FSA correspondence, box 75, file 4-FLT-R36, labor estimates; "Farm Labor Notes," June 20, 1942, NARA, RG 16, general correspondence, employment, 1–4 Farm, May 14–July 15, 1942; Hahamovitch, *The Fruits of Their Labor,* 163–66.

[9] Hahamovitch, *The Fruits of Their Labor,* 151–81.

camps as bases for impromptu strikes. Excluded also from the National Labor Relations or Wagner Act, field-workers did not enjoy the right of collective bargaining, but they could agree among themselves to delay entering the fields as crops ripened on the vine and growers became more open to persuasion. The more American farmworkers demanded higher wages, the louder agricultural employers demanded access to foreign labor.[10]

Federal officials capitulated to growers' demands in June of 1942. Secretary of Agriculture Claude R. Wickard left quietly for Mexico City, returning with an agreement that allowed Mexican laborers to work on American farms in the Southwest. To growers' dismay, however, the agreement came with strings attached by Mexican authorities. The FSA would transport the migrants and would use its extensive network of temporary and permanent camps to house them. Growers would have to provide cooking, sleeping, laundry, bathing, and waste disposal facilities to anyone not housed in FSA camps. Growers could charge rent for these conveniences but they would have to specify the amount before the workers signed their contracts. Even more, farm employers would have to pay a minimum wage of thirty cents an hour or the prevailing wage, whichever was higher. And, if a harvest was delayed and contracted workers sat idle, growers would have to pay them three-quarters of the minimum wage for each day they lost. It was an unprecedented agreement, one not at all like the First World War–era plan, which had simply allowed growers to pick up farmworkers at the Mexican border and drop them back there at the end of the season. The FSA began supplying farmers with Mexican workers in the fall of 1942, and within a few months, four thousand laborers from south of the border were working on California and Arizona farms.[11]

Aware that the federal government was supplying west coast growers with Mexicans, east coast producers demanded access to foreign workers as well. "Just 48 miles across the Gulf Stream," the Dade County Farm Bureau president testified before a Congressional hearing, "are some 18,000 men, willing laborers who want to come to Florida... and despite the fact that Mexican labor is permitted to enter this country—we haven't had one Bahamian laborer offered to us." The offer was not long in coming. In February, Edward, duke of Windsor, then governor of the Bahamas, traveled

---

[10] Ibid. See also telegram to Secretary of Agriculture Claude R. Wickard from Mrs. William J. Krome, January 29, 1943, NARA, RG 224, Office of Labor, FSA correspondence, 1943–44, box 75, file 4-FLT-R57; James W. Vann, Vienna, Maryland, camp manager, monthly report, August 1942, NARA, RG 96, general correspondence, box 16, file RP-M-85–183, monthly reports.

[11] Rasmussen, *History of the Emergency Farm Labor Supply Program*, 25–29, 200–201; Calavita, *Inside the State*, 18–25; Sidney Baldwin, *Poverty and Politics: The Rise and Decline of the Farm Security Administration* (Chapel Hill: University of North Carolina Press, 1968), 346–61.

to Washington and met with President Roosevelt to negotiate an agreement to import unemployed workers from that colony.[12]

Then, in April, Congress passed a remarkable bill that the nation's two most powerful growers' lobbies—the American Farm Bureau Federation and the Associated Farmers—had penned. The new law—Public Law 45—allowed for the expansion of the farm labor supply program, so long as federal funds were *not* used to improve the wages or conditions of *American* farmworkers. American farmworkers would have to stay where they were, unless their local county agricultural extension agent signed a release allowing them to take work elsewhere. The FSA's farm labor supply program would serve large farms or associations of farmers who could contract with foreign farmworkers under the terms negotiated by foreign governments.[13]

Bahamian men and women began departing for Florida almost immediately, and negotiations soon began to extend the migration program to Jamaicans who were available in far greater numbers.[14] Thus just at the point when American farmworkers had gained some power after twenty long years of depression wages, they found themselves thrown into competition with workers imported from abroad.

Just across the Gulf Stream

In 1943, Jamaicans were desperate to find work of any kind. Already devastated by the Great Depression, Jamaica's 1.2 million people had been pushed to the brink of starvation by the outbreak of the Second World War. While the war had recharged the U.S. economy, the dearth of commercial shipping vessels made it difficult for Caribbean exporters to unload their perishable produce. In November of 1940, the British government had prohibited the use of scarce ships to transport bananas, the principle cash crop of Jamaica's peasant farmers. Before the banana market collapsed, most Jamaicans had depended for their survival on a combination of wage labor and peasant farming. The coming of war thus forced them to buy goods at inflated wartime prices with nothing but their decreasing earnings from wage labor alone. "We were small farmers," one Jamaican explained to an American reporter, "but we were dumping our bananas because we had no market for them. There is no export now." A Jamaican

[12] Hahamovitch, "'Standing Idly By': 'Organized' Farmworkers in Florida during the Second World War," in *Organized Labor in the New South,* ed. Robert Zieger, 2d ed. (Knoxville: University of Tennessee Press, 1997), 15–36; Edward, duke of Windsor, governor of the Bahamas, to Oliver Stanley, secretary of state for the colonies, January 30, 1943, Public Record Office, London), Colonial Office Records (hereafter PRO, CO) 967/126.

[13] Rasmussen, *History of the Emergency Farm Labor Supply Program,* 42; Hahamovitch, *The Fruits of Their Labor,* 173–74; Baldwin, *Poverty and Politics,* 394.

[14] PRO, CO 318, 448/10, Recruitment of Labour for U.S.

seaman, who arrived in London in time for the first blitzkrieg after his ship was torpedoed, agreed: "There is no shipping...so we had to find other work."[15]

Jamaica's black majority had little hope of redressing its grievances through political channels. Most Jamaicans were excluded from political participation by property qualifications that reduced the electorate to the wealthiest 6 percent of the population...in effect, white Jamaicans and a small number of successful "browns." This tiny electorate chose fewer than half the members of Jamaica's legislative council: the "Electives." The remaining members, the "Officials," were appointed by the governor, who was himself appointed by the British prime minister. Only Officials could serve on the governor's executive council. As elsewhere in the British West Indies, what reform initiatives there were tended to come from above, from the British Parliament or Britain's Colonial Office. Jamaica's Electives saw their job as resisting reform in the interest of their class. This meant that black Jamaicans could usually improve their circumstances only by searching for work elsewhere. But when the Depression dried up the usual off-shore work opportunities in Cuba, Panama, and the United States, Jamaican workers dug in at home, organizing trade unions and public protests. Labor rebellions racked the British Caribbean in 1937 and 1938, strengthening reform forces in England and leading, in 1942, to the appointment of Oliver Stanley, a reformer, as secretary of state for the colonies.[16]

As a result of Stanley's pressure from above and popular pressure from below, by 1944 Jamaica had a new constitution that required secret bal-

---

[15] The Depression had caused world sugar prices to collapse, which resulted in falling wages on Jamaican plantations and dried up opportunities for some ten thousand Jamaican off-shore workers in places like Panama and Cuba, who had been bringing home £125,000 in remittances every year. Ken Post, *Strike the Iron*, vol. 1 (Atlantic Highlands, N.J.: Humanities Press, 1981); Cedric O. J. Matthews, *Labour Policies in the West Indies* (Geneva: International Labour Office, 1952), 52–53, 116; Dawn Marshall, "A History of West Indian Migrations: Overseas Opportunities and 'Safety-Valve' Policies," 15–31 in *The Caribbean Exodus*, ed. Barry B. Levine (New York: Praeger, 1987), 23–24; *Amsterdam News*, June 5, 1943, 13; Paul Blanshard, *Democracy and Empire in the Caribbean* (New York: Macmillan, 1947), 47, 91; Winston James, *Holding Aloft the Banner of Ethiopia: Caribbean Radicalism in Early Twentieth-Century America* (New York: Verso, 1998).

[16] According to census data, in 1943, Jamaica's black population made up 78.1 percent of the population. All nonwhites together accounted for 96% of the total population. G. W. Roberts, *The Population of Jamaica* (London: Cambridge University Press, 1957), 64–65; Blanshard, *Democracy and Empire*, 79. On the Depression era labor rebellions, see O. Nigel Bollard, *On the March: Labour Rebellions in the British Caribbean, 1934–39* (Kingston, Jamaica: Ian Randle Publishers, 1995) and Ken Post, *Arise Ye Starvelings: The Jamaican Labour Rebellion and Its Aftermath* (The Hague: Martinus Nijhoff, 1978). For a fascinating discussion of Jamaican politics during the war, see Trevor Munroe, *Politics of Constitutional Decolonisation, Jamaica, 1944–62*, (reprint ed., Mona: Institute of Social and Economic Research, University of the West Indies, 1983). And for a discussion of changing British attitudes towards colonialism during and after the Second World War, see John Darwin, *Britain and Decolonisation: The Retreat from Empire in the Post-War World* (London: Macmillan, 1988), 3–68.

loting and universal suffrage and that would make five of ten seats on the executive council elective. This did not constitute an end to colonial rule, but it did represent dramatic change nonetheless. Instead of having to appeal to an elite electorate of just 70,000, Jamaica's "Electives" would soon have to court the favor of 750,000 mostly black voters. Thus with constitutional reforms looming, white and elite "brown" Jamaicans did what they could to ensure their continued hegemony by forming the disingenuously named Democratic party. It was at this tumultuous moment in Jamaican history that U.S. State Department officials arrived bearing manna from heaven: a labor migration scheme that they predicted would create an estimated one hundred thousand jobs for Jamaicans in the United States, allowing Jamaican electives to reap political patronage even as they exported the destitute and the discontented.[17]

The Legislative Council thus approved the participation of Jamaican men (and men only) in the migration program and began distributing tickets in April of 1943. Rather than allow officials of Jamaica's Labour Department to give out the tickets by some equitable system, however, the Electives doled them out themselves, assuming (falsely, it turned out) that a ticket holder's gratitude would later translate into a vote. The Electives concentrated their recruitment activities in the countryside where the opposition parties were weakest and trade unionists rare, while at the same time avoiding men already employed on Jamaican plantations. They bypassed Kingston, Jamaica's largest city, entirely. Too anxious to wait for a ticket distributor to come to them, thousands of islanders began sending letters of inquiry to the Jamaican Department of Labour and to the United Fruit Company, whose president Samuel Zemurray had been asked by U.S. authorities to help screen the Jamaican recruits.[18]

Not everyone in Jamaica was so enthusiastic about the migration scheme. Some planters protested what they saw as competition for their labor supply, and the governor worried about the impact the migrants might have on Jamaican society at the end of their stint in the United States. "What will happen when these highly paid gentlemen return from the States God only knows," he wrote to an official in the Colonial Office in March of 1943. The leaders of the socialist People's National Party (PNP) and the Jamaican Labour Party accused the Democrats of denying tickets to their members, and both appealed unsuccessfully for the right to send trade union officials to the United States as the migrants' representatives.[19] Likewise, the

[17] Munroe, *Politics of Constitutional Decolonization*, 25–26; Blanshard, *Democracy and Empire*, 96; PRO, CO 859, 46/16, 12251/1, Minutes of Meetings, 1943.

[18] *Daily Gleaner*, April 8 and December 6, 1943; *Public Opinion*, April 15, 1944. United Fruit had long been recruiting Jamaicans for work on its Latin American plantations, so Zemurray was a sensible choice.

[19] Governor of Jamaica to Mr. Beckett, March 26, 1943, PRO, CO 448/10, Recruitment of Labour for U.S.; *Public Opinion*, April 1 and 12, 1943.

secretary of state for the colonies, as well as workers themselves, worried that the contract offered few guarantees that workers' rights would be protected. Still, the prospect of sending an estimated one hundred thousand unemployed West Indians to the United States left Stanley with little choice but to approve the scheme.[20]

Ultimately, Stanley set aside all his objections but one: he would not allow West Indian workers to be assigned to farms south of the Mason-Dixon line for fear that they would be abused. The contract devised by the Colonial Office, the Jamaican government, and the U.S. Department of State was otherwise similar to the Mexican deal in most details. The U.S. government would import Jamaican men and would guarantee them at least thirty cents an hour for a ten-hour day. Workers would pay a dollar a day—or a third of their minimum daily earnings—for food, and fifty cents a week to sleep in an FSA bunkhouse or an approved private labor camp. Another dollar a day would be deposited in a Jamaican bank as a compulsory savings program (and to ensure that workers returned home at the end of their contracts). If work was unavailable for any reason workers were to be paid for at least three-quarters of the period for which they had been contracted (though, unlike the Mexican deal, the Jamaican contract failed to specify how long a period of unemployment would have to last before this benefit took effect—an omission that would be the source of many later grievances). If local wages were higher than the thirty-cent minimum wage, the migrants would be entitled to the prevailing wage. On the other hand, workers who refused work for any reason would be subject to deportation.[21]

"Reaching Over": Jamaican Encounters in the Wartime North

News of the migration program and the publication of the contract in the *Daily Gleaner* met with great excitement in Jamaica. "For the past four weeks the question asked by the average man on the street is: Are you going to America?" one observer wrote to the *Gleaner* from May Pen. The men who got hold of the first tickets in North Clarendon were so nervous that they might miss their opportunity to work in the United States that they assembled at the embarkation point a full twenty-four hours before they were

[20] Telegram from secretary of state for the colonies to Barbados, April 20, 1943, PRO, CO 859, 12261/1/43, Conditions of Employment and International Labour Conventions, West Indies; Anglo-American Caribbean Commission (hereafter AACC) to secretary of state for the colonies, March 20, 1943, PRO, CO 318, 448/10, Recruitment of Labour for U.S.; *Daily Gleaner*, April 1, 1943.

[21] Telegram from secretary of state for the colonies to Barbados, April 20, 1943, PRO, CO 859, 12261/1/43, Conditions of Employment and International Labour Conventions, West Indies; AACC to secretary of state for the colonies, March 20, 1943, PRO, CO 318, 448/10, Recruitment of Labour for U.S.

scheduled to leave. Even in Maroon Town, where descendants of escaped slaves still lived in isolation from the rest of Jamaican society, a delegation called for the inclusion of two hundred Maroons in the migration scheme and the construction of a road to make it easier for recruiters to get to their mountain community. The PNP's paper, *Public Opinion*, soon began reporting a brisk trade in black-market recruitment tickets.[22]

As the first recruits prepared to leave for the United States in May of 1943, communities across the island organized alternately jubilant and solemn farewell ceremonies at which workers said special prayers, received pocket editions of the Bible, and feasted on curried goat. Men departing Buff Bay sang a chorus of "We all are jolly good fellows" before boarding the train that took them to the port at Kingston. Once at sea, however, everything that could go wrong did go wrong. The U.S. troop transport vessel, the SS *Shank,* which had been built to hold eighteen hundred men, was so overcrowded that the four thousand recruits aboard had to arrange shifts for meals, water, toilets, and bunks. George Pitt, a machinist from Spanish Town, wrote home to *Public Opinion* that men had to wait in line for hours to eat and were treated like prisoners by the military police who guarded the vessel. On their third day at sea, he and other observers reported, MPs turned a fire hose on the recruits. One man died on the voyage—by his own hand, according to the Jamaican official who investigated the incident, by accident, according to the U.S. Department of State, and at the hands of MPs, according to Jamaicans on the boat. In any case, it was an inauspicious beginning.[23]

Upon their arrival in New Orleans's port, the men were processed and fingerprinted before being sent north by train. Each man left with a pamphlet written by J. Harris, Jamaica's Labour Adviser, and Herbert MacDonald, who would be the workers' chief liaison to the Jamaican government while the men were in the United States Though assuring the men that they would be "among a friendly English-speaking people," the brochure warned them to expect habits and customs "somewhat different" from their own." "In the United States the word 'Negro' is not used to offend," the pamphlet explained, "but is used and accepted in the same way as the word 'coloured' in Jamaica." "Respect the 'Star Spangled Banner,'" the brochure admonished, and "try to recognize it whenever it is played...remember it is as sacred to Americans as 'God Save the King' is to us." "Try to save all of your surplus money," the pamphlet added in closing, "The more you have, the better off you will be when you go back home."[24]

---

[22] *Daily Gleaner,* April 30 and May 5–6, 1943.

[23] Ibid., May 5 and June 5, 1943; *Public Opinion,* September 25, 1943, 1; AACC to secretary of state for the colonies, May 22, 1943, PRO, CO 318/448/10.

[24] PRO, CO 318/448/10.

Jamaican migrants did find Americans friendly and certainly fascinated with them, though conditions varied enormously from place to place. Rupert Holn wrote from Burlington, New Jersey, that: "we have found the Americans a very fine lot. I am feeling very homely and would not mind if stay could be for all times...the experience that I have gathered could never be bought in a lifetime in Jamaica." Another recruit wrote his relatives from Bridgeton, Connecticut, that he and the other men on the boat "got over safely and have started to work. We are now in a place where the people are very fine and courteous to the Jamaicans." One man noted that they had been "treated royally" on their voyage from New Orleans to Bridgeton, remarking, hyperbolically, that Uncle Sam provided them beer to drink "every hour of the day." Ernest Pendley and thirty-four others were surprised to find a military band waiting to greet them when they arrived in Randolph, Wisconsin, in May of 1943. Pendley and the others were invited to attend various churches the following Sunday and were offered full use of the Randolph Country Club for as long as they were in the area picking the peas that had been planted on the golf course's fairways and greens. C. W. Creightney was amazed to find white locals willing to "come from miles with their cars to take us around and show us a good time." "They were not expecting us to be such fine fellows," he noted, and "we never expected to rub shoulders" with them in restaurants and stores. David Bent wrote a former teacher that his Wisconsin boss was a "gentleman." Samuel Gayle only wished he had come twenty years earlier. "It is just like a honeymoon to me.... Please tell them that life is given away in United States."[25]

Other recruits were not nearly as content with the conditions they found on northern farms and in hastily built farm labor camps. George Pitt recalled that after disembarking the "hell-ship" at New Orleans, and taking the long but "pleasant train trip" to Hebrant Camp in New Jersey, he worked over the next few days for three different employers, one of whom never paid him despite his complaints. After a week the FSA moved him to Swedesboro, where the recruits worked overtime (without overtime pay, he noted), and then the work slowed, until there was only enough for fifty of the four hundred men. Food and water supplies dwindled. Fourteen hundred and fifty workers sent to Michigan were without work for a month. While they waited, they lived off food bought on credit from the camp store. Because growers did not begin paying them the three-quarter wages that the Mexican contract would have demanded, some were reduced to demanding relief at police stations. "State of affairs... is deplorable and fraught with danger," the Jamaican governor telegraphed to Oliver Stanley. When they were finally put to work the following week, the men

---

[25] *Daily Gleaner,* May 29, June 4–7, 1943.

complained that they were paid less than prevailing wages and that they were the butt of race prejudice stemming from the recent race riots in Detroit. One hundred and sixty men insisted on returning to Jamaica. Another one hundred arrived in Centerville, Maryland, after an unusually long voyage to Norfolk during which a German submarine chased their ship and the delay caused the food on board to spoil. They arrived in Centerville so hungry that, when they discovered that the camp manager was not prepared for their arrival, "they broke into a neighboring orchard and consumed large quantities of green apples." After two weeks of work, with which "the farmers on the Eastern Shore of Maryland [were] very pleased," the men were quickly relocated when the Colonial Office discovered that Centerville was well south of the Mason-Dixon line.[26]

With the notable exceptions of Michigan, generally, and Swedesboro, New Jersey, in particular, most new arrivals experienced conditions in northern states that were satisfactory, if not luxurious, and the men were pleased and sometimes moved by the welcome they received from nearby communities. Four hundred Jamaicans working near Manhattan were treated to a tour of the city on Labor Day, which ended with a dinner and a cricket match between the Jamaican farmworkers and West Indian New Yorkers (the New Yorkers won). The Brant Labor Camp, near Buffalo, New York, held a celebration on August 1 to commemorate the abolition of slavery in Jamaica 105 years earlier, an event noted by the press as far away as Fort Wayne, Indiana. "Here they were in a country other than their own," Fort Wayne's *Protestant Voice* reported, "celebrating an event that happened thirty years before American negroes were freed. Their eloquence—the sheer beauty of their words in praising of ancestors who had won freedom for them—was surprising."[27]

Wherever Jamaicans worked in northern states, white Americans seemed similarly struck by the fact that they were black people—but not like black people they had known or read about. The white press, in particular, could not resist comparing the recruits to African Americans, at least implicitly. Arriving at Swedesboro, Waterbury *Republican* reporter Sigrid Arne remarked on the "queer sound" that could be heard coming from a long building that looked like an Army mess tent. "Dominoes," explained the

[26] *Public Opinion*, September 25, 1943, 1; Sir A. Richard, Jamaica, to secretary of state for the colonies, June 29, 1943, PRO, CO 318, 448/11, Recruitment of Labour for U.S.; Anglo-American Caribbean Commission to secretary of state for the colonies, July 7, 1943, PRO, CO 318, 448/11, Recruitment of Labour for U.S.; *Chicago Bee*, July 11, 1943, 2; Report to Mr. Middleton, July 1 1944, PRO, CO 318/460/1.

[27] The Labor Day celebration included a Jamaican-style dinner, during which public officials and members of New York's many West Indian civic organizations welcomed them to the area and the assembled guests sang both the American and British anthems. The dinner and the cricket match were broadcast on Jamaican radio stations. *Amsterdam News*, August 28, 1943, 4 and September 25, 1943, 4-A; *Daily Gleaner*, September 8, 1943, 1; The *Protestant Voice* story was reprinted in the *Daily Gleaner*, September 22, 1943, 4.

FSA official who was driving. "They play dominoes with a fine fury." Writing for a local population that had been hiring African Americans for sixty years, Arne explained that "The Jamaicans come from a Negro country," a place "without color prejudice." "It's a British colony," he noted, "a fact which lends to amusing situations when the Jersey farmer runs into his first Jamaican. Many of them have clipped, British accents that are quite surprising coming from a Negro field hand." "I was talking to one," he continued, "who told me, 'we're rather fond of cricket, you know. But we're having extreme difficulty acquiring the gear.' I could have closed my eyes and thought I was in a Park Avenue drawing room."[28]

In a story that found its way to Kingston's *Daily Gleaner*, the Humboldt, Iowa, paper also compared Jamaicans to African Americans. First noting where Jamaica was located, the paper described Humboldt's visitors as "happy men" who sang as they worked. "Sometimes, while they wait to start along the rows, they break into a soft shoe dance." "The only language the Jamaicans know is English," the paper noted, "However, among themselves they speak in rapid vernacular which no midwesterner ever could follow. But in talk with visitors, some become almost Oxfordian...." "In physical appearance," the reporter explained, "the Jamaican resembles the American Negro of the deep south. But they have enjoyed generations of equal social rights with white men in Jamaica.... There are no Jim Crow laws in Jamaica and some of the men, encountering racial prejudice for the first time in their lives, have been deeply hurt in several instances." "Their employers," the paper continued, "are defending Jamaicans loyally." As one farm manager noted to Chief Liaison, Herbert MacDonald, "We have had only one serious complaint about one of our boys." The "boy" had earned twenty-three dollars in one day, blocking beets (loosening the soil around the plant to allow it to grow bigger). "He is a real good boy; but he works too hard," the manager quipped.[29]

While compared by others to African Americans, the Jamaicans compared themselves to white Americans. In an open letter thanking the people of Humboldt City, for example, three Jamaican men wrote: "I suppose you all must have heard about us. We are from a British West Indies Island, a peaceful and law-abiding country as you are in Humboldt City." "I can assure you all that when we get back to our sunny Jamaica homes," the letter ended, "we will always remember America, especially Humboldt City where you have treated us so good that the only difference between us is colour and that's nature's work.... Men are judged by their minds." "We are made from the same clay," added Gerald Johnson, a cook from Port Antonio.[30]

[28] *Waterbury Republican*, June 27, 1943, 14.
[29] *Daily Gleaner*, August 6 and 28, 1943.
[30] Ibid., August 6 and September 8, 1943. For more comprehensive studies of West Indians' experience of Amerucan race relations, see among others Ira De A. Reid, *The Negro*

When Jamaicans encountered discrimination while working in northern states, moreover, they reacted to such affronts openly and sometimes aggressively—with few, if any, repercussions. For example, Renford Glanville, who came to the United States in 1943 at the age of nineteen, worked for a year alongside black and white Americans at Seabrook Farms in New Jersey, loading and unloading cartons of asparagus for fifty cents an hour, ten hours a day. The Americans had a union and the Jamaicans did not—"Since we were foreigners and on contract." "Still," he later recalled, "we were treated nicely." On one occasion, however, he and other Jamaicans stopped at a local restaurant on their way home from working in the fields. "We had worked all night, and some of the fellows wanted to get something to eat before we went home. The restaurant people wouldn't serve us. They served all of the other people before us." According to Glanville, the men "kept sitting there," but finally "some of the boys got mad. . . . So they jumped over the counter and started breaking up the dishes, tearing up the place. All for one and one for all, you know." Not knowing what to do, the restaurant staff called John Seabrook, who managed Seabrook Farms. Seabrook, by Glanville's telling, said, "Feed them. You better feed them." "So, that" according to Glanville, "was that."[31]

The fact that Jamaican farmworkers were being treated with more consideration than African American farmworkers was not lost on African American observers. African American reporters presumed a kinship with the Jamaican workers, reporting news of the program regularly and protesting cases of mistreatment with vigor. Yet, they keenly observed the special treatment accorded Caribbean workers. Roy Wilkins, writing for New York's *Amsterdam News*, noted that, when the government brought several thousand Jamaicans here to work as farm laborers, "it was careful to explain that these people were not accustomed to racial discrimination and must be handled accordingly." "But for its own Negroes . . . ," Wilkins complained, "the War Department says not a word." "Fair Wages Should Begin at Home," began a similar editorial in the Norfolk *Journal and Guide*. The author noted that West Indian laborers had been guaranteed a minimum wage of forty cents per hour and adequate housing, "which is much more than any U.S. Negro farm laborers are assured of making." "A minimum wage has been denied Negro or white farm labor in the United States," the author contin-

---

Immigrant (New York: Columbia University Press, 1939); Lennox Raphael, "West Indians and Afro-Americans," *Freedomways* (summer 1964): 438–45; Roy S. Bryce-Laporte, "Black Immigrants, the Experience of Invisibility and Inequality," *Journal of Black Studies* 3, no. 1 (1972): 29–56; Philip Kasinitz, *Caribbean New York* (Ithaca: Cornell University Press, 1992); and Milton Vickerman, *Crosscurrents: West Indian Immigrants and Race* (New York: Oxford University Press, 1999).

[31] Life History 2, in *Looking Back: Eleven Life Histories*, comp. Giles R. Wright (Trenton: New Jersey Historical Commission, Department of State, 1986), 18–24.

ued, though "the experiment points up what the farmers can do, and what our government can do when necessity demands that something be done."[32]

Jamaicans Jump Jim Crow: Encounters in the Wartime South

The first few months of the Emergency Farm Labor Importation Program did indeed reveal what governments could do to guarantee farmworkers decent conditions and fair treatment. As long as the Importation Program placed Jamaicans only in the North, and as long as FSA officials and the Jamaican liaisons responded promptly to workers' complaints, the scheme seemed useful to all concerned, and at least to some, a promising experiment in interracial cooperation. However, U.S. pressure on colonial officials to allow Jamaicans to venture south never relented, and the pressure increased as winter approached. Harvests in the North would soon come to an end, the War Food Administration (WFA) warned, and Jamaicans already in the United States would either have to work in the South or return home. "In avoiding districts like Delaware and Maryland in the Northeast and the 'deep south' where a rigid colour bar exists," as Jamaica's Labour Adviser put it, Jamaicans would soon run out of crops to harvest. "We tried hard... to have numbers of the men sent to California," Harris noted, "but this State is worked almost entirely by Mexicans." The director of the War Food Administration asked for permission to send Jamaicans to Texas to pick cotton, but Harris refused, enforcing the ban on work south of the Mason-Dixon line, though he checked again with the colonial secretary, just to be sure.[33]

Thus by the time the first Jamaican farm laborers were arriving in the United States in May of 1943, the recruitment scheme had already been suspended back home. On May 17, recruitment was postponed for an indefinite period, leaving men who had hoped to go "in a state of despondency." And on June 12 the recruitment staff disbanded. Over the next five months, the colonial secretary held his ground as anxious recruits gathered in Kingston, hoping the migration program would resume.[34]

Meanwhile, Florida growers continued to demand Caribbean workers, estimating, rather vaguely, that their labor supply would be "twenty-five to eighty-five percent" short during the coming winter harvest season. The "importation of labor from the British West Indies was the only chance of meeting the situation," according to the Florida Vegetable Committee. The

[32] *Amsterdam News,* May 22, 1944 (clipping in NARA, RG 224, box 25, file: Publications 1–1 Negro Press); *Norfolk Journal and Guide,* July 17, 1943.
[33] J. Harris, May 21, 1943 and Colonel Bruton, WFA, to Taussig, AACC, undated, PRO, CO 318, 448/11, Recruitment of Labour for U.S.; *Public Opinion,* May 17, 1943, 1.
[34] *Daily Gleaner,* May 17 and 19, 1943.

staff of the FSA's Office of Labor refuted such claims, citing field reports that suggested an adequate supply of labor. But while FSA officials argued that reports of labor scarcity were "considerably exaggerated," the director of the War Food Administration, the FSA's parent agency, chose to heed Florida's growers. Thus, U.S. officials added to the pressure on the colonial secretary to allow Jamaicans to work in the South by suspending further recruiting until he relented. [35]

While U.S. officials waited, pressure to resume transporting migrants mounted within Jamaica. The Jamaican press published heartbreaking tales of recruits who had spent what little they had to travel to the port at Kingston, only to discover that the program had been called off. Even the PNP, whose party organ, *Public Opinion,* had kept up a steady barrage of criticism against the program, could not help but notice how important the program was as a relief measure. *Public Opinion* reported that workers still in the United States had sent home remittances in the amount of twenty thousand pounds or one hundred thousand dollars for the month of June alone. Calling for the "fullest and most sincere and earnest provisions" to be made for the workers' protections, the PNP reluctantly endorsed the proposed change in policy. And, while the *Daily Gleaner* editorialized about the "real and serious difficulty" of sending Jamaicans to the U.S. South, its editors reasoned, that "if the men who volunteer for such a trial are made fully aware . . . of the realities of 'down South' conditions . . . the experiment might end satisfactorily." "Perhaps, too, as a racial experiment," the *Gleaner* added, "it may prove instructive, certainly enlightening."[36]

Colonial officials also feared what might happen if Jamaicans faced discrimination or violence in the U.S. South. But because Bahamians were already working in Florida under a separately negotiated contract, and because Barbadians and Puerto Ricans were clamoring to be included in the scheme, they worried that failure to comply with the U.S. demand might mean the loss of the offshore program to other Caribbean workers entirely. Thus, in September of 1943, Oliver Stanley reluctantly gave in, and Jamaican and War Food Administration officials drafted a new agreement that allowed Jamaican workers "to proceed south." The conditions of the agreement provided that only those recommended "for character and efficiency" would be allowed to stay in the United States for winter work in Florida. And those who chose to remain would have to be fully informed of the "racial and other conditions prevailing in the Southern States." To start, Jamaicans would only work in Florida, where they would be under the supervision of an expanded staff of Jamaican liaisons.[37]

---

[35] Ibid.
[36] *Public Opinion,* July 17, 1943; *Daily Gleaner,* September 22, 1943, 4.
[37] *Daily Gleaner,* September 21 and 29, 1943.

To smooth their way, Herbert MacDonald, the chief liaison, announced to the Miami press that Jamaicans were "good workers," "and only those who have made excellent records" would be given contracts for work in Florida." Though the Jamaicans' contract still stipulated that they would suffer no discrimination while at work in the United States, MacDonald announced unilaterally that "These men *want* to abide by the customs of the South." "They are not arrogant," he assured white readers, "and do not wish to get out of bounds." "If one should enter a restricted place, for example, it will be through a lack of knowledge of Southern customs, and he will leave immediately when he is reminded." So, while northern employers had been advised that they would have to adapt to black workers from Jamaica, and most seemed willing to do so, southern growers were assured that Jamaicans would adapt to them.[38]

Jamaicans began arriving in Florida to cut sugarcane for the U.S. Sugar Corporation on October 7, 1943. To ensure that the first 800 Jamaicans shifted south would in fact abide by the customs of the "Jim Crow"—that is the formally segregated—South, MacDonald insisted that the men agree to what the *Amsterdam News* dubbed the "Jim Crow Creed." MacDonald made it clear that "A distinction is made in Florida with colored people and you must be careful and endeavor to help the position, as by your conduct you will be judged." "It is well to tell you for the sake of general information," he continued, "that there is a law in many Southern States, including Florida, which makes the offense of rape punishable by death. This, of course, is a very serious offense anywhere, but down there it is viewed even more seriously." "There will be ample opportunity for you to make friends among the colored people," he assured them, "as every city, town and village has its colored section." "You are free to purchase wherever you wish, but there are certain places of amusement, restaurants and bars where you will not be allowed." MacDonald also noted that the new contract included "a misconduct and indiscipline clause," which gave the United States government the right to terminate the contract "if the worker misconducts himself." He exhorted the men to "behave themselves" because there was "a slight possibility that the success of the Florida venture might well influence any future recruitment in Jamaica." Those who refused to behave, he said in conclusion, would be turned over to the Immigration and Naturalization Service for "repatriation."[39]

In fact, the workers who began arriving in Florida from northern states and from Jamaica were not nearly as content to "abide by southern customs" as MacDonald had promised, nor were they at all satisfied with the wages and conditions offered by U.S. Sugar. While the city of Hartford,

[38] Emphasis mine. Reprinted in the *Daily Gleaner,* October 4, 1943.
[39] *Amsterdam News,* November 6, 1943, 7-B; *Pittsburgh Courier,* October 30, 1943.

Connecticut, held farewell ceremonies for Jamaican workers, congratulating them on the work they had done, 93 men arrived in Florida incensed at the "Jim Crow Creed" and upset that they were being sent to cut sugarcane. They "refused to get off the buses," MacDonald later reported, and when they did, "they refused to carry their own luggage." When they got to the mess hall, "they scraped their food on the ground & trampled on it...." and "abused everyone & everything in sight." The men were quickly shipped off to the Dade City jail to await deportation. Within two weeks the number of Jamaicans sitting in Florida jails had risen to seven hundred. "I must advise caution as they are in an ugly mood," Herbert MacDonald warned Jamaica's Labour Adviser.[40]

Still, many got to work, and Jamaicans harvested 65 percent of Florida's sugarcane in 1944. Those who had agreed to stay in Florida, however, quickly discovered that Bahamians and African Americans were working in nearby vegetable fields, earning three times as much for work that was far less difficult and dangerous. Their complaints went unheeded. One group of men recruited directly from Jamaica for work at U.S. Sugar accused MacDonald of "lying to them and of being in league with the sugar people to keep them in Florida."[41]

The conditions in U.S. Sugar's camps were also far worse than anything the recruits had experienced in places like Humboldt, Hartford, and Bridgeton. Upon their return to Jamaica, a group of men complained of abysmal conditions and racist camp officials in Florida. They told of "odorous" drinking water, a plague of mosquitoes, flies, snakes, and deadly insects, and of "sanitary conditions in their living quarters that were absolutely intolerable." Upon entering the U.S. Sugar Corporation barracks at Clewiston, Florida, Stanley Wilson discovered that he was expected to sleep on a bare mattress, without sheets, pillow, or blanket. When he and the other cane cutters protested, the camp superintendent exclaimed, "Pillows... you aren't serious! This is the first time in my life that I ever heard niggers slept with pillows, too." To make matters worse, the barracks adjoined a latrine that was in an "unimaginable" state of filth. Because the latrine stood directly across from the mess hall, swarms of flies "trafficked regularly between the food served to the workers and the deposits in the convenience." "Workers made the strongest representations against this condition," Wilson reported, "but could secure no redress." While in the

[40] *Daily Gleaner,* November 6, 1943, 15; *Palm Beach Post,* October 9 and 15–16, 1943, 12; Herbert G. McDonald [*sic*] to Labour Adviser, Labour Department, Kingston, Jamaica, Office of Censorship, U.S.A, October 21, 1943, PRO, CO 318/460/1.

[41] PRO, CO 318, 460/3; Sir J. Huggins (governor. of Jamaica) to secretary of state for the colonies, December 4, 1943, PRO, CO 318, 448/11; excerpt of letter from Herbert G. MacDonald to Labour Adviser, Labour Department, Kingston, Jamaica, Office of Censorship, U.S.A,, PRO, CO 318/460/1.

fields, the men were given water to drink that not only smelled rank but "changed the colour of any of the more delicate metals with which it came in contact." If Jamaican workers wanted the same water that white workers drank, they had to pay thirty-five cents a gallon for it. When they refused to work under these conditions, Wilson and fifty-eight others were loaded onto a truck and taken to jail, where they spend the next three weeks awaiting passage back to Jamaica.[42]

Rather than attempting to redress the conditions in Florida's labor camps, U.S. immigration officials jailed the Jamaicans who complained and then deported them. Detention was not meant as a punishment, though imprisonment certainly had that effect. Its purpose was to keep angry migrants awaiting their return to Jamaica from influencing newly arrived recruits, who had no experience in the United States with which to compare the conditions at U.S. Sugar. In December of 1944 the War Food Administration began to deport dissenters without imprisoning them by turning Fort Eustis in Virginia into a repatriation center, which housed only workers awaiting boats back to the Caribbean. That same month, however, the War Manpower Commission shifted almost two thousand West Indians into war industries, as industrial employers were willing to accept workers who had been blacklisted by the War Food Administration. When news spread at U.S. Sugar that workers facing repatriation in Virginia had been transferred to coveted industrial jobs in New Jersey and Wisconsin, four hundred sugar workers in Florida promptly threatened to strike. Their hope was that they would be transferred to Virginia for repatriation and that, once there, they too could sign up for industrial work. Its plan undone, the WFA closed the Fort Eustis Repatriation Center, and opened one at Camp Murphy, near West Palm Beach, Florida. There men who refused work, or who simply wanted to go back to Jamaica, waited impatiently for transportation, while they spent their savings on food and other necessities.[43]

The guards at Camp Murphy and the problem of securing transportation back to Jamaica remained sources of discontent for the remainder of the war. The *Christian Science Monitor* attributed a riot of 250 workers at Camp Murphy in August of 1945 to "the Negroes [sic] unwillingness to return to their comparatively drab former existence after sampling the high wages and luxury goods during their employment in the United States." In fact, it was a fight between Barbadians and Jamaicans as to which group would get to leave first.[44] And while discontent among Jamaicans in northern camps had sent managers scrambling to find cricket equipment and Jamaican-born cooks, the managers of Camp Murphy went scrambling for

[42] *Public Opinion*, June 20, 1944, 1.
[43] Report of Herbert MacDonald for December 1944, PRO, CO 318, 460/2.
[44] August 28, 1945, clipping in PRO, CO 318/460/2.

their guns. A week after the Camp Murphy riot, a white camp employee, Lacey A. Griffin, fired his weapon while chasing a Jamaican who had urinated against a building. Griffen lost his quarry and was taunted by a group of men, who dared him to enter their barracks. He went for help, telling Captain R. G. Ray, the camp manager, that he would quit before he took "such talk off of these men any further." Ray, Griffin, and two other camp employees then returned to the barrack armed, yelling at the men to stand up as they entered and beating with billy clubs those who moved too slowly. "If we did not behave ourselves," one worker later quoted Ray as having said that he would "shoot us and throw us in a hole." To make themselves clear, Ray shot his gun toward the floor and Griffin fired his through a window, hitting a man in the leg in another building. The military police sent to replace the camp's hired staff were "well received by the men," according to Herbert MacDonald, but a month later, another worker was shot, this time by the military police brought to maintain order.[45]

Delaware was no better than Florida, according to Nathaniel Allen, whose letter to his mother in Montego Bay caught the eye of an official in the Office of Imperial Censorship. Work was scarce, he complained, and dust plentiful: "No Latrines, no water to bathe, no beds to sleep in, no lights to sleep with and see at nights [*sic*] and worse than all, no work to do." "What this thing is going to lead up to I don't know," he wrote, "but what I can tell you is that every one is getting panicky...." "Mam, you can't imagine," he wrote. "This is a one man's place. Every where you look belongs to no one else but him, so then he runs the place and fixes the rates the people must work for.... I am not working because working here is only putting money in some one else's pocket."[46]

What Jamaicans were encountering, of course, were the conditions that African Americans had long faced as agricultural workers in the U.S. South. In the Vienna, Maryland, War Food Administration camp, for example, Jamaicans objected to the daily "shape up," complaining that only those who got in the trucks first got work. Jamaicans also resented having to arrive early in the fields and then wait without pay until the farm manager declared the fields dry enough for picking. Likewise, their organizing attempts brought an immediate, hostile response. When a white camp manager reported James Morrison to the local police as an "agitator," he was arrested and held at the Vienna, Maryland, police station, without so much as a warrant or a hearing. Though he was eventually released, he noted that two other workers had already been deported as "trouble-makers."[47]

---

[45] Depositions, September 10, 1945, PRO, CO 318/460/2; Chief Liaison's report for September 1945, PRO, CO 318, 460/2.

[46] PRO, CO 318/460/1.

[47] *Washington Bee*, July 22, 1944, 2.

How an Experiment Became an Institution

The more Jamaicans soured on the southern "experiment," the more the workers' distaste for working and living conditions seemed to spread northward. And the more dissatisfied they were, the more frustrated they became with Herbert MacDonald, the chief liaison, and he with them. In November of 1944, after quickly settling a Wadsworth, Ohio, strike over the phone, MacDonald remarked, "As far as I can see, the only reason these men had for striking was to keep in practice for the day when they return home." Likewise, in March of 1945, he reported that a worker had punched a Cleveland camp manager in the face "and got away with it." "I told the Camp Manager," MacDonald noted, "that he should have reported this and I would have taken responsibility [for] removing the man. Subsequently another worker abused him shamefully and was removed. The effect of this," MacDonald lamented, was that "the workers are under the impression that it is safer to punch the Camp Manager than to abuse him." "Men write home or go home and say they have never seen me," MacDonald added two months later; "that is their theme song," he complained. But he also estimated that it would take him nearly four years to visit every man.[48] MacDonald and the other liaisons on his staff would, of course, have been hard pressed to attend to every grievance made by their far-flung compatriots. However, with U.S. immigration authorities ready to deport importees who contested their wages and treatment, the workers could not redress their grievances themselves. By 1944, in effect, the federal government was serving not just as a crew leader for the nation's largest farms, but as an enforcer of workplace discipline.

Jamaican leaders did try to follow up on the migrants' complaints, but their desire to expand the program outweighed their concerns. While strikes in the United States became more frequent and workers in repatriation camps fought to return home, men and women in Jamaica and elsewhere in the Caribbean were struggling bitterly to get to the United States. In April of 1944, "bedlam, and minor damage to property" were the result when police used batons to beat back three thousand people trying to get the 180 available tickets at the Port Maria recruiting station. Even outrage that American doctors were requiring recruits to strip naked on Kingston's open pier for venereal disease examinations failed to put a damper on public enthusiasm for the program. Jamaicans may not have been receiving prevailing wages in the United States but they were sending more money home than Jamaican offshore workers had ever sent before, and that fed

[48] Extract of letter from Edon (?) to Hon. and Rev. Dr. P. G. Veitch, J.P., Legislative Council, Kingston, Jamaica, quoted by Imperial Censorship, Jamaica, July 10, 1944, and Chief Liaison's Report for Month Ending May 31, 1945, June 2, 1945, PRO, CO 318/460/1 and 2.

the program's popularity, no matter how bad the reports from the United States got.[49]

Jamaican officials were reluctant to attack the program, both because of its popularity and because they still stood to gain from it. 1944 brought Jamaica its new constitution, universal suffrage, and, therefore, the first democratic elections in its history. The Jamaican Labour party, the political wing of the Bustamente Industrial Trade Union (BITU), swept the polls, completely unseating the Democratic party and winning twenty-two seats to the PNP's five. The Democratic party's monopoly over the ticket distribution process had failed utterly in keeping white Jamaicans in power. Nonetheless, once ensconced in the new Jamaican House of Representatives, Alexander Bustamente, the BITU's "president for life," happily inherited the tickets and the patronage system that went along with them. In May of 1945, four opposition PNP members made a motion on the floor of the Jamaican House of Representatives to condemn the ticket distribution system, arguing that nonelected officials should distribute the tickets. But after a rancorous debate, the motion was defeated by twenty votes to four, and the migration program and the patronage system it spawned became permanent features of Jamaican political life.[50]

Citizens of other Caribbean colonies were also demanding to be included in the migration scheme, but in its first year the program remained restricted to Jamaicans, Bahamians, and Mexicans. United States officials were trying to avoid importing Puerto Ricans. "As they are United States citizens," an American diplomat explained in a letter to Oliver Stanley, "they could not be sent back to Puerto Rico against their will." "This cannot, of course, be stated," he added, so the "reason given is lack of shipping facilities." If workers were brought from Barbados or elsewhere, the "falsity of the reason given would be apparent." In the spring of 1944, however, the point became moot, as employers began importing Puerto Ricans on their own. The importation of Barbadians thus began immediately, and once the logjam broke, the governors of St. Lucia and the British Honduras insisted that their subjects be included as well, citing protests and demonstrations at home.[51]

With workers from many nations scrambling to work in the United States, American growers and officials had little incentive to improve conditions. Those who did not like them could simply leave. In the last year of the war,

---

[49] *Daily Gleaner,* August 28, 1944.

[50] The remaining five seats went to independents. *Public Opinion,* December 16, 1944; Monroe, *Politics of Constitutional Decolonisation,* 42.

[51] Governor (Sir) Grattan Bushe to the Colonial Office, June 29 and July 12, 1943, and decoded telegram from AACC to secretary of state for the colonies, March 11, 1944, PRO, CO 318, 448/10, Recruitment of Labour for U.S.; Sir A. Grimble, Windward Islands, to secretary of state for the colonies, August 30, 1944. PRO, CO 318, 448/11; telegram from AACC to secretary of state for the colonies, March 22, 1945, CO 318, 460/2.

38,000 Jamaicans, Barbadians, St. Lucians, and British Hondurans labored in the United States alongside almost 62,000 Mexicans, 5,800 Bahamians, 120,000 prisoners of war, and an undisclosed number of Puerto Ricans. Herbert MacDonald now supervised Jamaicans and the other British West Indians under the rubric of the British West Indies Central Labour Organisation, which had been set up jointly by the various British Caribbean governments (with the exception of the Bahamas).[52]

The end of the war came and went with little change in the "Emergency" Farm Labor Importation Program. Congress moved quickly to expel foreign workers from industrial jobs, but, at the urging of farm lobbyists, the agricultural program received an extension. In the year following the war, 39,630 guestworkers from the British West Indies worked in nearly fifteen hundred localities in thirty-six of the forty-eight states, and Jamaicans harvested most of Florida's sugar crop.[53]

Once the war ended the new secretary of state for the colonies, Fabian socialist Arthur Creech-Jones, demonstrated that he, at least, was still ambivalent about the migration program. In April of 1946, colonial officials insisted on pulling all Jamaican workers out of Florida for the same reason that the government of Mexico tried unsuccessfully to keep its citizens from working in Texas. Both of these state-sponsored strikes against poor working conditions and racist abuse failed, however. Mexican citizens undermined their government's effort by crossing the border illegally and taking whatever work Texas growers had to offer. The government of Barbados took advantage of Jamaica's "strike" against Florida to expand opportunities for its citizens in the United States The Emergency Farm Labor Importation program had, in essence, re-created the prewar labor surplus. Only it had created an international shape-up; if one nation's workers failed to climb on to the back of growers' trucks, another nation's workers would.[54]

Jamaicans and the Making of Agricultural Immigration Policy

Could the United States have fashioned a guestworker program or open-border policy that would have allowed foreign farmworkers temporary

---

[52] K. A. Butler, Acting Director of Labor, to Nathan Koenig, executive secretary to the secretary of agriculture, 1/24/46, NARA, RG 224, General Correspondence 1946, box 107, POWs.

[53] The *Norfolk Journal and Guide* (October 5, 1946) protested the continuation of the program, arguing that farm operators and the federal government were defeating any New Deal for agricultural workers by "continuing a war-inspired importation of foreign laborers when the conditions which made that imperative no longer exist." Protests such as this one were few, and they went unheeded.

[54] Annual Report of Chief Liaison, covering April 1, 1945 to March 31, 1946, PRO, CO 318, 460/3.

immigration status without subjecting them to the kind of conditions depicted here? Nothing in this tale precludes such a possibility. The mere presence of Jamaican workers in the United States did not account for the rapid decline in conditions described here. Indeed, Jamaicans raised the bar for other farmworkers when they first arrived in the North. The problem was not so much the fact of a temporary worker program but the combination of a program that put the authority to deport in the hands of growers with labor laws that denied farmworkers the right of collective bargaining. Had the INS insisted that Jamaicans could not be deported simply for protesting violations of their contracts, the last fifty years of agricultural history might have turned out quite differently.

Instead, what began in 1942 as an emergency measure became, in the aftermath of the war, a fixture of modern agriculture. The "jolly good fellows" from Jamaica turned out to be among the vanguard of a great migration, as monumental in scale and impact as any that had come before it. In the decades that followed, the wartime Labor Importation Program mutated into the Bracero Program on the West Coast and the H-2 program in the East, both of which continued to provide growers with temporary harvest labor without permitting the "migrants" to become "immigrants." In the 1950s U.S. growers hired ten times more temporary foreign workers than they had during the Second World War, though the federal government got out of the business of recruiting, transporting, feeding, and housing foreign workers, leaving those aspects of the program to private employers. Growers' associations were allowed to buy the FSA labor camps for a dollar apiece, and some remained in use thirty years later. Federal officials continued to set "prevailing wage" standards and deport those who caused trouble. As a section foreman supervising three hundred West Indian sugarcane cutters in Florida explained in 1966: "We bring the Jamaican here under contract. If he violates his contract we can send him home. So we've got leverage over that West Indian that we don't have over American workers. When that offshore comes in here, he's either going to cut cane or get sent home—or if he violates his immigration status and runs away from his employer, the law will get him."[55]

The agricultural guestworker programs came under attack repeatedly over the decades, but campaigns to end the use of braceros in the West and

---

[55] Peter Kramer, *The Offshores: A Study of Foreign Farm Labor in Florida* (St. Petersburg, Fla.: Community Action Fund, 1966), 39. For more on agricultural guestworkers in Florida since the Second World War see Alec Wilkinson, *Big Sugar: Seasons in the Cane Fields of Florida* (New York: Knopf, 1989); Josh DeWind, Tom Seidl, and Janet Shenk, "Caribbean Migration: Contract Labor in U.S. Agriculture," *NACLA Report on the Americas* 11, no. 8 (November–December 1977): 4–37; David Griffith, "Peasants in Reserve: Temporary West Indian Labor in the U.S. Farm Labor Market," *International Migration Review* 20, no. 4 (1986): 875–98; Charles H. Wood and Terry L. McCoy, "Migration, Remittances and Development: A Study of Caribbean Cane Cutters in Florida," ibid., 19, no. 2 (1985): 251–77.

scale back the number of H-2 workers in the East have only resulted in growers' increased use of illegal immigrants. Since penalties against employers
who hire undocumented workers have rarely been enforced on farms, the
undocumented workforce—which is much bigger than the H-2 workforce—functions as a sort of unofficial guestworker program, only without
the housing and prevailing wage guarantees. Both groups can be disciplined
by the threat of deportation. On the occasions when Congress has determined to roll back illegal immigration, it has tended to expand the H-2 program. The relationship forged by growers and the state during the Second
World War persists; the agricultural exception is alive and well.

Ernesto Galarza, Mexican Immigration, and Farm Labor Organizing in Postwar California

STEPHEN PITTI

"If Sherlock Holmes and Dr. Watson were around and could fix their celebrated private eyes on the California scene," the prominent Mexican American activist Ernesto Galarza speculated in 1960, "nothing would intrigue them more than the mysteries of its agricultural labor politics." It was a story of "missing bodies," he wrote, the "murder" of crops, and local workers driven to wandering "in a confusion of unemployment and poverty." The modern-day Moriarty was the government itself, Galarza believed, and he held both elected and appointed officials guilty of reorganizing the region's agricultural labor relations in seemingly criminal ways. In his long career as a political activist in California from the 1940s through the 1970s, this Mexican-born critic struggled hard both to expose the backroom machinations of government officials and to develop a grassroots union movement to counteract their crimes. Targeting the reorganization of agriculture in California in the years after World War II, he argued with policymakers in Washington and Mexico City, lectured to audiences in both the United States and Mexico, wrote more than a dozen articles, and published six books, including the aptly titled *Spiders in the House, Workers in the Fields,* which illustrated how officials in the House of Representatives and other government bodies had helped create the webs of hierarchy that constituted large-scale California agribusiness.[1]

---

[1] Galarza's publications on farm labor include *Spiders in the House and Workers in the Field* (Notre Dame, Ind.: University of Notre Dame Press, 1970); *Merchants of Labor: The Mexican Bracero Story* (Charlotte, S.C.: McNally and Loftin, 1964); *Mexican-Americans in the Southwest,* with Herman Gallegos and Julian Samora (Santa Barbara, Calif.: McNally and Loftin, 1969); *Strangers in Our Fields* (Washington, D.C.: U.S. Section, Joint United States–Mexico Trade Union Committee, 1956); *Alviso* (San Jose, Calif.: Mexican American Community Service

Calling government officials to task was not unusual among twentieth-century agricultural unionists, of course, but unlike most other crusading reformers who set their sights on California agriculture, Galarza understood that at least two national governments—of both the United States and Mexico—had helped to reshape that region since the early 1940s. In places like California, he argued, agricultural economies after World War II reflected strong ties to developments in Mexico, and Galarza's writings about the international nature of those seemingly local political economies have influenced scholars and activists ever since. As a leading voice in the American Federation of Labor in California during the 1940s and 1950s, moreover, he lobbied energetically to reform or end the Bracero Program, an international agreement between the United States and Mexico that orchestrated the temporary migration of millions of contracted Mexican laborers from 1942 until its conclusion in 1964. While most contemporary commentators in the U.S. press considered these contracted immigrants valuable allies in "saving the crops," Galarza carefully documented how the program also had allowed growers in California to keep wages low, displace local workers, and underpay even certified braceros.[2]

That international labor agreement became the focal point of Galarza's attack on the "crimes" of the U.S. and Mexican states during this transitional era, and the presence of contracted braceros in California fields framed his efforts to develop a rural, grassroots civil rights effort in the

---

Agency, 1973); *Tragedy at Chualar* (Santa Barbara, Calif.: McNally and Loftin, 1977); *Farm Workers and Agribusiness in California, 1947–1960* (Notre Dame, Ind.: University of Notre Dame Press, 1977). See also the dozen articles and speeches written between 1944 and 1960, in the Galarza Papers, Department of Special Collections, Green Library, Stanford University, box 1, folder 8.

[2] In addition to the works by Galarza, useful surveys in English of the Bracero Program include Ellis Hawley, "The Politics of the Mexican Labor Issue, 1950–1965," *Agricultural History* 40 (July 1966): 157–76; Richard B. Craig, *The Bracero Program: Interest Groups and Foreign Policy* (Austin: University of Texas, 1971); Otey M. Scruggs, *Braceros, "Wetbacks," and the Farm Labor Problem: Mexican Agricultural Labor in the United States, 1942–1954* (New York: Garland Press, 1988); Kitty Calavita, *Inside the State: The Bracero Program, Immigration, and the INS* (New York: Routledge, 1992); and Manuel García y Griego, "The Importation of Mexican Contract Laborers to the United States, 1942–1964," in *The Border That Joins: Mexican Migrants and U.S. Responsibility*, ed. Peter G. Brown and Henry Shue (Totowa, N.J.: Rowman and Littlefield, 1983), 49–98. The use of terminology to describe residents of Mexican descent in the United States poses a number of difficulties. For the purposes of this essay, I generally follow those proposed by David Gutiérrez which emphasize the formative role of citizenship status in shaping the identities of these residents. The term "ethnic Mexican" is used here as an umbrella term to refer to *all* residents of Mexican descent. "Mexican Americans," however, are those who, by birth or naturalization, are citizens of the United States. "Mexicans" and "*Mexicanos*" are used to designate immigrants from Mexico living in the United States. David G. Gutiérrez, *Walls and Mirrors: Mexican Americans, Mexican Immigrants, and the Politics of Ethnicity* (Berkeley: University of California Press, 1995), 219. The union that Galarza joined after World War II was known in 1948 as the National Farm Labor Union (NFLU), although it changed its name in the early 1950s to the National Agricultural Workers Union. For the purposes of clarity I refer to it in this essay by its former name.

region. While few historians or other commentators have paid attention to Galarza's career as a unionist during the 1940s and 1950s, his prolonged efforts in the context of labor's postwar internationalization would prove extremely influential in California's ethnic Mexican communities by the early 1950s. Although called by one scholar "a prelude to [César] Chávez," Galarza's efforts should not be seen as a mere precursor to the United Farm Workers organization that would blossom in the following decade. Forced (unlike later UFW activists) to contend with the presence of imported braceros in the fields of rural California, Galarza became politically active in Mexico and politicized Mexican cultural nationalism in ways that would not even be attempted by the UFW.[3]

In fact, Galarza's struggles against conservative government "villainy" in the early Cold War period may seem to anticipate patterns of transnational political activism now emerging in the twenty-first century. As scores of commentators have suggested, California's multiracial and multinational history makes that state a fruitful place to analyze themes of growing importance to the United States as a whole. Proposing one starting point for understanding more recent politics in rural areas, this essay in part illustrates the difficulty of organizing a union and confronting federal officials in the context of increased international migration. It is, however, also a story of one union's creative response to those political circumstances. Future generations of rural activists will certainly be pressed to follow Galarza's lead in organizing rural America's growing number of noncitizens whose shifting national allegiances often challenge established social movements in the United States. As he discovered in the late 1940s, both U.S. citizenship and transnational ties to other nations wield great influence on residents of the countryside, and scholarly engagements with those connections may help both to deepen analyses of twentieth-century politics and to fashion more forward-looking responses to social inequalities in the United States.

Wartime Critic

It was in the context of the wartime Bracero Program during the 1940s that Ernesto Galarza first became an internationally recognized spokesperson on U.S.–Mexico relations and Mexican immigration to the United

[3] Donald H. Grubbs, "Prelude to Chavez: The National Farm Labor Union in California," *Labor History* 16, no. 4 (May 1975): 454–55. For a useful survey of Galarza's life, see Joan London and Henry Anderson, *So Shall Ye Reap: The Story of Cesar Chavez and the Farm Workers' Movement* (New York: Thomas Y. Crowell, 1970), 115–40. Galarza's approach to politics breaks the mold that most historians have used to characterize the era's dominant style of political organizing, and he appears in less than a paragraph of Mario García's broad overview of the period, *Mexican Americans: Leadership, Ideology, and Identity, 1930–1960* (New Haven, Conn.: Yale University Press, 1989), 231.

States. Born in Mexico in 1905, Galarza had emigrated to California with his family, like many *Mexicanos* during this era, because of civil war and economic upheaval in his home country. His activities thereafter marked him as virtually unique among California's ethnic Mexican population. As his widely read autobiography *Barrio Boy* suggests, Galarza labored in California fields as a youth, distinguished himself in academic pursuits at an early age, and emerged as one of the few college-educated members of his generation. After completing his Ph.D. at Columbia University during the 1930s, Galarza was hired by the Pan American Union (PAU)—the forerunner of the Organization of American States—to monitor labor relations in the Americas. Since his college days, Galarza had often advocated the development of strong labor unions and registered deep concern about U.S. imperialism in the hemisphere. As a top official in the PAU, he sought to encourage the development of independent, democratic labor organizations throughout the Americas, and he urged the United States to encourage trade unionism and respect labor's right to organize. He therefore argued that the Axis would find few sympathizers if the United States influenced its neighbors to pass legislation similar to the Wagner Act, which had recently assured workers in the United States their own right to bargain collectively in organized unions.[4]

Galarza's interest in Latin American labor issues extended into the agricultural fields of the Southwest as well, and he used his position in the PAU to press the federal government to address anti-Mexican discrimination there. Virtually the only Mexican American holding political office in Washington during these years, he called attention to the segregated conditions that he and many other ethnic Mexicans in the Southwest had faced for generations, showing in the process a clear interest in holding the national state responsible for racial discrimination against local residents. Galarza warned policymakers in Washington that if they failed to improve the living and working conditions of ethnic Mexicans in the region, "Axis agents" who had infiltrated the United States might turn those communities against the Allied war effort. Criticizing both government and union officials in the United States for failing to address patterns of "economic" and racial discrimination against Mexicans in the region, he supported the development of a permanent but expanded Fair Employment Practices Commission that would address complaints by all racial minorities. "When it comes to discrimination, usually based on racial prejudices," he wrote in

---

[4] See Ernest Galarza, "Student File," Occidental College, Los Angeles; Ernest Galarza, *The Roman Catholic Church as a Factor in the Political and Social History of Mexico* (Sacramento, Calif.: The Capital Press, 1928); Carlos Muñoz, Jr., *Youth, Identity, Power: The Chicano Movement* (New York: Verso Press, 1989), 22; Ernesto Galarza, "Mexico and the World War" (M.A. thesis, Stanford University, 1932); and Ernesto Galarza, introduction to *La Junta Nacional de Relaciones del Trabajo* (Washington, D.C.: Oficina de Información Obrera y Social, Unión Panamericana, 1944).

the journal *The Pan American,* "no fine line of distinction is drawn between Negroes, Mexicans, Filipinos, Puerto Ricans and other 'minority groups.'" It was, he argued, the federal government's role to take an activist stance in addressing the racial discrimination he had known first-hand as a former resident of rural California.[5]

Because of his long-standing interest in assisting ethnic Mexican communities in the United States, Galarza also took it upon himself as a wartime PAU official to investigate the workings of the Bracero Program. Joining Carey McWilliams and other liberals during this period, Galarza initially approved of the international agreement because it seemed to promise that both the U.S. and Mexican governments would closely monitor immigrants' wages and working conditions.[6] The promise of government protections had long attracted unionists who bemoaned the tremendous power of growers in western states over their workforces, of course, and this agreement seemed to assure that both governments would take seriously reported violations of bracero contracts. In Galarza's view, moreover, this sort of international agreement might serve as a model in similar efforts to guarantee the rights of other international migrants in Latin America. Convinced that the agreement was an important test case, Galarza left his Washington office to visit over twenty camps in the rural West in 1944 and interview growers, labor contractors, government officials, and imported workers involved in the program.

He reported with disgust that Mexico and the United States had betrayed farmworkers' interests in their administration of the Bracero Program, and he angrily began thereafter to identify the outlines of the "crimes" that he would later imagine required the skills of Watson and Holmes. With considerable emotion, Galarza elaborated his findings in an August 1944 memorandum circulated within the Pan American Union and sent to Mexico's President Avila Camacho. Highlighting the discrimination accorded many braceros, he reported that "some local merchants will not accept Mexican trade" and that other residents of the United States. at times "display[ed] an attitude of hostility toward the Nationals." Galarza borrowed from Good Neighbor rhetoric to argue that such treatment had to be addressed, and he advised government officials that in coming years "the relation of Mexico to the United States after the war, inter-American cooperation, and the Good Neighbor policy will be looked at by the returning workers through a vivid prism of personal experiences." Galarza was troubled by the fact that the government of the United States had not

[5] Along with Galarza, the Democratic senator Dennis Chavez from New Mexico also lived in Washington, and Chavez would continue to serve in that capacity until 1962. Ernesto Galarza, "Pan-American Union Chief Speaks," *The Pan-American* (February 1945): 12–14.

[6] See, for instance, Carey McWilliams, "They Saved the Crops," *The Inter-American* (August 1943): 12–13.

provided imported workers with adequate living conditions and that contracted laborers in practice often enjoyed few of the rights guaranteed by the international contract. Contractual guarantees now seemed to him only "imposing... on paper," and his 1944 memorandum ominously predicted that, through the Bracero Program, the governments of the United States and Mexico were forging a new inter-American relationship that paid little attention to the rights of working people in either country.[7]

Most worrisome to Galarza was the fact that so many braceros reported that they rarely even saw their government representatives, and Galarza therefore concluded that the Mexican government had abandoned its responsibility to protect Mexican citizens living outside of that country's national borders. Because organized labor had been given no role in negotiating or monitoring the agreement in either the United States and Mexico, Galarza further worried, with great prescience, that "the question arises whether this kind of procedure sets a precedent for the future mobilization and migration of labor under government auspices across international boundaries." Instead of addressing contracted workers' grievances, officials commonly appealed to the wartime need for hemispheric unity in order to discourage bracero complaints, thereby turning the Good Neighbor policy into a tool for denying workers their contractual rights. The Mexican consular agents who did visit bracero camps frequently resorted to delivering "patriotic speeches" about the role of these war workers in uniting the two nations, and braceros who insisted on speaking to their government representatives about important matters were often forced to travel to faraway consular offices in Los Angeles, San Francisco, and other cities on their own, always at the risk of being "regarded as agitators" and deported since the international agreement stipulated that braceros could not wander from their workplaces without written permission.[8]

Postwar Unionist

By 1944, Galarza expressed great concern that officials in these neighboring countries had abandoned a vision of hemispheric relations beneficial to working people and were beginning to use the rhetoric of Pan-Americanism to undermine the rights of migrant farmworkers. When the U.S. State Department then organized a coup against Bolivia's trade union movement and president, Galarza declared himself disgusted with politically conservative, probusiness interventions in both the U.S. Southwest

<hr/>

[7] Galarza, "Personal and Confidential Memorandum," Galarza Papers, box 1, folder 8; David Richard Lessard, "Agrarianism and Nationalism: Mexico and the Bracero Program, 1942–1947" (Ph.D. diss., Tulane University, 1984), 131.
[8] Ibid.

and Latin America, "tired of constantly dealing with 'little men behind the big desks' in Washington," and convinced that a revived union movement needed to recapture political influence. With all this in mind, he left Washington in March 1948 and returned to California to work with the National Farm Labor Union, a group that had first made a name for itself in the South and Midwest in the 1930s as the Southern Tenant Farmers Union and had moved west in early 1947 to organize the southern farm workers who had migrated to California in the previous decade.[9]

Prior to Galarza's return to California, NFLU leaders had recently initiated the first union-management confrontation in postwar California agriculture, an action against the mammoth DiGiorgio Corporation in the San Joaquin Valley. In the midst of the nationwide strike wave that rocked urban and rural areas in the immediate aftermath of World War II, union president H. L. Mitchell and organizer Hank Hasiwar had sent a strong anti-Communist message to local workers in the area around Fresno where they started their organizing campaign, positioned themselves against the left wing of the Congress of Industrial Organizations (CIO), and cooperated with Dave Beck and his Teamsters, who also showed interest in organizing workers in agricultural processing industries.[10] Yet these southern white unionists had experienced great difficulty in the fields of racially and nationally diverse California, which were becoming "Latinized" with large numbers of Mexican and Mexican American workers by 1947.

In fact, NFLU organizers in California had done little work at the beginning of their strike to contact local ethnic Mexicans and instead had spent most of their energy mobilizing the area's more familiar southern whites and African Americans by making references to southern culture, sharing southern foods, and singing popular songs from the rural South. While leaders never preached the exclusion of Mexicans from the organization—racial divisions of this sort were dismissed as efforts to divide the working class—most knew and cared little about local "native Americans of Spanish descent," as many mistakenly called them. The union's demands that farmworkers be included under the protections of U.S. citizenship (through an expansion of the Wagner Act and other provisions) may also have contributed to its lack of initial success with local ethnic Mexicans, many of whom were immigrants or the children of immigrants, lived in

---

[9] "Ernesto Galarza, Director of Research and Education," (biographical sketch), at end of 1951, Southern Tenant Farmers Union Papers (hereafter STFU Papers), University of North Carolina, Chapel Hill, reel 36; Mitchell to Milton Plumb, August 9, 1957, STFU Papers, reel 40; Grubbs, "Prelude to Chavez," 454–55. For an introduction to the spirit of reformism during these years, see George Lipsitz, *Rainbow at Midnight: Labor and Culture in the 1940s* (Chicago: University of Illinois Press, 1994).

[10] Bob Hartley to Mitchell, April 29 and May 5, 1947, Galarza Papers, box 7, folder 6.

segregated communities, spoke only Spanish, and considered themselves culturally "Mexican."[11]

It became clear within the first weeks of the DiGiorgio confrontation, however, that ethnic Mexican farmworkers would play a critical role in the NFLU's future, and one union official sympathetic to the Mexican work-force lamented in March 1948 that "I doubt whether we have 50 Mexican members." While all of the braceros working at DiGiorgio when the strike began joined the union's walkout on the first day, government agents re-turned them to work for the next six weeks thanks in part to intimidation by the local sheriff. White unionists' animosity towards these ethnic Mexi-cans and others in the San Joaquin Valley increased when, shortly after the beginning of the strike, the DiGiorgio Corporation shuttled other work-ers of Mexican descent across the union's picket lines. During the thirty-month confrontation, in fact, workers of Mexican descent imported from Texas, from other areas of California, and from across the international border constituted a majority of the reviled "scabs" who crossed union picket lines. Perhaps not surprisingly, some unionists therefore blamed Mexicans for the NFLU's eventual defeat in the struggle for a closed shop at DiGiorgio, and the organization therefore argued strenuously for the need to limit immigration from Mexico to the United States.[12]

Under these conditions, racial violence seemed an imminent possibility as many white members, self-described "citizens of our Country," voiced growing resentment about the Latinization of the farm labor force. Within the ranks of the NFLU, for example, rumors spread "that the company plans to replace all the 'whites' in the ranch with Mexican American em-ployees," that ethnic Mexicans were content to live with low wages, and that Mexican immigrants never supported unions. Some union members began to use the epithets "scab" and "spic" interchangeably, and NFLU leaders hoped that Galarza's arrival would calm these frayed nerves. But while many union members expected Galarza to focus on simply discouraging

---

[11] NFLU meetings traditionally featured songs like "We Shall Not Be Moved" (the official song of the Union), "Roll the Union On" (to the tune of "Polly-Wolly-Doodle All Day"), and the spirituals "No More Mourning," "Swing Low, Sweet Chariot," and "It's A-Me, O Lord." The national conventions ended with the "Ceremony of the Men of the Land," in which "each delegate marches around a large table, picks up a handful of dirt from his native state and mingles it with the soil of all states represented in the meeting." "Report of the Executive Council," January 13, 1947, and Mitchell to the *American Federationist*, December 14, 1947, STFU Papers, reel 32; "Memorandum—Plans for Organization of Agricultural Labor," 1947, STFU Papers, reel 33. See also Galarza, *Spiders in the House*, 18–23, and Walter Goldschmidt, *As You Sow: Three Studies in the Social Consequences of Agribusiness* (Montclair, N.J.: Allanhead, Osmun, 1978), 232.

[12] [Author unknown], "Confidential Memo" (n.d.[1948?]), Galarza Papers, box 9, folder 10; Galarza, *Farm Workers and Agribusiness in California*, 99–105.

"scabism" among ethnic Mexicans, his response to the ethnic Mexicans outside the NFLU was, predictably, more complex.[13]

Beginning in March 1948, Galarza took a prominent role as the NFLU official charged with educating unionists about ethnic Mexicans to discourage such "race prejudice," on the one hand, and with encouraging Mexicans and Mexican Americans to join the union, on the other. Addressing whites already in the union, he consistently stressed that "local" Mexican workers deserved full inclusion into the NFLU and other institutions in the United States, regardless of their citizenship status. "The idea of special work with Mexicans," he assured red-baiters and other potential critics, "is that it should be continued only until in each local good working relations between them and Negroes and Okies" had been achieved. Drawing on his wartime experience, he also educated white unionists about the ways in which the U.S. and Mexican governments contributed to agribusiness coffers in California and perpetuated low wages among rural workers in both countries. As part of his program attacking racial prejudice among rural whites, Galarza urged California unionists to imagine their common cause with ethnic Mexicans "as workers and citizens of the Americas." To illustrate the conditions that prompted many Mexicans to migrate to the United States, he showed white unionists slides of rural conditions in Latin America, believing that those who understood the extent of rural poverty in Latin America would better understand the Mexican immigrant community in California.[14]

[13] Jim Wrightson to Mitchell, March 5, 1948, STFU Papers, Reel 32; *DiGiorgio Strike Bulletin*, no. 20 (March 20, 1948), STFU Papers, reel 32; F. R. Betton to Arthur C. Churchill, October 16, 1948, STFU Papers, reel 34; transcript of interview by Anne Loftis with Hank Hasiwar, November 25, 1975, Anne Loftis Papers, box 1, folder 8, Department of Special Collections, Stanford University. While unionists primarily expressed fear of job competition with Mexicans, they also worried about Asian American workers. The California State Federation of Labor reported that "Numerous rumors have been afloat that efforts were being made to recruit Japanese, Mexicans and Filipinos" as strikebreakers. *DiGiorgio Strike Bulletin*, no. 3 (November 13–15, 1947), STFU Papers, reel 33. "DiGiorgio Strike Faces Crucial Development," *Weekly Newsletter from California State Federation of Labor,* November 19, 1947, STFU Papers, reel 33.

[14] For one example of opposition to Galarza's focus on organizing ethnic Mexicans, see Mitchell to Becker, November 21, 1952, STFU Papers, reel 36. See also Galarza to Mitchell, October 31, 1949, Galarza Papers, box 7, folder 6; Ernesto Galarza, "Mexican–United States Labor Relations and Problems," Galarza Papers, box 1, folder 8; Galarza to Mitchell, July 18, 1948, STFU Papers, reel 34; Ernesto Galarza, "Big Farm Strike: A Report on the Labor Dispute at the DiGiorgio's," *Commonweal,* June 4, 1948, 182. Mitchell's anticommunism, for example, shaped his antipathy toward race-based organizing, as he noted that in Louisiana, the NFLU was competing for workers' loyalties with the Packinghouse Workers: "Another indication of communist domination of UPWA is their constant appeal to the Negroes, not on a trade union basis but on the basis of race alone. The UPWA so-called Anti-Discrimination Program is designed to inflame the Negro worker against the white, just as the White Citizens Councils make their appeals to the prejudices of the white against the Negro." He wrote to Galarza that "I am afraid what the UPWA intends to do with Mexicans is to exploit them as they do the Negro here in the South." Mitchell to Meany, June 18, 1957, STFU Papers, reel 39. Mitchell to Galarza, June 28, 1957, STFU Papers, reel 39.

As he pushed a Pan-American union consciousness among local white farmworkers, Galarza dedicated himself to lobbying the U.S. government on issues of concern to those residents, as well. As the union's director of education, Galarza in fact demanded that government agencies in the United States pay greater attention to the complaints of the region's multi-racial farm labor force. Drawing attention to rural California's declining wages and working conditions in a number of articles published throughout the country, he emphatically echoed his wartime call that the United States establish a better system for monitoring labor rights for both immigrants and citizens of that state. Noting the active support given agribusiness by the officials in California, however, Galarza pressed policymakers in Sacramento to abolish the Farm Placement Service, an agency that played an important role in assigning braceros to growers, and he also went on to attack the U.S. Labor, Justice, and State departments for their roles in the program. Hoping for an improved system of hemispheric labor protections, he argued for the establishment of a binational committee to protect collective bargaining rights among all farmworkers living in California, an international organization that would include both government officials and "full and equal representation for the free trade unions of Mexico and the United States."[15]

In emphasizing the need for these changes, Galarza clearly hoped to leverage U.S. officials' desires for international business cooperation with Mexico as a way to develop new labor protections for migrant farmworkers. Demanding that existing government agencies pay greater attention to the economic poverty and racial discrimination that California farmworkers experienced, he led the NFLU's drive in 1948 to persuade California Governor Earl Warren to follow the lead of Texas and establish a Good Neighbor Commission that would "look into the various forms of exploitation that California workers of Mexican ancestry are subject to." Believing that Warren might fear jeopardizing California's relatively unblemished reputation in Latin America, Galarza told the governor that companies like DiGiorgio practiced racial discrimination that "feeds racial animosity and other un-American attitudes," and "violate[s] systematically the spirit of the Good Neighbor policy."[16]

Echoing the disgust of his 1944 memorandum to the Pan American Union, Galarza also increasingly registered anger after World War II at "the kidnapping of the Good Neighbor Symbolism by those who have shut the door of the House of the Americas on the workers," and he continued to

---

[15] "Talk by Dr. Ernesto Galarza at UFW boycott office," Anne Loftis Papers, box 1, folder 10; H. L. Mitchell to Sindicato Americano Nacional de Trabajadores Agrícolas, March 16, 1949, STFU Papers, reel 34.
[16] Galarza to Mitchell, August 7, 1948, and Mitchell to Warren, 10 August 1948, STFU Papers, reel 34.

believe that officials in Washington would only listen to farmworker complaints if the NFLU developed a base of power in California. Big business had captured control of the federal state, he felt certain, and Galarza complained to H. L. Mitchell in 1953:

> When I am putting in ten days or two weeks in waiting at the church door on Constitution avenue [in Washington] holding a tin cup to these guys, they know godam [*sic*] well that's ten days of less heat they will eventually get from the grassroots. I believe our forces—few as they are—will be poorly used this way.... I have no business going into a meeting in which some sleazy, eviscerated junk fed bureaucratic pimp for the millionaires will blandly lie with me sitting right there.

While H. L. Mitchell attributed such hostility to a "Latin temperament," Galarza continued to prefer working outside of policy circles among ethnic Mexicans in California, understanding first-hand that those residents had a complicated relationship to national identity and civil rights struggles in California. The recently arrived unionist believed that these factors explained the reluctance of ethnic Mexican farm workers to join the NFLU during the DiGiorgio strike, and his discussions with rural residents revealed that ethnic Mexican California farmworkers commonly maintained political concerns distinct from those of the AFL. While some told Galarza about their troubles with police brutality in the late 1940s and early 1950s, for example, others mentioned difficulties with the postwar housing crisis, and still more discussed the lingering presence of segregation in their public schools. Heartened by those conversations, Galarza reported witnessing "much more young leadership than is generally recognized" throughout the state, including the emergence of small groups of Mexican American professionals "active in various community enterprises," and he therefore set out to develop a new movement in California which would reflect those residents' concerns.[17]

To design an approach more attentive to those residents, he instructed other NFLU officials that unionists would have to abandon their trade union structure imported from the South and Midwest. The AFL had long spurned Mexicans and Mexican Americans, Galarza knew, and his meetings with members of Mexican mutual aid societies and *comisiones honoríficas,* influential organizations that promoted the observance of Mexican

[17] *Common Ground* 10, no. 3 (summer 1949); Galarza to Mitchell, January 20, 1953, STFU Papers, reel 37; Mitchell to Hasiwar, December 29, 1952, STFU Papers, reel 36; Mitchell to Becker, March 14, 1952, Galarza Papers, box 7, folder 6. Galarza was familiar with similar political developments among ethnic Mexicans in urban California. In Los Angeles, for example, he reported in 1948 meeting a lawyer who "is particularly interested in fighting police brutality in LA county, concerning which he is going to send me material. I'm convinced that a persistent job with this type of person is quite necessary and not too difficult to get going." Galarza to Mitchell, July 26, 1948, STFU Papers, reel 34.

national holidays, further illustrated to him that a successful union movement in rural California would have to take seriously the distinct political
and cultural concerns of ethnic Mexicans. In part because ethnic Mexicans in California were "moving on several fronts at once—economic organization, political education, civil liberties and the like," Galarza contended that an "orthodox organization technique" was destined to fail and
that the NFLU would need to "keep a balance between workers, young
people, community leaders, store keepers, cafe owners and other types...
who represent the core of [ethnic Mexican] community organization."[18]

Only this sort of partnership between unions and existing ethnic Mexican community groups would attract locals who remembered the AFL's
"historic race policy," he believed, and Galarza struggled to cement a partnership between the NFLU and local ethnic Mexican activists by establishing what he called NFLU "Mexican committees," separate organizations
for Mexicans and Mexican Americans that would work closely with every
union chapter. Also known by their suggestive acronym in Spanish, SANTA
(Sindicato Americano Nacional de Trabajadores Agrícolas), these auxiliaries would provide a connection to existing community groups, participate in the issues that already concerned ethnic Mexicans, and create a
new civil rights movement with the help of Spanish-speaking church leaders and other nonunionists. In the years after they began in early 1948, the
Mexican committees held separate meetings in Spanish, fostered pride in
the *raza mexicana,* and met frequently with other NFLU members to ensure that white unionists would not forget ethnic Mexicans' distinct concerns. Although few records remain documenting the development of the
Mexican committees, former members recall that several dozen chapters
existed around the state by the early 1950s, and in November 1952
Mitchell estimated that twenty-four hundred "Mexican-Americans whose
place of origin was the Imperial [Valley]" had been members. Each local
organization also maintained links with similar committees around the
state with the help of an informational network designed by Galarza.[19]

---

[18] Galarza to Mitchell, July 18, 1948, STFU Papers, reel 34; Galarza to Mitchell, July 26,
1948, STFU Papers, reel 34; Galarza to Mitchell, August 7, 1948, STFU Papers, eel 34; Galarza
to Mitchell, July 5, 1948; and Galarza to Mitchell, July 18, 1948, STFU Papers, reel 34.

[19] In conversations with Galarza, ethnic Mexicans in rural California expressed "fear, left
over from previous wildcat strikes, that they will not receive outside support when and if there
is a major strike." Galarza to Mitchell, July 5, 1948 STFU Papers, reel 34. Galarza, "Supplementary [report]," December 24, 1949, STFU Papers, reel 34. Galarza knew that it was not
only Mexicans who were suspicious of U.S. unions, noting that a longtime Filipino activist in
the Sacramento area was "a bit miffed on the AFL's historic race policy." Galarza, "Supplementary [report]," December 24, 1949, STFU Papers, Reel 34; Galarza to Mitchell, July 5,
1948; Galarza and Hasiwar, "Confidential Memo," February–May 1951, STFU Papers, reel
35. He organized local "Mexican workers" in a given area by first calling "a general public
meeting to explain the general aims of the Union," and then creating "a Mexican organizing

Critics of Two States

Perhaps most importantly, while those organizations attempted to improve race relations between union members, the separate Mexican committees articulated political ideas that pushed the NFLU to embrace Mexican cultural nationalism and to criticize the Mexican government's role in remaking California agriculture. Rather than attempt to rally all farmworkers around a common "Americanism" based in southern culture and the rights of U.S. citizenship, as the NFLU had done prior to Galarza's arrival, these organizations became a vehicle for emphasizing to Spanish-speaking audiences that ethnic Mexican participation in the NFLU was an extension of the long-standing political struggles of the Mexican people. Connecting local union activities with the wider currents in Mexican nationalism, the onetime NFLU member Luis Manríquez remembered that "Galarza's union allowed the Mexican people to be very Mexican [and] gave everybody a sense that we could be *Mexicanos* and also demand our rights as residents of California." The Mexican committees organized in the racially segregated spaces of rural California, and when seeking new recruits, Galarza and other members of these committees focused most of their attention on the bars where local men congregated after work—"the beer joints where the Mexicans seem to do most of their politicking"—and attempted to persuade male patrons that the union would help men protect their families and communities, regardless of citizenship status. Organizers for the Mexican committees encouraged ethnic Mexicans to join the union, for instance, "if you demand an wage adequate to meet your needs as a man and as the father of a family," and Galarza argued that both U.S.–born Mexican Americans and Mexican-born immigrants needed to carry forward Mexico's political legacy "AS MEN FILLED WITH THE SPIRIT OF MEXICO."[20]

That "spirit of Mexico" clearly transcended the U.S.–Mexican border, and NFLU activists used that cultural framework to promote a sense of allegiance to the wider Mexican national community. With slogans such as "Union-Protection-*Patria*," Galarza and others argued that as residents *en el extran-*

committee" of five or six workers who would form the nucleus of a "Mexican committee" within the local union branch. One or two members of the Mexican committee were expected to join the Executive Board and all permanent committees of the union local. Galarza to Mitchell, July 5, 1948, STFU Papers, reel 34; Castro interview, May 14, 1996; interview with Manuel Hurtado, San Jose, April 2, 1996; Mitchell to Galarza, November 26, 1952, STFU Papers, reel 36; Galarza to Mitchell, June 9, 1950, STFU Papers, reel 35.

[20] Interview with Luis Manríquez by the author, San Jose, May 12, 1996; Galarza to Mitchell, August 7, 1948, STFU Papers, reel 34; "Ahora es Cuando Los Trabajadores Agrícolas de California Deben Entrar en el Sindicato Americano Nacional de Trabajadores Agrícolas" (pamphlet), in Galarza Papers, box 8, folder 5; "Anuncio Oficial de la Union de Trabajadores de Rancho A.F. of L. No Sea Usted Esquirol!!!" (December 2, [1948?]), Galarza Papers, box 8, folder 5. See also "Triunfos de la Unión" (flier printed in the Imperial Valley in 1951 or 1952), Galarza Papers, box 8, folder 5.

jero (outside national borders) they remained members of the Mexican "nation." Relying on the political symbols of the 1910 Mexican Revolution, Galarza soon displayed Mexico's national flag to rally *Mexicanos* and Mexican Americans at his meetings, printed union posters with prominent images of Mexico's nationalist iconography, and informed strikebreakers at DiGiorgio and elsewhere that crossing picket lines constituted a betrayal of the Mexican people. Rather than promoting a cultural nationalism divorced from class politics, these residents promoted a vision of *mexicanidad* that marked California agribusiness as a new enemy of the Mexican people, an enemy that even the Mexican government had begun to support. In making sense of the ways in which growers maintained low wages and poor working conditions, for example, Galarza called agribusiness agents in California the new *encomenderos*, a throwback to Mexico's brutal landowners of an earlier period who had once oppressed mestizos, prohibited Mexico from developing in democratic ways, and met popular opposition after Mexican independence. A 1951 organizing pamphlet in the Imperial Valley argued that agribusiness owed much to officials in Mexico City, and that while

The encomiendas of 1551 were granted by the king.

The encomiendas of 1951 are being granted by the Governments [of Mexico and the United States]....

The worker bound to the encomiendas is the contract bracero who cannot force them to comply with his contract.[21]

Cultural nationalism here provided Galarza and other ethnic Mexicans a mode for critiquing the Mexican state's choice to move "back" to institutionalize earlier forms of inequality rather than to promote more enlightened civil rights concerns in the postwar period. The Mexican government's practice of supplying California's "encomenderos" with imported, low-wage Mexican immigrants constituted an act of betrayal of the deeply held ideals of the Mexican people, Galarza and others contended, and members of the Mexican committees stressed that it was the Mexican government that had flooded the California labor market with imported braceros, lowered agricultural wages for all workers in that state, and allowed local agribusiness to exploit both U.S. and Mexican citizens. The NFLU's Mexican committees claimed that officials in Mexico City had sent braceros to California "to share in the misery of their counterparts on this side of the Rio Bravo," and ethnic Mexican unionists in northern and southern California circulated handbills in the 1950s publiciz-

[21]"Anuncio Oficial de la Union de Trabajadores de Rancho A.F. of L. No Sea Usted Esquirol!!!" (December 2, [1948?]), Galarza Papers, box 8, folder 5; "Triunfos de la Unión" (flier printed in the Imperial Valley in 1951 or 1952), Galarza Papers, box 8, folder 5; "Los Encomenderos de 1951" (flier), Galarza Papers, box 8, folder 5.

ing the fact that the Mexican government was paid for each bracero who worked in U.S. fields, what the NFLU called the *"sale of cattle at ten dollars per head."*[22]

While they also drew attention to the culpability of United States officials in bringing about these developments, members of the Mexican auxiliaries emphasized that what they called the Mexican government's "business in brown flesh" signaled that state's conservative turn against both its working-class citizens and the long national tradition of agricultural reform. Calling to mind well-established traditions of agrarian radicalism in Mexico, these unionists clung to the ideals and language of their "imagined" national homeland, contending that officials in Mexico City no longer represented the concerns of the Mexican people. Stressing that the state "burrocracia" had abandoned members of the Mexican nation living both inside and outside Mexico, for example, Galarza further lambasted the Mexican consulate in 1951 for "the economic war being carried out against the resident farm workers of our race" and for putting imported workers "in competition with sons of the same *patria.*" A 1952 strike song from the Imperial Valley further illustrated the Mexican committees' internationalist efforts to oppose the administration of the Bracero Program:

No me tomen por rival
Del bracero contratado
Pero también me hace mal
Que me dejen desplazado
Donde hay trabajo para uno
Les gusta poner de a tres
Así no come ninguno
Y se mueren de una vez.
Y como el gallo en su casa
Sacude su roja cresta
Yo le contaré a mi raza
Las glorias de nuestra gesta.[23]

Do not take me for the rival
Of the contracted bracero
Although it hits me hard

[22] "A $10 dólares por cabeza!," "En Hermosillo están Contratando Braceros," and "Detrás de la Cortina de Humo, Miguel Alemán" (fliers from 1951 or 1952), Galarza Papers, box 8, folder 5; statement of the Sindicato Americano Nacional de Trabajadores Agrícolas, AFL, Bakersfield, January 21, 1949, in Galarza Papers, box 8, folder 5; *El Organizador del Campo,* March 3, 1951 (emphasis in original).
[23] Galarza to Elías Colunga, April 14, 1951, STFU Papers, reel 35; statement of the Sindicato Americano Nacional Agrícola, AFL, Bakersfield, January 21, 1949, Galarza Papers, box 8, folder 5; "Atención, Atención, Atención" (flier), Galarza Papers, box 8, folder 5; "Corrido del Valle Imperial," Galarza Papers, box 19, folder 6.

That they leave me displaced
Where there is only work for one
They want to send three
So that no one will eat
And they will all soon pass away.
And as the rooster in his house
Shakes his red crest
I will tell my people
About the glories of our effort.

Moreover, when Mexican officials showed a periodic hostility to the NFLU's "glorious effort," their official animosity only seemed to prove the conservatism of that nation's ruling party. In July 1949, for example, Mexico's Consul General Salvador Duttant ordered the NFLU to cease using the Mexican flag at union rallies, threatening to sue Mexican members of the union because "your organization not being Mexican has no right whatsoever to the use of the Mexican national colors." Publicizing Duttant's threats, Galarza asked *Mexicanos* and Mexican Americans in California to consider how the consulate could oppose agrarian reform and unionization (which had a powerful legacy in twentieth-century Mexico) in the name of Mexican nationalism. He quickly sent letters to Mexican communities around the state, urging them "to give the Mexican Government all the Chile [*sic*] its been begging for," and Galarza subsequently rallied their anger each time the Mexican government renewed the Bracero agreement.[24]

The language and symbols of Mexican nationalism continued to shape NFLU politics during the 1950s, providing a means for ethnic Mexican unionists to identify and attack the betrayal of Mexican officials, and many members accordingly expressed opposition to the Bracero Program directly to Mexican politicians. Some Mexican farmworkers in the NFLU who were unable to travel to Mexico City made their opposition to Mexican policies heard by picketing Mexican consuls in urban California, while others wrote letters to local Spanish-language newspapers in the state as well as to the press in Mexico City, informing journalists that the Bracero Program represented the betrayal of the Mexican people on both sides of the border. Mexican committee members also frequently participated in, and in some cases helped to organize, the *fiestas patrias*, patriotic celebrations that brought ethnic Mexican workers in rural California together several times a year during the 1950s, and under their direction these events

[24] Telegram from Salvador Duttant, consul general of Mexico, to Galarza, August 5, 1949, Galarza Papers, box 7, folder 6. In 1952, moreover, Galarza wrote Mitchell from the Imperial Valley that "We are keeping up a running fire on the Mexican consuls and Alemán." Galarza to Mitchell, January 19, 1949, STFU Papers, reel 34. Galarza to Mitchell, May 26, 1952, Galarza Papers, box 7, folder 6.

at times also took on an antigovernment tone. In the town of Tracy, at least, Galarza even held NFLU meetings in the hall of the consulate-sponsored *Comisión Honorífica Mexicana* in order to encourage that group to pay greater attention to union issues. In a similar way, Mexican unionists in San Jose and other communities met with consular agents to stress that the Bracero Program violated provisions of the Mexican Constitution of 1917 guaranteeing the right of workers to organize collectively, and Galarza traveled to Mexico on a number of occasions to voice these same complaints. With the abuses of that founding document in mind, he also wrote politicians in the United States. that "there should be no restriction on the right of collective bargaining by Mexican Nationals. They have this right in Mexico and no international agreement should abrogate it."[25]

Recruiting Braceros

While members of the Mexican committees struggled to influence consular agents in California and policymakers in Mexico, Galarza also emphasized that braceros had to be included in the NFLU's ranks in order to counterbalance the influence of agribusiness interests on the Bracero Program. As with the unionization of local ethnic Mexican workers in California, Galarza developed this effort against the interests of a Mexican state that seemed intent on denying contracted workers the right to join unions in the United States. By establishing a closed shop in California agriculture that braceros would enter as union members, however, the NFLU hoped to wield some control over when and where the program's administrators would send certified immigrant workers. But involving braceros was a tall order—a daunting task in part because the Mexican and United States governments dissuaded those immigrants from political activities. As they had during World War II, Mexican government officials in the 1950s used the language of "Good Neighborliness" to instruct braceros that they "represent Mexico and should behave," and some contracted workers who accordingly worried about deportation spurned union outreach efforts and insisted instead that

---

[25] Castro interview, May 14, 1996; Galarza to Mitchell, September 11, 1952, STFU Papers, reel 36; Galarza to Mitchell, January 17, 1951, and May 8, 1951, STFU Papers, reel 35; "Atenta Invitación" (flier), August 11, 1951, Galarza Papers, box 8, folder 5; "Statement of the National Farm Labor Union on the Importation of Agricultural Workers from Mexico," June 4, 1948, STFU Papers, reel 32; Galarza to Bob Jones, November 28, 1950, STFU Papers, reel 35. On the Mexico City press, see Galarza to Mitchell, January 1954, STFU Papers, reel 37. Galarza wrote Mitchell from Mexico City in 1951 that "I have been in touch with several deputies (congressmen) some are old friends.... We can have some speeches in Congress if we want them." Galarza to Mitchell, February 4, 1951, STFU Papers, reel 35. Galarza to Bob Jones, November 28, 1950, STFU Papers, reel 35. National Farm Labor Union press release, June 4, 1948, STFU Papers, reel 33.

"we came here to work." The cultural geography of California agriculture also mitigated against NFLU efforts to involve braceros. Most imported workers during the 1950s never even saw a union organizer, in part because their government sent them to rural labor camps far from main roads and other settlements, and Galarza later regretted that in many cases "we couldn't get to them. I lost track of the number of times I was thrown out of [a] camp talking with braceros."[26]

But because braceros were hardly "subservient and submissive workers," Galarza believed that their ongoing acts of protest against both growers and government officials—the hidden transcript developing in the context of labor's internationalization—could be channeled into the NFLU. As he later remembered,

> the conversations in the camps, the work stoppages in the fields, the desertions, the violations which were obvious even to casual observers, the private legal actions by a few braceros, the quantity of mail addressed to their consuls, the pilgrimages of men from their camps to nearby towns in search of advice from anyone who would listen to them – all were symptoms of a distress which was not officially recorded.

Optimistic about braceros' interest in unionization, Galarza here noted that government disinterest in farmworker complaints might help the union effort by compelling contracted immigrants to seek aid from the NFLU. Writing H. L. Mitchell in the late 1950s, he therefore announced with delight that "I am told all over the place that the braceros themselves want to join the union because they simply cannot get compliance service from the consuls or anybody else," and his conversations with them allowed Galarza to encourage antistatist, pro-union sentiments among at least some contracted braceros.[27]

As he aimed to internationalize the membership base of the NFLU by involving braceros, Galarza also sought to bring together the U.S. and Mexican labor movements in order to contest the conservative tendencies of national policymakers. Ever attentive to Pan-American labor issues, Galarza argued that the organizing of Mexican immigrants in California would strengthen the AFL's influence in Latin America by providing a human bridge to distant unions in Mexico. Envisioning the West's agricultural industries as a natural point of cooperation for the hemisphere's labor movements, he organized a series of meetings between high-ranking AFL officials and representatives of Mexican unions between 1948 and

---

[26] Galarza to Bob Jones, November 28, 1950, STFU Papers, reel 35; Galarza, "N. Misc." (handwritten notes), September 15, 1955, Galarza Papers, box 3, folder 1; "Talk by Dr. Ernesto Galarza at UFW boycott office," Anne Loftis Papers, box 1, folder 10.

[27] Galarza, interview with nine nationals in Terminous, October 20, 1955, Galarza Papers, box 18, folder 7; Galarza quoted in Sam Kushner, *Long Road to Delano* (New York: International Publishers, 1975), 101; Galarza to Mitchell, June 22, 1957, STFU Papers, reel 39.

1957. Galarza planned the first such occasion for October 1948, an event in Laredo, Texas in which Galarza acted as translator and sponsored a resolution that Mexican immigrants be allowed to join U.S. unions without fear of deportation. At his urging, the NFLU agreed that its locals would automatically recognize all braceros who were already affiliated with Mexican unions, both sides called for binational union involvement in the administration of the Bracero Program, and labor officials from Mexico and the United States declared their opposition to "discrimination based on Mexican nationality and call[ed] for equal conditions of employment regardless of nationality."[28]

Despite these proclamations, it soon became clear that most national labor leaders at the meetings remained unwilling to push for such radical reform of the Bracero Program. Increasingly frustrated that few unionists in either country had committed resources to cross-border organizing projects, Galarza complained bitterly about Serafino Romualdi, the AFL's Latin American representative, who seemed too timid a negotiator in meetings with Mexican unionists. He also expressed anger that the Confederation of Mexican Workers' Secretary-General Fidel Velázquez feared that opposing the administration of the labor agreement would imperil his union's relationship with Mexican government officials, a charge that likened the Mexican unionist to corrupt AFL labor bureaucrats equally entrenched in U.S. policy circles. Noting the pact between the CTM and Mexico's ruling political party, Galarza called Velázquez "a smooth guy who is out for number 1. He's a politician primarily and what he does will depend in good part on what the government will allow." In subsequent years and months, Velázquez often did not respond to Galarza's letters, and Galarza predicted before one meeting in Mexico City that "the Mexicans [union officials] will... do their usual number of defending the government's laxness," and "are going to do precisely nothing about protecting the bracero." Years later, Galarza angrily remembered that the union movement in Mexico had already become "part of the political machinery of the state and so you see secretaries [and] presidents of unions are rewarded by seats in Congress."[29]

Rather than relying on Mexico's mainstream labor movement, Galarza attempted to work closely with the Alianza de Braceros Nacionales de México, a small organization based in Mexico City that had attempted in-

[28] Ernesto Galarza, "They Work for Pennies," *American Federationist* (April 1952): 29. See also "Memorandum from Ernesto Galarza, Subject: A New Approach to Latin American Relations" (1954), STFU Papers, reel 38; Galarza, "Report on Activities," January 6, 1949, STFU Papers, reel 35; Galarza, "Move Against Illegal Importation of Agricultural Workers to the United States," Galarza Papers, box 1, folder 8.

[29] "Supplementary Report, 1954–1955," STFU Papers, reel 39; see, too, the letters written in January 1949, STFU Papers, reel 34; Galarza to Mitchell, April 29, 1953, STFU Papers, reel 37; Galarza to Mitchell, June 17, 1953, STFU Papers, reel 37; Galarza to Frank Noakes, June 3, 1956, STFU Papers, reel 39; Galarza to Mitchell, March 11, 1957, STFU Papers, reel 42; Joe García, "Solidarity Forever.... Report on the Conference of the Mexican and American

termittently since World War II to unionize these certified emigrants before they left Mexico. The small number of braceros who joined either the NFLU or the Alianza were automatically made members of the other organization, but Galarza remained frustrated with this arrangement, aware that the Alianza did not wield much influence in Mexico. Despite the lack of strong support in either country, Galarza helped members of local Mexican committees and imported Mexican workers to form coalitions with one another in the 1950s, and dozens of braceros joined the National Farm Labor Union in the Salinas and Imperial Valleys during these years.[30]

The "delicate" compacts between these two national labor movements and their respective governments made the NFLU's work in California much more difficult throughout the 1950s. With little support from top officials in either country for Galarza's efforts, the few successful cases of bracero unionization often represented a tremendous investment of his time and energy. In the Imperial Valley during the early 1950s, for example, he met secretly with braceros after work and passed them small slips of paper explaining the union's interest in defending their rights as contract workers. When a group of braceros there joined the NFLU and were subsequently targeted for deportation in 1952, Galarza hid these men in an El Centro hotel, trying without success to force the U.S. government to issue a direct statement confirming the right of braceros to join unions in California, until agents of the Department of Labor arrived. After approximately one hundred of the four hundred braceros working near Salinas joined his organization in September 1952, Galarza confronted Mexican American foremen in the area who began to tell braceros that "they can't join a union" and that their involvement would lead to deportation. And when on another occasion a local growers' association dispersed immigrant "troublemakers" to work in other parts of the state, Galarza paid for one of the braceros, Francisco Cano, to go instead to Washington in order to publicize his story. Borrowing Galarza's only hat for his trip across the country, Cano made the pages of the *San Francisco Chronicle* and became a topic of discussion on California's Spanish-language radio stations, but the Mexican consulate in Fresno attempted to frighten Cano upon his return to the state by asking "who sent him" to Washington, calling him a "Wandering Jew," and telling him "he had no right to apply for membership [or] seek help from an American Union." With little support from

---

Union Leaders Held in Mexico City, December 14, 15, 16, 1953, extracts from *The Industrial Worker*," STFU Papers, reel 37; "Talk by Dr. Ernesto Galarza at UFW boycott office," Anne Loftis Papers, box 1, folder 10.

[30] Minutes of the First California Council of Agricultural Unions Meeting, September 14–15, 1951, STFU Papers, reel 36. See the extensive correspondence regarding the Alianza in Galarza Papers, box 50, folder 3; Galarza to Dawes, October 2, 1951, STFU Papers, reel 36.

other union officials in either country, however, few policymakers even heard Galarza's protests.[31]

Demanding State Controls

Despite considerable interest among California's ethnic Mexicans in joining a farm labor movement, Galarza never found the success he anticipated in organizing either braceros or "local" ethnic Mexicans long resident in the state by the early 1950s. Most importantly, the conservative ties between AFL and CTM officials and their national states left Galarza scrambling for resources and paying for many organizing trips out of his own pocket, and by 1955 the impoverished NFLU made Galarza the lone official charged with "servicing 17 locals from Mexicali to the Oregon border." Correctly or not, Galarza continued to interpret his union's financial desperation as a sign of the AFL's conservative pact with the state and federal governments. He charged that the California State Federation of Labor, for example, had taken a less than accommodating stance toward farm labor unionization because those union leaders were afraid of disrupting the "delicate 'relationships'" which they had established in Sacramento. And as the Bracero Program continued to displace local farmworkers, rural California's tremendous economic instability also presented great difficulties for Galarza's unionization efforts. The arrival of contracted braceros continued to displace more established workers from local employment, for example, and regional cities such as San Jose and Los Angeles became the new homes of thousands of urbanizing farmworkers during the 1950s, including members of Mexican committees who expressed regret about leaving their fellow unionists behind.[32]

Faced with these difficult conditions and with little support from labor unions in either country, Galarza and others in the NFLU argued for a new type of state intervention, this time to control the arrival of "illegal" immigrants who seemed to threaten the stability of local labor markets. Following migration patterns established by state-certified braceros since the early 1940s, undocumented workers were flocking to California at extraordinary rates by the early 1950s to seek agricultural employment. In

---

[31] Galarza to Mitchell, May 8, 1951, STFU Papers, reel 35; Galarza to Mitchell, September 2, 8, and 11, 1952; and "notes on Francisco Cano," September 15, 1952, STFU Papers, reel 36.

[32] "Talk by Dr. Ernesto Galarza at UFW boycott office," Anne Loftis Papers, box 1, folder 10; Galarza to Mitchell, December 10, 1957, STFU Papers, reel 40. On the commitment of the AFL and AFL-CIO to organizing ethnic Mexican workers during this period, see Juan Gómez-Quiñones, *Mexican American Labor, 1790–1990* (Albuquerque: University of New Mexico Press, 1994), 208; Leo Grebler, Jean W. Moore, and Ralph C. Guzmán, *The Mexican American People* (New York: The Free Press, 1970), 90; Galarza, *Farm Workers and Agribusiness in California*, 243.

his effort to stop this trend, Galarza and other members of the Mexican committees rather ironically found common cause with official government rhetoric in Mexico City about the departure of that country's so-called "wetbacks" who left without their government's permission. Many officials and pundits in Mexico City had long viewed this "traffic" as a threat to Mexico's future, and labor unionists and intellectuals there had worried since the 1920s that emigration drained their country of labor power and other necessary resources. In 1929 Galarza had also called upon the Mexican government to play a role in controlling this exodus, and he continued to make this case as a union official in the years after World War II.[33]

Driven by a concern for labor markets in California, Galarza argued that stopping illegal border crossing was critical for the development of the political Left in Mexico. Convinced that potential critics of the Mexican state fled that country to work in the United States instead of investing their energies in domestic reform, Galarza pushed for both greater border regulation and widespread deportations as a way to change "policy in Mexico that created such terrible poverty conditions that the wetback was a natural product of this burgeoning Mexican capitalism." In Galarza's view, the Mexican government would only address the rural poverty that caused migration to the United States if that country ceased to be a convenient "safety valve" for releasing political pressure against the state. Migration was, as he later argued in his 1964 study *Merchants of Labor,* "a failure of roots" attributable to Mexican government policies that had favored exporting labor rather than developing new industries and improving agricultural production, and he argued for restricting immigration in order to force the governments of both countries to be more responsive to the needs of their rural inhabitants.[34] Deportation drives and border enforcement seemed a critical first step, and with few government agencies actively addressing farmworker poverty in either rural California or Mexico, Galarza therefore attempted to make the Immigration Service his ally by calling on that agency to create the conditions that would allow the Mexican people to reform their own state.[35]

[33] Galarza emphasized the need for government control of "the chaos of the seasonal labor supply" in his 1929 presentation to the National Conference of Social Work. Ernest Galarza, "Life in the United States for Mexican People: Out of the Experience of a Mexican," *Proceedings of the National Conference of Social Work* (Chicago: University of Chicago Press, 1930), 399–404.
[34] Galarza informed unionists in the United States in 1954, for instance, that "The President of Mexico, in his last message to Congress on the state of the Union, frankly admitted that his country considers this situation as the answer to the fact that the Mexican population increases at the rate of 800,000 a year." "A Report from Ernesto Galarza: Where the Labor Movement Stands with Respect to Infiltration by Wetbacks and Contract Workers Imported from Mexico, October 22, 1954," STFU Papers, reel 38. The quote is from Galarza, *Merchants of Labor,* 14.
[35] Galarza supported these deportation drives for reasons different from those expressed by many other Mexican Americans who also supported "closing the border" at this time.

Because of heightened concerns about both regional labor markets and Mexico's political future, Galarza began energetically to summon U.S. immigration agents to help keep uncertified emigrants in Mexico. Most members of the Mexican committees likely followed Galarza's lead primarily out of a concern for local jobs. The farmworker Sal Ortega, for example, wrote in 1950 from the rural community of Heber that he had gone "all over the vall[ey] for about a month looking for work and couldn't find it," concluding his letter with a request that Galarza "for god's sake please prevent this situation by sending these wets and contract nationals to their own country to get out of our way so that's the best way to prevent bad situations, then wages will be put up some, treatments will be better to all." Later that year, Galarza noted with interest that "in California it is the local, resident Mexican farm worker who has taken the lead in opposing the 'wetback,'" and two hundred ethnic Mexican residents of Delano therefore sent a petition to the INS in December 1951 requesting the removal of undocumented *Mexicanos* from their area, including with their demand "a list of the places where the local people believe wetbacks to be." Capitalizing on growing cold war concerns about national security, Galarza subsequently distributed the following form letter to all union locals in the state to make it easier for members to report suspected "wetbacks" to the Immigration Service:

Dear Sir:

Members of this Local have reported to the Executive Board that persons who entered this country illegally are working, living or generally being harbored on the premises indicated below.

It is our understanding that the Alien Registration Act of 1940, as amended by the National Internal Security Act of 1950, required the registration and fingerprinting of these persons.

Since we have reason to believe that these requirements have not been met in the present case; and further since it appears that the presence of these unregistered aliens suggests fraudulent arrangements to violate Federal laws, we request that the Department of Justice investigate these premises without delay to the end that the Alien Registration Act and the National Internal Security Act be complied with.

Sincerely yours,

_____

President

Compare, for example, Galarza's international concerns with those of the American G.I. Forum during these years. See American G.I. Forum of Texas and Texas State Federation of Labor, *What Price Wetbacks?* (Austin: G.I. Forum of Texas, 1954). See also Gutiérrez, *Walls and Mirrors*, 152–78.

The widespread deportation drives in California that followed the NFLU's efforts—what INS Commissioner Joseph Swing called "Operation Wetback"—sent hundreds of thousands of captured undocumented immigrants (and untold numbers of U.S. citizens) to Mexico. This seems to have been a price that Galarza was willing to pay in order to restrict the agricultural labor market and change the politics of rural Mexico, but it also marked a bitter denouement to the NFLU's ongoing efforts to build a transnational social movement uniting farmworkers in the U.S. and Mexico during this period.[36]

"Re-Stating" the Case

Contradictory though it may seem, the story of Galarza's involvement in the agricultural politics of 1940s and 1950s California reveals critical if little-studied trends in rural history. Perhaps most obviously, the NFLU's work illustrated the multiracial nature of the U.S. countryside, and Galarza certainly recognized the importance of Asian Americans, Latinos and African Americans to nineteenth- and twentieth-century developments throughout the rural United States. Galarza also knew that more than one nation-state helped to control the fate of those rural Americans, and his union organizing work raised difficult questions about the extent to which the Mexican government was helping to redefine labor relations in California. Like other observers familiar with that state, Galarza came to understand that local political battles over agriculture remained in many ways mysterious, often violent, and just the stuff that required the ingenuity of Sherlock Holmes to understand by the 1940s.

Due to renewed international labor migrations from Mexico, the NFLU's struggles also came to illustrate the importance of distinct political identities among California's rural workers. Hemispheric economic integration reshaped the "contradictions of ethnic politics" for Mexicans and Mexican Americans during the immediate postwar era, and Galarza began to combat agribusiness's cozy relationship to both Washington and Mexico City by building a new social movement that would capture the "spirit" of an inclusive and antistatist Mexican cultural nationalism. With Mexico's rural past and future in mind, members of the NFLU's Mexican committees therefore came to be among the first post–World War II Californians to make strong political claims against the Mexican state as members of a broader, diasporic

---

[36] Sal Ortega to Galarza, March 11, 1950, Galarza Papers, box 10, folder 4; Galarza to Beth Biderman, July 25, 1950, Galarza Papers, box 12, folder 4; blank letter on NFLU stationary (n.d.), Galarza Papers, box 8, folder 5. The best general study of the deportations of the 1950s remains Juan Ramón García, *Operation Wetback: The Mass Deportation of Mexican Undocumented Workers in 1954* (Westport, Conn.: Greenwood Press, 1980).

Mexican "nation" in California. These trends have continued in the U.S. countryside. More recently, for example, Mixtec immigrants from southern Mexico have fashioned their own political demands out of a growing sense that common indigenous ties link them to other Indians' rural struggles in Latin America, and in the process those residents have elaborated an antistatist politics of their own. In the case of NFLU and Mixtec efforts, the circulation of the dominant political symbols of twentieth-century Mexico and the claims to indigenous political rights certainly ought to remind scholars that a multitude of agrarian traditions have influenced the modern countryside in the twentieth-century United States.[37]

While rural Californians in the NFLU and similar organizations have therefore made transnational political demands since the 1940s, others have opposed that trend by reasserting the primacy of U.S. national borders and the sanctity of its imagined national culture. Rejecting regional visions of a working-class coalition *sin fronteras* (without borders), these movements have favored a language of "alien" exclusion that privileges U.S. citizenship as a basis for making political claims. The attractions of such an approach remain strong in part because of the continuing power of the federal state in rural America, but new trends also suggest that such restrictionism may not retain its popularity in the countryside for long. In fact, the weekly arrival of thousands of new foreign-born residents, the rapid institutionalization of the North American Free Trade Agreement, and the greater ethnic diversity of the AFL-CIO seem in some ways ready to challenge more xenophobic political traditions. We might therefore imagine that if Holmes and Watson returned to "fix their celebrated eyes" on rural America in the year 2020, they might discover even greater numbers of immigrants involved in rural labor unions, and Galarza himself might return to learn that new generations of activists were also drawing on imagined ties to other homelands as a basis for political organizing in the United States. While rural political organizers will no doubt remain concerned to influence U.S. policymakers in the twenty-first century, Galarza's activist legacy will also continue to urge rural Americans to develop more sophisticated and transnational approaches to the countryside in the age of modern states.

[37] Gutiérrez, *Walls and Mirrors,* 117–51.

PART 3

Constructing the Modern State

Accounting for Change

Farmers and the Modernizing State

DEBORAH FITZGERALD

Between 1910 and 1940, the way that American farmers operated their farms changed definitively. In 1910 most American farmers were small-scale, used animals for power, relied on family labor, produced for subsistence as well as regional markets, and were very lightly capitalized. By 1940 farmers had larger farms and more output, used machines such as trucks, tractors, and combines, and produced for international rather than local markets. But while most scholars of agriculture can agree that these changes occurred, virtually no one has explained why this change occurred—why, in other words, farmers "become modern." The observation that it happened is not the same as an explanation for how and why it happened. Economic historians argue that farmers made these changes because it was in their economic self-interest to do so. It just made sense, they argue, for a farmer to acquire more land, or replace his horse with a tractor. They suggest that, as businessmen, farmers had to consider the bottom line, and smart farmers were eager to invest in improving their productive capacity.[1]

But while an economic interpretation aptly describes most farms in 1940, it does little to explain the ragged and uneven pace at which farmers made such changes after World War I, or the marked differences between farmers in different parts of the country, or those with different farm products or economic circumstances. And it certainly does not explain why farmers changed their minds and their practices. Indeed, for many farmers it made little sense to become modern in the 1920s. Most farmers did not have the money or the credit to expand their farms, even if they had wanted to, be-

[1] See, for example, Jeremy Atack and Fred Bateman, *To Their Own Soil: Agriculture in the Antebellum North* (Ames: Iowa State University Press, 1987).

cause of the severe farm depression immediately following the war. In many rural areas credit was scarce or nonexistent, markets for farm products were poor, and prices were high. Tractors were not standardized, and other sorts of machines such as combines and even heavy trucks were not much beyond the experimental stage until the late 1920s. There were no reliable repairmen, company-trained mechanics, or spare parts to support the new industry. Indeed, most farmers who bought machines kept their horses, partly for backup power, partly for doing jobs that machines such as tractors were not very good at, and partly for the company.[2]

What happened on American farms in the early twentieth century, and particularly in the 1920s, was that farmers were persuaded by urban leaders, bankers, and emerging professionals in engineering and economics to industrialize their farms. Experts observed that other sources of American productivity, such as factories, and other workforces, such as industrial laborers, had at last been tamed and rationalized by scientific and technological means and methods, and they thought that farmers should follow suit. Innovations such as scientific management, the moving assembly line, standardized parts manufacturing, the use of high-speed tool steel, and specialization in both product and work assignments, had transformed industrial production and, it seemed to many, could be adapted more or less to agricultural production. As economist E. G. Nourse put it, "the essential features of economic organization which have brought efficiency into industrial pursuits must be incorporated into agriculture." While the specific correlations between factory and farm might have seemed obscure, many engineers wondered: why couldn't farmers make oranges or wheat or bacon like Ford made cars or Remington made typewriters? Particularly for investors who had little exposure to farm life, such a proposition made great sense.[3]

World War I was an important hinge point for American farmers, marking what turned out to be a crucial separation between the traditional, prewar farm and the proto-industrial, postwar farm. As prices for agricultural goods rose, farmers found it profitable to invest in more land to produce more goods, which found a ready market abroad. The critical shortage of some commodities, such as wheat, encouraged farmers to break ground further

[2] Hal Barron's fine study *Mixed Harvest: The Second Great Transformation in the Rural North, 1870–1930* (Chapel Hill: University of North Carolina Press, 1997), captures the sense of this shift but focuses largely upon the markets and business elites rather than technological innovations and ideologies. David Danbom has also addressed such questions in his excellent *The Resisted Revolution: Urban America and the Industrialization of Agriculture, 1900–1930* (Ames: Iowa State University Press, 1979) and *Born in the Country* (Baltimore: Johns Hopkins University Press, 1995). For tractors see Robert C. Williams, *Fordson, Farmall, and Poppin' Johnny* (Urbana: University of Illinois Press, 1987).

[3] E. G. Nourse, "The Revolution in Farming," *Yale Review* 8 (October 1918): 93; Raymond Olney, "The Farm Power House: A Factory Idea," *Power Farming*, November 1917, 7; David Hounshell, *From the American System to Mass Production* (Baltimore: Johns Hopkins University Press, 1984).

west and north, in places that presented ecological conditions quite different from those faced by farmers in other regions. In addition, the war created serious shortages of farm laborers; many of the men on the home front
found that they could earn better wages in the cities than on the farm. But
at the end of the war, farmers discovered that the prosperity of the last ten
or fifteen years marked, not the beginning of stability and abundance as they
had thought, but rather an anomalous blip in their precarious lives. With
the closure of foreign agricultural markets and abruptly falling prices for
their goods, farmers found themselves dropping into an economic abyss that
would last through the 1920s. Farm bankruptcies were the most visible and
wrenching result, as farmers found themselves holding massive amounts of
grain and livestock that could not be sold, and facing as well bank payments
for the land they had bought to increase production during the war.[4]

The resulting wave of farm foreclosures had several effects that were important in rearranging the rural landscape and in establishing a relationship between the banks, the farm population, and the academic departments at state universities. First, when farmers lost their farms through
foreclosure, the farms themselves reverted to the banks or insurance companies repossessed them. Bankers did not particularly want to own hundreds of abandoned farms, especially in a dead market, and were thus
forced into thinking about how to manage many disparate farms with a
minimum of effort and cash; indeed, these institutions were almost acci-
dentally at the forefront of the drive to rationalize and standardize farms.
Second, recent graduates of the agricultural colleges, especially students in
farm economics, found that the crisis among rural financial institutions
provided them with an employment opportunity. Many found attractive
positions working for the banks and insurance companies as managers of
the abandoned farms, an experience that provided valuable data for their
academic mentors. Similarly, young agricultural scientists found that abandoned and repossessed farms were virtual laboratories for studying different agricultural methods and practices, sites for comparing, e.g., animals
versus machines in harvesting, or the cost of production on a big farm versus a small farm, or the income differences between raising oats and corn.[5]

[4] The classic work on the postwar farm depression is James Shideler, *Farm Crisis, 1919–1923*
(Berkeley: University of California Press, 1957).

[5] C. L. Holmes, "Prospective Displacement of the Independent Family Farm by Larger
Farms or Estate Management," *Journal of Farm Management* 11 (April 29, 1929): 227–47; "Will
Build Up North Dakota Farms," *Commercial West* 56 (October 19, 1929): 19; "Are We Coming
to Corporation Farming?" *Power Farming*, February 1927, 5, 9; E. H. Taylor, "How Many Farms
Can One Man Run?" *Country Gentleman* 93 (October 1928): 3–4, 120, 123; Wayne Gard,
"Agriculture's Industrial Revolution," *Current History* 34 (September 1931): 853–57; Robert
Stewart, "Mass Production on the Farm," *New Republic* 59 (June 17, 1927): 230–32; Stewart,
"When a Bank Turns Farmer," *Journal of the American Bankers' Association* (February 1929):
726–27, 816.

Urban investors and rural leaders were forced by the relentless nature of the agricultural depression to consider how agriculture might be reconstituted. Some felt that the federal government should enact farm policies that fixed the price that farmers received for their commodities; the McNary-Haugen Bill was an unsuccessful attempt to achieve this parity price. Still others felt that farm practice itself should change, and that farmers should follow new, more modern models of production. One such model in the early 1920s was the factory, which, thanks to Henry Ford and Frederick Taylor, had been rationalizing and standardizing both processes and employees for about ten years. Many commentators agreed with Charles O'Neal that "it is a stupendous fallacy to hold that farming can only be conducted independently by millions of individuals, each struggling to eke out a bare living under the most expensive methods of production." Indeed, those who looked at farming simply as an industrial and managerial problem could consider unorthodox solutions. For example, quite a few American farmers and agricultural leaders were intrigued by the Soviet collective farm, which sprang to life in 1928. To those who went to the Soviet Union to assist, the Soviet farms were attractive not for their political novelty, but rather for the giant experiment in applying rational management techniques to farming they represented.[6]

In trying to understand, then, what happened on farms in the 1920s, we need to consider both the large, national phenomena such as economic differences between city and farm, the war, international markets, and legislative politics, as well as the small, local stories that illustrate how a revolution like this one played out in real time. How did the facts, theories, and models of scientific and technical elites actually make their way from the laboratories and boardrooms and into the kitchens of farm families who each year decided which of their farm practices they would retain, and which they would abandon? What was the "framework of persuasion" by which ordinary people were inclined to change the way they did things, and in particular to adopt a product or practice that was developed or promoted by a rationalizing elite? Farmers have always made choices about which farming practices to follow according to their own circumstances, needs, and beliefs. But the transformation that began in the 1920s created a new context of decision making for farmers. While farmers were free to adopt or reject new innovations such as tractors and combines, cost accounting, or expanded farm size, the consequences of these decisions became more sharply defined.

Accounting for the changes that farmers made in the 1920s and beyond requires that we move past economic analyses of markets and productivity,

[6] On the ill-fated McNary-Haugen Bill, see Gilbert C. Fite, *George N. Peek and the Fight for Farm Parity* (Norman: University of Oklahoma Press, 1954), and David Hamilton's brief but very helpful remarks in his *From New Day to New Deal* (Chapel Hill: University of North Carolina Press, 1991), 20–21. See Charles D. O'Neal, "Solving the Farm Problem," *Manufacturer's Record* 90 (August 26, 1926): 67–69; Shideler, *Farm Crisis.*

although these are crucial, to a recognition that the twentieth-century transformations were fundamentally scientific and technological. This scientific and technological dimension of rural life was apparent not only in the things farm families bought and used in productive and recreational activities, but in the very way their worlds were structured and their choices defined. In its most fundamental form, this dimension refers to what James Scott calls "a high modernist ideology,... best conceived as a strong, one might even say muscle-bound, version of the self-confidence about scientific and technological progress, the expansion of production, the growing satisfaction of human needs, the mastery of nature (including human nature), and above all, the rational design of social order commensurate with the scientific understanding of natural laws." As farmers tried to sort out for themselves what parts of modernity they wanted, business and the state plowed ahead, transforming rural America into a legible countryside.[7]

Quantifying Farm Success

Social change in early twentieth-century America frequently was set in motion by emerging professional elites. Particularly where scientific and engineering experts have been concerned, members of the first generation have tended to cast about for a meaty social, economic, or cultural problem that would respond to the new techniques and ideas such experts offered, not coincidentally providing such experts with the gleam of respectable and incontrovertible authority. In the 1910s and 1920s, agriculture was dominated by the agricultural economists and engineers, and they carried the high modernist message most forcibly. Both groups were trained in economics or mechanical engineering rather than agriculture per se, and both wanted to graft the general principles of those disciplines onto the more mundane problems of agriculture. Thus, the agricultural economists would attend to the urban, industrial issues that shaped national and international markets and trends, and would develop the theories that accounted for their observations. Similarly, good engineering practice was based on evaluating specific cases and shaving off the idiosyncratic and particular dimensions, leaving those elements that were more or less similar, and then abstracting these similarities into general principles and recommendations. An agricultural expert would never get anywhere, so the logic went, by always being focused on specific crops, soil types, horse breeds, disc plow designs, and so

---

[7] See, e.g., James A. Henretta, "Families and Farms: *Mentalités* in Preindustrial America," *William and Mary Quarterly*, 3d ser., 35 (1978): 3–32; James C. Scott, *Seeing Like a State: How Certain Schemes to Improve the Human Condition Have Failed* (New Haven, Conn.: Yale University Press, 1998), 4; David Harvey, *The Condition of Postmodernity: An Enquiry into the Origins of Social Change* (Oxford: Basil Blackwell, 1989).

forth. And when new agricultural economists and engineers looked around for models of rational, predictable, and prosperous production practices in the late 1910s and early 1920s, they often looked beyond the chaotic farm toward the apparently serene and rational factory, and particularly to Fordism and Taylorism.[8]

The agricultural economists who flooded the U.S. Department of Agriculture (USDA) and the agricultural colleges in the early 1920s were among the first professional groups to argue that one did not need to be a farmer to understand agriculture. They did not need to be farmers themselves, but did need to learn what farmers knew. Farmers, according to many economists, lacked both the training and the objectivity to understand "the big picture" and their own role in it. Farmers themselves were thus helpless either in understanding agricultural conditions or in effecting change. "It would seem a self-evident proposition," wrote Nourse, "that in no field of human endeavor could it be expected that leaving managerial decisions to two-thirds of all the workers could result in anything but inefficiency almost medieval in character." Agricultural economists argued that, since they could speak in a numerical and quantitative voice, they could rise above the romantic and impractical ideas that seemed to guide farm practice. Economists such as John D. Black at Harvard University and Henry C. Taylor at the new Bureau of Agricultural Economics in the USDA were leaders in the effort to quantify, measure, weigh, bracket, and tame agricultural production practices. Others, such as George Warren at Cornell and M. L. Wilson at Montana State University, tried to effect change more directly as professors of farm management. Such experts were involved in the immediate collection of "facts" about farms and the manipulation of facts into models, paradigms, and programs that abstracted the individual and regional experience of farmers into general, quantitative principles. But the real shock troops of rural transformation were farm management experts located within rural banks and in agricultural college extension divisions. In evaluating both farmers themselves as credit risks and farmers' habits and practices on the farm, they determined what constituted best practice in agriculture, and how farmers could be made to comply.[9]

[8] On professionalization see Thomas Haskell, *The Authority of Experts* (Bloomington: Indiana University Press, 1984); on agricultural professionalization see Lawrence Busch and William Lacy, *Science, Agriculture, and the Politics of Research* (Boulder: Westview Press, 1983); and Margaret Rossiter, *The Emergence of Agricultural Science: Justus Liebig and the Americans* (New Haven, Conn.: Yale University Press, 1975).

[9] E. G. Nourse, "Economic Issues of Large-Scale Farming," *Agricultural Engineering* 10 (January 1929): 13–17; The Bureau of Agricultural Economics opened its doors in 1922; see Henry C. and Anne Dewees Taylor, *The Story of Agricultural Economics in the United States, 1840–1931* (Ames: Iowa State University Press, 1952); Henry Charles Taylor, *A Farm Economist in Washington, 1919–1925* (Evanston, Ill, 1926; reprint ed., Madison: Department of Agricultural Economics, University of Wisconsin, 1992); Richard Lowitt, ed., *Journal of a Tamed Bureaucrat: Nils A. Olsen and the Bureau of Agricultural Economics, 1925–1935* (Ames: Iowa State University Press, 1980).

Agricultural economists were also similar to other nascent agricultural experts in that their expertise was based in part upon substantial local knowledge. Although they began from the firm foundation of economic theory, they quickly realized that farmers themselves had the upper hand where tradition, practice, and experience were concerned. If the new economists hoped to gain credibility in the farm community and agricultural colleges, then it became essential for them to extract local knowledge from farmers. What crops and livestock did farmers produce, and why? How much did farmers produce, and how did they decide this? How much cash was needed to run a farm for a year? How many people? What did land cost, and what accounted for different prices?

Rural Americans had a long history of enumerating their possessions, sales, and other transactions, and of course the state followed tabulating practices in taking the census and producing probate inventories. But at the beginning of the twentieth century, economists also began taking notice of what farmers had, what they did, and what it added up to. In 1901 economists at the University of Minnesota located fifteen dairy farmers who agreed to provide farm data to a student "fieldman" who collected the data from each farm daily. Funded by the USDA's Bureau of Statistics, this exercise was to collect information that would generate a snapshot of Minnesota agricultural conditions; the fieldman was instructed to never offer advice or assistance, since it was not scientifically known what constituted proper farm practice. Similar work was undertaken by George Warren at Cornell University in 1906. His famous Tompkins County survey, conducted from 1907 to 1911, became the model for the survey method of collecting farm information to find out which types of farms were most productive. There were several different methods of obtaining information. One approach was to get lists of farmers' names from the local Farm Bureau, and send each farmer a questionnaire asking for information regarding his farm. A second approach was to have the county agent personally visit each farmer in his county, explaining the need for information and perhaps helping the farmer figure out how to calculate his expenses and income. In large states, or states in which farmers had become enthusiastic about the project, the county agent might arrange meetings at which he could discuss the tally sheets with a group of farmers all at once. A third approach, which was particularly effective, was for the local rural banks to distribute account books to farmers directly.[10]

---

[10] Winifred Barr Rothenberg, *From Market-Places to a Market Economy: The Transformation of Rural Massachusetts, 1750–1850* (Chicago: University of Chicago Press, 1992). As one Bureau of Agricultural Economics field worker reported back to Washington, "when the work first began farmers had a feeling that it was being conducted because of the information which the colleges wished to secure from them rather than to give them any considerable amount of

While most farmers had a pretty good idea of what they possessed and what they lacked, few could report on how much it really cost them to raise twenty dairy cows, whether hired help was cost-effective, or whether sidelines such as cutting lumber or beekeeping actually brought in extra money once land, labor, and other elements were considered. Thus, the most fundamental work in farm economics before the New Deal was showing farmers how to keep track of their income and expenses, and how to study their own actions and assign values to them, something that few average farmers had bothered with on a day-to-day basis. Encouraged by the USDA's need for quantitative data, and especially by the new income tax law, which for the first time required that farmers report their incomes and expenses, between 1916 and 1921 economists at the state colleges began grappling with farm accounts. In Wisconsin, for example, county agents helped farmers categorize and tally their expenses and receipts. The initial reports tended to list everything a farmer could quantify. For instance, Neil Simon's account sheet for 1924 was typical in listing expenses within categories such as "crop," "feeds," "livestock supplies," "machinery—new," "real estate expenses," and so forth. Within real estate repairs he listed a new silo costing $695.50, but also a door hinge at 59 cents. Under new machinery he listed a $6.00 incubator, but also a $5.00 horse blanket, an unusual definition of "machine." In Carl Waldson's 1925 account, the "livestock purchased" category included not just a nine-hundred-pound bull for $250, but also a Queen bee for $1.25. In Montana, county agents showed farmers how to figure their accounts and then offered advice on improving their "efficiency." After going over a Montana farmer's receipts and expenses, one county agent wrote, "Your labor income is a little too low and I expect you realize this as well as anybody else. If I were you I would raise more cash crops, increase the numbers of acres of wheat and oats." Thus were farmers brought into the quantitative world, one by one.[11]

---

help in the operation of their farms" (H. C. M. Case to H. C. Taylor, report on a trip to visit Utah farmers, October 27, 1919, National Archives, RG 83, box 2, series 124). George Warren, "President's Address," *Proceedings of the American Farm Management Association* (November 1913): 9–13; Willard Cochrane, *Agricultural Economics at the University of Minnesota, 1886–1979*, Minnesota Agricultural Experiment Station Miscellaneous Publication no. 21(1983), 5–6, 18; M. C. Burritt, "Farm Management Demonstrations—Past, Present, and Future," *Journal of Farm Economics 1* (September 1919): 57–64. G. E. Warren, K. C. Livermore, et al., *An Agricultural Survey—Townships of Ithaca, Dryden, Danby, and Lansing, Tompkins County, New York,* Cornell Agricultural Experiment Station Bulletin no. 295 (1911).

[11] The state-by-state development of farm account work is described in H. C. M. Case's trip reports sent to H. C. Taylor, October 27, 1919, February 11, 1920, February 27, 1920, June 10, 1921, and February 17, 1921, all in National Archives, RG 83, box 2, series 124; Wisconsin data are in College of Agriculture–Agricultural Economics, University of Wisconsin Archives, Steenbock Library, box 9/2/6-2, Miscellaneous Files, folder "Cost Surveys"; F. Josiah Chase, *Report of Farm Management Demonstration,* Montana State College of Agriculture Cooperative Extension Circular no. 8 (December 1915); "Results of Demonstrations in Missoula County," M. L. Wilson Papers, box 22, file T-18, Montana State University Archives.

It was not enough, however, for a farmer merely to know where his economic strengths and weaknesses were—whether he should have raised more oats, sold fewer calves, or spent less money on fencing, painting the barn, and newspapers. For the agricultural establishment, it was equally important that each farmer's facts be comparable to those of his neighbor, and that lenders take an active part in this ostensibly educational campaign. Although in nearly every state it was the agricultural college demonstration agent who first designed and distributed the account sheets or books, most agents turned this part of the operations over to local banks within a few years. The perennially overworked agents were anxious to enroll other leaders in their counties in the tedious job of contacting all farmers. Bankers also were part of the larger network of interested parties, which included the tax revenue agencies, state and federal officials, and the national banking associations, all of whom favored standardizing efforts. And banks were the most essential turnstile for farmers as they figured out their farming plans each year. Banks could offer or withhold farm loans depending on whatever calculus was handy, and the account books served as a sort of economic confessional for farmers seeking credit. Bankers gave blank books to farmers, the farmers filled them out, and then showed them to bankers in hopes of appearing creditworthy. In such a way did the state, the college, and the banks convince farmers to operate in a rational manner.[12]

Another method farm economists used to help farmers visualize modernization was to show farmers exactly what a modern farm looked like. Beginning in about 1920, some agricultural extension economists decided that many farmers were not going to adopt more businesslike, modern practices unless they had a tangible understanding in their heads of the ideal farm. Building upon years of cost accounting, a Purdue economist suggested holding farm management contests through the state fairs, but got bogged down in the administrative difficulties of evaluating farms. In Illinois, the county agent used the county fairs to show three farm models, each twelve feet square and representing different combinations of crops and livestock. What made these models real conversation pieces was the fact that each model had real crops growing in its "fields," as well as charts explaining how certain practices would increase yields and income, while certain other practices might actually reduce profits. The enterprising Illinois agent also offered farmers annual tours of farms that could demonstrate clever arrangements of buildings, crops, and livestock, and innovative combinations of work schedules, sources of income, and productive

---

[12] On the role of banks see, e.g., H. C. M. Case to H. C. Taylor, August 23, 1919, National Archives, RG 83, box 2, series 124; on the situation in Ohio see R. F. Taber, "Farm Management Extension Work," *Journal of Farm Economics* 1 (September 1919): 50–51; for Montana see Arthur Copeland, "Farm Management Annual Report, July 1, 1920–June 30, 1921," M. L. Wilson Papers, box 22, folder T-20.

efforts. This, it was hoped, would give other farmers ideas regarding how to readjust their own, presumably less efficient, farm practices.[13]

Engineering the Farm

For the agricultural engineers, the impetus of high modernism was not so much with accounting as with machines and factory practices. They found the similarities between farms and factories a common source of discussion and inspiration, and they used them as the basis for a general rationalizing campaign. Certainly the design and operation of specialized machinery was one component of this, but equally important was the obsession with farm layout, standardization, and efficiency. To scientific management experts such as Frederick Taylor, the physical arrangement of buildings and work sites on the farm, like the arrangement of these things on the factory floor, was very important. They felt that linear rather than circuitous movement of men and materials through a factory guaranteed the orderliness of all other factory operations. Just as the rational arrangement of machinery could prevent the worker from wasting time and money by wandering around the factory looking for lost tools, delivering materials, or chatting with friends in other areas, so the orderly arrangement of buildings on the farm could save the farmer from wasting time backtracking. They studied how ordinary farmers actually spent their time, outdoors as well as in the barn and machine shop. Distances between the barn and the house, or house and fields, or fields and shed, were tallied up and evaluated with an eye toward eliminating wasted movement. Engineers, like economists, erected models of ideal farmsteads at the state and county fairs to illustrate their ideas to visitors, especially farm families.[14]

Agricultural engineers were also concerned about standardization, although it often seemed even more difficult to manage than farm layout. For the engineers, standardization on the farm relied on a prior standardization in factories that produced tools and machines for farmers. Until

[13] G. I. Christie to H. C. Taylor, March 9, 1920, and Taylor to Christie, March 12, 1920, National Archives, RG 83, entry 124, box 2; M. L. Mosher, "Farm Management and the County Agent's Program" (Complete Report of the Farm Management Section of the Conference of Extension Workers of the Corn Belt States, May 16–18, 1923), 26–27, National Archives, RG 23, box 2, series 124; H. C. M. Case to H. C. Taylor, October 11, 1920, National Archives, RG 83, box 2, series 124.

[14] Robert Stewart, *Seven Decades That Changed America: A History of the American Society of Agricultural Engineers* (St. Joseph, Mo.: ASAE, 1979); E. B. McCormick, "How Engineering May Help Farm Life," *United States Department of Agriculture Yearbook of Agriculture, 1915* (Washington, D.C.: Government Printing Office, 1916), 101–12; L. W. Chase, "Farm Building Location as a Factor Affecting Farm Labor Efficiency," *Transactions of the American Society of Agricultural Engineers* 6 (1912): 96–116.

World War I, however, there was very little standardization among implement manufacturers. Before the war, for instance, one engineer counted
226 types and sizes of steel walking plows, which were reduced to 39 by war's
end thanks to the government's recommendation to manufacturers to standardize.[15] For most of these engineers, the question of standardization and
farm layout centered on an emerging notion of efficiency. While the word
"efficiency" had been around a long time, its meaning became both more
flexible and more powerful under the direction of Taylor and his efficiency
experts. But although engineers could agree that it was the key unifying
concept in their endeavor to modernize farming, they had difficulty settling
on any single definition of efficiency because the work farmers did was so
variable. Measuring something so seemingly straightforward as the efficiency
of tractive power was almost immediately confused by the recognition that
different soil types would have big effects on how much resistance the tractor encountered, and hence would affect the tractor's efficiency.[16]

The farm tractor offers a good example of the tension between farmers'
own attempts to economize and the pressures exerted by bankers and the
state. Before the 1910s, the tractor market was fairly small. During the
"golden years" of agricultural production in the 1910s—when markets in
Europe and South America were expanding, farmers were optimistic and
expansionist, federal and state regulations on manufacturers were few, and
automobile manufacturers like Henry Ford were demonstrating both the
virtues of mass production and the apparent affordability of car ownership—tractor manufacturers sprang up like toadstools. Hundreds of new
manufacturers began putting out small lines of implements or sometimes
single models, many of them unreliable, without standardized parts or speci-
fications, and without factory support should machines break down. Farmers whose tractors fell apart during the crucial days of harvesting or planting, or who waited for days or weeks for parts to be fashioned or delivered,
grew fonder of their horses. Before the war, most farmers resisted buying
tractors because they were too expensive, generally too large to turn around
in small fields, and useful only for big seasonal events such as the harvest.[17]

[15] A. B. Dinneen, "Standardization of Farm Machinery," *Transactions of the American Society
of Agricultural Engineers* 12 (1918): 151–59; Theo Brown, "Standardization in the Implement
Industry," ibid., 17 (1923): 115–19.

[16] L. W. Ellis, "Tractive Efficiency," *Transactions of the American Society of Agricultural Engineers* 4 (1910): 172–85 (a lengthy discussion followed this paper); J. B. Davidson, "Laboratory Efficiency," ibid., 7 (1913): 220–35.

[17] W. F. MacGregor, "The Combined Harvester-Thresher," ibid., 19 (1925): 40–47; C.
Parker Holt, "Early Developments of the Holt Manufacturing Company" (manuscript, June
26, 1935), in F. Hal Higgins Collection, D-56, box 28, file 15, Special Collections, Shields Library, University of California at Davis, 14–15; Ann Foley Scheuring, *A Learned Profession:
A History of Agriculture at the University of California*, Working Paper no. 61, July 1990, Agricultural History Center, University of California, Davis; Alan L. Olmstead and Paul Rhode, "An

As the sod-busting farmers and ranchers of the western states brought the last arable land under cultivation around 1913–14, manufacturers of heavy, expensive machinery realized that they needed to develop new machines and new markets. Smaller tractors that had both wide adaptability and the capacity for belt work—connecting the tractor engine with belting to run grinders, sharpening stones, and pumps—seemed the most likely market, a view reinforced by the Allies' need for food supplies from American farmers. During this period of ready markets, high prices, and a dwindling supply of horses (which were in demand from the military), farmers expanded their farms and many bought tractors. But again, many farmers were caught out by unscrupulous tractor manufacturers, who sold machines "because... they looked like tractors," but which were poorly designed, cheaply built, and impossible to repair. By war's end, the lack of standardized models, the failure of tractor firms and the resulting evaporation of dealerships and repairmen, the economic depression in agriculture generally, and Henry Ford's dumping of a hundred thousand cheap Fordsons on the market together strained what little credibility the tractor industry had ever had. This situation led the agricultural engineers in Nebraska, in collaboration with the state legislature, to frame a law in 1919 that mandated all tractor manufacturers planning to sell their tractors in the state to submit their machines to the Nebraska Tractor Test, conducted at the state university. The thrust of the test was to ensure that new tractors operated as advertised, and that the manufacturer could supply spare parts and advice to customers. It was widely emulated by other agricultural states.[18]

Throughout the 1920s, most engineers and farmers followed the middle road to mechanization, favoring a combination of tractors and horses on the typical farm. In this way they embraced modernization at their own pace. Tractors were used for belt work, while horses were used to pull implements such as cultivators, weeders, and manure spreaders. The combination seemed most reasonable because, even by the end of the decade, it was difficult for most farmers to calculate the most economical option in comparing the expense of the tractor, including initial cost, gasoline, repairs, and insurance, against the expense of hired help, who needed room and board, and horses, which needed feeding, stabling, and veterinary visits. Further, it was hard to calculate this against farm size, expected farm income from crops and livestock, and real day-to-day power needs.

Overview of California Agricultural Mechanization, 1870–1930," *Agricultural History* 62 (1988): 86–112; "Farm Power Conference," October 1919, sponsored by the United States Department of Agriculture, National Archives, RG 83, entry 124, Box 4.

[18] Reynold Wik, "Henry Ford's Tractors and American Agriculture," *Agricultural History* 38 (April 1964): 79–86; Conference on Farm Organization and Farm Equipment, Office of Farm Management, Bureau of Agricultural Economics, April 17–19, 1919, National Archives, RG 83, series 3, box 124; L. J. Fletcher, "Factors Influencing Tractor Development," *Transactions of the American Society of Agricultural Engineers* 15 (1921): 142–49.

With little or no training in this sort of accounting and forecasting, most farmers were hard pressed to follow economists' advice about rational farming, and they tended to do the best they could by following their neighbors' examples.

But by 1929 and 1930, farmers discovered that their decisions were being made for them in this regard, as bankers began evaluating whether a farmer was a good credit risk or not according to the degree to which he was using power machinery such as tractors and combines. As one banker who managed thirty-three midwestern farms reported that he would always choose a new tenant who owned a tractor over one who did not, figuring that such a tenant would be more likely to get the crops in and out quickly in poor weather. Likewise, rural bankers in Montana worked with the agricultural college advisors to create a scorecard that bankers could use to evaluate farmers as credit risks. Farmers who owned machinery, expanded their land holdings, and got rid of their horses, among many other features, were considered more progressive and promising than those who did not.[19]

Large-Scale Farms

Almost immediately following the war, new types of farms emerged that borrowed both implicitly and explicitly from factory production methods. Some of these farms were extremely large in acreage, some large in output alone. Some farmers figured out how to mechanize nearly all the operations on the farm, while some focused on highly routinized managerial techniques. Often referred to as "corporate farms," because they were so big—few were legally incorporated—these farms were numerous enough by early 1929 to warrant becoming the focus of a large U.S. Chamber of Commerce study. In many cases, corporate farming was initiated not by traditional farmers, but by investors anxious to demonstrate the power of industrial and business ideas through farming, and with the money to invest in long-term gambles. After all, while the countryside was littered with abandoned farms and broken farmers, the cities had plenty of affluent business leaders looking for a sound investment. If farming could be made predictable, rational, and profitable, then investors would be interested in supporting it.[20]

Treating the farm as if it were a factory meant focusing on the patterns, motions, and routine activities that took place on farms, rather than on

[19] C. D. Kinsman, "Summary of the National Farm Power Survey," *Transactions of the American Society of Agricultural Engineers* 18 (1924): 101–13; John A. Hopkins, *Horses, Tractors, and Farm Equipment,* Iowa State University Agricultural Experiment Station Bulletin no. 264 (June 1929); J. E. Johnson, "He Prefers Tenants Who Have Tractors," *Farm Implement News* 53 (February 4, 1932): 28–29.
[20] United States Chamber of Commerce, Agricultural Service Department, *Large–Scale Farming* (Washington, D.C., July 1929).

the clearly uncontrollable dimensions such as droughts, plagues of locusts, and plant diseases. It also meant mechanizing ordinary activities such as planting and harvesting; standardizing tools and procedures; and reducing complexity through monocropping and cost accounting. Corporate farm enthusiasts railed against farmers' irrational, romantic, nearly childlike absorption in farm life itself, their interest in the "way of life" aspects of farming rather than the production aspects, and against farmers' highly irregular work habits. As Ford himself liked to say, the actual productive work a typical farmer did amounted to no more than about thirty days per year; and this suggested to urbanites a grossly inefficient mode of work that, with industrial expertise, could be vastly improved. But just as in industrial production, the use of automatic machinery was but one part of the ultimate solution to agricultural production; and it would take the equally important components of rationalization and standardization to make the transition successful.[21]

Corporate farms tended to follow one of several designs. One of the earliest, called "chain farms," consisted of centrally located farms repossessed by insurance companies and banks, many of which were operated as specialized parts of a larger whole. For instance, one Indiana firm arranged to divide the various tasks of hog raising among its farms, with farrowing on one group of farms, fattening on another, and so forth. Another type of corporate farm was modeled on the industrially-based company town, in which a large industry oversaw not only the working lives of employees, but also the employees' free time and family time. The Taft Ranch in Texas, for instance, consisted of 100,000 acres and four small towns housing forty-five hundred workers. The enterprise was mainly involved in cattle ranching, and all aspects of raising, slaughtering, and shipping meat were conducted on the property. The company provided housing that boasted modern conveniences such as indoor plumbing, electricity, and telephones, and also provided churches, schools, hospitals, roads, and railways. In a similar vein, retail king J. C. Penney established the J. C. Penney–Gwinn Corporation Farms in 1924 in Florida, which grew to 125,000 acres divided up into tiny, 20-acre farms, each owned by a family but tightly controlled by Penney's managers, who also ran the cannery, chicken hatchery, and agricultural school. These and other corporate farming company towns bore a striking resemblance to industrial company towns, and were designed to solve some of the same, anticipated problems of shifting from traditional, artisanal work to industrialized work. Farmers were perceived in many ways as similar to immigrants and low-skill industrial workers—uneducated, rural, backward, and

[21] Henry Ford, *Today and Tomorrow* (Garden City, N.J.: Doubleday, 1926), 211–12; Edgar L. Smith, "Corporate Farming," *Proceedings of the American Farm Management Association* (1917): 47–57.

in need of civilizing. The company towns were thought to provide the ac-
coutrements of the modern world—electricity, indoor plumbing, schools—
that agricultural leaders and businessmen assumed rural people wanted, and
also offered a controlled, paternalistic environment crucial to reeducation.[22]

Other corporate farms were based explicitly upon technological innovations that allowed farmers to avoid employing laborers, to expand their
acreage, or to consolidate operations. The Johnson poultry farm in Texas,
for example, was based on a particular type of chicken—the White
Leghorn—that was tolerant of a "mass production environment." Made
possible by the invention of the Hall incubator, the Johnson farm com-
prised a million square feet of floor space in eighty-six buildings, where
75,000 chickens and 112,000 eggs in incubators were processed in 1926.
Likewise, the production of hay, which had traditionally been highly labor-
intensive, was mechanized quite suddenly in 1927 with the introduction
of hay dryers and other equipment. It was not, however, for the struggling
farmer: the initial capital investment was over $21,000, and annual costs
were estimated at around $22,000 more.[23]

Certainly the most dramatic example of industrial farming was the farm
operated by Thomas Campbell in southeastern Montana beginning in
1918. The Montana Farming Corporation was to ordinary farms as Ford's
River Rouge factory was to a corner store. At the time of Campbell's death
in 1966, it was the largest wheat farm in the world. Campbell, who had a
master's degree in mechanical engineering and a background in wheat
farming, originally intended to use industrial methods to raise wheat for
the war effort. He discussed his ideas with Herbert Hoover and President
Coolidge, and ultimately arranged with the Interior Department to lease
land from several Native American tribes in Montana. In addition, his employer in Pasadena, California, J. S. Torrance, introduced him to J. P.
Morgan, who agreed to loan Campbell two million dollars. According to
Campbell, "Mr. Morgan says it is the most interesting, romantic, profitable
and at the same time patriotic enterprise which he has had put up to him
since the war began." Campbell assembled a total of ninety-five thousand
acres, and began turning the sod in the spring of 1918. "If it succeeds,"
said Campbell, "it will prove that agriculture has reached a stage of devel-

[22] On banks and insurance companies see L. L. Holmes, "Prospective Displacement of the
Independent Family Farms by Larger Farms or Estate Management," *Journal of Farm Manage-
ment* 11 (April 1929): 227–47; Taylor, "How Many Farms Can One Man Run?"; Stewart, "Mass
Production on the Farm"; A. Roy Stephens, *The Taft Ranch: A Texas Principality* (Austin: Uni-
versity of Texas Press, 1964); "The Unique Farm Project of James C. Penney" (Green Cove
Springs, Fla.: The J. C. Penney–Gwinn Corporation Farms, 1927), in Penney Archives, Dallas.
[23] Clotilde Grunsky, "Where Hoover Meets the Farm Problem from Within," *Magazine of
Business* 55 (April 1929): 415, 474–75; John E. Pickett, "The New President's Kern County
Farm," *Pacific Rural Press* 117 (February 23, 1929): 238, 247; Frank L. Platt, "The Biggest
Poultry Farm in the World," *American Poultry Journal* 58 (January 1927): 11, 88–92, 94–97.

opment which makes it possible to organize it similarly to other industrial enterprises."[24]

What was industrial about Campbell's farm? The first thing that drew attention was simply the size of Campbell's holdings. His ninety-five thousand acres were not, as some had expected, arranged contiguously, but rather in sections or units, each of which was managed and operated as a semiautonomous farm. By the time Joseph Howard visited the farm in 1949, he could see twenty-eight miles of wheat, all of it Campbell's, stretching away to the mountains. Because the units were so large, and because they were scattered, Campbell built bunkhouses, kitchens and dining halls, machine shops, and eventually showers for the workers at each unit, and hired a manager responsible for every aspect of work and life on his own unit. Since farmwork was seasonal, the number of people living on the units also varied, peaking to several hundred during harvest and falling to only a few hands over the winter. Other than the cook, there were no women or children on the units—"our camps are run on the army style," wrote a Campbell recruiter—and workers with families housed them in Hardin, where the company office was located.[25]

The large scale of the farm also required heavy machinery. As discussed above, the relation between farm size and machinery was reciprocal: farmers could not operate large farms without a great deal of either horses or machinery, and machinery in turn could not be paid for without large farms that provided large yields. Campbell was an enthusiastic engineer, buying millions of dollars worth of tractors, trucks, combines, disc plows, and so forth. By about the third year of operation, Campbell was on familiar terms with the manufacturers as well, writing long letters reporting on the shortcomings and happy surprises each machine offered. His interactions with one company, the Stinson Tractor Company, nicely illustrate the difficulties of early industrialization in farming. After receiving a number of tractors in July of 1918, Campbell complained to the company that they appeared to have been assembled by "by a lot of Amateurs," and felt that the company should have sent an expert out to the farm with the tractors as Holt and Deere had done. Manufacturers often did this to help assemble the machinery and train the laborers in the finer points of operating and maintaining the machines; for many field hands, this was their first experience with engines. But where Stinson blamed the "disinterested, city schooled boy[s]" Campbell hired to drive the tractors, Campbell blamed the Stinson tractor designers who had ignored harsh Montana con-

[24] Philip Rose, "Biggest Wheat Farm in the World," *Country Gentleman* 83 (October 26, 1918): 6; Joseph K. Howard, "Tom Campbell: Farmer of Two Continents," *Harpers*, March 1949, 55–63.

[25] J. R. Torrance to Matt Michels, March 14, 1928, Thomas Campbell Papers, box 5, Montana Historical Society, Helena.

ditions. After eight months, and a heated, voluminous correspondence on the subject, Campbell's farm was littered with the broken remains of Stinson tractors.[26]

Campbell also had difficulty convincing his laborers that they were industrial workers, although many young men begged to work on the farm because they were interested in the big machines. Some of the job applicants were trained in one of the automobile and tractor driving schools that sprang up during this period, while others were college students studying mechanical engineering. Still others were itinerant farm workers, and many were themselves farmers who had lost everything in the wave of bankruptcies and foreclosures. Campbell paid good wages—in 1919 the wage scale was set at between $80 and $120 per month for engine operators plus 25 cents per mile as noted on the mile recorder attached to all machines, and the men received free room and board on the unit farms. But Campbell also rejected many of the perquisites and prerogatives of traditional ranching life, set firm rules for his workers, and expected absolute compliance. A teetotaler himself, Campbell railed at a town councilman in nearby Hardin when he found some of his men and local Crow Indians drunk on bootleg whiskey on a Saturday night. He insisted that his harvest crew work an eleven-hour day, something even his best manager, Fred Gale, strongly objected to, pointing out that other businesses in the area only worked ten hours per day, and Campbell's employees had to add considerable travel time to and from the fields to those eleven hours. Said Gale, "You may recall that last June, when we put the eleven hour day into effect, we had to get practically a entirely new crew."[27]

For Campbell, the actual fieldwork also required eternal vigilance, which was difficult due to the distances between the units. Campbell visited the units frequently in his Stutz Bearcat, sent memos to the unit managers sometimes several times a day, and complained to them frequently about the incorrect or slipshod manner of both the laborers' work and of their own oversight. Campbell complained about the truck drivers to manager Tom Hart: "Do not let the men pile up on the front end and running boards. Insist that they sit in the back part of the truck. There is no objection to this now with pneumatic tires.... Please ask the fellows to keep the hoods over the engines. It looks very badly to see our trucks running

[26] Campbell to Stinson Tractor Company, July 4 and 18 August, 1918; W. B. Gleason to Campbell, August 24, 1918; Campbell to Stinson Tractor Company, August 29 and October 24, 1918; all in Campbell Papers, box 3. Campbell corresponded regularly with manufacturers large and small, usually to suggest design changes in equipment.

[27] My remarks on job applicants are based on general correspondence and a collection of over one hundred applications dating from 1928, Campbell Papers, box 5. On wages see Fred Gale to Campbell, September 25, 1919, and Campbell to Gordon, Hart, and Keyes (all unit managers), March 2, 1920, both in Campbell Papers, box 5; on drinking see Campbell to D. L. Egness, October 13, 1927, Campbell Papers, box 7.

around without covers over the engines." Campbell also had an engineer's abhorrence of waste, urging Fred Gordon: "Do not let any of the threshing machines remain idle anywhere one day; for instance, if Sam can't thresh his spring wheat until day after tomorrow, start threshing at Wolf's or George's or Beal's tomorrow.... Move at night, if necessary, but under no circumstances permit any one machine to be idle one day." Campbell could be a difficult boss, micromanaging everything on the farm. But his grand vision of industrial farming outweighed all criticism, at least in his mind. "This farm is a factory," he told Malcolm Cutting. "It is operated on exactly the same principles of mass production, cost accounting, specialized machinery, and skilled mechanical labor as any great industrial organization in the country."[28]

As critics pointed out, Campbell had several unusual advantages. He had been adequately capitalized to hire laborers, buy machinery, pay freight rates, and build housing. His lease of Native American land, as one critic put it, amounted to "a government subsidy." The crops Campbell chose— wheat with some flax—were fairly low-maintenance between planting and harvest, especially because Campbell did not believe in fertilizing newly broken fields. Both the crop and the land were amenable to mechanization. Miles of flat land without pesky creeks, trees, buildings, and roads made machine planting and harvesting straightforward. These three factors—capital, type of farm product, and geography—were absolutely crucial to industrial farming. Farms that were small in acreage or broken up by obstacles and hills were not suited to industrial farming of this sort. Farms that centered on crops or livestock that for some reason could not be mechanized, or at least highly routinized, were difficult to industrialize. And farmers who could not get the money to invest in land, machines, and experts were not likely to become industrial agriculturalists.[29]

For these reasons, industrial farming also tended to succeed in the wheat regions of Washington, California, North Dakota, Oklahoma, and especially Kansas and Montana. In Kansas, for example, following the introduction of the combined harvester-thresher in 1917, many farms consolidated their land or broke new land for wheat farming; in the late 1920s over ten million acres of virgin prairie were broken in the southwestern

[28] Campbell to Tom Hart, August 6, 1920, Campbell Papers, box 1; Campbell to Fred Gordon, September 7, 1920, Campbell Papers, box 1; Malcolm Cutting, "A Manufacturer of Wheat," *Country Gentleman* 44 (August 1926): 18.

[29] Gard, "Agriculture's Industrial Revolution"; John D. Black, *Agricultural Reform* (New York: McGraw-Hill, 1929), 371–72; M. L. Wilson, "Large-Scale Farming Problems Discussed," *Agricultural Engineering* 10 (January 1929): 31–34; Howard, "Tom Campbell." Negotiations between Campbell and the Interior Department, including the various leases, are in the National Archives, RG 48, Department of the Interior, Office of the Secretary, Indian Agencies—Crow, Leases, Thomas D. Campbell, file 5-1, part I, and in the Campbell Papers.

edge of the winter wheat belt, thanks to mechanization. Rural towns began to vanish as small farmers sold out to larger farmers or moved to an expanded farm. Indeed, the short-term impact on rural communities was so serious that several agricultural states passed or attempted to pass legislation designed to slow down the shift to industrialized farming.[30] Without a doubt, the development of the combine and the improvements made to trucks and tractors by the mid to late 1920s were extremely important to the rapid industrialization of wheat production. Whereas in 1915 there were just under twenty-five hundred tractors in the hard winter wheat belt, by 1926 there were nearly thirty-four thousand. Combine capacity also shifted upwards; a top of the line combine in 1917 was nine feet wide, but by 1927 it was forty-eight feet wide. Stories abounded of farmers in Kansas pooling their resources and their land to create huge wheat ranches; the most famous was the Wheat Farm Corporation in Kansas City, which hired workers for the planting and harvest, installed time clocks on the tractors and combines, and worked drivers in three shifts, round the clock.[31]

Collective Farms as Models

A final example of the high modernist impulse comes from an unexpected place—the collective farms of the Soviet Union. In the late 1920s an organization called Amtorg, the trade office of the Soviet goivernment located in New York City, began placing advertisements in the farm papers seeking specialists in hog raising, wheat growing, and a host of other agricultural activities. They were promised a high salary if they would move to the Soviet Union for a year or two to help establish modern farming operations on what came to be known as the collective farms. While no figures are available, anecdotal evidence suggests that quite a few bankrupt farmers jumped at the chance. And some observers, including Henry A. Wallace, began to wonder if maybe the Soviets' agricultural scheme might hold lessons for American agriculture as well.

In 1928, Soviet leaders sent agriculturalists to the United States to buy farm implements and observe the industrial operations of farmers like Thomas Campbell, all in preparation for breaking land on the huge

[30] W. E. Grimes, "Social and Economic Effects of Large Scale Farming in the Wheat Belt," *Journal of Farm Economics* 13 (January 1931): 21–26; Herman Steen, "Corporations Farm Many American Acres," *New York Times Sunday Magazine*, May 26, 1929, 11.

[31] M. L. Wilson to John D. Black, April 11, 1928, John D. Black Papers, box 1, April–May 1928, Historical Society of Wisconsin; M. L. Wilson, "Report of the Secretary and Managing Director to the Board of Directors, Fairway Farms, for the Years 1925–1926," 14–16, M. L. Wilson Papers, box 36, folder AH-16; W. E. Grimes, "Effects of Improved Machinery and Production Methods on the Organization of Farms in the Hard Winter Wheat Belt," *Journal of Farm Economics* 10 (April 1928): 225–31; Gard, "Agriculture's Industrial Revolution."

collective farms. The Soviets also hired a number of American agricultural engineers and economists to help organize and establish these farm units, paying them a handsome salary for staying on the farms for several months or several years. This was not a highly systematic, well-organized transfer of technical skill from one culture to another; indeed, in some ways it was nearly random. No educational or governmental institutions were officially involved, and aside from the groups of tractor assemblers sent by manufacturers, the Americans traveled individually and did not know each other until arriving in Moscow. And they were never a large group; although exact numbers are elusive, an educated guess would be less than ten experts who had or would have national reputations in American agriculture (among them M. L. Wilson and Mordecai Ezekiel), with another twenty or so from the manufacturing and business community. None of these Americans wrote a biographical or critical account, although several wrote articles for the farm press. How could such a little-known and randomly experienced interlude have any real impact on the industrial revolution in agriculture?

The answer to this lies in the historical confluence of several trends. First, the Soviets had decided that the best way to raise money to pay for urban industrialization was to grow as much wheat as possible as quickly as possible for sale on the world market. Enamored of the internationally acclaimed factory system in the United States, exemplified by Ford and International Harvester, and capable of devoting almost unlimited land and peasant labor to the effort, the Soviets sent delegations to America to study agricultural methods and purchase farm machinery. Second, by this time American advocates of large-scale industrial farming had developed systems of wheat growing that relied upon an industrial logic of high mechanization, large land units, careful organization and management, and, increasingly, a separation between farming as a way of life and farming as a productive industry. If the Soviets had come ten years earlier, they would have seen little industrial farming in America, but by 1928 they saw enough to be convinced of its viability. Third, although manufacturers did not develop reliable farm machinery for ordinary, small-scale farms until after about 1924, they had been making large-scale machines such as threshers, reapers, and rollers for the international grain market for many years. Places such as California's Central Valley, Argentina, and Canada had the right geography for this. Indeed, such places were emblematic of the idealized, abstract place that advocates had in mind when they discussed the virtues of industrial farming. And the northern Caucasus fit this template perfectly; Montana experts like Wilson and Campbell remarked on the similarity of landscapes.[32]

---

[32] There is no overview of the American agriculturalists in the Soviet Union, but see Deborah Fitzgerald, "Blinded by Technology: American Agriculture in the Soviet Union,

Most of the Americans worked at State Farm no. 2, also called "Verblud" (the Russian word for "camel"—perhaps an ironical reference to the customary beast of burden in the northern Caucasus where the farm was located). It consisted of a field headquarters—a boomtown of modern buildings, many of them built out of the packing crates in which unassembled tractors were shipped, and in which all farm business and agricultural education were carried out—and 375,000 acres of land for wheat growing. Because the fields were very large and removed from the town itself, they were divided into eight separate field units, on which farm workers lived while planting and harvesting the wheat.

Before going to the Soviet Union, Wilson had prepared a highly detailed plan for orchestrating the first wheat crop. It included graphs and charts explaining the day-by-day locations and work schedules of all the machines and humans involved in the effort, a schedule reminiscent of Frederick Taylor's routing charts for materials in factories. Wilson's plan was based on the summer fallow system of wheat growing, which necessitated putting one-third of the land "in fallow," or keeping it unplanted, each year as a moisture conservation measure. The Soviets followed Wilson's plan, as well as his method using specialized machines to break the sod, plant the wheat, cultivate and weed, and harvest. Because of the size of the farm, the most crucial task was coordinating the laborers, the machines, and the fields so that the highly time-sensitive field operations could be managed effectively, without work stoppages due to broken machines, workers arriving late, and travel problems getting to the fields that were so typical of large farming operations in general. Wilson's system was thus as much about management as it was about agronomy; the biggest problems were managerial rather than biological.[33]

Not surprisingly, many aspects of the Soviet farming system resembled the American ideas and practices. The ideas that the only sensible way to raise wheat was on a huge scale, using huge machines and quite a few laborers to drive and repair the machines; that the land should be broken up into units, each with its own living arrangements; and that production schedules should follow a precise choreography that even seasoned factory workers would find difficult, came directly from the growing American

---

1928–1932," *Agricultural History* 70 (summer 1996): 459–86; Guy Bush, "Nine Out of Ten Pigs Died," *Wallaces' Farmer*, November 14, 1931, 1179, 1202; Bush, "Where Hired Men Issue Orders," ibid., November 28, 1931, 1218, 1231; Bush, "What Is Russia's Major Vice?" ibid., December 26, 1931, 1271, 1276; Mordecai Ezekiel, "In the Grain Belt of the New Russia," ibid., July 11, 1931, 825, 840. Unpublished correspondence in the M. L. Wilson Papers provided much of the material for my understanding of this episode.

[33] Harold Ware, M. L. Wilson, and Guy Riggin, "Tentative Plan for Organizing Factory Wheat Farm for Grain Trust at Verblude, North Caucues [*sic*], U.S.S.R.," n.d. (February 1929), Wilson Papers, box 10, file F-22; E. J. Stirniman, "An Agricultural Engineer Looks at Mechanized Farming in Russia," (manuscript of speech given at the World Grain Conference, Regina, Saskatchewan, 1933); thanks to Ann Stirniman for sharing this document with me.

fixation on precision, rationality, and order in agriculture as in other production systems. Certainly the notion that American farming practice and theory were sufficiently stable and universal simply to transplant to the Russian countryside, just as Singer Sewing Machine and International Harvester had transferred their factories, machine tools, and mass-production techniques to Moscow, was based on a stunning confidence in the reliability of scientized, routinized production practices. The fact that such transfers had rarely proceeded as planned, that the mentality of Soviet peasants was not exactly comparable to that of American farmers, and that no Americans had actually seen a farm as large as Verblud, never mind managed one—all such worries fell away in light of high modernist promises of ultimate mastery over such situations.

The main business of the farm, in addition to planting and harvesting, was twofold: educating peasants and students in modern agricultural methods, and assembling and maintaining the farm implements that arrived daily from America and Germany. To the Americans, the Soviet educational system and educational philosophy were surprisingly devoid of a practical dimension. The Americans found no Soviet counterpart to the American agricultural engineer or economist. The most prominent agriculturalists, the "agronomes," had been trained at colleges or institutes and often had been directors of pre-Revolutionary estates. But they usually had very little practical field experience, having been educated in theoretical and abstract strains of biology, chemistry, and botany. They were also not experienced in mechanical and technical issues, such as tractor design or principles behind the internal combustion engine, which made the training of students especially difficult. This lack of experience with machinery was also apparent in tractor and combine assembly. The Americans all commented on the Soviets' mistrust of American instructions, and their preference for assembling the machines as they saw fit, including using fewer parts than the Americans thought necessary.[34]

From the perspective of the Soviet people, this project had decidedly mixed results. While a tremendous amount of wheat was raised, it was virtually all confiscated by the government, contributing to the infamous rural famine that killed millions of people. The techoscientific practices, machines, and ideologies that Americans brought to the Soviet Union both worked and failed to work in this respect. But from the American perspective, the project was in many ways a big success, because the American goals had nothing to do with feeding Soviet citizens, or even with

[34] Dana Dalrymple, "The Stalingrad Tractor Plant in Early Soviet Planning," *Soviet Studies* 18 (October 1966): 164–68; Dalrymple, "The American Tractor Comes to Soviet Agriculture: The Transfer of a Technology," *Technology and Culture* 5 (1964): 191–214.

modernizing the Soviet Union.[35] Rather, most of the engineers went to the Soviet Union for the paycheck and adventure. Professional men such as Wilson returned to the United States with new knowledge based on the agricultural demonstration of factory farming. For Wilson, the project was an experiment in a new and revolutionary type of farming, and most importantly, affirmed his own theories regarding the need for large scale, mechanization, and overall modernization in American agriculture. Despite the vast differences between the Soviet Union and the United States, for Wilson the project was evidence that factory farming was the wave of the future, and he promoted his ideas with vigor in Montana and Washington following his trip.[36]

✿

Conclusion

What happened on American farms in the 1920s did not really look like politics to farm families or their urban counterparts, but it was. The stirrings of a revolution in American agricultural practice, shaped extensively by technocratic and scientific approaches created and endorsed by the state, was ultimately more profoundly political than most of the legislation passed in the name of farmers in that decade. Even where there is little evidence of "hardware" or explicit scientific theories, the shaping force of high modernist ideas is everywhere apparent. Innovations such as tractors with internal combustion engines and income tax forms were alien and opaque to the first generation of farmers who encountered them. It was simply not self-evident to those who had never seen a tractor before what to do if the tractor would not start, or how to figure out the overhead on growing fifty acres of oats. Such innovations removed a great deal of personal decision making from farm families and replaced it with industrial/university authority.[37]

Further, farm families were less and less able to make independent decisions regarding farm size, whether to diversify or concentrate on single commodities, whether to mechanize fieldwork or the home, whether to electrify, or how much debt to carry. As college officials, bankers, engineers, urban investors, and the state began organizing the direction of

---

[35] An important exception to this statement was a group of American Communists led by Hal Ware; see Lement Harris, *My Tale of Two Worlds* (New York: International Publishers, 1986).

[36] Wilson to C. S. Noble, November 6, 1929; Wilson to J. V. Bennett, November 8, 1929, and Wilson to E. C. Leedy, November 15, 1929, all in Wilson Papers, box 10, file F-19.

[37] For examples of the difficulties farmers faced in changing their farm practices, see, e.g., Deborah Fitzgerald, *The Business of Breeding: Hybrid Corn in Illinois, 1890–1940* (Ithaca: Cornell University Press, 1990), and Fitzgerald, "Exporting American Agriculture: The Rockefeller Foundation in Mexico," *Social Studies of Science* 16 (1986): 457–83.

American agriculture, more rules and regulations were put in place that strongly pressured families to move toward industrializing their farms. The Depression highlighted this trend, as the economic disaster was visited on most farmers by 1930 by both local bankers and international markets. Despite some economists' belief that farmers just recognized their own self-interest in purchasing land, machinery, plumbing, and electrification for their barns and homes, the facts show that rural banks effectively forced farmers to modernize as a sign of their creditworthiness. State and federal regulations of various sorts have long disguised the iron hand of force in the velvet glove of persuasion. In agriculture, one can see this in standardization measures among implement manufacturers as well as dairy producers and citrus growers. The fact that, where issues of public health and convenience are concerned, we tend to approve of such regulations, does not make such regulations any less exemplars of high modernism.

Agrarian Intellectuals in a Democratizing State

A Collective Biography of USDA Leaders in the Intended New Deal

JESS GILBERT

> *Those who voice the loudest objections to the planning now being done*
> *[in the New Deal] are the disappointed politicians, the orthodox*
> *economists, and the business men who think their interests are likely to*
> *be adversely affected by any plans made by farmers, workers, and un-*
> *conventional economists.*

> —USDA Economist Bushrod Allin (1937)

New Deal Agrarian Intellectuals in Theory and History

The agricultural New Deal and its "policy intellectuals" have become major subjects for innovative research and theorizing about the modern state. Social scientists Theda Skocpol and Kenneth Finegold draw attention to statist agrarian institutions such as land-grant colleges and the U.S. Department of

An earlier version of this essay was presented at the annual meeting of the Social Science History Association, Washington, D.C., October 1997. Financial support for this research came from the Wisconsin Agricultural Experiment Station, College of Agricultural and Life Sciences, University of Wisconsin—Madison. Thanks to Margaret Christie, David Lachman, and Spencer D. Wood for research assistance, and to Deborah Fitzgerald, Robert Johnston, Olaf Larson, Alice O'Connor, Cathy Stock, Mary Summers, Vicky Woeste, and Spencer Wood for all their good suggestions.

A much shorter version of the collective biography in this essay appears, together with a group biography of Rexford Tugwell, Jerome Frank, Alger Hiss, and three others, in Jess Gilbert, "Eastern Urban Liberals and Midwestern Agrarian Intellectuals: Two Group Portraits of Progressives in the New Deal Department of Agriculture," *Agricultural History* 74 (2000): 162–80.

Agriculture (USDA) that produced "state-centered" and "autonomous" New Deal experts like M. L. Wilson and Howard R. Tolley. Historian Catherine McNicol Stock employs sophisticated class theory to criticize the "intellectual imperialism" of policymakers such as USDA Secretary Henry A. Wallace who planned but, she says, did not understand farm life. And in this volume, historian of science Deborah Fitzgerald suggests that these New Dealers were "high modernists," that is, agricultural rationalizers and vigorous advocates of technology.[1] In this essay, however, I wish to present an alternative interpretation that stresses the agrarian intellectuals' work for family farmers, progressive reform, and democratizing policies.

Skocpol and Finegold, Stock, and Fitzgerald all offer insights into New Deal agricultural policy, but ultimately each provides a one-sided view. Skocpol and Finegold, for example, posit the subordination of individuals to institutions. And they are so intent on establishing the autonomy from "society" of state actors and institutions that they overlook the distinctive class position of family farmers (landowning producers without wage labor)—precisely the social class that yielded the agrarian intellectuals. In turn, Stock acknowledges that the New Dealers were "distant friends and relations" of the Dakota farmers she studies. But she asserts that they, USDA's "new middle class," were antidemocratic bureaucrats who favored centralized planning—even though these department leaders explicitly rejected such elitism. Stock even refers to Henry Wallace and M. L. Wilson as "urban outsiders," and writes as if rural people had nothing to do with creating the New Deal. Finally, Fitzgerald focuses on the twenties rather than the thirties; I note only that Wallace and Wilson, as good pragmatists, learned from experience and changed priorities considerably over the decades—in a less "scientistic," more democratic direction. However, Fitzgerald's chief theoretical source, James Scott, classifies Wilson with others as "high modernist" planners during the New Deal, meaning that they were industrializing rationalists consistently opposed to historical tradition and local cultures. Further, Scott and others seem to deny the possibility, or at least the likelihood, of meaningful social reform and a democratizing state.[2]

---

[1] Kenneth Finegold and Theda Skocpol, *State and Party in America's New Deal* (Madison: University of Wisconsin Press, 1995); Catherine McNicol Stock, *Main Street in Crisis: The Great Depression and the Old Middle Class on the Northern Plains* (Chapel Hill: University of North Carolina Press, 1992); Deborah Fitzgerald, "Accounting for Change: Farmers and the Modernizing State," this volume. Another current perspective is reflected in Mary Summers's chapter in this collection; I agree substantially with it and with her other work on the New Deal such as "The New Deal Farm Programs: Looking for Reconstruction in American Agriculture," *Agricultural History* 74 (2000): 241–57.

[2] Finegold and Skocpol, *State and Party*, 60; Stock, *Main Street*, 97–118; Stock, *Rural Radicals: Righteous Rage in the American Grain* (Ithaca: Cornell University Press, 1996), 79; Fitzgerald, "Accounting for Change"; James C. Scott, *Seeing Like a State: How Certain Schemes to Improve*

Other historians present more differentiated views of policy intellectuals and the modern state. David Hamilton sees that USDA officials and farm economists were indeed a "new elite"—but one with a difference. Such agrarian modernizers built an antibureaucratic "associational state," based on voluntary, cooperative planning by public agencies and private economic groups, without centralized administration. Labor historian Leon Fink treats the New Deal only slightly and agriculture not at all, yet his work on activist intellectuals is also relevant. While not without "new middle class" faults, Progressives such as Jane Addams and John Dewey believed that they could connect with a democratic public and reform society together. The new social sciences tended to distance experts from their subjects, but this was not universally true. For instance, Fink points to labor education organizations and even the odd university (like the one in Madison, Wisconsin) that fought this technocratic trend. Both Fink and Hamilton investigate various ways in which intellectuals related to citizens and the state, advocating and even celebrating their "democratic commitments."[3]

I side with Hamilton and Fink and hope to put into question the analyses of Skocpol, Finegold, Stock, Scott, and Fitzgerald. The New Deal agrarian intellectuals not only arose from but worked in the interests of midwestern family farmers. They also advanced programs for and visions of a rural America that would be modern as well as participatory-democratic. This was the "Third" or "Intended New Deal," to use Otis L. Graham's label, the one envisioned and implemented in the late thirties but soon destroyed.[4] Rather than being simply "autonomous" and "urban outsiders," the USDA leaders at this time were organic intellectuals who proposed what we might call (in response to Scott's and Fitzgerald's concept-cum-epithet) "low modernism."

---

the Human Condition Have Failed (New Haven, Conn.: Yale University Press, 1998), 87–102, 199–201. For my earlier critique of Skocpol and Finegold, see Jess Gilbert and Carolyn Howe, "Beyond 'State vs. Society': Theories of the State and New Deal Agricultural Policy," *American Sociological Review* 56 (1991): 204–20; and their response in Finegold and Skocpol, *State and Party*, 181–96. See also Fitzgerald on M. L. Wilson's 1929 work in the USSR, "Blinded by Technology: American Agriculture in the Soviet Union, 1928–1932," *Agricultural History* 70 (1996): 459–86.

[3] David E. Hamilton, *From New Day to New Deal: American Farm Policy from Hoover to Roosevelt, 1928–1933* (Chapel Hill: University of North Carolina Press, 1991); Hamilton, "Building the Associative State: The Department of Agriculture and American State-Building," *Agricultural History* 64 (1990): 207–18; Leon Fink, *Progressive Intellectuals and the Dilemmas of Democratic Commitment* (Cambridge, Mass.: Harvard University Press, 1997), 20–51.

[4] Otis L. Graham, Jr., "Franklin Roosevelt and the Intended New Deal," in *Essays in Honor of James MacGregor Burns*, ed. Michael R. Beschloss and Thomas E. Cronin (Englewood Cliffs, N.J.: Prentice-Hall, 1989), 78. See also Barry D. Karl, *The Uneasy State: The United States from 1915 to 1945* (Chicago: University of Chicago Press, 1983), 155–81; and Karl, "Constitution and General Planning: The Third New Deal Revisited," *Supreme Court Review* (1988): 163–201. For an excellent overview of the historiography, see John W. Jeffries, "A 'Third New Deal'? Liberal Policy and the American State, 1937–1945," *Journal of Policy History* 8 (1996): 387–409. None of these sources treat agricultural policy to any degree.

The heart of this matter doubtless transcends academic debate over warring labels, conflicting evidence, or multidisciplinary use of social-scientific concepts—important as those are. Rather, it concerns core political issues of modern capitalist society. How are public intellectuals and local citizens connected to one another? What does this relationship mean for the possibility of democracy? Indeed, is there even room, as Leon Fink says, for serious "democratic-intellectual engagement" in the modern world? Despite often condescending scholarly tones (and tomes) toward Progressives and New Dealers alike, we have still not resolved these problems any more, and probably less, than they did.[5] Statist agrarian intellectuals (because of their distinctive social background, ideological visions, and actual programmatic achievements) therefore provide a key opportunity to reexamine such pressing political as well as theoretical issues.

Formative Influences:
Family Farms, Institutional Economics, and the BAE

We should first ask: Where did the ideas for the New Deal agrarian reforms come from? What kind of people, from what backgrounds, developed and carried out such progressive programs? How were they connected to rural America? My approach to these questions emphasizes collective biography; I focus on six of the major policy intellectuals in the New Deal's USDA. They were not representative of all departmental employees but instead were the leaders of its most innovative reforms, particularly of the Intended New Deal.

The top three choices are obvious: Henry A. Wallace, secretary of agriculture; M. L. Wilson, undersecretary of agriculture and later director of Federal Extension; and Howard R. Tolley, administrator of the Agricultural Adjustment Administration and later Bureau of Agricultural Economics (BAE) chief. In addition to their official positions, they provided general intellectual leadership to the New Deal. The second three also played major roles in the influential BAE during the late 1930s, when the Intended New Deal thrived: Lewis C. Gray, head of the Division of Land Economics and assistant BAE chief; Carl C. Taylor, head of the Division of Farm Population and Rural Welfare; and Bushrod W. Allin, head of the Division of State and Local Planning, which led the BAE's democratic planning effort.

The following collective biography emphasizes three formative periods in the lives of these agrarian intellectuals before the New Deal—childhood, education, and early career. As a preview, let me mention the prototype of these New Dealers: Henry C. Taylor. He came from the previous generation but exemplified all of the characteristics (absent the

---

[5] Fink, *Progressive Intellectuals*, 11–12, 280.

participatory-democratic sensibility, admittedly a large exception) in the group portrait sketched below. Born in 1873 and reared on a Scots-Irish family farm in rural Iowa, he was smart, ambitious, and self-assured. He graduated in agriculture from Iowa State College in 1896. Taylor then entered the University of Wisconsin to study with Richard T. Ely, a famous and unorthodox (some even said radical) political economist. After earning a Ph.D. in 1902, he joined Ely's department, but soon founded his own Department of Agricultural Economics, the first in the country. Later he moved to the USDA in Washington, and in 1922 established the department's core BAE. He was fired in 1925 by Calvin Coolidge for supporting farm legislation that the president vetoed, but his organizations continued. As disciplinary founder, land-grant professor, institution builder, policy advisor, and general "ideas man," Taylor mentored all the economists who became agrarian New Dealers, and his biographical pattern was repeated in the six lives below.[6] Table 1 outlines the group's paths leading to the USDA and the Intended New Deal.

Social Origins: Midwestern Family Farm Boys

All but one of the future New Dealers were born in the same time and place: the rural Midwest of the 1880s. (Allin, born in Kentucky in 1899, was the exception.) They were reared on family farms in northern Missouri (Gray), Indiana (Tolley), and Iowa (Wallace, Wilson, and Taylor). This social and family background plainly helped determine their careers as students of rural society. More than that, though, three related features of late nineteenth-century Midwestern family farming are relevant to their later work and politics: an ingrained one-class view of society, civic republicanism, and a reforming Protestant spirit. These earliest influences are the root sources of the Intended New Deal in agriculture.[7]

---

[6] Thanks to the editorial work of Kenneth H. Parsons, Taylor's previously unpublished memoir written in 1926, *A Farm Economist in Washington, 1919–1925*, is now available (Madison: Department of Agricultural Economics, University of Wisconsin–Madison, 1992). In addition to Taylor's informative and revealing text, Parsons appended some useful short pieces, including his own "Henry Charles Taylor, 1873–1969: Organizer and First Head of USDA's Bureau of Agricultural Economics," ibid., 256–63. See also two more critical articles by Harry C. McDean, "Professionalism, Policy, and Farm Economists in the Early Bureau of Agricultural Economics," *Agricultural History* 57 (1983): 64–82, and "Professionalism in the Rural Social Sciences, 1896–1919," ibid., 58 (1984): 373–92; and also Jess Gilbert and Ellen Baker, "Wisconsin Economists and New Deal Agricultural Policy: The Legacy of Progressive Professors," *Wisconsin Magazine of History* 80 (1997): 280–312, which treats Ely, John R. Commons, Henry Taylor, Gray, Wilson, and Allin. Most of the material below on Wisconsin comes from this latter article.

[7] For Gray, biographical details may be found in Henry C. Taylor, "L. C. Gray, Agricultural Historian and Land Economist," *Agricultural History* 26 (1952): 165; E. H. W. and H. C. T., "Lewis Cecil Gray, 1881–1952," *Journal of Farm Economics* 35 (1953): 157. On Taylor, see Joseph Knapp, "Carl C. Taylor," in *Biographical Sketches of 101 Major Pioneers in Cooperative*

TABLE 9-1 SOCIAL PROFILE OF THE
AGRARIAN INTELLECTUALS IN THE NEW DEAL USDA

	Birth Place / Year	Education	Early Career (1920s)	Position in the New Deal
Henry A. Wallace	1888 Iowa	Iowa State '10 Iowa State M.S. '20	Iowa farm editor, geneticist, statistician, economist; BAE consultant	Secretary of Agriculture, 1933–40; U.S. Vice President, 1941–45
M. L. Wilson	1885 Iowa	Iowa State '06 U. Wisconsin M.S. '20	Montana State agricultural economist; BAE	AAA Wheat Section Head, 1933; Subsistence Homesteads Division Director, 1933–34; Assistant Secretary of Agriculture, 1934–35; Under Secretary of Agriculture, 1936–40; Federal Extension Director, 1940–52
Howard R. Tolley	1889 Indiana	U. Indiana '10	BAE; U. Cal. agricultural economist	AAA Specialty Crops Section Head, 1933; AAA Program Planning Division Head 1933–34; AAA Administrator, 1936–38; BAE Chief, 1938–46

Name	Birth	Education	Position	Career
L. C. Gray	1881 Missouri	William Jewell (Mo.) '00 U. Wisconsin Ph.D. '11	BAE land economist	Founder and Head of BAE Land Economics Division, 1919–37; AAA Land Policy Section Head, 1933–35; RA Assistant Administrator, 1935–37; Assistant BAE Chief, 1937–40
Carl C. Taylor	1884 Iowa	Drake (Iowa) '11 U. Missouri Ph.D. '18	N.C. State rural sociologist	In Subsistence Homesteads Division, 1933–34; RA Rural Resettlement Division Head, 1935; BAE Farm Population and Rural Welfare Division Head, 1935–53
Bushrod W. Allin	1899 Kentucky	U. Wisconsin '21 U. Wisconsin Ph.D. '26	U. Wisconsin agricultural economist; BAE	In AAA Program Planning Division and the Secretary's Office of Land Use Coordination, 1934–38; BAE State and Local Planning Division Head, 1938–42

Note: BAE = Bureau of Agricultural Economics
AAA = Agricultural Adjustment Administration
RA = Resettlement Administration

Capitalism is a social system based on the class division between property owners and wage workers. But family farming does not match that mold. In the words of Harriet Friedmann, it is a form of "household commodity production in the era of wage labor." Unlike the industrializing urban North or the plantation South, the nineteenth-century rural Midwest was substantially a one-class society. That is, most farm families operated their own land—or rather, family labor worked the land owned by the husband/father. There were gender and age inequalities to be sure, but no class divisions within the enterprise, and relatively few in rural communities. Wage labor existed but was not the norm on midwestern farms. The modern family farm, then, was an anomaly in the emerging capitalist society: property and labor (the basic parameters of class) were combined within the same household. Some farmers owned more land than others, yet there was a basically egalitarian distribution of wealth, especially in comparison to cities and plantations. The point is simply that the rural Midwest at this time was not a deeply class-divided society.[8]

Family farming did not altogether fit, either structurally or ideologically, into the rising urban-industrial capitalism of the United States. Tensions persisted between these two forms of social production and reproduction. In 1965, after a long career of public agrarian work, M. L. Wilson confessed:

Everyone is a creature of his home environment, and as a child he develops in his mind stereotypes which he carries with him throughout his life. I was

Development, ed. Joseph Knapp (Washington, D.C., 1967), 489–95; Olaf F. Larson and Julie N. Zimmerman, with Edward O. Moe, *Sociology in Government: The Galpin-Taylor Years in the United States Department of Agriculture, 1919–1953* (Boulder, Colo.: Westview Press, forthcoming); Margaret M. Christie, "Carl C. Taylor, 'Organic Intellectual' in the New Deal Department of Agriculture" (M S. thesis, University of Wisconsin—Madison, 1996). On Wilson, see O. E. Baker, Ralph Borsodi, and M. L. Wilson, *Agriculture in Modern Life* (New York: Harper & Bros., 1939), 215–81; Wilson, "M. L. Wilson," in *American Spiritual Autobiographies*, ed. Louis Finkelstein (New York: Harper, 1948), 1–24; "The Reminiscences of Milburn Lincoln Wilson," Columbia Oral History Collection, Columbia University; Harry Carson McDean, "M. L. Wilson and Agricultural Reform in Twentieth Century America" (Ph.D. diss., University of California—Los Angeles, 1969). On Wallace, see Russell Lord, *The Wallaces of Iowa* (Boston: Houghton Mifflin, 1947); Graham White and John Maze, *Henry A. Wallace: His Search for a New World Order* (Chapel Hill: University of North Carolina Press, 1995); Edward L. Schapsmeier and Frederick H. Schapsmeier, *Henry A. Wallace of Iowa: The Agrarian Years, 1910–1940* (Ames: Iowa State University Press, 1968); and John C. Culver and John Hyde, *American Dreamer: The Life and Times of Henry A. Wallace* (New York: Norton, 2000). On Tolley, see M. R. Benedict and M. L. Wilson, "Howard Ross Tolley, 1889–1958," *Journal of Farm Economics* 41 (1959): 1–2; "The Reminiscences of Howard R. Tolley," Columbia Oral History Collection, Columbia University. On Allin, see "The Agricultural-Business Conflict" (draft ms., 1958), Bushrod W. Allin Papers (box 4), Parks Library Special Collections, Iowa State University, Ames.

[8] Harriet Friedmann, "World Market, State, and Family Farm: Social Bases of Household Production in the Era of Wage Labor," *Comparative Studies in Society and History* 20 (1978): 545–86; Jake Temple Kirby, *Rural Worlds Lost: The American South, 1920–1960* (Baton Rouge: Louisiana State University), 1–22, 49; Kirby, "Rural Culture in the American Middle West: Jefferson to Jane Smiley," *Agriculture History* 70 (1996): 581–97. Deborah Fink gives a different class view in *Cutting into the Meatpacking Line: Workers and Change in the Rural Midwest* (Chapel Hill: University of North Carolina Press, 1998).

born in a community of corn belt farmers where the farms ranged from quarter to half-sections in size [i.e., 160 to 320 acres]. Therefore, instinctively when I am talking about farmers, I am actually thinking about the kind of farmers and farm families that live on the farms that you look down upon when you fly over the Corn Belt.

Growing up in such a cultural milieu, farm boys developed certain images of normal social relations, daily community life, and the "good society"—predispositions that led them readily to transform the nation's political economy for the benefit of farmers such as they sprang from.[9]

This nineteenth-century family farm culture, of course, was the kind that Thomas Jefferson extolled as the agrarian ideal. His political economy required self-sufficient property owners in order to meet the prerequisites of democracy. Jefferson and other American revolutionaries were "civic republicans" who asserted that common citizens (not just elites) could direct society, including their government; indeed, such citizens had a duty to do so. This democratic faith held that a virtuous citizenry would advance the common good—a belief whose last great political exemplar was Abraham Lincoln. The material base for this republican ideal had disappeared from most of America by the late nineteenth century, giving way to industrial urbanism, scientific expertise, and the specialized professions. However, it lived on in supposedly backward regions of the country like the rural Midwest. As youngsters, Henry Wallace and the others thus imbibed fading and unfashionable values (such as participatory democracy and citizen action) and later carried them into the New Deal. Not for nothing was M. L. Wilson's middle name "Lincoln"; in addition to his day jobs, he was a lifelong and world-class collector of Lincoln memorabilia.[10]

The other critical element in the farm boys' background was a Protestant upbringing, as Scots-Irish Presbyterians, Disciples of Christ, or Methodists. In addition to duty to God, they also learned a certain responsibility to fellow citizens and society at large. M. L. Wilson's "spiritual autobiography" relates his youthful churchgoing and his parents' religious teachings. His father was Presbyterian and his mother Quaker; to them he attributed

[9] M. L. Wilson, "The Communication and Utilization of the Results of Agricultural Research by American Farmers: A Case History, 1900–1950," in Charles Y. Glock et al., *Case Studies in Bringing Behavioral Science into Use* (Stanford, Calif.: Stanford University Institute for Communication Research, 1961), 79. See also Christie, "Carl C. Taylor," and Wilson and Tolley, Columbia Oral History Collection.

[10] Kirby, "Rural Culture"; McDean, "M. L. Wilson"; Mary O. Furner, "The Republican Tradition and the New Liberalism: Social Investigation, State Building, and Social Learning in the Gilded Age," in *The State and Social Investigation in Britain and the United States,* ed. Michael J. Lacey and Mary O. Furner (Washington, D.C.: Woodrow Wilson Center Press, 1993), 171–241; Joyce Appleby, *Liberalism and Republicanism in the Historical Imagination* (Cambridge, Mass.: Harvard University Press, 1992); Appleby, "Commercial Farming and the 'Agrarian Myth' in the Early Republic," *Journal of American History* 68 (1982): 833–49, which opens with M. L. Wilson quoting Henry A. Wallace in 1943; William M. Sullivan, *Reconstructing Public Philosophy* (Berkeley: University of California Press, 1986); Robert N. Bellah, Richard Madsen, William M. Sullivan, Ann Swidler, and Steven M. Tipton, *The Good Society* (New York: Knopf, 1991).

whatever goodwill and tolerance he later exhibited (it was considerable). Howard Tolley's family was quite active in the local church, and during his teenage years his own interest in Christianity rekindled. Beyond their local experiences, all the agrarian New Dealers were touched by the Social Gospel movement. In fact, some of their future professors as well as Carl Taylor's older brother were national leaders in this Protestant effort to apply biblical precepts of social justice toward the betterment of society. Crusading Christianity easily melded into a social reformism.[11]

Henry A. Wallace's childhood was an exaggerated version of all these social influences in the rural Midwest—exaggerated, in part, because of the unusually strong impact of his grandfather. "Uncle Henry," as he signed his magazine column to Iowa farm boys, was father to one USDA secretary (Henry C.) and grandfather to another (Henry A.). Presbyterian minister and farmer turned agrarian journalist and editor, this "first Henry Wallace" (1836–1916) supported President Lincoln and the Radical Republicans, the Farmers' Alliance and Progressive Republicans, scientific agriculture and Protestant faith, agrarianism and industrial modernization. He opposed railroads and other corporate monopolies that exploited farmers and deserved state regulation. Henry A. Wallace later admitted that his grandfather had "more influence [on me] than anybody else" in matters ranging from agriculture to politics to religion. The elder Wallace spotted something special in "Young Henry" and consciously strove to shape the life and mind of his grandson. Thus the New Deal secretary of agriculture had three generations of midwestern agrarian experiences and resources—intellectual, cultural, political, spiritual—to draw upon. Nor was he alone, for as M. L. Wilson recalled, "The Wallaces helped form my mind and character, just as they did for hundreds of thousands of other folks in Iowa."[12]

After a half-century of advancing rural reform at home and abroad, Wilson spoke of a certain "consciousness of kind," or "guild-like social structure in American rural society," between public agricultural workers and midwestern family farmers. Land-grant teachers, researchers, and extension agents were usually from such families. He noted the "lack of any social or psychological gulf between the people in professional agriculture and working farmers." Agricultural professors and researchers, he added, "feel a sort of moral responsibility for keeping in close touch with the farmers of their state." Allowing for some class bias here (the farmers in his mind were landowning, commercially successful, and probably above av-

---

[11] Wilson, "M. L. Wilson"; Tolley, Columbia Oral History Collection; Christie, "Carl C. Taylor"; Ronald C. White, Jr., and C. Howard Hopkins, *The Social Gospel: Religion and Reform in Changing America* (Philadelphia: Temple University Press, 1976); Gary Dorrien, *Soul in Society: The Making and Renewal of Social Christianity* (Minneapolis: Fortress Press, 1995).

[12] Richard S. Kirkendall, *Uncle Henry: A Documentary Profile of the First Henry Wallace* (Ames: Iowa State University Press, 1993), 219 passim.

erage), Wilson's point still applies to the connection between the agrarian New Dealers and midwestern farmers of the 1930s. They were cut from the same cloth. The six people investigated here, that is, continued by and large to represent the type of farm families from whom they came. The concept of "organic intellectual" thus captures much truth about these Midwestern farm boys made good—an interpretation elaborated in my conclusion.[13]

Education: Agricultural Colleges and Institutional Economics

Still, these bright farm boys did leave the farm and become social scientists. They attended college in their home states, except for Allin who ventured even as an undergraduate to the University of Wisconsin. Two of them graduated from Protestant liberal arts institutions (Gray from William Jewell College northeast of Kansas City, Taylor from Drake University in Des Moines). Three finished in technical agriculture from midwestern land-grant colleges (Iowa State and Wisconsin); Tolley, from Indiana University. Four earned graduate degrees in the "new social sciences" at leading state agricultural universities in the region. Henry Wallace continued his formal education in animal science; original work in genetics and statistics, economics and journalism, soon marked him as an unusually adept intellect. Most significantly, all six students learned the radical reformism and public policy lessons of institutional economics from the two reigning geniuses of the field. Thorstein Veblen and John R. Commons taught this alternative kind of economics that emphasized a historical, statist, and problem-solving orientation. Even during Wallace's undergraduate studies at Iowa State, a Wisconsin economist introduced him to institutionalism, especially Veblen's ideas, which appealed to him for the rest of his life.[14]

Three of the others—Gray, Wilson, and Allin—obtained graduate degrees from the University of Wisconsin, where they acquired a distinctive education in institutional economics. The "neoclassical revolution" swept through American economics around World War I, but Wisconsin rejected it in favor of an empirical, ethical, and policy-driven approach to the nation's political economy. A leading social scientist of the age, Richard T. Ely

---

[13] M. L. Wilson, "Communication and Utilization," 80. A USDA colleague during the New Deal wrote: "Many rural sociologists and other professionals in the field of agriculture grew up on family-sized farms and tend to entertain a bias for that sized holding, as against the hacienda and the 'factory farm.'" Charles P. Loomis and Zona Kemp Loomis, "Rural Sociology," in *The Uses of Sociology*, ed. Paul F. Lazarsfeld, William H. Sewell, and Harold L. Wilensky (New York: Basic Books, 1967), 660.

[14] Allin grew up mostly in Texas on a family farm. In high school, he asked his agriculture teacher what was the best college for farm boys to attend. His teacher said Iowa State or Wisconsin, so at age seventeen Allin began his long career in Madison (telephone conversation with Thelma Allin, February 27, 1992).

had come to the university in 1892 to direct a new School of Economics, Political Science, and History, which included Frederick Jackson Turner (his former student at Johns Hopkins). They taught Iowan Henry C. Taylor, who joined their faculty in 1902. Within four years, Ely had hired two other of his earlier and more radical doctoral students: sociologist Edward A. Ross and economist John R. Commons. In 1909, Henry Taylor founded the Department of Agricultural Economics at Wisconsin, into which he soon hired the first American rural sociologist (Charles J. Galpin) and another rural Iowan and Ely/Turner graduate (Benjamin H. Hibbard). These professors formed the unique Wisconsin school of institutional and agricultural economics.[15]

The Progressive professors in Madison, as elsewhere, were confronting some massive problems of modern capitalist society. How were the conflicting industrial classes (owners and workers) to coexist? What was the proper role of the state? What reforms were needed to assist the laboring classes, especially wage workers and farmers? Ely, Ross, Commons, and Taylor focused on these issues in their teaching and research. Their answers all involved a "middle way" between laissez-faire capitalism and revolutionary socialism. Government had major and permanent roles in the economy. Collective action and long-range structural reforms were necessary, and new institutions must be created by scientists and citizens working together. Many of these precepts defined the "Wisconsin Idea" which made the state a Progressive showcase for social legislation. Most important here was labor historian, policy expert, and institutional economist John R. Commons, whose graduate students largely developed the New Deal's measures for social security, labor relations, and agriculture. Prominent in the latter work were agricultural economists Gray, Wilson, and Allin.[16]

Late in their careers, all three old New Dealers spoke of Madison's influence. Gray recalled that when he had been in graduate school, "laissez-faire" ruled the minds of economists, and no "public action" countered the traditional land policy of rapid privatization: "At the University of Wisconsin, however, under the inspiration of Richard T. Ely and H. C. Taylor, far more attention was then given to land and its problems than in any other American institution." Wilson similarly remembered his graduate days:

> At that time, the University of Wisconsin was called a very liberal institution in its economics, sociology, and political science, and these were views that I got pretty much there.... The things that fundamentally affected my thinking were these institutional ideas from Professor Commons's courses, social psychology and social behavior from Ross's course, and Ely's philosophy, which was to quite an extent this historical-institutional type.

[15] Gilbert and Baker, "Wisconsin Economists."
[16] Ibid.

In a 1931 letter to Allin, Wilson wrote that John R. Commons was "one of the great original and inventive minds of his period." Allin himself considered Commons "to be the genius of our age." Upon FDR's choosing of Henry A. Wallace as USDA secretary, Allin wrote to Wilson: "If Wallace will surround himself with men of your philosophy—the philosophy of John R.—he will teach some economics to a lot of economic illiterates in high places. He must do so." Doubtless "John R." was proud of his Wisconsin students in the New Deal.[17]

Carl Taylor studied with the other major institutional economist, Thorstein Veblen, who was more radical but less policy-oriented than Commons. Earlier, Taylor had attended two Disciples of Christ colleges and earned a master's degree at the University of Texas, where he worked part-time as a preacher. In 1914, Taylor entered the doctoral program in sociology at the University of Missouri, largely to study with Veblen. The two shared an office, which helped Taylor get beyond the economist's notoriously gruff manner with students, as did their common background from midwestern family farms. They also shared a personal dislike of land speculation, which had hurt both their families. From Veblen, Taylor gained a radical critique of the modern "price and market economy," including Veblen's disequilibrium theory of social change ("cultural lag") and a penchant for historical class analysis. Reminiscent of Wilson's and Allin's praise for Commons, Taylor called Veblen "one of the greatest intellectuals in the world." Like the Wisconsin students, Taylor had other outstanding professors. He worked briefly with national rural leader Kenyon Butterfield at the Massachusetts State College of Agriculture, sociologist Franklin Giddings at Columbia University, and race relations expert Robert E. Park of the "Chicago School" of sociology. Taylor finished his Ph.D. at Missouri in 1918.[18]

A related intellectual current also affected the agrarian New Dealers: American pragmatism. John Dewey's ideas specifically were connected to those of institutionalists Veblen and Commons. But Dewey and William James had additional influence on Henry Wallace and M. L. Wilson (and Carl Taylor: Robert Park had studied with Dewey). James's *Varieties of Religious Experience* had a profound impact on both New Dealers-to-be; it helped them maintain a Christian faith in light of modern thought. Dewey was more consequential, especially for Wilson, who claimed the pragmatist as his favorite philosopher. In 1920, Wilson took Professor Commons's

[17] Gray, "Evolution of the Land Use Program of the United States Department of Agriculture," March 29, 1939, National Archives, Washington, D.C., RG 83, entry 213, box 1; Wilson, Columbia Oral History Collection, 579; Wilson to Allin, August 27, 1931, and Allin to Wilson, February 27, 1933, both in M. L. Wilson Papers, file E-69, Montana State University Library, Bozeman; Allin to B. M. Selekman, January 8, 1952, Allin Papers; John R. Commons, *Myself: The Autobiography of John R. Commons* (1934; reprint ed., Madison: University of Wisconsin Press, 1964), 74–77.
[18] Christie, "Carl C. Taylor."

advice and began doctoral work in philosophy at the University of Chicago, where he studied with Dewey's collaborator and fellow Progressive James H. Tufts. Although Wilson never finished the degree, he did keep up with Dewey's inspiring "public-intellectual" output during the twenties and thirties. Later as USDA assistant secretary, he hired one of his former philosophy professors to direct discussion groups for farmers and schools of philosophy for extension workers. Predictably, these large-scale educational programs had a strong bias toward pragmatic philosophy. What Wilson called "a practical and peculiarly American philosophy of social reform," based on pragmatism and institutionalism, thus underlay much of the New Deal in agriculture.[19]

The future New Dealers, in sum, received excellent graduate educations, but of a particular sort. They studied with some of America's best and most radical social scientists, who also happened to be public intellectuals. Whether themselves rural-oriented or not, their students applied the knowledge gleaned to the problems of farmers in the context of the land-grant colleges of agriculture. Of especial importance was their in-service training among the largest concentration of social scientists anywhere in the federal government—perhaps in the world.

Early Careers in the 1920s: Activist Professors and Statist Social Scientists

Howard Tolley did not attend the University of Wisconsin but attained its distinctive institutionalist education by other means. He joined the USDA in 1915 and learned agricultural economics after Henry Taylor became his supervisor. He was tutored by Taylor himself, L. C. Gray, and other Wisconsin economists who were in and out of the Bureau of Agricultural Economics during the twenties, notably John D. Black and M. L. Wilson. Tolley first applied his quantitative skills to the development of new techniques, multiple correlation analysis and input-output studies. He rose rapidly in the bureau, becoming first head of the Division of Farm Management and assistant BAE chief for research in 1928. Two years later he became director of the new Giannini Foundation of Agricultural Economics at the University of California in Berkeley. In 1933, he was

[19] Henry A. Wallace, *Statesmanship and Religion* (New York: Round Table Press, 1934); Mark L. Kleinman, "Searching for the 'Inner Light': The Development of Henry A. Wallace's Experimental Spiritualism," *Annals of Iowa* 53 (1994): 195–218; M. L. Wilson, Columbia Oral History Collection, 1018, 2091; Wilson, "Beyond Economics," in *The Yearbook of Agriculture, 1940* (Washington, D.C.: Government Printing Office, 1940), 936–37. On the BAE farmer discussion groups and schools of philosophy, see BAE division head Carl F. Taeusch, "Schools of Philosophy for Farmers," ibid., 1111–24; McDean, "M. L. Wilson," 414–25, 484–88; Richard S. Kirkendall, *Social Scientists and Farm Politics in the Age of Roosevelt* (Columbia: University of Missouri Press, 1966), 140–43, 170, 187–90.

president of the American Farm Economic Association. Tolley was only one case, however impressive, of the BAE's nurturing and molding of a first-rate social scientist who assumed a major university post and, of course, top government jobs in the thirties and forties. This remarkable federal agency, in short, provided the final training ground for the economists who would lead the agrarian New Deal.[20]

President Harding's secretary of agriculture Henry C. Wallace and Wisconsin economist Henry C. Taylor (both redheaded Scots-Irishmen from rural Iowa) founded the BAE in 1922. Earlier, Taylor had placed three of his doctoral students in key social science positions within USDA, including L. C. Gray as head of the Division of Land Economics. He also brought his departmental colleague from Wisconsin, Charles Galpin, to lead the Division of Farm Population and Rural Life (the sociology unit that Carl Taylor later directed). In 1919 Taylor played a central role in organizing the American Farm Economic Association and became its second president. He and other BAE members dominated its annual meetings as well as the new *Journal of Farm Economics*. In the 1920s, it is little exaggeration to say, the BAE essentially developed the new fields of land economics, agricultural history, rural sociology, and agricultural economics. This extremely large group of social scientists aimed to expand not only their own professional status, but also the welfare of farmers, especially those of moderate property and from the Midwest.[21]

Based on a Progressive faith in social-scientific enlightenment, the BAE of the twenties sought to "make facts useful to farmers." It gathered and publicized crop and livestock statistics, set and enforced uniform commodity standards, conducted farm management and "rural life" studies, centralized and disseminated information on cooperatives, investigated foreign markets, and improved domestic marketing (with inspections and a news service that included the latest technology, that of radio). A major development was the Outlook Reports, begun in 1923. To assist farmers in adjusting their production, Howard Tolley, Henry A. Wallace (son of the then secretary), and other statistical economists forecast the future supply, demand, and prices of agricultural commodities. About this innovative applied research effort, which continues today, Taylor said: "The farmers were

[20] Richard S. Kirkendall, " Howard Tolley and Agricultural Planning in the 1930s," *Agricultural History* 39 (1966): 25–33; Kirkendall, *Social Scientists,* 15–17; Benedict and Wilson, "Howard Ross Tolley." At Berkeley, Tolley taught agricultural economics to Canadian farm boy John Kenneth Galbraith. Another famous academic who perfected his skills in the BAE (as a sample surveyor and division head) was Rensis Likert, who left USDA in 1946 to found the Institute for Social Research at the University of Michigan.

[21] Henry C. Taylor, *A Farm Economist in Washington;* Gilbert and Baker, "Wisconsin Economists"; McDean, "Professionalism"; Donald L. Winters, "The Persistence of Progressivism: Henry Cantwell Wallace and the Movement for Agricultural Economics," *Agricultural History* 41 (1967): 109–20.

not told what to do but given the facts they needed in order to act intelligently." In its early days, then, the BAE, while being an activist state agency, was still individualist and somewhat paternalistic: farmers could improve their situation if they followed the advice of the USDA experts.[22]

Of the six agrarian intellectuals portrayed here, L. C. Gray was closest to Henry Taylor in age, training, and technocratic leanings. As students, both worked closely with Richard T. Ely and Frederick Jackson Turner, and Taylor was Gray's dissertation advisor. After getting his Ph.D., Gray taught for several years in Wisconsin's two economics departments—Ely's and Taylor's. When Taylor went to work at USDA in 1919, Gray accompanied him. The Division of Land Economics, which Gray led for twenty years, was the numerical and theoretical core of the BAE. In 1928 Gray became president of the American Farm Economic Association. As one of the leading land economists in the country and the top land use planner in USDA, Gray made sure that his research throughout the twenties fed directly into the New Deal land programs, most of which he directed.[23]

Gary never espoused participatory democracy as the others, particularly M. L. Wilson, did. After graduating from Iowa State, he trekked to the Great Plains as a pioneer on several farms. He then began working for Montana's new Extension Service and became head of the agency in 1915. All told, Wilson spent twelve years in the West prior to his graduate education at Wisconsin, after which he chaired agricultural economics at Montana State College. Henry Taylor brought him in to lead the BAE's Division of Farm Management and Costs in the midtwenties, when Wilson also served as president of the American Farm Economic Association. He returned to Montana State in 1926 and oversaw an experiment in large-scale wheat farming and alternative land tenure arrangements. This project, Fairway Farms, became a model for later New Deal land reforms that turned tenants into owners. In 1929, Wilson spent six months in the Soviet Union as advisor to a gigantic wheat farm (evidence for Fitzgerald and Scott that he was a "high modernist"). Yet by the thirties (and possibly in part as a reaction to what he saw in Russia), Wilson had become the USDA's main apostle of grassroots democracy, his career evincing a deep faith in common citizens.[24]

[22] See sources in note 21; Donald L. Winters, *Henry Cantwell Wallace as Secretary of Agriculture, 1921–1924* (Urbana: University of Illinois Press, 1970), 109–44. David Hamilton, *From New Day to New Deal*, is particularly good at showing the continuities between the BAE of the 1920s and the New Deal.

[23] Richard S. Kirkendall, "L. C. Gray and the Supply of Agricultural Land," *Agricultural History* 37 (1963): 206–14; Kirkendall, *Social Scientists*, 21, 39; Gilbert and Baker, "Wisconsin Economists."

[24] Gilbert and Baker, "Wisconsin Economists"; Fitzgerald, "Accounting for Change" and "Blinded by Technology"; Scott, *Seeing Like a State*, 199–201. Thanks to Mary Summers for suggesting this link between Wilson's USSR experience and his democratic localism.

Henry A. Wallace, the only nonacademic in the group, had an extremely quick and broad mind. His genetic experiments with corn, beginning at age sixteen, culminated in 1923 with the first commercialization of hybrid seed and his subsequent founding of Hi-Bred Corn Company. He taught himself statistics and then popularized the subject to Iowa State faculty. A leading early farm economist, his *Agricultural Prices* (1920), using correlation and regression analyses, was one of the first econometric studies. He often visited the pre–New Deal BAE, founded by his father. From 1910 to 1933, furthermore, "Young Henry" worked on *Wallaces' Farmer,* the family journal. When Henry C. died unexpectedly in 1924 (during his tenure as USDA secretary), Henry A. became senior editor of the magazine his grandfather had established. He crusaded for collective action to counter the farm crisis of the 1920s and emerged as a national leader for the agrarian cause. Although he remained officially Republican until 1936, he was instrumental in convincing midwestern farmers to vote for Democratic candidate Franklin Roosevelt in 1932. As secretary of the New Deal USDA, of course, he was ultimately responsible for all its programs and policies.[25]

Carl Taylor did not join the BAE until the New Deal. Instead, after earning his Ph.D. from Missouri, he taught economics and sociology there for two years. He was considered "radical" by the administration, which did not object to his moving to North Carolina State College. In 1922 he was promoted to dean of the new Graduate School at North Carolina State. He continued his research on farm tenancy, conferring with USDA's land economist L. C. Gray. He wrote an early textbook in an emerging field, *Rural Sociology* (1926), which proposed a progressive land tax to reduce tenancy. Taylor both studied and led rural reform movements. He advocated such causes as tobacco marketing cooperatives in more than two hundred speeches to farmers; in turn, he wrote sociological papers that upheld class as a fundamental category of analysis. Taylor's outspoken radical reformist views did not sit well with some of the state's elite. According to the American Association of University Professors, Taylor was North Carolina State's "most distinguished" faculty member when, in 1931, he was dismissed by the college amidst charges that he was "a communist, anarchist, or socialist."[26]

Early in the Depression, then, Carl Taylor was without steady work for more than two years. He began writing a book, arguing that there had been a single agrarian protest movement throughout American history, analogous to "*the* labor movement." He drew on Commons's labor history and

[25] See books on Wallace in note 8 above, and Mordecai Ezekiel, "Henry A. Wallace, Agricultural Economist," *Journal of Farm Economics* 48 (1966): 789–802; Richard S. Kirkendall, "The Mind of a Farm Leader," *Annals of Iowa* 47 (1983): 138–53.
[26] Christie, "Carl C. Taylor"; Olaf F. Larson, Robin M. Williams, Jr., and Ronald C. Wimberley, "The Dismissal of a Sociologist: The AAUP Report on Carl C. Taylor," *Rural Sociology* 64 (1999): 533–53.

Veblen's critical analysis of capitalism. Before taking over and expanding the BAE's rural sociology unit, he worked in the earlier New Deal for M. L. Wilson in the Subsistence Homesteads Division, for L. C. Gray in the Agricultural Adjustment Administration's (AAA) Land Policy Section, and as head of Rural Resettlement in Rexford Tugwell's Resettlement Administration. Thanks to a delay that some writers can appreciate, his large and still impressive historical study (*The Farmers' Movement, 1620–1920*) appeared just as he retired from USDA in 1953, some twenty years later![27]

The youngest of the agrarian intellectuals, Bushrod Allin, received his Ph.D. in 1926 and remained at Wisconsin for two more years teaching land economics and the history of farmer movements. After winning his dean's disapproval for criticizing land speculation, he worked for the U.S. Forest Service, then joined the BAE in 1930. Henry Taylor had already been fired, but Allin still felt his presence. In response to some remarks by John Kenneth Galbraith in the *Journal of Farm Economics* years later, Allin recalled the BAE's early days:

> Because [H. C. Taylor's] Bureau was intermittently called upon to make analyses to provide a basis for action, its lasting and continuing service was its influence in giving research men the will to action by modifying their college-bred laissez-faire assumptions. These men can be found in influential and strategic positions throughout the government, in farm organizations, and in private business. Some of them have even gone back to the universities where they are teaching men to think about action as well as justifications for inaction.

This passage sums up what the young economists gained by their work in the BAE before 1933: detailed information on the entire agricultural sector certainly, but also a dedication to activist public service on its behalf. This knowledge and commitment proved to be excellent preparation for the New Deal soon to come.[28]

The Intended New Deal in Agriculture

Due significantly to these agrarian intellectuals, by 1940 New Deal agricultural policies offered an unprecedented opportunity for progressive

---

[27] Christie, "Carl C. Taylor."

[28] Bushrod W. Allin, "Galbraith's Stinger," *Journal of Farm Economics* 38 (1956): 1055; Allin, "The Agricultural-Business Conflict," 23–38; Gilbert and Baker, "Wisconsin Economists." After World War II, as the New Dealers were retiring, Allin fought a losing battle for institutionalism in economics. His presidential address to the American Farm Economic Association urged agricultural economists to live up to their activist heritage, citing Henry C. Taylor, John R. Commons, and M. L. Wilson; see Allin, "Relevant Farm Economics," *Journal of Farm Economics* 43 (1961): 1007–18.

social reform in the rural United States. In 1933, the AAA had introduced some degree of economic stability, although its programs were biased against the rural poor. Partly as a result, the Farm Security Administration (FSA) worked on behalf of small farmers, sharecroppers, and farm workers. In addition to the services provided by these and other USDA agencies (such as the Soil Conservation Service), nearly one million rural residents participated in their local administration. Such decentralization involved citizens in government in an extremely innovative way. Most important for the long term, the New Dealers thought, was the county land use planning program of the Bureau of Agricultural Economics. Between 1938 and 1942, over two hundred thousand farm men and women served on community and county committees that adapted and coordinated New Deal programs throughout rural America. USDA leaders lauded this planning initiative as "economic democracy in action." In the early forties, then, they believed that all of these new policies and institutions would eventually modernize and democratize the countryside—as the agrarian wing, perhaps, of a European-style social democracy for America.[29]

This picture of the New Deal in agriculture is not the one usually painted. Yet it was the one *intended* by the core policy intellectuals who conceived, designed, and implemented most of the measures. Their intentions are not well known today because they failed, or rather were defeated politically, and their vision was forgotten. Local and regional elites (notably the American Farm Bureau Federation), as well as some agencies within USDA itself, opposed such planning and reform for rural social change. In the middle of World War II, then, a conservative anti–New Deal Congress killed the BAE's participatory planning program and gutted the radical reformist Farm Security Administration. Only the less ambitious, more politically acceptable programs survived the war and thus became the *unintended* legacy of the New Deal in agriculture.[30]

---

[29] Anthony J. Badger, *The New Deal: The Depression Years, 1933–1940* (New York: Farrar, Straus & Giroux, 1989), 147–89, provides an excellent overview of all the agricultural programs. A good longer treatment is Theodore Saloutos, *The American Farmer and the New Deal* (Ames: Iowa State University Press, 1982). On the BAE's planning effort, see Jess Gilbert, "Democratic Planning in Agricultural Policy: The Federal/County Land-Use Planning Program, 1938–1942," *Agricultural History* 70 (1996): 233–50. Fumiaki Kubo has an outstanding article on the late New Deal from the viewpoint of the USDA Secretary: "Henry A. Wallace and Radical Politics in the New Deal: Farm Programs and a Vision of the New American Political Economy," *Japanese Journal of American Studies* 4 (1991): 37–76. For something of the breadth and feel of the late New Deal USDA, see the remarkable *Farmers in a Changing World: Yearbook of Agriculture, 1940* (Washington, D.C.: Government Printing Office, 1940). In *Dust Bowl: The Southern Plains in the 1930's* (New York: Oxford University Press, 1979), 188–96, Donald Worster gives a suggestive interpretation of L. C. Gray's New Deal activities as "social-democratic," but he underplays the significance of Gray's like-minded colleagues in USDA.

[30] Charles M. Hardin, "The Bureau of Agricultural Economics under Fire: A Study in Valuation Conflicts," *Journal of Farm Economics* 28 (1946): 635–68; Hardin, *Freedom in Agricultural Education* (Chicago: University of Chicago Press, 1955), 155–85; Kirkendall, *Social*

This eventuality paralleled the fate of broader reforms of the Intended New Deal," the one President Roosevelt envisioned in his second term but never realized. It encompassed FDR's Executive Reorganization bill of 1937, which included calls for a powerful national planning board; more regional planning authorities ("seven little TVAs"), federal judicial reform ("court packing"), and the 1938 attempt to purge some conservative southerners from Congress. This last New Deal merged the interests of the first two in sectoral self-government and social reform, respectively, but emphasized more governmental coordination, administrative management, and economic planning. The distinguishing mark of the Intended or Third New Deal is that it failed; not one of these initiatives came to fruition. The parallel with the agricultural New Deal applies further in that, as Graham notes, "Americans have forgotten or misremembered Roosevelt's ideas," just as we have those of the agrarians. Yet the parallel also misleads because only in agriculture did this last, best New Deal actually get off the drawing board and into the field—in the form of the BAE's county/federal land use planning and related programs. After a few years, though, it too succumbed to conservative forces in rural society and in the state.[31]

But until Congress destroyed it all in the middle of World War II, what did the agrarian New Dealers have in mind and on the ground? A little background may be useful. In 1933, when FDR became president, the immediate farm problem called for economic relief and recovery. The First New Deal established the Agricultural Adjustment Administration within the USDA. The AAA made "benefit payments" to farmers who planted fewer acres of certain crops; this production control plan succeeded somewhat in raising farm prices. Montana State professor M. L. Wilson and a few other USDA economists developed this "voluntary domestic allotment plan" as a stopgap measure to address the farm emergency. Wilson also proposed that farmers in every county administer the crop reductions locally. Secretary of Agriculture Henry Wallace agreed, and they gained the aid of the decentralized Extension Service, based in each state land-grant college. Led by the county agents, farmer committees "signed up" millions of farmers in the AAA commodity programs. It was an impressive political and administrative feat, but one with certain victims as well.[32]

The AAA was aimed at the commercially successful farmers who benefited most from higher crop prices. In places like Wallace's Iowa and Wilson's Montana, and generally where family farms prevailed, the First

Scientists, 195–240; Sidney Baldwin, *Poverty and Politics: The Rise and Fall of the Farm Security Administration* (Chapel Hill: University of North Carolina Press, 1968).

[31] Otis L. Graham has a good half-sentence on the BAE's county planning program as part of FDR's Third New Deal; "Comment," in *Soviet-American Dialogue on the New Deal,* ed. Graham (Columbia: University of Missouri Press, 1989), 289.

[32] Badger, *The New Deal,* 147–89.

New Deal helped most farmers. But in class-based systems such as in California and the plantation South, the AAA worked for larger farmers and against farm workers, sharecroppers, and tenants. Particularly in the Mississippi Delta, the AAA's cotton reduction program empowered planters and displaced many landless farmers. Historian Pete Daniel cites a small southern farmer who accused the New Dealers, accurately enough, of "trying to make an Iowa plan fit Louisiana." The USDA's early program did not assist, and often harmed, the "lower third" in rural America.[33]

Could, then, the New Deal treat persistent poverty on the farm? President Roosevelt responded with the agrarian part of the Second New Deal in 1935: the Resettlement Administration (RA), led by economist-planner and USDA Undersecretary Rexford G. Tugwell. One of the most radical of all federal agencies, it tried to reform both poor land and poor people. Back in 1933, M. L. Wilson had directed a utopian-agrarian Subsistence Homesteads Division, and USDA economist Lewis Gray had started a massive land retirement and federal purchase program. The new RA absorbed both these programs, and Gray became the agency's leader for land utilization. In late 1936, Wallace chaired and Gray directed the President's Committee on Farm Tenancy, which also included Tugwell, Wilson, and their mentor, Henry C. Taylor. The 1937 Farm Tenancy Report constituted a profound critique of American individualism and the private land tenure system; it is one of the most radical official documents ever issued by the U.S. Government. Following Congressional legislation later that year, Secretary Wallace and Undersecretary Wilson reorganized the RA as the Farm Security Administration. The FSA continued the controversial Second New Deal in agriculture, with small farmer loans and a tenant purchase program as its main activities. For the next five years, the FSA and the AAA were the USDA's largest action agencies, with quite different (and frequently antagonistic) leadership, field staffs, constituents, and ideologies.[34]

By 1938, then, the USDA offered a wide variety of new programs, and these sometimes worked at cross-purposes. The AAA, for example, paid farmers not to plant while the FSA encouraged more production. Enter the Third New Deal, which aimed to coordinate the first two. Secretary Wallace reorganized the huge USDA to foster a new initiative in cooperative land use planning. He elevated a "new" Bureau of Agricultural Economics as the central planning agency for the entire department and moved Howard Tolley from AAA head to Bureau chief. In late 1938, that

[33] Baldwin, *Poverty and Politics*, 47–58, 76–84; Gilbert and Howe, "Beyond 'State vs. Society,'" 212–13; Pete Daniel, "The Legal Basis of Agrarian Capitalism: The South since 1933," in *Race and Class in the American South since 1890*, ed. Melvyn Stokes and Rick Halpern (Oxford: Oxford University Press, 1994), 96, 86–87.

[34] Baldwin, *Poverty and Politics*, 85–192; Gilbert and Howe, "Beyond 'State vs. Society,'" 214–15. Smaller but more controversial FSA programs included migrant labor camps, greenbelt communities, cooperative farms, and the nation's first group health care plans.

JESS GILBERT

is, Wallace, Wilson, Tolley, and the others set out to democratize agricultural policy through a national program of local planning committees. Farmers formed the majority of each county-level committee, which also included the local administrators of the USDA "action agencies" (such as AAA, Soil Conservation, and FSA) and social as well as natural scientists from the land-grant college. Together the farmers, bureaucrats, and technicians sought to unify the federal programs at the county level, address problems as they arose, and develop new policies. BAE assistant chief L. C. Gray oversaw the agency's land use specialists based in each agricultural college; they worked with statewide planning committees of farmers and officials, who reviewed and integrated the county-level work. At the federal level, the planning program was handled by a new BAE division, led by young "unconventional" economist Bushrod Allin.[35]

Other BAE divisions supported this innovative program. One, led by Carl F. Taeusch, a pragmatist philosopher from the University of Chicago and Harvard, organized thousands of local discussion groups for farmers and hundreds of weeklong schools of philosophy for extension workers. Topics included "Do farmers want the federal government to deal with farm problems?" "Is it in the interest of the nation to have more or fewer people living on the land?" "Is the farm laborer getting a square deal?" "The place of government in modern society," and "A critique of our present economy." Materials and lecturers presented different sides of such issues. Wallace and Wilson knew that departmental leaders themselves needed continuing education, so they held numerous enlightening conferences in Washington. In 1938, for instance, Wilson sponsored fifteen weekly lectures on democracy by some of America's leading public intellectuals. About one thousand USDA workers heard preeminent historian (and New Deal critic) Charles A. Beard, Yale law professor Thurman Arnold (*The Folklore of Capitalism*), public opinion expert George Gallup (*The Pulse of Democracy*), and social anthropologist Ruth Benedict (*Patterns of Culture*). Back on the farm, Carl Taylor's BAE division of nearly sixty sociologists and anthropologists engaged local citizens in "participatory action research," aimed to increase community organization and involvement in the county planning process. Lewis Gray's division of land economists worked with farm people on land classification studies to assist the county planning committees. In these ways the BAE units collaborated with many thousands of rural people in order to

[35] Gilbert, "Democratic Planning"; Kirkendall, *Social Scientists*, 165–92. The best single analysis of the county planning program is by political scientist Ellen Sorge Parks, "Experiment in the Planning of Public Agricultural Activity" (Ph.D. diss., University of Wisconsin, Madison, 1947). The summary material presented in this and the next two paragraphs is elaborated in Jess Gilbert, "Democratic Rationalization: The Ideology of Agrarian Intellectuals in the Third New Deal," paper presented to the Social Science History Association, 1996.

advance the larger land use planning program of the Intended New Deal.[36]

The federal/county land use planning program, overseen for the BAE by Bushrod Allin, was something new in American history: a formal cooperative partnership between representatives of an entire sector (agriculture), government administrators, and applied scientists, seeking to shape and reform public policy. By 1941 it was underway in nearly twenty-two hundred counties, over two-thirds of all those in the United States. More than two hundred thousand farm men and women were involved in this network of planning committees, extending from neighborhoods, communities, and counties to states and Washington, D. C. Far from being "the end of reform," as Alan Brinkley has argued, the early 1940s thus marked the peak of the New Deal in agriculture.[37] To the agrarian intellectuals, this last New Deal was the culmination of their vision of progressive social reform and gradual cultural change in the countryside; we might even call it participatory modernization. They saw such activities as the best way to democratize the agricultural policy process and to counter the growing opposition from a powerful conservative coalition. This, in a nutshell, was their Intended New Deal.

It did not, of course, turn out exactly as they intended. The county planning committees were neither very representative of all local farmers nor fully participatory for the citizen members. Larger, wealthier farmers were overrepresented on the committees, and even they were frequently dom-

[36] Only two historians treat the educational effort in any detail: Kirkendall, *Social Scientists,* 140–43, 170, 187–90; and McDean, "M. L. Wilson," 414–25, 484–88. The most complete history and analysis is David Lachman, "Democratic Ideology and Agricultural Policy: 'Program Study and Discussion' in the U. S. Department of Agriculture, 1934–1946" (M.S. thesis, University of Wisconsin, Madison, 1991); see also David Lachman and Jess Gilbert, "Democratic Ideology in Agricultural Policy: 'Program Study and Discussion' in the U. S. Department of Agriculture, 1934–1946," paper presented to the Rural Sociological Society, 1992. The philosopher in charge, Carl F. Taeusch, summarized the program in "Schools of Philosophy for Farmers." M. L. Wilson edited the lecture series as *Democracy Has Roots* (New York: Carrick & Evans, 1939), with a glowing preface by Charles Beard. Another of the USDA conferences was a three-day event on agricultural history chaired by Populist historian John D. Hicks. Other attendees were Kathleen Bruce, Avery Craven, Paul W. Gates, and Caroline F. Ware. See "The U. S. Department of Agriculture Agricultural History Conference," *Agricultural History* 13 (1939): 221–22; and Jess Gilbert, "A Usable Past: New Dealers Henry A. Wallace and M. L. Wilson Reclaim the American Agrarian Tradition," in *Rationality and the Liberal Spirit: A Festschrift Honoring Ira Lee Morgan,* ed. Centenary College Department of English (Shreveport, La.: Centenary College, 1997), 134–42. On Taylor's and Gray's divisions, see Carl Taylor, "Social Science and Social Action in Agriculture," *Social Forces* 20 (1941): 157; Taylor, "The Work of the Division of Farm Population and Rural Life," *Rural Sociology* 4 (1939): 221–28; John D. Lewis, "Democratic Planning in Agriculture, I," *American Political Science Review* 35 (1941): 241–44; BAE Division of State and Local Planning, "Operating Report Covering the Cooperative Land-Use Planning Program for the Year Ended June 30, 1940," National Archives, RG 83, entry 215, Box 1; Gilbert, "Democratic Planning," 241–42, 248–49.

[37] Gilbert, "Democratic Planning," 233, 241; contra Alan Brinkley, *The End of Reform: New Deal Liberalism in Recession and War* (New York: Knopf, 1995).

inated by the expert members. The low modernist program, then, did not achieve its full democratic promise. However, the committees were becoming increasingly effective and citizen-oriented when they were abolished in 1942 by those, like the Farm Bureau, who saw them as an organizational and ideological threat. Moreover, in comparison to the dominant power structure in rural America (built around the AAA committees and large-farm groups), the federal/county land use program was remarkably more open and less elitist.

In the end, it was the enemies of mass participation and reformist planning, much more than the program's own ideological limitations, that cut short its potential. We must remember, in the words of Leon Fink, that "No grand plan for a dialogue between intellectuals and a mass audience has ever been put into practice." Few grander plans, however, have ever been envisioned and implemented in the United States than the Intended New Deal in agriculture. Despite its overall failure and defeat, we can still learn from such earlier "examples of commitment" and practical efforts to secure democratic public policy.[38]

Organic Intellectuals, Low Modernists, and the Lost Tradition

I have specified a progressive midwestern tradition of agrarian social science and public policy. Reared on family farms, so to speak, it drew from the ideologies of Jefferson and Lincoln which insisted on equality, citizenship, and public service. The rural Midwest in the late nineteenth century was a relatively egalitarian and very Protestant place; such religious and class origins stayed with the farm boys as they left home for higher education. At the land-grant universities in Missouri and Wisconsin, they learned from the brilliant progenitors of a peculiarly American brand of historical, statist, reformist economics called institutionalism. Some also picked up lifelong commitments to American philosophical pragmatism. Due to the state building of their mentors (Henry C. Wallace and Henry C. Taylor), they inherited organizational encouragement for applied research on public issues in the USDA's new Bureau of Agricultural Economics. Once thorough apprenticeships sharpened their professional and policy skills in the BAE and land-grant colleges, they were ready to reform agriculture in the New Deal. Thus the six subjects of this chapter (along with others, to be sure) invented an "alternative tradition" of agrarian reform in an activist state. Their Intended New Deal sought simultaneously to modernize and democratize rural America.

[38] Gilbert, "Democratic Planning," 246–50; Fink, *Progressive Intellectuals*, 50–51.

This tradition was not one of "autonomous intellectuals" or "urban outsiders." On the contrary, I suggest another interpretation based on the background and subsequent careers of the six social scientists. They were organic intellectuals of the Midwestern family-farming class. The Italian Marxist philosopher Antonio Gramsci defines intellectuals broadly as people who educate, organize, or lead various social classes. "Organic intellectuals" are linked closely with the class from which they emerge and which they serve. They create and promote an alternative interpretation of reality that challenges the dominant society.[39] This certainly applies to the New Dealers. They came from and never forgot—indeed, they worked primarily for—the interests of midsize propertied family farmers. Unlike most policy intellectuals, they maintained close ties to their roots. Their connection with such farmers was institutionally enabled, even required, by the entire land-grant/USDA system of applied research, teaching, and extension. As much as Marxist intellectuals, they tried to integrate theory and practice but aimed for reform, not revolution. They put forth a pointed political analysis of a unitary "farming class" that was exploited by the modern industrial economy and therefore deserved special assistance from the federal government. In this way we can understand the intentions behind the price-raising Agricultural Adjustment Administration as well as the emphasis on citizens' localization of national policies in the BAE's county land use planning program.

The agrarian New Dealers were not "tied" to all farmers, though, but only to the peculiar class of modern, successful, landowning family farmers from which they arose. What most of them lacked, especially before the late 1930s, was a class analysis of U.S. farming itself, an appreciation of quite different groups such as southern sharecroppers and western farmworkers. Carl Taylor's sojourn in biracial North Carolina and Howard Tolley's in class-divided rural California must have influenced their later work,[40] but generally the South and the West were not the agrarians' regions and hence were too often outside their vision. As M. L. Wilson admitted late in life, to him "farmer" always meant the property-owning kind he grew up with in Iowa. This ingrained family farm image was a serious limitation, politically as well as ideologically. The midwestern background of the group (on family farms and in land-grant colleges), as well as their Progressive science in the early BAE, equipped them ill to understand and transform much of U.S. agriculture. Their

---

[39] Antonio Gramsci, *Selections from the Prison Notebooks,* ed. Quintin Hoare and Geoffrey Nowell Smith (New York: International Publishers, 1971), 1–25, 325–34. Margaret Christie and I first applied this concept only to Carl Taylor. Leon Fink uses it to interpret A. Philip Randolph's relationship to his followers (*Progressive Intellectuals,* 212–13).

[40] Thanks to Mary Summers and Olaf Larson for pointing this out.

middle-class assumption of classlessness helps explain, for example, how class-conscious capitalist farmers and southern planters routed them during World War II. Wilson and the others thought mainly of midwestern family farmers when, in fact, rural America was much more varied, conflictual, and inegalitarian. Of course, they knew this in their heads, but it was not part of their deeper, instinctive knowledge of rural life, which otherwise was so beneficial. And when they did seek to turn tenants into landowners, as with the Farm Security Administration, political-economic elites attacked and defeated them.

Admittedly, however, the USDA leaders were only partially "organic" intellectuals. For they were also modernizing social scientists. They drank deeply from the well of scientific Progressivism. Early in their careers particularly, some of the New Dealers-to-be touted farm industrialization. Understandably Deborah Fitzgerald and James Scott call them high modernists, but, when we look closely at their roots and politics, we can see that this is an exaggeration. Instead, they were much more "low modernists." The agrarian intellectuals promoted planning and rationalization but with grassroots, participatory twists. They favored a larger state but also devolved much power to local farmers, upon whom they depended for essential knowledge and action. They believed that philosophy and religion were more important than science and technology, and, with Jefferson and Dewey, that democracy required continuing civic education for experts, administrators, and citizens alike. They actually thought that Americans could achieve—were achieving—democratic planning. Finally, there is the New Dealers' strong preference for family farms over large-scale industrial enterprises. A comparison with their high modernist USDA colleague, Rexford Tugwell—Resettlement Administrator—effectively makes the point. Tugwell disapproved of most of the small-scale features that they endorsed, and he disdained both spiritual mysticism (which Wallace practiced) and folk cultures (which Wilson and Carl Taylor exalted). More or less like farmers, they were also characteristically humble, in contrast to Tugwell's typical and self-styled arrogance.[41]

Half organic intellectual and half low modernist as the agrarian intellectuals were, the tradition they created was short-lived. It suffered a political death at the hands of Congress in the mid-1940s, at least domestically. Many social scientists who trained in this manner pursued international careers after 1945, either with the government or with foundations concerned with land reform and rural development

---

[41] Gilbert, "Eastern Urban Liberals," although I do not employ the concepts of high or low modernism there.

abroad.[42] In the United States, though, such proposals were no longer acceptable and would remain off the policy table for decades. For this reason, the "revolution" in American agriculture of the fifties and sixties was fundamentally chaotic and unplanned. The massive changes wrought in postwar rural society received little policy attention, and no assistance was given to the millions of farmers and other rural residents displaced. The New Deal planners had intended to slow and ease such social transformations, but their plans had been demolished. Most significantly, not just particular policy streams and institutional creations were lost. Rather, an entire way of political-economic thinking effectively disappeared from public discussion. Conservatives suppressed institutional economists and progressive sociologists in land-grant colleges and the USDA. The once dominant statist agrarian tradition of reform had a brief life: The two world wars signaled its rise and fall. Now, however, it is time for us to reclaim and reinvent that tradition in the service of democracy, agrarian and otherwise.

---

[42] In 1946, Howard Tolley finally got fed up with Congressional oversight—or rather political repression—of the BAE, so he resigned as its chief. He had helped organize the Food and Agriculture Conference in 1943, and he served as chief economist in the United Nations Food and Agriculture Organization from 1946 to 1951. He took some of the brightest minds in the USDA with him (e.g., economist Mordecai Ezekiel). M. L. Wilson and Carl Taylor both stayed in the USDA until the Republican administration came in in 1953 and the new secretary abolished the BAE. Both men then had late careers in international rural development, especially with the Ford Foundation in India, which was run by Wilson's former assistant in the New Deal, rural sociologist Douglas Ensminger. Taylor also spent a year in South America during World War II and published the classic *Rural Life in Argentina* in 1948. See Taylor, "Early Rural Sociological Research in Latin America," *Rural Sociology* 25 (1960): 1–8, and his "The Development of Rural Sociology Abroad," ibid., 30 (1965): 462–73. Such connections between New Dealers and international development are fascinating and underresearched.

An "Enviable Tradition" of Patriarchy

New Deal Investigations of Women's Work in the Amish Farm Family

KATHERINE JELLISON

In 1940, O. E. Baker, a senior agricultural economist assigned to the Bureau of Agricultural Economics (BAE) in the United States Department of Agriculture (USDA), traveled to Lancaster County, Pennsylvania, where his colleague Walter M. Kollmorgen was conducting research among the Old Order Amish. In his work for the BAE's Division of Farm Population and Rural Welfare, Baker had long argued that the success of American agriculture depended upon large farm families to produce agricultural products and sizable off-farm families to purchase and consume those items. Noting that the Amish had weathered the Great Depression more successfully than other farming communities, Baker predictably attributed this fact to their reliance on large family work units that employed the labor of all able-bodied men, women, and children. Following his visit to Kollmorgen, Baker became convinced that the Amish farm family would serve as an appropriate model for his own household, particularly in its reliance on women as workforce reproducers and farm laborers. Years later, after leaving the Department of Agriculture and taking a university teaching position, Baker purchased a house at the edge of town, where he introduced his family to the practices of Old Order Amish life. Focusing particular attention on one child, Baker made the girl raise chickens in the backyard and forced her to dress in home-made, Amish-style clothing, which she would discretely exchange for more fashionable wear at school when safely out of her father's sight.[1]

[1] Walter M. Kollmorgen, interview with Katherine Jellison and Steven D. Reschly, Lawrence, Kans., March 20, 1994; Walter M. Kollmorgen, "Kollmorgen as a Bureaucrat," *Annals of the*

Baker's attempt to hold his daughter to the standards of rural Amish life, and the girl's resistance to that agenda, paralleled the larger battle that he and other key members of the BAE had waged within the USDA during the New Deal era. While most Department of Agriculture agencies had continued their decades-long commitment to modern, capital-intensive agriculture, the BAE included personnel, like Baker, who maintained that depression conditions demonstrated the merits of traditional, labor-intensive agriculture. Baker and other social scientists who worked under the direction of Carl C. Taylor at the BAE's Division of Farm Population and Rural Welfare subscribed to the notion that employment of farm family labor rather than investment in mechanized farm equipment was the means to efficient agricultural production. Depression conditions and the failure of many heavily capitalized farming operations simply confirmed their existing philosophy. In selecting the Amish farm family as the ideal model for the nation's farm families in general, and for his own family in particular, Baker was, however, choosing a family structure in which the husband and father held firm and obvious control over the labor and behavior of all other family members. In Baker's own family, he attempted to extend this control even to the type of clothing his young daughter could wear to school.[2]

Perhaps the highly structured, religiously sanctioned patriarchy under which Amish women live and work has rendered them an unattractive subject of study for many contemporary scholars, but in Baker's day, those very conditions made Amish women a fascinating focus of investigation. In the New Deal era, researchers in the BAE and in the USDA's Bureau of Home Economics recognized and even celebrated the fact that Amish women's continued participation in farm production contributed to the economic survival of their families and themselves. At the same time, even though their efforts ultimately served the interests of patriarchy, the Amish patriarchy acknowledged and respected those efforts, providing Amish women with a sense of worth and accomplishment that other farm women often lacked.[3]

Association of American Geographers 69 (March 1979): 84; O. E. Baker, "Will More or Fewer People Live on the Land?" address delivered to the National Catholic Rural Life Conference, Fargo, N.D., October 13, 1936, National Archives II, College Park, Md., RG 83, General Correspondence (1923–1946), O. E. Baker Folder (1936–1940), box 62 (hereafter Baker Folder).

[2] During much of the New Deal era, the BAE organization in which Baker worked, the Division of Farm Population and Rural Welfare, went by another name—the Division of Farm Population and Rural Life. During the period in which the BAE's study of the Old Order Amish community was researched and published, however, the organization went by the title of the Division of Farm Population and Rural Welfare, and that will be the name used throughout this essay.

[3] In the past twenty-five years, published scholarship on the Amish community has rarely focused on Amish women or gender roles. Among the few studies that have dealt with these topics are Richard A. Wright, "A Comparative Analysis of Economic Roles Within the Family: Amish and Contemporary American Women," *International Journal of Sociology and the Family* 7 (January–June 1977): 55–60; Julia Ericksen and Gary Klein, "Women's Roles and Family Production Among the Old Order Amish," *Rural Sociology* 46 (summer 1981): 282–96; Steven

By the time of Baker's visit to Lancaster County, members of the Old Order Amish faith had been living there for generations. Like other Anabaptists who lived in the county—such as Mennonites, the so-called "Car" Amish, and members of other "plain" denominations—they were descendants of religious dissenters who had opposed infant baptism and other aspects of mainstream Protestant belief in sixteenth- and seventeenth-century Switzerland, Germany, and the Netherlands. After years of exile and persecution, these dissidents had finally left Europe altogether, finding a haven in colonial Pennsylvania. Among the various Anabaptist sects whose members resided in Lancaster County, the Old Order Amish were the most traditional, having remained committed to many aspects of the culture they had brought with them to Pennsylvania in the early modern period. They continued to speak a German dialect, referred to as "Pennsylvania Dutch," and refused to adopt modern communication, transportation, housekeeping, and contraceptive technologies, forgoing ownership of telephones, radios, automobiles, electrical appliances, and birth control devices. At a time when a high school education was becoming a universal experience throughout the rest of the northern United States, the Old Order Amish refused to send their children to school beyond the eighth grade. Members of the sect also dressed in a decidedly "plain" and unfashionable manner, with the men sporting full beards and flat black hats and the women wearing modest head coverings and aprons. Most significantly, in urban, industrial America, the Old Order Amish remained committed to an agricultural way of life. They farmed in Lancaster County and other areas of Amish settlement without the benefit of tractors—relying instead on the power of horses and mules—and at a time when other farmers were increasingly specializing in production of a few major cash crops, the Old Order Amish continued their tradition of general, diversified farming to provide for the agricultural market and at the same time feed their own families. Old Order Amish men and women believed that the Bible sanctioned their devotion to an agrarian way of life, just as it did their other distinctive practices. As a Lancaster County Amish man told Walter M. Kollmorgen in 1940, "[T]he Lord told Adam to replenish the earth and to rule over the animals and the land—you can't do that in cities."[4]

D. Reschly and Katherine Jellison, "Production Patterns, Consumption Strategies, and Gender Relations in Amish and Non-Amish Farm Households in Lancaster County, Pennsylvania, 1935–1936," *Agricultural History* 67 (spring 1993): 134–62; Marc A. Olshan and Kimberly D. Schmidt, "Amish Women and the Feminist Conundrum," in *The Amish Struggle with Modernity*, ed. Donald B. Kraybill and Marc A. Olshan (Hanover, N.H.: University Press of New England, 1994), 215–29.

[4] Jane C. Getz, "The Economic Organization and Practices of the Old Order Amish of Lancaster County, Pennsylvania," *Mennonite Quarterly Review* 20 (January 1946): 59. Getz quotes here from Walter M. Kollmorgen's field notes. For an overview of Amish culture and history,

Given the modernization efforts of many New Deal programs that focused on rural America, such as the Rural Electrification Administration, government researchers like Kollmorgen might have been expected to view Amish women as quaint, outmoded—even subversive—hangers-on to the obsolete traditions of another era. Amish rejection of automobiles, selective use of mechanized farm equipment and household technology, and avoidance of commercial entertainment certainly made them atypical members of northern rural society in the 1930s, but it was their very uniqueness that rendered the Old Order Amish such a desirable population to study for the scholars under Taylor's direction. The Amish community's successful reliance on an older way of agrarian life, at a time when many "modern" farms were failing, intrigued these investigators. They suspected that perhaps traditional Amish family farming, in which both male and female members continued to play an active role in farm production, represented a viable alternative to mechanized, business-oriented agriculture. This point of view placed Taylor and many other BAE employees in opposition to the dominant New Deal stance regarding American agriculture.

Taylor's conception of a stable and successful agrarian life differed significantly from the vision of "industrialized agriculture" that most officials within the USDA had been promoting since the turn of the century. As Deborah Fitzgerald notes elsewhere in this volume, the Department of Agriculture, along with personnel at the nation's agricultural colleges, had been promoting the modernization of American agriculture for several decades. According to this plan, the nation's farm families should adopt an urban, middle-class household model, in which farm men used mechanized equipment to produce a few major cash crops and farm women became full-time homemakers and consumers who used labor-saving domestic appliances within the home. In contrast, the BAE harbored personnel who remained committed to the principle that had guided federal agricultural policy in the nineteenth century: the idea that successful agriculture required the productive efforts of every member of the patriarchal farm family. Persons who subscribed to this older model of family farming viewed it as highly efficient; farms that relied on family labor did not require the major cash outlays of mechanized farms or those that depended on hired labor, and the farm family work unit came under the full-time authority, supervision, and control of the husband/father. Adherents to traditional farming argued that the "separate spheres" model of family farming, in which women relinquished their role in farm production to become consumers of manufactured goods, was one that only the nation's

see Donald B. Kraybill, *The Riddle of Amish Culture* (Baltimore: Johns Hopkins University Press, 1989); Steven M. Nolt, *A History of the Amish* (Intercourse, Pa.: Good Books, 1992); and John A. Hostetler, *Amish Society* (Baltimore: Johns Hopkins University Press, 1993).

243

most prosperous farm families could successfully afford to adopt. Its critics also charged that with its emphasis on the purchase of manufactured equipment, the modern farm family model potentially benefited American industry more than it did American agriculture.[5]

Rejecting the notion of mechanized, capital-intensive agriculture in favor of traditional, labor-intensive family farming, Taylor thus embarked in 1940 on one of the most ambitious projects in the BAE's eighteen-year history as the USDA's economic research unit. He sent social scientists working under his direction in the BAE's Division of Farm Population and Rural Welfare to six geographically diverse rural communities. A chief objective of the project was to determine the impact of New Deal programs on these communities and to provide guidance for future government planning in rural America.[6] From the beginning, Taylor and his associates envisioned the six communities lying along a continuum from most stable to least stable, with the Old Order Amish of Lancaster County on one end and the Dust Bowl residents of Sublette, Kansas, on the other. In between these two extremes lay the communities of El Cerrito, New Mexico; Irwin, Iowa; Harmony, Georgia; and Landaff, New Hampshire. Taylor's "community stability-instability study" would require each primary "participant-observer," including cultural geographer Walter M. Kollmorgen, to conduct intensive fieldwork in his assigned community for nearly a six-month period.[7]

Taylor and his colleagues assumed that community stability and quality of life depended on a variety of cultural, historical, and sociopsychological

[5] See Fitzgerald's essay, "Accounting for Change: Farmers and the Modernizing State," in this volume. For further discussion of the USDA's attempts to promote an "industrialized" agriculture, see David B. Danbom, *The Resisted Revolution: Urban America and the Industrialization of Agriculture, 1900–1930* (Ames: Iowa State University Press, 1979). For examination of the USDA's "separate spheres" agenda for American farm families, see Katherine Jellison, *Entitled to Power: Farm Women and Technology, 1913–1963* (Chapel Hill: University of North Carolina Press, 1993), chap. 1. For discussion of the BAE during the New Deal era, see Richard S. Kirkendall, *Social Scientists and Farm Politics in the Age of Roosevelt* (Columbia: University of Missouri Press, 1966). For examination of the central role of the patriarchal farm family in nineteenth-century agriculture, see David B. Danbom, *Born in the Country: A History of Rural America* (Baltimore: Johns Hopkins University Press, 1995), 87–90. For analysis of nineteenth-century USDA policies promoting labor-intensive family farming, see Deborah Fink, *Open Country, Iowa: Rural Women, Tradition and Change* (Albany: State University of New York Press, 1986), 23–25.

[6] Ironically, in championing the Amish, the members of Taylor's research team were promoting the practices of a group who had very little use for the BAE or any other government agency. The self-reliance that Taylor and his colleagues so admired among the Amish made them the very kind of people who did not cooperate with New Deal social welfare and agricultural programs.

[7] Kollmorgen interview; Kollmorgen, "Kollmorgen as a Bureaucrat," 84; "Opinions, Attitudes, and Values in Self-Sufficing and in Commercial Agriculture," December 19, 1939, and Carl C. Taylor, "My Memory of the Conceptual Development of the Community Stability-Instability Study," August 28, 1944, National Archives II, RG 83, General Correspondence (1923–1946), American Farm Community Study Project files (1941–1946), box 538 (hereafter AFCS Project Files).

factors, in addition to the economic and geographical conditions that investigators typically examined in USDA studies. To guide their field research, Taylor and his team of social scientists developed a set of criteria to define community stability or instability that reflected their commitment to traditional family farming. According to their scheme, the stable rural community depended upon a long-established economic base that had remained constant or had changed slowly over time, was isolated from outside influences and divergent cultures, practiced a system of values in which some noneconomic value dominated all others, and was a community that experienced little in- or out-migration. In contrast, the unstable rural community depended upon a widely varying agricultural income, had experienced a disaster to its economic base and thus had shifted to a new means of support, had encountered disturbing cultural influences from the outside, had accepted new agricultural techniques or tools that had disrupted the established class structure, and had experienced broad fluctuation in its population numbers. Given these criteria, the self-sufficient, highly religious Old Order Amish indeed seemed the very model of community stability, in direct contrast to the cash-dependent, drought-plagued residents of Sublette, Kansas.[8]

Taylor's group believed before they started their research that the Old Order Amish would provide a model of community stability and Jeffersonian agrarianism for the rest of rural America. In outlining his philosophy on rural life to a colleague, Taylor clearly acknowledged his own commitment to Jefferson's agrarian ideal: "[T]here are inherently good traits in the rural way of life,... there are spiritual, cultural, esthetic, and social values which attach themselves to... the closer association of family and community which are typical of the simpler rural cultures." In contrast, he noted, as a society "grows more complex, becomes more mechanical and more mercenary, it tends to lose its spiritual, cultural, esthetic, and creative nature."[9] When Taylor sent field investigators to the six communities to be studied, he was envisioning a series of reports that would ultimately demonstrate the merits of many aspects of the Amish belief system—their commitment to traditional family farming, their rejection of expensive technology, and their view of farming as a superior way of life rather than as a mere business enterprise. In instructing Walter M. Kollmorgen how to achieve the cooperation of his Lancaster County informants, Taylor advised the young scholar to "try to convince these Amish people that we believe that many of their characteristics are praiseworthy and that rather than pry into their individual beliefs, we are anxious to discover the good things in their whole system and reveal these good things to other

[8] Earl H. Bell to Carl C. Taylor, October 16, 1944, AFCS Project Files.
[9] Carl C. Taylor to O. E. Baker, November 22, 1937, Baker Folder.

KATHERINE JELLISON

people."[10] Incorporating this strategy, Kollmorgen informed his contacts among the Old Order Amish that the BAE considered Lancaster County the "garden spot of the country," admired Amish self-sufficiency, and wanted to know the reasons for their great success as agriculturalists.[11]

Not surprisingly, then, Kollmorgen's final report, published in 1942, cast Old Order Amish practices in a favorable light. He closed his study with an analysis of the Old Order Amish formula for success:

> A group that has survived centuries of persecution in Europe and has so far resisted many of the onslaughts of factories, with their standardized products, and the appeals of higher education must have qualities that make for survival. Important among these qualities are a tradition of hard work, a willingness to make sacrifices for the good of others, and an enviable tradition of constructive diversified agriculture.[12]

Noted throughout Kollmorgen's study was another key to the success of the Old Order Amish community—women's work. In line with the federal government's nineteenth-century philosophy that prosperous American agriculture required the efforts of both the farm husband and wife, Kollmorgen's discussion of large family work units and women's labor in the garden and home highlighted the Amish woman's role as reproducer and producer. Kollmorgen acknowledged, though, that Old Order Amish women functioned within a highly structured, patriarchal system: "[T]he man is distinctly the head of the household and in most cases directs the affairs of the family. Neither on the family level nor on the community level does the wife initiate or direct important activities."[13]

Kollmorgen and the other members of Taylor's research team were not the only USDA investigators interested in Amish women and the patriarchal farm family. The USDA's Bureau of Home Economics (BHE) had also conducted research among the Old Order Amish of Lancaster County during the New Deal years. At a time when women around the country were necessarily searching for ways to limit consumer spending, the BHE had put on hold its longtime commitment to farm home modernization and instead was concentrating on ways that women could retrieve or expand upon traditional methods of home and farm production. The BHE, working with the Bureau of Labor Statistics in the Department of Labor, had chosen the Old Order Amish of Lancaster County as one of the population groups surveyed in their massive 1935–36 Study of Consumer Purchases.

[10] Carl C. Taylor to Walter M. Kollmorgen, April 8, 1940, AFCS Project Files.
[11] Kollmorgen interview.
[12] Walter M. Kollmorgen, *Culture of a Contemporary Rural Community: The Old Order Amish of Lancaster County, Pennsylvania*, Rural Life Studies, vol. 4 (Washington, D.C.: Government Printing Office, 1942), 105.
[13] Ibid., 78.

Under the auspices of the BHE and the Bureau of Labor Statistics, Works Progress Administration workers had interviewed women in three hundred thousand families in cities, small towns, and rural areas throughout the nation. Rural participants were to be nuclear families in which both the husband and wife were present; they were not to receive relief benefits during the survey year; and outside the South only white farm families were eligible to participate in the study, apparently because organizers considered the number of non-Caucasians living in the rural North to be statistically negligible. Lancaster County Amish families, whose race, family organization, and religiously based refusal to participate in social welfare programs made them a perfect fit for the Study of Consumer Purchases, thus participated significantly in the project. Of the 1,200 farm households surveyed in Lancaster County, 105 were Old Order Amish families, and the comments of Amish women regarding farm crops and income, family size, home production, and dietary habits further demonstrated the role that they played in the economic health of the Amish community. Information from the BAE report and the Consumer Purchases Study indicated that Old Order Amish families relied heavily on women's economic contributions both within the home and on the farm.[14]

Results of the government-sponsored Study of Consumer Purchases showed that Old Order Amish women played a vital role in keeping their farm families clothed and supplied with other necessary textile items. According to the survey data, 97.1 percent of Old Order Amish women in the county owned their own sewing machines, and, as other sources of evidence suggest, they put that equipment to particularly hard use during winter months when there were few outdoor farming responsibilities. Examination of Amish diaries of the period reveals that some women spent up to half the month of February engaged in sewing activities. Old Order Amish informant Fannie Esch has estimated that she could work on as many as twelve or thirteen dresses during lengthy sewing sessions in which her young daughters performed all the other household tasks. Esch also made pillowcases, bedsheets, and tablecloths out of discarded feedbags. Amish woman Lydia Stoltzfus remembers using her treadle sewing machine to make twenty pairs of pants every winter. Along with construction of new clothing, repair of old clothes took up a considerable amount of time for the average Amish woman. Naomi Fisher remembers her mother frequently writing the words "I was patching all day," in her Depression era diary. Old Order Amish women's sewing activities ensured that they spent

---

[14] "General Instructions for Field Agents," March 18, 1936, National Archives II, RG 176, Consumer Purchase Study Records (1935–36), box 2, folder 2. For extensive discussion of the Study of Consumer Purchases and Old Order Amish responses, see Reschly and Jellison, "Production Patterns," 134–62.

less money per person on clothing their families than did their non-Amish counterparts.[15]

New Deal era investigators were also interested in Amish women's food production and processing activities. Gardening, canning, preserving meat, and churning butter filled many hours for Amish farm women and allowed them to provide for their families in ways that city women—and even some other farm women—did not. Lydia Stoltzfus's memories of the period are typical: "We raised everything we needed on our own farm. In the garden. We made our own butter. We bought only staples at [the grocery store], and occasionally some candy. That's just how things were." As Consumer Purchase Study findings indicated, with abundant fruits, vegetables, meat, and dairy products already available on their farms, Old Order Amish families purchased only a few basic items, including coffee, sugar, salt, and prepared cereals. The cash value of women's food production for home consumption was significant. In Old Order Amish families during the mid-1930s, the monetary value of women's food production for household use averaged $422 a year, more than twice the amount spent on purchased groceries.[16]

Government-sponsored research also celebrated the fact that in addition to producing foods for the family, Amish women sold food items to city dwellers door-to-door, at curbside, or at central markets in the city of Lancaster or in smaller area towns. Sometimes women also exchanged items such as eggs or cans of lard directly for groceries at local stores. According to her mother's 1933 diary, Naomi Fisher's family went to the Southern Market in Lancaster every Tuesday, Friday, and Saturday. Every Monday, Fisher and her mother prepared their market products, making forty gallons of apple butter or milking the cows and then making cup cheese—or *Schmierkäse*—to be placed in small cardboard containers and sold for ten cents a carton. The family's major market specialty, however, was fresh-baked pie sold at twenty-five cents apiece. In Fisher's words, "Mother figured that if she made one hundred pies, she had $25. We paid nineteen cents for a twelve-pound bag of flour and three cents for one

[15] Patricia T. Herr, "Quilts within the Amish Culture," in *A Quiet Spirit: Amish Quilts from the Collection of Cindy Tietze and Stuart Hodosh* (Los Angeles: UCLA Fowler Museum of Cultural History, 1996), 52–53; Fannie Esch, interview with Katherine Jellison and Steven D. Reschly, Lancaster County, January 10, 1997; Fannie Esch, interview with Louise Stoltzfus, Lancaster County, April 29, 1995; Lydia Stoltzfus, interview with Louise Stoltzfus, Lancaster County, April 17, 1995; Naomi Fisher, interview with Louise Stoltzfus, Lancaster County, April 29, 1995. Because of the Old Order Amish aversion to prideful behavior or somehow setting oneself outside the rest of the group, the names of all Old Order Amish interview subjects used in this essay are pseudonyms. Lydia Stoltzfus, who was a member of the Old Order Amish during the Depression years, is now a member of a less traditional "Car" Amish sect and has agreed that her real name may be used. For further information on family size, clothing purchase, and sewing statistics taken from the 1935–36 Study of Consumer Purchases, see Reschly and Jellison, "Production Patterns," 148, 152–58.

[16] Stoltzfus interview; Reschly and Jellison, "Production Patterns," 152.

pound of lard. We baked one hundred pies at a time. We got up early and started. The range baked four pies at a time. When it was hot, we just done it. There was no such thing as it being too hot. We just went and did it." Such determined efforts on the part of Fisher and her mother yielded important cash resources that could be used for grocery staples, farming expenses, or other necessities.[17]

As both the Consumer Purchases Study and the BAE report indicated, Old Order Amish women also played a major role in the production of cash crops and livestock on Lancaster County farms. While all women took a turn at work in the potato, tobacco, or corn fields during busy periods, many of them also performed other "outdoor" work on a regular basis. Women who had a fondness for animals frequently worked with the large livestock, and girls from predominantly female families worked in the farm fields alongside their fathers every day. Scattered responses to the government's Consumer Purchases survey likewise indicated that Old Order Amish men sometimes involved themselves with domestic concerns. This is a theme reiterated in oral history testimony. For instance, Daniel Zook tearily remembered his father's distress over the hard work his mother performed in caring for her seven children during the Depression years. Over the protests of Zook's mother, his father spent scarce cash resources to buy her a gasoline-powered Maytag washing machine, telling her, "I have a [hay] binder that stays in the barn and I use twice a year; you use the washing machine every week." A husband's contributions to domestic labor, however, could extend beyond supplying his wife with the appropriate household equipment. Fannie Esch, for instance, characterizes her Depression era marriage as an ideal cooperative relationship. She and her husband made all decisions that affected the farm family together, and they shared work on both sides of the farmhouse threshold. He frequently looked after the children; she hoed weeds, milked cows, and shocked wheat. This spirit of cooperation began on the day the couple married in 1929 and continued until her husband's death in 1989.[18]

Old Order Amish families were not the only ones in Lancaster County to rely substantially on farm women's contributions to survive the hard times of the Great Depression. As data from the Consumer Purchases Study indicate, however, women played a larger role in the Old Order Amish family economy than they did in other Lancaster County households. According to survey results, Old Order Amish women's productive efforts

[17] Fisher interview.

[18] Daniel Zook, interview with Katherine Jellison, Lancaster County, July 22, 1997; Esch interview with Louise Stoltzfus. For discussion of the mutuality of men's and women's work on farms in other regions of the country, see Nancy Grey Osterud, *Bonds of Community: The Lives of Farm Women in Nineteenth-Century New York* (Ithaca: Cornell University Press, 1991), and Mary Neth, *Preserving the Family Farm: Women, Community, and the Foundations of Agribusiness in the Midwest, 1900–1940* (Baltimore: Johns Hopkins University Press, 1995).

surpassed average output for the county's women in every category of analysis. Old Order Amish women canned thirty more quarts of fruits and vegetables a year than the statistically average Lancaster County farm woman. The dollar value of the vegetables Old Order Amish women raised exceeded the county average by \$24 a year, and the total value of Old Order Amish women's home food production outstripped that of the average Lancaster County woman by \$63 a year. The typical Old Order Amish woman also contributed more workers to the farm labor force than did the average Lancaster County woman, helping to limit hired labor costs. While the average county farm woman who responded to the Consumer Purchases Study had 2.53 children living at home in 1935–36, the typical Old Order Amish respondent had 3.34 children in her household at the time of the survey. As a result, annual hired labor costs for Old Order Amish families totaled \$175 as compared to \$184 for the average Lancaster County family. According to results of the government's Consumer Purchases survey, these various contributions to the farm family economy by Old Order Amish women helped their families realize \$1,000 a year in net farm profit as compared to \$878 for the average county farm family.[19]

Just as he had intended, Taylor's stability-instability study—particularly in its juxtaposition of Lancaster County and Sublette, Kansas, data— showed even more clearly than the results of the Consumer Purchases Study the advantages that Amish farm families gained from women's contributions. BAE participant-observer Earl H. Bell found in his examination of Sublette that residents there relied heavily on a single cash crop–winter wheat. Area families, many of whom had resided in the region only since the World War I wheat boom, found themselves at the mercy of wheat market fluctuations, and during the drought of the 1930s, this meant that they lived precariously, with few other home and farm production activities in existence to supplement their dismal wheat income. With the exception of the area's small Mennonite community, in which women engaged in more diversified and traditional practices, female residents of Sublette did not contribute significantly to their family economies by way of garden and home production activities. In 1939, a year before Bell's arrival in Sublette, one-fourth of the farms in the county had sold, traded, or used less than \$250 worth of farm products. At the same time, among the Old Order Amish of Lancaster County, annual value of farm products sold, traded, or used averaged \$1,444, with women making a sizable contribution to this total. While virtually all Old Order Amish women raised poultry and kept gardens—canning, on yearly average, 345 quarts of fruits and vegetables per woman—Sublette women raised poultry on only 56.7 percent of farms in the region and tended gardens on only 13

---

[19] Reschly and Jellison, "Production Patterns," 148, 150–52.

percent of farms. Sublette area farm women instead spent scarce family resources to purchase dairy, poultry, and produce items at the local grocery
store, and frequently earned the necessary cash to do so by holding wage-
earning "town jobs" at the courthouse or in local retail establishments.
Women's travel to these jobs in turn required that scant cash resources be
spent on gasoline and automobile maintenance. Women also employed
family automobiles to pursue nonproductive leisure activities—such as
club meetings—which Bell considered an inappropriate use of resources.[20]

By the time that Kollmorgen, Bell, and the other BAE investigators published their findings, the federal government had shifted its primary policy agenda. "Dr. Win-the-War" had now replaced "Dr. New Deal." As a result, upon publication of the six community studies in 1942, the reports
were not as widely distributed as originally planned. Although fifteen thousand copies of Kollmorgen's study were eventually printed and distributed,
the BAE was unable to keep up with demand for the report—particularly
among rural sociology students and faculty on college campuses, and
Amish people who wanted to read the geographer's positive assessment of
their community—because additional printings were not deemed necessary to the war effort. The war also interrupted efforts to produce an additional volume in the stability-instability series that would have synthe-
sized the six community studies and made clear the advantages of the
Amish community's labor-intensive diversified agriculture over capital-
intensive monoculture—and additionally would have reinforced the significance of Amish women's productive activities. Wartime distractions likewise halted plans to publish an extensive volume of photographs to ac-
company each of the community studies. Among the images to have been
included in the volume on Lancaster County were photographs that documented the results of Amish women's work in the kitchen, sewing room,
garden, dairy barn, and farmers' market.[21]

Hostile reaction to the BAE's praise for traditional family farming and its
criticism of farming as big business also surfaced at this time among conservative members of the U.S. Congress and agencies within the Department of Agriculture that promoted industrialized agriculture. Antagonism
toward BAE policies on the part of other government officials and agencies
demonstrated once again that the state possessed complex and varied

[20] See Earl H. Bell, *Culture of a Contemporary Rural Community: Sublette, Kansas,* Rural Life
Studies, vol. 2 (Washington, D.C.: Government Printing Office, 1942). For further discussion
of Bell's study and his analysis of farm women's activities in the Sublette area, see Jellison, *Entitled to Power,* chap. 4. Statistics for the Old Order Amish community derive from Reschly and
Jellison, "Production Patterns," 150, 152.
[21] Kollmorgen, "Kollmorgen as a Bureaucrat," 84; Kollmorgen interview; Peter H. DeVries
to Charles Suter, April 27, 1943, Carl C. Taylor to Charles P. Loomis, November 6, 1941, Carl
C. Taylor to E. W. Burgess, August 2, 1944, Ralph R. Nichols to Wayne C. Neely. September
26. 1944, Conrad Taeuber to Ray E. Wakeley. June 22, 1942, AFCS Project Files.

attitudes toward rural America and its problems and reinforced the reality that the Taylor group's commitment to small-scale, diversified farming represented a minority position among federal policymakers. Ultimately, opposition to such philosophies resulted in budget cuts for the BAE and censorship of some of its publications, further ensuring that the agency's research would not be widely disseminated during and after the war.[22]

Limited distribution of BAE findings muted the message of Taylor's group that women's work was central to the long-term success of agriculture and was particularly crucial during hard economic times. In contrast to the farm families of Sublette, Kansas, where women had largely relinquished their part in home and farm production, Old Order Amish women had retained the traditional, multifaceted role of women on the family farm. As numerous recent studies have shown, Amish farm families were not entirely unique in this regard. Farm women in many American communities continued to participate in farm and home production in the twentieth century, even in the face of USDA advice to limit their activities to homemaking. With the exception of communities like Sublette, where women had completed the transition to a modern consumer ethos, millions of farm women throughout the nation stepped up their home production activities and decreased their reliance on purchased goods to aid their families in times of economic crisis. In particular, farm communities in many regions witnessed a substantial increase in women's gardening and poultry-raising activities in the 1930s as compared to the 1920s. By the 1930s, however, most of these women's families were in a period of transition between the general family farming practices of the nineteenth century and the greater crop specialization, mechanization, and reliance on consumer goods that farm journals, agricultural college farm and home extension services, and most USDA agencies had urged upon them. For the Old Order Amish, in contrast, productive activities represented a continuation rather than a resumption or extension of earlier practices. As Kollmorgen had noted, the Old Order Amish belief that the Lord had commanded them to lead a labor-intensive life on the land lay behind their strong and sustained commitment to productive activities that involved all members of the farm family. Hard work distracted family members from worldly influences outside the Amish community, and home production ensured that members of the Old Order Amish sect—with their history of

[22] Evidence suggests that wartime budgetary concerns and staff cutbacks resulted in the elimination or reduction of some proposed BAE publications. Evidence also suggests, however, that some BAE studies were altered before publication to eliminate or soften criticism of other USDA agencies. In the case of Earl H. Bell's study of Sublette, Kansas, for instance, both wartime conditions and censorship of his criticism of the Agricultural Adjustment Administration resulted in major alterations of his manuscript before publication. Kimball Young to Carl C. Taylor, June 29, 1942, Kimball Young to Conrad Taeuber, August 2, 1942, Earl H. Bell to E. A. Ross, November 27, 1942, AFCS Project Files.

religious persecution—could remain relatively self-reliant and independent of potentially dangerous outsiders. For Old Order Amish women, a central role in home and farm production thus represented a permanent way of life rather than a temporary survival strategy or the final stage of reliance on the practices of an earlier era before continuing down the road toward "modern," mechanized farming when the economy revived. Old Order Amish women's long-established and wide-ranging production efforts, and their limited involvement in consumer activities, served their households well during the crisis years of the Great Depression and helped them weather depression conditions more successfully than most other farm families.[23]

Amish women performed this necessary labor within the constraints of a long-established patriarchal system. Kollmorgen was correct in noting that women generally had limited decision-making power within the Amish household and relied on the good will of sympathetic husbands for the purchase of new household equipment (as in the case of Daniel Zook's father) or cooperation in child-rearing activities (as in the case of Fannie Esch's husband). The Taylor group's fascination with the Old Order Amish, after all, stemmed in part from the sect's seeming adherence to the rules of the nineteenth-century farm family. The family patriarch controlled and organized the labor of all family members, from the youngest child to the wife and mother. In other words, Taylor's research team embraced patriarchy as central to their vision of successful American agriculture and thus celebrated patriarchal control within the Amish farm family.

In contrast, the Taylor group viewed the farm families of Sublette, Kansas, as existing in chaos. In this corner of the Dust Bowl, Earl H. Bell found few families outside the area's small Mennonite community who maintained an allegiance to the traditions of diversified farming and family labor. Instead, the children of Sublette frequently traveled off the farm to attend ball games or movies with their schoolmates, and wives motored away to earn town wages, shop, or attend Farm Bureau meetings. Bell's disgust with what he presumed to be a lack of patriarchal control in

---

[23] For the transition to a more modern model of farming during this period, see Fitzgerald, "Accounting for Change." For information on farm women's activities in other areas of the North during the Great Depression, see Deborah Fink, *Agrarian Women: Wives and Mothers in Rural Nebraska, 1880–1940* (Chapel Hill: University of North Carolina Press, 1992), chaps. 5, 7; Catherine McNicol Stock, *Main Street in Crisis: The Great Depression and the Old Middle Class on the Northern Plains* (Chapel Hill: University of North Carolina Press, 1992), chap. 6; and Neth, *Preserving the Family Farm*, passim. For discussion of farm women's Depression era production efforts in the Irwin, Iowa, community, see Jellison, *Entitled to Power*, chap. 4. For extensive examination of the greater long-term success enjoyed by farming communities that practice farming as a way of life rather than as a business enterprise, see Sonya Salamon, *Prairie Patrimony: Family, Farming, and Community in the Midwest* (Chapel Hill: University of North Carolina Press, 1992).

KATHERINE JELLISON

Sublette led him to portray the area's farm men as worn-out and emascu-
lated, and to characterize Sublette's women as the "real leaders" of the
community. The women of Sublette, however, no less than the women of
the Old Order Amish community, functioned within a patriarchal structure. Women largely put their wages, their automobiles, and their political
skills at the service of the male-headed family farm. Within a gendered
labor system that viewed men as the true farmers, women were the help-
mates who necessarily absented themselves from the farm to earn wages to
pay for farming expenses, to purchase supplies for the farm and household, and to attend meetings where agricultural policies were discussed.[24]

While on the surface the car-driving, job-holding women of Sublette
seemed to possess greater freedom than their Amish counterparts, they
merely served a patriarchal farm family that had adapted itself more completely to an urban, industrial economy. As Deborah Fink has noted in her
study of farm women in Depression era Nebraska, women there who took
off-farm jobs to support the farming operation "helped expand the
agrarian base of the rural economy. But in each case the family economy
was modeled on the family farm, where each person's work derived from
that of the male household head.... women were rural wives, but they were
rural wives in a new way. The economic hardships of the 1930s removed
the possibility of their being 'only' farm wives."[25] In other words, gender
roles in Sublette conformed more closely to those of the "modernized" patriarchal farm family that most members of the USDA had been promoting since the Progressive era. For Bell, however, who clung to the older
nineteenth-century model of family farming, this updated version was dis-
organized, inefficient, and wasteful of family resources.

Results of government-sponsored research also demonstrated that the
apparently "liberated" women of Sublette remained less satisfied with farm
life than their supposedly "oppressed" Amish sisters. Women in Sublette
and elsewhere on mechanized plains farms lacked the sense of achievement and recognition that Amish women found in their capacity as farm
producers. Earl H. Bell was not the only person who did not recognize the
significant economic role that the women of Sublette continued to play in
the life of their family farms, even after the transition to mechanized monoculture. Many of the women themselves failed to recognize the true worth
of their contribution to the farm. For example, oral history informant
Marguerite Rooney chiefly characterized her family's Depression era experience near Sublette as one in which her husband farmed wheat while

[24] Historian Donald Worster reiterates Bell's characterization of Sublette-area women in
Dust Bowl: The Southern Plains in the 1930s (New York: Oxford University Press, 1979), 171–73.
For an alternative interpretation of women's experience in the Kansas dust bowl, see Jellison,
Entitled to Power, chap. 4.
[25] Fink, *Agrarian Women*, 109–10.

she worked in a local grocery store. When pressed, however, she noted that she and her husband had used a portion of her grocery store earnings to develop a successful turkey-raising operation that was key to their survival as family farmers. In contrast, Old Order Amish women, whose economic contributions to the family farm were more direct and visible than those of their Sublette counterparts, readily acknowledged their part in the success of the family farm during the Depression years. The work that Amish women described in detail to government investigators had a direct impact on their families' standard of living and status in the community. It was not unusual, for instance, for the entire Amish community to watch the progress of a woman's thriving kitchen garden, thereby conferring prestige on the woman herself and her family.[26]

Although Old Order Amish women lived in a highly structured religious patriarchy, their families and neighbors greatly valued Amish women as farm producers for market and household and for their labor in limiting consumer expenditures for food and clothing. In contrast to many other farm women of the period, such as those in the Sublette area whose contributions to successful farming were increasingly behind the scenes and therefore unacknowledged, New Deal era Amish women apparently remained satisfied with life on the farm. Fannie Esch's memories of the Depression are emblematic: "[My husband and I] had so much fun on the farm. We would get up to do the milking in the morning and the moon would be shining.... Oh, we had so much fun."[27]

In the years following World War II, the majority of American women who remained on the farm followed more in the footsteps of the women of Sublette than of the Old Order Amish women of Lancaster County. During this time, the Taylor group's minority voice within the Department of Agriculture became silent, the USDA continued its decades-long campaign to encourage greater specialization and capital investment on the nation's farms, and increasing numbers of farm women began to define themselves more as consumers than as producers. With a return to greater prosperity on the farm in the post–World War II era, the thrifty, self-sufficient Amish model held little appeal for the government agencies that advised farm families or for the families themselves, which were now experiencing a

[26] For further discussion of Marguerite Rooney's experiences, see Jellison, *Entitled to Power*, 118–20, 122–24. For analysis of plainswomen's relative discontent with farm life, see Katherine Jellison, "Women and Technology on the Great Plains, 1910–1940," *Great Plains Quarterly* 8 (summer 1988): 145–57, and Fink, *Agrarian Women*, passim. For further examination of Amish women's satisfaction and prestige within their community, see Olshan and Schmidt, "Amish Women and the Feminist Conundrum," 215–29. See also the anecdotal evidence in Louise Stoltzfus, *Amish Women: Lives and Stories* (Intercourse, Pa: Good Books, 1994), and Sue Bender, *Plain and Simple: A Woman's Journey to the Amish* (San Francisco: Harper & Row, 1989). For analysis of the "invisibility" of women's contributions to modern agriculture, see Carolyn E. Sachs, *The Invisible Farmers: Women in Agricultural Production* (Totowa, N.J.: Rowman and Allanheld, 1983).

[27] Esch interview with Louise Stoltzfus.

higher income and full integration into the nation's consumer culture. As USDA advice manuals and articles in farm periodicals urged families to invest in attractive labor-saving farm and household technology, most rural households responded. The state, particularly in the form of the Department of Agriculture, had little use for the Amish, no matter what their level of agricultural success. Agrarian author Wendell Berry has speculated that this neglect resulted from two primary reasons: the Amish were poor consumers of the technology produced by agribusiness industries which influenced federal farm policies; and the success of Amish agriculture disproved the wisdom of the USDA's long-standing dominant philosophy that bigger, more capital-intensive agriculture was better.[28]

In contrast, Carl C. Taylor and the other New Deal era investigators involved in the BAE stability-instability studies had consistently championed Amish farm women and their families. Wartime disruptions and conservative opposition, however, had prevented widespread distribution of these scholars' findings, which concluded that women's productive and reproductive efforts were vital for the success of an agricultural community in the closing years of the Great Depression and the New Deal. These researchers argued that Old Order Amish women's wide-ranging work—on both sides of the farmhouse threshold—contributed to their families' relative economic stability during the Depression years. While they acknowledged that Amish women performed this labor within the boundaries of the patriarchal family, these researchers noted that it was a family in which each member played an assigned and valued role. In contrast, the "modern" farm women of Sublette, Kansas, functioned within the boundaries of a patriarchal farm family in which they no longer had a clearly defined and appreciated position. As they worked in town-based office or retail jobs, Sublette area women may have questioned the extent to which they were any longer farm women at all, even if they invested their wages in the farm's maintenance and improvement. Women's contributions to the farm family economy had become "invisible," lessening their sense of satisfaction and purpose in life on the farm.

Given the USDA's long-standing commitment to policies that promoted patriarchal control on the farm, the Taylor team's adherence to this concept was predictable and probably inevitable. What was not so predictable was their promotion of a brand of rural patriarchy more in line with USDA standards of the 1800s than of the twentieth century. The paper trail that Taylor, Baker, Kollmorgen, Bell and other members of the team have left behind demonstrates that the USDA was not a monolith. It contained personnel who voiced an opposing point of view to the dominant notion that farm men should be rural businessmen and farm women rural housewives.

---

[28] Wendell Berry, *The Unsettling of America: Culture and Agriculture* (San Francisco: Sierra Club Books, 1977), 216–17. For extended analysis of mainstream farm women's lives in the years following World War II, see Fink, *Open Country, Iowa*, and Jellison, *Entitled to Power*, chap. 6.

Instead, the Taylor contingent promoted a way of life more in line with the one that the majority of farm families were still living in the 1930s and early 1940s, a system in which all members of the family remained actively engaged in agricultural production. By the time the stability-instability case studies were published in 1942, the old system's days were already numbered because farm state politicians, land-grant colleges, and most members of the USDA had rejected it as the model for twentieth-century American agriculture. The work that Taylor and his colleagues produced in the waning days of the New Deal, however, remained in many ways a blueprint for subsequent dissenters who challenged the hegemony of modern agribusiness. Participants in the stability-instability investigation nurtured a debate that continued throughout the remainder of the twentieth century and achieved a particularly high profile among back-to-the-land advocates of the 1960s and 1970s counterculture, family farm activists of the 1980s farm crisis period, and family values proponents and sustainable agriculture supporters of the 1990s. For such diverse groups as these, Amish rejection of the military draft, crop reduction payments, public schools, Social Security, and the "big agriculture" dictates of the USDA rendered them a model of self-sufficiency and independence from the state. The debate to which Taylor and his colleagues contributed continues even today as observers discuss the questionable outcomes of such late twentieth-century developments as the Freedom to Farm Act and the globalization of agricultural markets and production.[29]

Whether it was Taylor's vision of labor-intensive family farming or the more dominant notion that separate spheres should reign supreme on the family farm, the USDA remained committed to patriarchy in the New Deal era. USDA bureaucrats of the twentieth century, like their counterparts in the 1800s, adhered to the principle that successful family farming rested on male control and female assistance. The only variation was the form in which that female "help" manifested itself. According to the nineteenth-century farm family ideal, the "helpmate" was a producer; in the updated version, she was a consumer. In perpetuating the older patriarchal model, members of Taylor's research team at least advocated a system that functioned sufficiently in hard economic times and contributed to women's self-esteem and feeling of purpose, as the words of Lydia Stoltzfus clearly illustrate:[30] "On our farm I did whatever needed to be done. I stripped tobacco. I mixed doughnuts. I papered the house. Whatever needed to be done, I did it."

---

[29] For discussion of Old Order Amish efforts to limit state intrusions into their lives, see Hostetler, *Amish Society,* 255–76, and the various essays in Donald B. Kraybill, ed., *The Amish and the State* (Baltimore: Johns Hopkins University Press, 1993). For information on attempts since the mid-1960s by people disaffected with mainstream society to model themselves on the Amish, see Hostetler, *Amish Society,* 397–99.
[30] Stoltzfus interview.

Remaking Red Bird

Isolation and the War on Poverty in a Rural Appalachian Locality

ROBERT S. WEISE

In November of 1966, representatives of the United States Forest Service and the Council of the Southern Mountains met with angry and worried residents of the Red Bird River valley at the Jack's Creek Church in Leslie County, Kentucky. These citizens feared the loss of their homes, because the land on which they lived was soon to become part of the Daniel Boone National Forest. Enabled by legislation to purchase land within a 591,000-acre territory in the mountainous southeastern portion of the state, the Forest Service was in the process of buying a 60,000-acre tract along the Red Bird River, in Clay and Leslie counties, owned by the Red Bird Timber Company. Individuals who owned land within the Red Bird Purchase Unit, as the larger territory was called, also voiced their concerns, having heard rumors to the effect that, as described by a Forest Service official, "the U.S. Forest Service is going to buy land all over the... area regardless of whether the people want to sell." At the 1966 meeting and for months thereafter, the Forest Service tried to dispel those rumors, saying that it would forgo its power of eminent domain and buy only from willing sellers, and that it had no plans to evict any of its new tenants. It would instead follow a policy of attrition, removing homes when people left them but not forcing anybody to move. Despite those efforts, as statements from the Council of the Southern Mountains acknowledged, "people who live up in the hollows are resisting any attempts to get them to move." At the same time, limitations the Forest Service placed on people's actions in order to prevent fires and enforce hunting regulations had been "met with an attitude of resistance."[1]

[1] *Manchester (Ky.) Enterprise*, March 23, 1967; "That They, Too, Shall Live in Dignity," *Mountain Life and Work* 43, no. 1 (spring 1967): 22; "Program Development in Red Bird to Date," n.d.—probably summer 1968, Records of the Council of the Southern Mountains, series V, box 185, folder 6, p. 5. Special Collections, Hutchins Library, Berea College, Berea, Kentucky

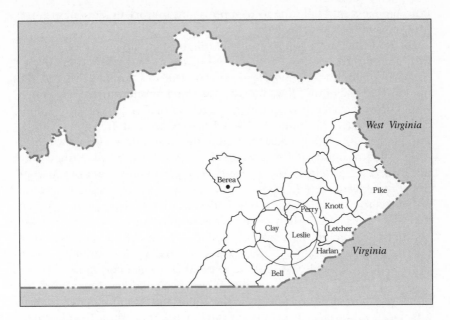

Red Bird Purchase Unit, Kentucky

The Forest Service and the Council of the Southern Mountains worked cooperatively in Red Bird as arms of the federal War on Poverty, defined broadly here to include the entire gamut of antipoverty actions undertaken by the Kennedy and Johnson administrations. The Forest Service, delivering federally-based resource management programs to promote development, provided means of economic restructuring, while the council, a private organization in partnership with Sargent Shriver's Office of Economic Opportunity (OEO), took on the role of human development. The council, housed on the fringes of the Kentucky mountains at Berea College, was an umbrella organization formed in 1913 that connected various church missions and settlement schools that had been established throughout the Appalachians. In the 1960s, foundation grants and an influx of federal funds from the OEO allowed the council to play a crucial part in the War on Poverty, funneling OEO money, assisting in organizing Community Ac-

(hereafter CSM). Robert F. Collins, *A History of the Daniel Boone National Forest, 1770–1970* (Winchester, Ky.: United States Forest Service, 1975); *The Thousandsticks,* July 22, 1965; January 12, 1967; October 19, 1967; *Manchester Enterprise,* July 15, 1965; August 5, 1965; June 23, 1966; January 12, 1967; March 23, 1967; September 14, 1967; October 19, 1967; November 9, 1967; February 22, 1968.

tion Agencies, and tailoring its own programs to work in tandem with the programs of the Great Society.[2]

For Red Bird, near where council affiliates had already been working with community groups, council administrators and researchers began preparing ambitious proposals to relocate the 115 families living in the 60,000-acre tract into "New Towns"—planned, modern urban areas that would provide an alluring alternative to rural isolation and poverty. Council representatives promoted the New Towns concept at the 1966 meeting, hoping that the comforts and amenities the towns offered would win over disgruntled residents and encourage them to move even when they were not forced. An article in *Mountain Life & Work,* a periodical published by the council, reflected that hope, maintaining that most residents would not object to moving as long as they had a place to go. The article reported that one "housewife," when seeing slides of low-cost homes to which she and her family might have access, replied, "'I want you to get me out of here as quick as possible.'" Other residents, the article continued, "have expressed this same desire, and there are likely to be many more."[3]

Red Bird's War on Poverty experience reveals the key components of public policy toward rural poverty in the 1960s: the assumption that poverty was the result of isolation from national economic, political, consumer, and cultural networks; and that, as a consequence, solving poverty in rural areas often required relocating people into urban areas, thereby integrating them into the main currents of modern, national life.[4] The federal government's policy of economic integration grew out of a Progressive tradition of pursuing rural betterment through social and environmental engineering. In the eyes of Progressives, the rural South represented a

[2] John Glen, "The War on Poverty in Appalachia—A Preliminary Report." *Register of the Kentucky Historical Society* 87 (winter 1989): 40–57. David E. Whisnant, *Modernizing the Mountaineer: People, Power, and Planning in Appalachia* (Boone, Ky.: Appalachian Consortium Press, 1980), 3–39.

[3] "That They, Too, Shall Live in Dignity," 22. The council was a conglomeration of many different people and groups from throughout the mountain South who often held contradictory political viewpoints. The council as a whole never voted on or approved the proposal, and council administrators never considered it an official document.

[4] On the War on Poverty, see Charles Murray, *Losing Ground: American Social Policy, 1950–1980* (New York: Basic Books, 1984); Lawrence Mead, *Beyond Entitlement: The Social Obligations of Citizenship* (New York: The Free Press, 1986); Gareth Davies, *From Opportunity to Entitlement: The Transformation and Decline of Great Society Liberalism* (Lawrence: University of Kansas Press, 1996); Irwin Unger, *The Best of Intentions: The Triumphs and Failures of the Great Society Under Kennedy, Johnson, and Nixon* (New York: Doubleday, 1996); Alice O'Connor, "Modernization and the Rural Poor: Some Lessons from History," in *Rural Poverty in America,* ed. Cynthia M. Duncan (New York: Auburn House, 1992), 215–35; Michael Katz, *The Undeserving Poor: From the War on Poverty to the War on Welfare* (New York: Pantheon, 1989); Oscar Lewis, "The Culture of Poverty," in *On Understanding Poverty,* ed. Daniel Patrick Moynihan (New York: Basic Books, 1969), 187–220; Allen J. Matusow, *The Unraveling of America: American Liberalism during the 1960s* (New York: Harper and Row, 1984). See also Carl Brauer, "Kennedy, Johnson, and the War on Poverty," *Journal of American History* 69, no. 1 (June 1982): 98–119.

national problem, an obstacle to the achievement of national goals of prosperity and modernity. Toward those ends, particularly in the decades surrounding the New Deal, Progressives in both North and South tried to rationalize the South's agriculture, upgrade its standards of living, and modernize its social relationships.[5]

Another strain of Progressive thought, overlapping with but also at odds with the first, pursued local revitalization as well as modernization. Most associated with the New Deal's Resettlement Administration and the Bureau of Agricultural Economics, revitalization efforts respected the vitality of local cultures and saw regional diversity as a source of national strength.[6] Those ideals lost favor in the 1940s, but they reemerged in the War on Poverty, especially in the OEO and among some elements of the diverse Council of the Southern Mountains. The New Towns proposal for Red Bird reflected the struggle between these two ideals, though it weighed in solidly in favor of integration over revitalization.

As directed toward rural areas of the South, and especially Appalachia, the War on Poverty was more properly a War on Provincialism. To most postwar liberals, rural isolation conjured images of social pathology: poverty, poor health, ignorance, closed-mindedness, constricted opportunities for personal growth, and, as the Deep South proved all too well, violent racial hatred. Relocating and urbanizing rural people would place them in touch with the blessings of modern living and would reaffirm in the minds of middle-class Americans that the country was and ought to be urban and cosmopolitan rather than rural, isolated, and provincial. Poverty itself seemed out of place in a generally affluent nation and was

[5] Michael J. McDonald and John Muldowny, *TVA and the Dispossessed: The Resettlement of Population in the Norris Dam Area* (Knoxville: University of Tennessee Press, 1982); David L. Carlton and Peter A. Coclanis, eds., *Confronting Poverty in the Great Depression: The Report on Economic Conditions of the South with Related Documents* (Boston: Bedford Books of St. Martin's Press, 1996); David L. Carlton and Peter A. Coclanis, "Another 'Great Migration': From Region to Race in Southern Liberalism, 1938–1945," *Southern Cultures* 3, no. 4 (winter 1997): 37–62; Larry J. Griffin and Don H. Doyle, *The South as an American Problem* (Athens: University of Georgia Press, 1995); Bruce Schulman, *From Cotton Belt to Sunbelt: Federal Policy, Economic Development, and the Transformation of the South, 1938–1980* (New York: Oxford University Press, 1991); Robert Gough, *Farming the Cutover: A Social History of Northern Wisconsin, 1900–1940* (Lawrence: University Press of Kansas, 1997); Thomas A. Lyson and William W. Falk, eds., *Forgotten Places: Uneven Development in Rural America* (Lawrence: University Press of Kansas, 1993).

[6] Donald Holley, *Uncle Sam's Farmers: The New Deal Communities in the Lower Mississippi Valley* (Urbana: University of Illinois Press, 1975); Paul E. Mertz, *New Deal Policy and Southern Rural Poverty* (Baton Rouge: Louisiana State University Press, 1978); Richard S. Kirkendall, *Social Scientists and Farm Politics in the Age of Roosevelt* (Columbia: University of Missouri Press, 1966); Robert L. Dorman, *Revolt of the Provinces: The Regionalist Movement in the United States, 1920–1945* (Chapel Hill: University of North Carolina Press, 1993); Jane S. Becker, *Selling Tradition: Appalachia and the Construction of an American Folk, 1930–1940* (Chapel Hill: University of North Carolina Press, 1998); Jess Gilbert and Alice O'Connor, "Leaving the Land Behind: Struggles for Land Reform in U.S. Federal Policy, 1933–1965," Land Tenure Center Paper no. 156, Land Tenure Center, University of Wisconsin—Madison, 1996.

more than a little embarrassing for a nation that advertised its prosperity to the Third World in its Cold War competition with communism. Reflecting the postwar faith in capitalism to produce wealth, media and politics presented poverty as a separation from the normal workings of the American economy rather than as a consequence of it. For these reasons, "isolation" became a code word for poverty during the 1960s, and it implied not only material deprivation but economic, cultural, and social deprivation as well. In the rhetoric of its rediscovery in the early 1960s and the subsequent war upon it, poverty, especially in its rural form, was only partially about standards of living and economics; more importantly, it was a shorthand for talking about modernity, progress, and the essential character of the United States.

The American public rediscovered Appalachia in the early 1960s, when John Kennedy toured the West Virginia coalfields as part of his 1960 presidential campaign. A national curiosity during the union wars of the 1920s and 1930s, the region had fallen out of national consciousness in the next generation. But now Appalachia emerged again as both a curiosity and a problem, and it quickly became a symbol of rural poverty for urban, middle-class Americans. Writers, journalists, and television producers feasted on Appalachian poverty, expressing a romantic fascination that emphasized otherness and isolation as the region's defining characteristics. Michael Harrington's *The Other America* included a section on Appalachia, and following that came a flurry of other books, most notably *Night Comes to the Cumberlands,* written by lawyer Harry Caudill from Whitesburg in Letcher County, Kentucky, and the Reverend Jack E. Weller's *Yesterday's People,* published by the Council of the Southern Mountains. By early 1964, at least six television news programs on major networks appeared featuring eastern Kentucky counties. British television also ran a piece on the region, as did countless newspapers and magazines, including *Time, Newsweek, Life, Look, The New York Times, The Washington Post,* and the communist *Progressive Labor.*[7]

---

[7] Robert F. Mann, "The Latest Rediscovery of Appalachia," *Mountain Life and Work* 40, no. 3 (fall 1965): 10–12; Dan Wakefield, "In Hazard," in *Appalachia in the Sixties: Decade of Reawakening,* ed. David S. Walls and John B. Stephenson (Lexington: University Press of Kentucky, 1972); Michael Harrington, *The Other America: Poverty in the United States* (Baltimore: Penguin Books, 1969), 44, 45; Harry M. Caudill, *Night Comes to the Cumberlands: A Biography of A Depressed Area* (Boston: Little, Brown, 1963); Jack Weller, *Yesterday's People: Life in Contemporary Appalachia* (Lexington: University of Kentucky Press, 1966); John Fetterman, *Stinking Creek* (New York: E. P. Dutton, 1967); Homer Bigart, "Kentucky Miners: A Grim Winter," *New York Times,* October 20, 1963; John Dominis and Michael Murphy, "The Valley of Poverty," *Life,* January 31, 1964, 54–64; *The Mountain Eagle,* February 27, 1964, 1.

Every journalist and writer who contributed to the rediscovery remarked on the paradoxes of poverty in Appalachia: that such pockets of poverty could exist in a wealthy nation; that a region so blessed in natural resources could be so poor. Equally perplexing was the persistence of poverty among people of northern European origin—white people whose ancestry could be traced to the British Isles. The author of a 1971 analysis of governmental policy encapsulated a decade of common wisdom:

> Appalachia is an American enigma. It is a region rich in natural beauty and resources lying close to the vast industrial-urban complexes of the Midwest and Northeast . . . and it is inhabited largely by people who represent the American archetype in terms of ethnicity, religion, patriotism, and a ruggedly independent lifestyle. Yet these same people, many of colonial stock, have not shared fully in their nation's social and economic progress for nearly two centuries. Appalachia is a depressed region.[8]

The importance of whiteness and the Anglo-Saxon, pioneer heritage enhanced the region's mystique as an anachronistic, anomalous place that did not follow the same historical course as the rest of the country.

Poverty was no media invention. Appalachian Kentucky had no large cities and few towns, hundreds of miles of unpaved roads, and an unmechanized farming sector that provided little in the way of profits or income. When the coal industry mechanized after the Second World War, tens of thousands of miners lost their jobs. And when the coal industry as a whole collapsed around 1960, those who remained had little to substitute for lost mining wages. Tens of thousands of people left the region in search of better opportunities elsewhere; the rest tried to survive in decomposing company towns and on uncommercialized farms. Even with out-migration, eastern Kentucky counties still suffered from the highest levels of unemployment and underemployment in the country. Thousands of families, often headed by occasional or disabled miners, survived on the margins of the formal economy—from the produce of small farms, unreported wage work, illegal activity such as moonshining, and welfare. One reporter estimated that one-third of the people in one county lived on government assistance, as did 70 percent of families in Red Bird.[9] By the early 1960s,

[8] Donald N. Rothblatt, *Regional Planning: The Appalachian Experience* (Lexington, Mass.: D. C. Heath, 1971), 1. According to the 1960 population census, Leslie County, one of the Red Bird counties, had no nonwhite inhabitants at all, and Clay County, the other Red Bird county, had a nonwhite population of 455 out of 20,748, none of whom lived in the Red Bird area. U.S. Bureau of the Census, *Census of Population: 1960.* vol. 1: *Characteristics of the Population,* pt. 19, Kentucky (Washington D.C.: U.S. Government Printing Office, 1963).

[9] Julie Sheriff, "Report of Conference on Planned Relocation, New Housing, and Local Employment in Eastern Kentucky," 23 Aug. 1966, CSM, series 2, box 264, folder 16. At its peak in 1950, the eastern Kentucky coal industry employed nearly sixty thousand workers. That number had dropped to just over twenty-five thousand in 1960. Mary Jean Bowman and

neither the farming nor the industrial sector of the Appalachian economy could sustain standards of living that even came close to levels most Americans, including those in the Kennedy and Johnson administrations, considered acceptable.

John Kennedy's astonishment at the conditions that he saw in West Virginia, interpreted through his sense of nationalism and public purpose, prompted him to consider the situation as a weakness in the national economy that required national solutions. In 1963, Kennedy established the President's Appalachian Regional Commission (PARC) to study the situation and develop proposals for governmental action. President Johnson expanded on his predecessor's sense of national purpose by following through on the PARC's recommendations and, through the 1965 Appalachian Regional Development Act, by establishing the Appalachian Regional Commission (ARC) as a permanent body. While the ARC addressed the structural weaknesses in the regional economy, the Office of Economic Opportunity, the most visible weapon in the War on Poverty, dealt with the human and personal aspects of poverty.

The federal government's plan for rebuilding the Appalachian economy was rooted firmly in an isolation analysis. In a statement for *Mountain Life & Work,* the two senators most responsible for the 1965 Act, John Sherman Cooper of Kentucky and Jennings Randolph of West Virginia, described their hope that "the developed power of millions will be geared into the national economy and culture. Appalachia will no longer be the Isolated Country."[10] Like the rest of the War on Poverty, the Appalachian Act was intended to replace "handout" forms of government assistance, such as food commodity distribution, with genuine opportunities— defined as participation in national life as an improvement over the constricted experiences available on the local, provincial level.

In support of those goals, PARC and ARC proposed institutions and tools designed to break down isolation and produce long-term structural change. PARC and ARC officials hoped that federal programs would improve Appalachia's competitive position in the national economy and lead to an expansion of urban "growth poles," which would provide jobs and services to a shrinking rural hinterland. In the PARC report, the integration of rural life began with transportation, especially improved roads. Most of the initial ARC program budget, over $800 million out of slightly more

---

W. Warren Haynes, *Resources and People in East Kentucky: Problems and Potentials of a Lagging Economy* (Baltimore: Johns Hopkins University Press, 1963), 64; U.S. Bureau of the Census, *U.S. Census of Population: 1960.* On moonshine, see the *Manchester Enterprise* July 23, 1964; June 24, 1965; July 8, 1965; August 6, 1965; August 19, 1965; etc.

   [10] John Sherman Cooper and Jennings Randolph, "The Appalachian Development Act: A Statement for the 40th Anniversary of *Mountain Life & Work,*" *Mountain Life & Work* 40, no. 2 (summer 1965): 31–32.

than $1 billion, went into "developmental roads," designed to penetrate terrain barriers and link the mountains with the national transportation system. After roads, the PARC report listed efficient resource management, especially in coal, timber, and water and flood control, as the next highest priority. Decades of intense exploitation, PARC said, had severely compromised the sustainability of logging and mining. In addition, improper management carried with it serious consequences. Most of eastern Kentucky, including the Red Bird area, had been cut over several times by the 1960s. The scraggly forest, combined with strip mining for coal, led to mudslides, acid runoffs into streams, erosion, and soil depletion. The lesson that unmanaged exploitation of natural resources could bring disaster became all too apparent in 1957 and 1963, when heavy rains caused massive flooding, not just in the mountains, but far down river in cities like Frankfort as well. Twelve people died in the 1957 flood, which also caused damage amounting to more than $50 million.[11]

The proper management of resources, according to PARC, would not only protect the state from disaster but would in itself create wealth and employment. PARC's suggestions for maximizing the benefits of the mountains' abundant resources were "directed at the creation of new growth by [creating] a new employment of the region's natural riches, by orienting their utilization to emerging national and regional needs and by... new combinations of resource activity." For water resources, PARC recommended construction of several dams to create lakes, not only for flood control and soil preservation, but also for recreational and tourism purposes. As for timber, PARC recommended establishing national forests in areas "of depleted forest or strip-mined land which need to be restored to full productivity." PARC contended that, in depleted areas, private owners of small tracts had no incentive to practice conservation, but that "these same areas, under consolidated management, would serve recreational and wildlife uses and could eventually produce timber of high quality."[12]

The United States Forest Service established the Red Bird Purchase Unit in 1965 as a part of both resource management and economic restructuring. The Kentucky legislature's memorandum of approval for the creation of the forest made clear its role in regional development. Without blaming coal or timber companies directly, the memorandum complained that "natural resources have been exploited and abused," and listed the effects of inefficient agricultural, logging, and mining practices on the water

[11] The Whitesburg *Mountain Eagle* reprinted the whole of PARC's report over several issues in April and May of 1964. Monroe Newman, *The Political Economy of Appalachia: A Case Study of Regional Integration* (Lexington, Mass.: D. C. Heath, 1972); Rothblatt, *Regional Planning*. See also *The Thousandsticks*, September 1, 1966; *Manchester Enterprise* July 14, 1966, June 1, 1967.

[12] Report of the President's Appalachian Regional Commission, reprinted in the *Mountain Eagle*, April 30, 1964.

supply and the soils. The memorandum then noted the extreme poverty in Clay and Leslie counties: depopulation, high unemployment, and a per capita income that was from one-third to one-half the national average. The memorandum concluded that "there is an urgent need to restore the basic forest, water and wildlife resources as part of a comprehensive program to build up the economic base of this area." Rehabilitation and management of the Red Bird watershed "can make a substantial contribution to the permanent economic recovery of eastern Kentucky through long range programs" which "will help restore forest resources, enhance local economies, and advance national programs of resource conservation and betterment of rural areas."[13]

Had PARC and the Forest Service been willing to identify the coal and timber industries as the primary sources of environmental damage, they might have called into question some of the basic assumptions of the rediscovery literature and of War on Poverty policy. As PARC's analysis implied, economic isolation in Red Bird was more the product of land use policies by the coal and timber companies than a natural, self-evident, and ahistorical condition of scattered rural settlement. The Forest Service purchased the land from the Red Bird Timber Company, which had recently purchased it from a longtime owner, the Ford Motor Company. Red Bird's inhabitants had been tenant farmers rather than landowners for more than two generations. Surely the history of tenancy and monopolization of resources contributed to a low standard of living, simultaneously preventing economic diversification and squelching whatever entrepreneurial spirit had developed among the inhabitants. Red Bird was certainly isolated; until the mid-1960s, the area had no paved roads and no telephones. The lack of these components and symbols of modern life, however, did not indicate a disconnection from modern economic structures. Instead, isolation was the result of the Ford Motor Company's decisions regarding the management of its property.

When Ford took control of the land around 1920, it enlisted the help of its tenants, as a condition of settlement and often in place of cash rent, in protecting the timber supply. Tenants on the property paid very little in rent. Many paid nothing at all for a one-year lease; others paid one or five or ten dollars. All, however, were required to provide "Care of Property," which primarily meant maintaining the stands of timber that made the land valuable to Ford. In addition, the leases prevented tenants from engaging in moneymaking endeavors that might compromise the company's interests. They prevented tenants from making or selling illegal liquor or cutting trees, and they required company permission before a tenant could

[13] Memorandum to the National Forest Reservation Commission, February 24, 1965; copy on display at the Peabody Ranger Station, Peabody, Ky.

clear additional land for farming, haul trees cut elsewhere over the leased land, cut small timber for home repair, or build chicken coops, barns, pens, or other structures to house livestock. The leases also required tenants to guard against forest fires, help put out forest fires on nearby tracts, and, most importantly, to "look after and protect the interests of lessor in said premises... by preventing all trespassing on same by others, by timbercutting or other wise, and to make prompt report to lessor... of any and all such attempts at trespass."[14]

The Ford Motor Company had little desire to be in the landlord business at all; since it made no money from holding tenants, it wanted to limit its investment. Like the Forest Service, Ford did not allow tenants or prospective tenants to build new houses, and it did not repair houses once they became unlivable. As the company manager, Christopher Queen, put it in a letter to a tenant, "I appreciate the fact that you could probably build a small house without using any timber of particular value. However, as a general proposition we do not want any more houses on our land." Only the necessity of protecting its investment and forging good relationships with people living in the vicinity compelled the company to keep tenants. The selection of tenants depended to a large extent on their usefulness to the company. "This [woman's] father has been a great friend to the company and is very popular in his section of the country," a Ford official wrote. "In those leases we must stand by our friends in the past." Conversely, the company held grudges against troublemakers and their families: "We have had two law suits with [resident] over nothing, and he has cost us considerable money without any claim on his part of any sort.... if this cost is not paid, I shall certainly object to making any lease to [same resident] or either of his sons."[15] In both cases, Ford was concerned primarily with creating a tenantry that, over the long run, would be unlikely to contest the company's dominating presence in the community.

With due respect to Ford's integrity in managing its property, corporate control of land nonetheless precluded both the agrarian vision of household independence and the liberal vision of material development. Neither the War on Poverty nor groups affiliated with it understood the role that Ford played in the creation of rural poverty. The only sign that corporate

[14] The Red Bird Purchase Unit ranger station, located at Peabody, Ky., contains legal documents, leases, and correspondence on every tract of land it owns, much of it absorbed from files maintained by the Ford Motor Company. This description of leases comes from a lease granted in 1958 and from one granted in 1916, which are nearly identical. Chris Queen to Lawrence Roark, July 23, 1930, Tract files, no. 70; Ford Motor Company to Ruth Roark, October 6, 1947, Lease files, no. 175, Red Bird Ranger Station (hereafter RBRS).

[15] Chris Queen to Doc Nolan, January 2, 1930, Lease files, no. 183; Thomas A. Bird to E. H. Moulds, November 28, 1918, Lease files, no. 179; Syndicate to Mat Asher, November 29, 1920, Lease files, no. 173; all RBRS. See also Thomas Bird to John C. Roark, December 22, 1920, Lease files, no. 184; Chris Queen to Wiley Sizemore, December 6, 1932, Lease files, no. 183; Chris Queen to Burley Sizemore, December 7, 1934, Lease files, no. 176; all RBRS.

ownership of vast amounts of land might have contributed specifically to Red Bird's moribund economy came from a single article in a Leslie County newspaper that commented on an irony that the Ford Foundation had funded many of the antipoverty efforts in the region that the Council of the Southern Mountains and other groups had undertaken. Erroneously equating the Ford Foundation with the Ford Motor Company, the article pointed out Ford's "dual role as profiteer and humanitarian" and commented on an incongruity that "the Ford Foundation should be involved in making grants to study the ills of our area and the solutions to our problems when at the same time it is partially responsible." The article may have mistakenly linked the foundation to the policies of the Ford corporation, but it nonetheless provided an important alternative analysis of poverty: that poverty in the Appalachian coalfields resulted from the region's unfavorable position within capitalist development rather than its exclusion from it.[16]

People living in eastern Kentucky responded to federal intervention with a mixture of hope and skepticism. Many of the region's strongest voices saw the federal government as the only solution to persistent poverty, and they welcomed television crews as a means of generating nationwide support for an aggressive public policy. Tom Gish and Pat Gish, the editors of Letcher County's progressive newspaper, *The Mountain Eagle*, pushed strongly for a War on Poverty and reprinted the entire PARC report when it was made available. The Gishes, fellow Whitesburg resident Harry Caudill, and Leslie County judge-executive George Wooten all advocated federal intervention more massive than Kennedy, Johnson, or Shriver ever suggested; Caudill and the Gishes even called for the construction of publicly-owned power generators modeled after the Tennessee Valley Authority. But the structural side of the War on Poverty proved too willing to sacrifice local communities for national goals, and much of that support eroded. The Gishes, especially, ended the 1960s as vocal critics of the War

---

[16] Newspaper clipping from unspecified Leslie County newspaper, probably *The Thousandsticks* February 3, 1966, CSM, series V, box 185, folder 1. This argument is by now almost universally accepted among scholars of the Southern Appalachians. See especially Whisnant, *Modernizing the Mountaineer;* Helen Matthews Lewis, Linda Johnson, and Donald Askins, *Colonialism in Modern America: The Appalachian Case* (Boone, Ky.: The Appalachian Consortium Press, 1978); Ronald D. Eller, *Miners, Millhands, and Mountaineers: Industrialization of the Appalachian South, 1880–1930* (Knoxville: University of Tennessee Press, 1982); Ronald L. Lewis and Dwight B. Billings, "Appalachian Culture and Economic Development: A Retrospective View on the Theory and Literature," *Journal of Appalachian Studies* 3, no. 1 (spring 1997): 3–42; Ada F. Haynes, *Poverty in Central Appalachia: Underdevelopment and Exploitation* (New York: Garland Publishing, 1997).

on Poverty, though they retained their progressive faith in the positive potential of governmental action.

The skepticism that eastern Kentucky residents expressed in the 1960s reflected a rejection of neither economic development nor the legitimacy of federal programs. Instead, it reflected a reassertion of the validity of rural life, an often conservative defense of provincialism, cultural particularism, and local identities and attachments—the very things that the War on Poverty, with its emphasis on cosmopolitan and urban living, aimed to eliminate. A letter writer to the *Mountain Eagle,* one of the many irritated at the intense media scrutiny of regional poverty, expressed a characteristically conservative view of self-help combined with a concern for local integrity. She complained that the media were exploiting poverty for their own use and purposely excluding the middle class from their reports. "You are laying bare the souls of humanity, throwing their plight and poverty open upon the TV screens and magazine pages, making it appear to the world outside who do not understand us that this is the typical southeastern Kentucky," she wrote. "When you take away our pride and self-respect, you haven't much left upon which you could build a civilization that you would be proud for your children to inherit." The letter contrasted the deserving poor in her area—the disabled and elderly, who warranted public sympathy—from the undeserving, the "parasites," who "no matter what opportunity comes their way or any amount of money they will still remain in the same rut for they like it that way." Charity, the woman continued, would only perpetuate the laziness of the undeserving poor and continue eroding the values, self-respect, and reputation that the region's people possessed.[17]

Localism sometimes meant an appropriation of the terms of derision applied to mountain people, who transformed the terms into symbols of regional cultural pride. "Us hillbillies is a queer breed. We are," as a *New Yorker* reporter heard one woman put it. "I'm not making any apologies when I say that. Us hillbillies is a queer breed, and I'm just as proud as punch to be one." The woman, a county court clerk, made that comment in response to a violent incident that occurred in Letcher County. In September of 1967, a landowner, Hobart Ison, shot and killed a Canadian filmmaker named Hugh O'Connor. The crew was interviewing Ison's tenants in their homes in the hamlet of Jeremiah. Ison heard that the crew was on his property without his permission, and he angrily went to the scene with a gun. While the crew prepared to leave, Ison shot wildly three times, the third shot hitting and killing O'Connor. About one hundred people attended Ison's bond hearing, and, according to the county newspaper, "feeling in the Jeremiah [*sic*] is running high on Ison's behalf." Apparently, many residents shared Ison's anger at having his property, his world, invaded by what

---

[17] *Mountain Eagle,* February 6, 1964; February 13, 1964; April 9, 1964.

he thought was a hostile entity. "I think that the old man thought they were laughing and making fun of him, and it was more than he could take," the clerk continued. When asked if Ison nonetheless had the right to kill, the woman replied, "Well, no.... But us hillbillies, we don't bother nobody. We go out of our way to help people. We don't want nobody pushing us around. Now, that's the code of the hills. And... that old man felt like— he was being pushed around. You know, it's like I told those men: 'I wouldn't have gone on that old man's land to pick me a mess of greens without I'd asked him.' They said, 'We didn't know all this.' I said, 'I bet you know it now. I bet you know it now.'"[18] Local residents defended Ison not because they approved of murder and not because of an innate, clannish suspiciousness of outsiders, but because they perceived the prying eyes of reporters to be an assault on manners, common decency, and the integrity of their communities.

Local people were especially angry about the many relocation plans developed in the 1960s. Federal agencies assumed that national interests and local interests coincided, that the rehabilitation of watersheds and the impounding of creeks to form lakes would benefit everyone involved. In the long run, and within the isolation framework for understanding poverty, relocation had merit. People would leave rural areas that could not sustain a high standard of living and which did not allow inhabitants to contribute properly to the national economy. Marginal land could be devoted to more efficient and profitable pursuits, while the people could enter more fully the urban world of material and consumer prosperity.[19] In the short run, however, the lives of the people who happened to live in these areas would be turned upside down. The problem, of course, was that people did not always want to leave their homes, especially when their removal would take place long before those vibrant urban growth centers materialized to soak up the displaced population.

Letcher County's *Mountain Eagle* sounded an early alarm over the prospect of removals in various places in eastern Kentucky. Tom and Pat Gish loudly opposed removal plans, saying that they sacrificed local people for the sake of economic efficiency. PARC, for example, had recommended establishing a Mountaineer National Forest on over one million acres of land in eastern Kentucky. The report, the Gishes said, contained "no mention of any plan for housing those who would be moved out to make room

[18] Calvin Trillin, "A Stranger With a Camera," *New Yorker,* April 29, 1969, reprinted in Walls and Stephenson, *Appalachia in the Sixties,* 201. *Mountain Eagle,* 21 September 21, 1967. See also Elizabeth Barret and Judy Jennings, *Stranger With a Camera* (Whitesburg: Appalshop films, 2000).

[19] An earlier study on conditions in Appalachia had already made that same point. L. C. Gray, C. F. Clayton, Bureau of Agricultural Economics, Bureau of Home Economics, and Forest Service, *Economic and Social Problems and Conditions of the Southern Appalachians* (Washington, D.C.: United States Government Printing Office, 1935).

for a forest." Later, when the Forest Service announced its plans to create the Red Bird Purchase Unit, the Gishes' newspaper reported, without citation, that "the forestry acquisitions are viewed as part of a calculated policy of the Appalachian Development Commission [*sic*] to force mountain families out of their rural homes." Red Bird, the article warned, was the first step in the Forest Service's campaign to purchase just about all of eastern Kentucky.[20]

The *Mountain Eagle*'s warnings about the Forest Service may seem farfetched in retrospect, but other forms of resource development did raise the problem of relocation. Dam construction posed immediate threats to rural communities that would soon be under water. The Army Corps of Engineers, which, before the War on Poverty, had already created several lakes in eastern Kentucky, now had a federal mandate to do more of the same. Recognizing the value of flood control and recreational development, most residents did not oppose dam construction as such. They did, however, mourn the loss of their homeplaces, and they expected at least a fair compensation in return. When, in 1967, the Corps began condemnation proceedings on the Carrs Fork of the Kentucky River, residents repeatedly complained that that Corps agents offered prices for land below the market price and below what it would cost to purchase comparable land elsewhere. Those who refused to sell received threats of condemnation unless they accepted the Corps' price. "I've been robbed," one long-time resident said, whose meager compensation did not allow him to purchase a new tract of land. "They've took a notion to come in and steal what people have. I've got my life here, all I wanted was enough out of it to buy me another little home." That same year, the Army Corps of Engineers planned to build a dam on the Kentucky River that promised to flood one-third of Letcher County. The *Mountain Eagle* led a crusade against the 1967 project, and dozens of letters-to-the-editor supported the paper's stance. Letter writers worried that the dam would provide a disincentive for industry to come to Letcher County, warned of the problems Carrs Fork residents experienced, lamented displacement, and directed some scorn at their downriver neighbors in Perry County who had originally requested the dam. The mobilization of public opinion, which included "almost every business firm, every civic club, every public official within the county, as well as ... thousands of residents," forced the Corps to cancel its plans.[21]

[20] *Mountain Eagle*, February 13, 1964; July 22, 1965. The *Mountain Eagle's* reprinting of PARC's report listed the proposed Kentucky forest at more than four million acres.

[21] *Mountain Eagle*, September 21, 1967; October 5, 1967; March 28, 1968; November 14, 1968. See also *Manchester Enterprise*, December 17, 1964; December 24, 1964; January 7, 1965; August 25, 1966; *Mountain Eagle*, September 28, 1967; October 19, 1967; December 7, 1967; December 28, 1967; January 18, 1968; February 1, 1968; February 22, 1968; May 9, 1968; October 17, 1968.

The opposition to the Letcher County dam came from a desire to channel federal policies in directions most beneficial to local people. While the ARC and the Army Corps of Engineers considered integration—the creation of strong, national economic structures—the highest priority, the *Mountain Eagle* considered integration a means to the end of local rehabilitation. By the early 1970s, the Gishes and Harry Caudill condemned further government appropriation of land and potential ARC relocation efforts in the strongest terms. In 1972, Caudill claimed that "depopulation is part of ARC's scheme, not because it will benefit people but because it will clear the land for a new round of exploitation by the absentee companies." Tom Gish said much the same thing: "Make no mistake about it. The [ARC] is planning genocide in the mountains.... No mountain residents, no mountain poverty, no problems."[22] In considering the goals of national integration and local betterment, the Gishes and Caudill, unlike the organs of the War on Poverty, perceived a contradiction between the two, and they opted for the needs of their communities.

The Council of the Southern Mountains' New Towns proposal tried to reconcile an integrationist agenda with renewed concerns for local revitalization. These concerns had emerged partly because Red Bird residents had voiced them loudly enough to force the Forest Service to take them seriously, but they mostly grew out of events taking place within the council itself. Council affiliates—particularly a unit of young members, predominantly from outside the mountains, called the Appalachian Volunteers (AVs)—had become heavily involved in the OEO's Community Action Program, the most democratic of Great Society initiatives. For the AVs, in keeping with the radicalism of the late 1960s, community organizing became a vehicle for generating opposition politics around issues such as welfare rights, black lung disease, and strip mining. Their realization that many of the eastern Kentucky poor had very strong opinions on political subjects caused the AVs to reject the passive images portrayed in the rediscovery literature. How passive could people be, who, with no prodding from outsiders at all, held strip miners and their bulldozers off at the gunpoint or by lying down in front of them, as several eastern Kentucky locals had done? The AVs' confrontational philosophy and success in organizing gained them many supporters, including the progressive *Mountain Eagle*. They also gained many powerful enemies, especially among local political figures and officials in the coal industry, who fumed at the challenge to

---

[22] Quoted in Whisnant, *Modernizing the Mountaineer,* 249.

their power and the fact that they paid for it through tax dollars. In 1967, angry officials in Pike County had several AVs arrested and tried in state courts for sedition. The AVs had limited political impact in eastern Kentucky, but they did force a reconsideration of the isolation interpretation and considerable soul-searching among council administrators to find a more precise rationale for community organizing.[23]

The New Towns proposal promised that the creation of the Purchase Unit, in contrast to the other relocation threats, would ultimately work to the benefit of local people. The final version recalled the planned communities of the Resettlement Administration, insisting that the New Towns would remain in rural settings, outside the major growth areas that the ARC projected. But the proposal was still so thoroughly grounded in the isolation motif that its nod in the direction of rural revitalization seemed strained at best. Early discussions of the plan among council members placed the greatest hopes on very large communities. Suggestions for towns holding up to twenty-five thousand people had circulated among New Towns planners, including a plan the University of Kentucky's architecture department offered in 1960 to a state commission. Only a large town, that plan argued, could "counteract the unprofitable and inefficient scatteration of people and work places throughout the mountain area in which it is to be located." Bowing to the mood of the residents, however, and perhaps to funding considerations as well, the council's final proposal advocated much smaller settlements, namely clusters of communities as small as fifteen houses each. Small settlements could appeal to Red Bird residents, the proposal argued, since they would maintain the rural character of the community, especially "the warm, personal, face-to-face, primary relationships which rural people in general and mountain people in particular value so highly." Isolation would no longer define these pseudorural communities, according to the proposal, since the clustered homes would bring families together and the towns' location on good roads would give them easy access to opportunities located elsewhere in the region.[24] Whatever its practical utility, replacing the actual presence of services in the New

[23] Douglas O'Neil Arnett, "Eastern Kentucky: The Politics of Dependency and Underdevelopment" (Ph.D. diss., Duke University, 1978); Guy and Candie Carawan, *Voices From the Mountains* (Urbana: University of Illinois Press, 1982), 44–49, 158–59, 164–71; Thomas J. Kiffmeyer, "From Self-Help to Sedition: The Appalachian Volunteers in Eastern Kentucky, 1964–1970," *Journal of Southern History* 44, no. 1 (February 1998): 65–94.

[24] *New Towns for the Appalachian Region: A Case Study Located In Eastern Kentucky* (Lexington: University of Kentucky Department of Architecture, 1960), 43, 45, in CSM, series VIII, box 291, folder 7; "Proposal," 11, in CSM, series 5, box 185, folder 3; Sheriff, "Report of Conference," 1, 4; Thomas Parrish to Dr. S. M. Miller, June 7, 1967, 5, in CSM, series V, box 185, folder 1. The council also hired a landscape architect from Pennsylvania to conduct a feasibility study for a site in Leslie County that could hold all 115 Red Bird families, with room to spare. "That They, Too, Shall Live in Dignity," 20–24.

Towns with access to them via improved transportation undercut the logical integrity of the proposal.

The proposal also incorporated political organizing into its objectives. Under what it called "community process development," the project pursued the growth of "true autonomy within local groups" and tried to create a "truly local decision-making process." While scattered rural settlement prevented residents from organizing, exercising an effective political voice, and, consequently, gaining access to resources needed "to achieve satisfactory levels of living," bringing people together into New Towns would, if properly facilitated by hired community workers, promote genuine political empowerment.[25] In stating empowerment as its goal, the proposal absorbed the more radical political ideas that had inspired groups like the Appalachian Volunteers. It reflected the reawakened concern for a participatory democracy in which people had some control over their own lives, as opposed to the elitist version of power that had motivated policy toward the rural poor.

Nevertheless, the proposal placed empowerment firmly within the framework of isolation. It located the source of powerlessness in rural people's generally narrow, limited perceptions of life and their place in it, and in their disconnection from the normal workings of American democracy. It made no mention of other sources of powerlessness, such as tenancy, the monopolization of resources, and a corrupt local political system, that strip mine opponents and unemployed coal miners might have mentioned. Rural isolation, according to Council of the Southern Mountains community developers, inhibited a political voice among Red Bird residents by preventing them from learning how to organize themselves formally for a collective purpose. Understanding power through an interest group model, council workers in Red Bird associated poverty with an inability to enter the political marketplace to influence elections and legislation for their own benefit. "A problem which has contributed to poverty in Southern Appalachia," one Red Bird worker noted in 1966, "is the inexperience of the people in 'negotiating the system.' For example, the people lack experience in working together as a community, serving together on committees, making decisions as a group, threading their way through the intricacies of the government and political system." As the New Towns proposal put it, "we see in Red Bird an absolute lack of what we generally regard as civic action or civic-mindedness. . . . There seems to be a lack not only of group-decision making mechanisms but simply of

[25] "Proposal," 28, 11. "Program Development in Red Bird to Date," n.d.—probably summer of 1968, 3, CSM, series V, box 185, folder 6; Ernest Walker, "Proposal," August 26, 1968, CSM, series V, box 185, folder 6.

purposeful groups."[26] Groups were purposeful if they connected people with the organizational networks that made up the American economic and political system, so that people who lacked such groups were irrelevant in national life.

Because of the recent challenges to the isolation analysis of poverty, Red Bird project leaders sought to express it in a more precise, sociologically grounded way. To that end, the proposal's authors adopted the concept of "scale," which promised to provide a quantifiable measurement of isolation. The broadest goal of the New Towns proposal was not to improve material conditions or enhance political power, but to enlarge the residents' scale of experiences and relationships. Scale measured the relative "*range* and *intensity* of a person's dependent relationships with other persons," with highly dependent and intense relationships defined as small in scale and more diffuse, less dependent and intense relationships defined as large in scale. The larger their scale, the more control people had over the situation in which they lived, and the more control they had over their own lives. A large scale, then, meant empowerment, while a small scale meant constriction, dependence, and lack of control. Living effectively in the modern United States necessitated a large scale, since it implied connectedness with national political and economic networks; enhanced political power, economic improvement, and self-esteem all flowed from an increase in scale.[27]

Red Bird community workers conceived of scale as a tool to diagnose weaknesses in a population and to evaluate their improvement under new conditions, such as relocation from rural areas to New Towns. The proposal's authors developed a questionnaire that, when scored, would reveal a person's relative scale level in three different areas of life: the social, the ideological, and the technological. Project workers, not surprisingly, found Red Bird residents to live on the small end of scale in all three areas. The social area referred to civic-mindedness, a person's sense that he or she is part of a larger, interdependent, national community. In Red Bird, people responded to conflicts or participated in projects "almost purely on a personal basis" rather than through formal processes, and they identified themselves not even with their county, but as residents of "Mud Lick or Lower Elk or Jack's Creek." Community organizing for specific goals would have the larger effect of increasing social scale through extending people's range of organizational contacts and enhancing their ability "'to act as a unit.'" The ideological area referred to people's access to information and

[26] Julie Sheriff, memorandum on community programs in Red Bird, October 25, 1966), in CSM, series V, box 268, folder 10; "Proposal," 25.

[27] According to the proposal, the concept of scale came from the work of C. T. Hobhouse, Godfrey and Monica Wilson, and O. Norman Simpkins. The proposal did not identify their work specifically. "Proposal," 12–13.

their receptivity to new ideas. Questionnaires evaluated literacy and the frequency of reading; "Books (great scale-expanders) are not highly valued" in Red Bird, the proposal said. To enlarge ideological scale, the Council of the Southern Mountains proposed a program of community education to expose people "to the best products of world civilization."[28]

Questions in the technological area measured job skills and the level of "scientific" rather than "magical" thinking, or the extent to which people believed they had control over their environment, a necessary component of modern economic success. Job creation and small business development provided the keys to expanding technological scale. The council considered several possibilities for locally owned businesses, including the building and repairing of the modular homes to be used in the towns (for which the council had already contracted with the Rhode Island School of Design), a bookbinding plant that would employ twenty-five people, and the cultivation of marketable cash crops such as tomatoes and strawberries. The goal of economic development was to build "economic roles for citizens... *within the context of the national economy*" and "to increase the understanding and application of scientific principles and procedures in general."[29] The connections created through relocation to New Towns created the opportunity for enlargement of scale in all four areas, by promoting organization over social disarray, liberal arts education over ignorance, and science over superstition.

With the concept of scale, the New Towns proposal leant an air of scientific objectivity to the isolation interpretation of poverty. It quantified the cultural lag suffered by rural Appalachian people, and, by maintaining an ahistorical analysis of the Red Bird situation, made the lag appear as a natural outgrowth of ruralness that could only be altered through outside intervention. The authors of the New Towns proposal saw nothing coercive or demeaning in their plans to engineer a better life for Red Bird inhabitants. Nor did they see their efforts as a plan to impose the values of middle-class urban culture on a rural culture. In anticipation of such charges, and in the realization that Red Bird residents preferred rural living to urban living, the proposal stated that it did not advocate "a conversion of the Red Bird native from perversity to middle-class righteousness." Instead, an expansion of scale would finally allow people free choice in their lives, creating an atmosphere in which individuals could select what they wanted from rural and urban cultures. The proposal advocated a rural-friendly version of New

---

[28] "Proposal," 26, 28, 29. The embedded quotation is not specifically cited.

[29] "Proposal," 38 (original emphasis); 17–18, 26, 36, 38–51; "That They, Too, Shall Live in Dignity," 20–24. Questions that measured scientific versus magical thinking included (with the respondent answering "yes" or "no") "Certain lines in a person's hand foretell his future," "Red-haired people have high tempers," and "A very smart person has a high forehead" (64–65).

Towns, "in which valuable elements of the traditional culture will be preserved while building effective roles for individuals in modern industrial society."[30] The proposal's special pleading in this case renders unclear exactly what aspects of traditional culture might remain after so much of it had been declared ignorance or superstition.

Despite all the time, effort, and planning that went into it, the Red Bird project never came into being. In early 1969, the Ford Foundation officially denied it funding, putting an end to the council's effort to link revitalization with integration. The Ford Foundation made its decision on the grounds that, by the late 1960s, as a representative of the foundation wrote to the council's executive director, "the community process point has been made several times over," and "the point has not taken significantly." Even the concept of scale, the representative said, was not new. Given what she considered the uninspiring quality of the proposal, the representative questioned "whether Red Bird is truly a priority item in the context of social development in Appalachia and the Council's role in that development."[31] The decision to deny funding for the New Towns proposal signaled that, in the political turmoil of the decade's later years, and with the new commitment to rights-based, oppositional organizing, social engineering had ceased to capture the progressive imagination.

※

On its own terms of ending poverty and isolation, the War on Poverty in Appalachian Kentucky has had some success. Isolation no longer bears the impressionistic reality in eastern Kentucky that it did in the 1960s, as paved roads, strip mines, and various National Forests and dam projects have both encouraged and forced people out of the hollows onto better-traveled routes. Four-lane highways provide easy access to modern shopping facilities, consisting of mega-chain stores that have brought national consumerism to the mountains while undermining local retailers. The Forest Service has succeeded admirably in repairing the Red Bird watershed, which now offers beautiful scenery and recreation to tourists. The town of Pikeville, following a multibillion-dollar water project completed in the 1980s, has emerged as the region's major "growth pole," and its banking industry rivals in assets banks in Lexington and Louisville. But if eastern Kentucky is no longer isolated, it is still, relative to national averages, very poor. Years of federal integration projects notwithstanding, the Kentucky

---

[30] "Proposal," 26, 27.
[31] Letter from Hilary S. Feldstein, Assistant Program Officer, Ford Foundation, to Loyal Jones, April 4, 1969, CSM, series V, box 185, folder 6.

mountains still suffer from high unemployment rates, low per capita income, and low educational achievement.[32]

Despite its mixed results as a foundation for antipoverty policy, isolation thinking still permeates public policy to the near-total exclusion of other perspectives. President Bill Clinton's New Markets Initiative, for example, launched in a 1999 speech at Hazard, Kentucky, rests entirely on the faulty premise that rural areas of the United States remain incompletely connected to market networks. Clinton's initiative involves little federal commitment, and it says nothing about tenancy, low wages, or the ownership of resources. Instead of plans for relocation or the development of growth poles, the initiative promises economic integration through tax cuts and market penetration. Concerns for the vitality of rural life have disappeared from public discussions entirely and are relegated now to sustainable-development activists on the left and antigovernment groups on the right. The irony of the War on Poverty is that in allowing nationalist integration and relocation policies to overshadow revitalization, policymakers undercut the initial support they had from target populations. Consequently, they gave ammunition to conservative groups that see only a limited role for the state in American life.

---

[32] Andrew M. Isserman, "Appalachia Then and Now: An Update of 'The Realities of Deprivation' Report to the President in 1964," *Journal of Appalachian Studies* 3, no. 1 (spring 1997): 43–70.

PART 4

Contemporary Rural Politics

Call of the Mild

Colorado Ski Resorts
and the Politics of Rural Tourism

ANNIE GILBERT COLEMAN

Look at any advertisement for a ski resort and you will see a leisure utopia. Joyous people slide down beautiful snow in scenic mountains. This vision represents a conscious effort on the part of ski area developers and managers to create appealing destination resorts out of isolated rural landscapes. Such harmony between tourists and landscapes, however, has always proven difficult to achieve in real life. When the chairlifts first opened in Aspen, Colorado, skiers had few choices of how they would descend Aspen Mountain. A few bypass runs let them avoid the steepest sections of the racing trail called the Roch Run, but that was not always enough. One resident recalled observing a woman descend the trail that first season in 1947. "She was sliding down the corkscrew with her hands out in front of her," he remembered, "and she was yelling 'You son of a bitch, why did you bring me here!' " This was not quite the experience the young Aspen Skiing Corporation was hoping to foster. A few years later one expert convinced the company to bulldoze some terrain and open it up to less experienced skiers. "Having done that," a director recalled, "you couldn't keep the skiers away—it was the best damned skiing in the world."[1]

The management of skiing landscapes and western tourism has been going on for over half a century. Since World War II destination ski

A portion of this paper was presented at the American Historical Association meeting in New York City, 1997. Thanks to Elizabeth Blackmar and Philip J. Deloria for their comments. Thanks also to Robert Johnston, Catherine Stock, Karl Jacoby, the anonymous reader for Cornell University Press, and—above all—Jon T. Coleman.

[1] Steve Knowlton, interview by the author, October 19, 1994, Denver, Colorado, tape recording and manuscript, 3, Aspen Historical Society (hereafter AHS); Paul Nitze, interview by the author, July 20, 1994, Aspen, Colorado, tape recording and transcript, AHS, 4.

With its wider intermediate trail only partly complete and no beginner terrain at all, Aspen Mountain c. 1947 posed challenges to skiers making their way down the winding Roch Run as well as to managers hoping to create an enjoyable experience without altering the mountain landscape too visibly. Photo courtesy of Aspen Historical Society.

resorts—areas where people stay to ski for more than a few days at a time—grew up from defunct mining towns, sleepy ranching communities, and un-inhabited land across the Rocky Mountains. Aspen, Breckenridge, and Tel-luride, Steamboat Springs, Snowmass, and Vail, among others, acquired new identities and cachet from their resorts. By this time Colorado and the American West had a long-established tradition of tourism. Images of nat-ural wonders, exotic natives, and the Wild West attracted tourists to the re-gion in the late nineteenth century and through the twentieth. Visitors rode railroad cars and later drove themselves to Yellowstone, the Grand Canyon, Santa Fe, and points across the region to participate in those images.[2]

Such scenes of the mythic West, which emphasized rugged individualism and freedom from the social, political, and environmental constraints of eastern society, were at odds with the dominant role the federal govern-ment played in the region. In organizing and developing the West the gov-ernment grew in power and influence, leading Richard White to charac-terize the region as the "kindergarten of the American state."[3] This was true especially in the twentieth century and since World War II. It played out in the ski industry through the U.S. Forest Service's changing role, first as a promoter and then an increasingly bureaucratic regulator of ski area development. Federal involvement in the West was accompanied, more-over, by the simultaneous fantasy that being in the West would free Ameri-cans from the federal government's grasp. This problematic but influen-tial notion became part of the appeal of the mythic West, as Patty Limerick has pointed out, and resort towns that described themselves with mythic images took advantage of it.[4]

For many rural communities in the American West—and across the globe—tourism also offered a way to capitalize on aspects of their ruralness. Isolation, limited economic development, and a small population held ap-peal as a scenic alternative to urban residents looking for vacation destina-tions. This appeal, scholars of tourism note, has grown more significant in re-cent decades as traditional rural economies have declined. High-paying

[2] See Elliott West, *The Way West: Essays on the Central Plains* (Albuquerque: University of New Mexico Press, 1995) for a discussion of how these images attracted settlers and tourists to the West since the nineteenth century. The most recent and comprehensive work on western tourism is Hal Rothman's *Devil's Bargains: Tourism in the Twentieth-Century American West* (Lawrence: University of Kansas Press, 1998). See also Marguerite S. Shaffer, "'See America First': Re-Envisioning Nation and Region through Western Tourism," *Pacific Historical Review* 54 (1996): 559–81; Anne Farrar Hyde, *An American Vision: Far West Landscapes and National Culture, 1820–1920* (New York: New York University Press, 1990); and the classic book by Earl Pomeroy, *In Search of the Golden West: The Tourist in Western America* (Lincoln: University of Nebraska Press, 1957).

[3] Richard White, *"It's Your Misfortune and None of My Own": A New History of the American West* (Norman: University of Oklahoma Press, 1991), 58.

[4] Patricia Nelson Limerick, *The Legacy of Conquest: The Unbroken Past of the American West* (New York: W. W. Norton, 1987), 89.

urban jobs reduced the permanent population; improved access from cities increased the number of temporary, weekend residents; the rise of agribusiness threatened the family farm; and new corporate and individual landowners exercised closer control over rural landscapes. In more recent years the increasing mobility of people and goods, specialized use of rural land, and the rise of nonrural residents and visitors blurred the lines separating urban from rural and outsider from insider.[5] From an economic perspective, changes in the past few decades have ushered in a "new era for rural people." Declining industry (including agriculture) and a perpetually weak service sector in rural areas meant that economies could no longer succeed through traditional means. In this new era, according to Mark Drabenstott and Tim Smith, scenic amenities and proximity to urban areas determined success.[6]

The demographic and economic transformations that have shaken rural areas in recent decades have long been visible in the history of the ski industry. Since World War II, skiing has reshaped the mountain West. Rural tourism, as Butler, Hall, and Jenkins note, has become increasingly characterized by active, competitive, fashionable, and hi-tech recreational pursuits.[7] Skiing epitomizes this tourism, and promotes the demographic and economic transformations that have made rural communities more complex places in the past few decades. It also raises problems about rural identity. Tourists want the rural. They want to experience quaintness, scenery, isolation, and even "wilderness." These are some of the elements that make rural places attractive, but packaging them for tourist consumption transforms the meaning of "rural" at the same time that it transforms the physical environment.[8]

[5] There is a substantial and growing literature on tourism by sociologists, geographers, economists, planners, social anthropologists, and political scientists. Their research spans the globe and together forms the increasingly popular discipline of "Tourism Studies." The most recent works relevant to the issues in this essay include Richard Butler, C. Michael Hall, and John Jenkins, eds., *Tourism and Recreation in Rural Areas* (New York: Wiley, 1998); Colin Michael Hall, *Tourism and Politics: Policy, Power and Place* (New York: Wiley, 1994); C. M. Hall and S. J. Page, *The Geography of Tourism and Recreation: Environment, Place and Space* (New York: Routledge, 1999); and John Urrey, *Consuming Places* (New York: Routledge, 1995). For an excellent collection of essays on tourism in developing countries see Douglas G. Pearce and Richard W. Butler, eds., *Contemporary Issues in Tourism Development* (New York: Routledge, 1999), and for a more general overview see Gareth Shaw and Allan M. Williams, *Critical Issues in Tourism: A Geographical Perspective* (Oxford: Blackwell, 1994). For a discussion of changes in rural communities see Butler, Hall, and Jenkins, *Tourism and Recreation*, 6, and Hall and Page, *Geography of Tourism and Recreation*, 180.

[6] Mark Drabenstott and Tim R. Smith, "Finding Rural Success: The New Rural Economic Landscape and Its Implications," in *The Changing American Countryside: Rural People and Places*, ed. Emery N. Castle (Lawrence: University Press of Kansas, 1995), 180–82.

[7] Butler, Hall, and Jenkins, *Tourism and Recreation*, 10. Rothman traces this trend historically in the West by showing how recreational and entertainment tourism gradually superseded cultural or heritage tourism. See *Devil's Bargains*, 23–25.

[8] Scholars of tourism have treated this issue in at least two ways: through the concepts of "sustainable tourism" and "carrying capacity," and by exploring the more cultural repercussions of commodifying "rurality." See especially Hall and Page, *Geography of Tourism and Recreation*, 180; Butler, Hall, and Jenkins, *Tourism and Recreation*, 14, 254–55; and Urrey, *Consuming Places*.

Negotiating this tension puts resort town residents, developers and managers, and visitors in a struggle for power over local resources, their use, and, most importantly, how they are represented. In this sense rural tourism has always been a playground for a symbolic politics rooted in the notion of place. In the world of Colorado's destination ski resorts, tourism's contradictions manifested themselves largely in the mountains. Mountain landscapes offered skiers physical freedom to explore the "wilderness" as individuals and without interference from crowds of people or overdevelopment. Recreational tourism commodified ski resort landscapes and turned them into highly contested spaces just as it has other resorts across the developed world. Skiing tourists wanted charming, western towns and wild, adventurous mountains at the same time as they expected comfortable accommodations, good food, and a safe, pleasurable skiing experience. In order to accomplish this feat, ski resort managers and developers refined a central strategy: they worked hard to build appealing ski areas and resort communities, then they tried to erase all signs of their labor from the landscape. Developers created the image of "wild" and rural places for their clients at a time when those categories became increasingly difficult to discern in reality. Their success helped the ski industry grow, and it led activists interested in protecting wilderness and the rural to focus their attention on destination resorts. Ski areas have thus become important arenas for rural politics, and, along with other kinds of destination resorts, they have redefined those politics as a contest over powerful images of place.

Mountain Landscapes

To those not acquainted with the sport, skiing can seem a strange and often uncomfortable pastime. By piling into snowbanks and dashing like the wind, skiers have come into close contact with the mountain landscape since the nineteenth century. "The ski has an unpleasant way of running in opposite directions, of getting crossed, and finally of piling the pupil in a snow-bank," one outdoorsman admitted in 1898, "but," he continued, "to one who is persistent the joys of jumping and running with the ski are finally opened." These joys, elusive as they may be, offer an interesting way to explore landscapes of leisure. A skier in 1905 liked to "dash down the crusted hillsides with the speed of the wind," with an "exhilaration and excitement," he claimed, "that positively knows no equal." Later skiers shared his sentiments. One Denver man who took up the sport in the 1930s said his favorite part of skiing was "being in the mountains." He liked "the feeling of rhythm," he said, and "to some extent the speed, but mostly [he liked] the feeling of being able to come into synchrony with the mountains and the snow." Expert skier Dolores LaChappelle described this same kind of experience in 1993. "Once this rhythmic relationship to snow and gravity is established on a steep slope," she wrote, "there is no longer an I and snow and the mountain, but a continuous flowing interaction."[9]

Even LaChappelle's "relationship to snow and gravity," however, were not as natural as they seemed to her. They reflected, instead, human efforts to control and commodify the landscape—efforts that altered not only the mountains themselves, but their meaning as well. Before World War II skiers usually climbed up mountain trails on foot and could make only one or two runs down in a day. The implicit danger that skiers faced, from skiing fast and from the mountains themselves, added to their sense of adventure. This physical landscape changed, however, after World War II. As the sport grew in popularity and became the center of its own tourist industry, destination ski resorts took shape throughout Colorado's Rocky Mountains and managed skiers' movement down the slopes. Needing to provide a fun, intimate skiing experience to large groups of people, ski area designers and managers had to think carefully about the ways landscape produced exhilaration and adventure in order to reproduce them for their customers.

Ski area development after the war could not replicate the kind of physical and solitary relationship to the landscape that earlier skiers knew as they climbed and schussed. Designers and developers could, however, accentuate attractive aspects of that experience. Mountain scenery became a natural resource, for instance; skiers' views of the surrounding mountains, something to plan and frame. Lodges and restaurants sprouted up accordingly—even on mountain tops—featuring picture windows and architectural equivalents to the highway signs that announced "scenic overlook" to every passing vehicle. Arapahoe Basin built its "Snow Plume Refuge" atop a narrow ridge, so that "its huge picture windows [could] ... revel [sic] in the splendid panorama of the Gore Range, Tenmile Range, and the Mount of the Holy Cross far to the West." Chairlifts and gondolas, too, offered passengers aerial visions of impressive landscapes on every ride. Even those who had once hiked to ski appreciated the views from the lifts. "To be able to ride the lift at Berthoud," one man recalled, "and get that view down the west side of the Indian Peaks, was a great thrill. I looked forward to each ride because I could get that view."[10] The presence of chair-

[9] Rolf W. Jackson, "A New Year's Day Ski Run," *Outing* 31 (January 1898): 395; Theodore A. Johnsen, *The Winter Sport of Skeeing* (Portland, Maine: Theo. A. Johnsen Company, 1905; reprint ed., New Hartford, Conn.: The International Skiing History Association, 1994, 6; Giles D. Toll, interview by the author, February 2, 1996, Denver, Colorado, tape recording and transcript, 5; Dolores LaChappelle, *Deep Powder Snow: 40 Years of Ecstatic Skiing, Avalanches, and Earth Wisdom* (Durango, Colo.: Kivaki Press, 1993), 101.

[10] Larry Jump, "Arapahoe Basin—The Promised Land," *Rocky Mountain Life*, January 1947, 38; even the U.S. Forest Service, in its *Planning Considerations for Winter Sports Resort Development*, recognized that while "lifts should be located to serve the best skiing terrain," and

lifts and gondolas, by offering better and more frequent views than hikers could enjoy, increased the impact of mountain scenery and transformed skiers' relationship to the landscape in the process.

Ski area developers crafted the visual impact of mountain scenery to help skiers feel connected to "nature" at the same time as they constructed an increasingly built landscape in those mountains.[11] Views from lifts mesmerized passengers on their way up the mountain, attracted their attention to the pristine "wilderness" that lay just beyond the ski area boundary, and overpowered the visual impact of lifts, lodges, and access roads immediately around them. Through their eyes, skiers experienced the mountain landscape as a wild and natural "other." And on their skis, moving through the snow and down the mountain, skiers could believe that they were "in synchrony with the mountains and the snow," embraced by a "natural" landscape that, if they were to stop and look around, flashed "manmade" like a neon sign.

Ski area managers struggled to provide this downhill experience, which had once been relatively solitary, for as many skiers as possible. Simply cutting trees down was enough to build more trails; but managers quickly learned that not just any trail would do. While Aspen's Roch Run had earned a national reputation among downhill competitors even before the war, for example, postwar managers knew they would have to cut some easier trails to sell more lift tickets. Vail opened in 1962 with skiing terrain consciously designed for skiers of all levels, and other Colorado areas followed suit. In contrast to the "historic and pioneering days," when "the

---

"seldom should the type of lift dictate the location of ski trails," nevertheless "a lift intended to provide both ski trail access and scenic views for summer [and presumably winter] tourists is one exception to this principle." U.S. Department of Agriculture Forest Service and the National Ski Areas Association, *Planning Considerations for Winter Sports Resort Development* (Washington, D.C.: Government Printing Office, 1973), 15. Ski area planners had been noting that exception for some time. One developer of Snowmass attributed the resort's first-year success to its scenic appeal. By virtue of its terrain and lift placement, "even the weaker skiers... can get to the top of Elk Camp and the Burn, and it's almost as if they can get a Sir Edmund Hillary complex," he said; "they're on top of the world." Jim Snobble, interview by the author, July 11, 1994, Aspen, Colorado, tape recording and transcript, 2, AHS; see also Toll interview, 9.

[11] Ski areas convinced visitors—to at least some degree—that the landscape around them was indeed natural. City dwellers especially connected the meaning of "nature" with that of "scenic mountain landscapes," sometimes with the help of the ski industry. One marketing director wrote, "The more hectic cities become, the greater the drive toward Nature, a reward for skiers." He went on to equate Nature (with a capital "N") to "the vast sweep of snowbowls, the play of sun and shade, [and] the changing colors of the winter sky at dusk." Todd Martin, foreword to Curtis W. Casewit, *Skiing Colorado* (Old Greenwich, Conn.: The Chatham Press, 1975). As the ski industry attracted middle-class Americans farther and farther away from the Rocky Mountain West to Colorado's mountains, it became easier to accept the marketing director's figuring. For suburban Chicagoans, Dallas businessmen, or New Jersey housewives, Colorado's national forests represented rugged wilderness beyond compare—a perfectly accurate perception, in light of where they were from.

general trend was toward the big mountain with steep, narrow, expert slopes," Winter Park's manager argued that well-groomed easy and intermediate slopes, balanced with a few expert trails, characterized the ideal ski area of the 1960s.[12] This new kind of ski resort landscape reflected the industry's desire to attract a broader clientele to the slopes, and it led skiers to expect easily negotiable terrain—even to understand such managed and controlled spaces as part of the "natural" mountain landscape.

Flocks of new skiers supported the growth of the postwar ski industry, but offering them an intimate mountain experience grew increasingly difficult for ski area developers. They responded to this dilemma by trying to create trails that would visually lessen the impact of crowds. Through the U.S. Forest Service and its mandate to promote varied use of national forests, the state supported such management. When Friedl Pfeifer cut the first new trails on Aspen Mountain for its grand opening, he said, he "[removed] trees only when necessary [and] left much of the mountain untouched, so that skiing would feel like a backcountry tour." Twenty-five years later the Forest Service recommended such planning for all ski areas. If a mountain is designed correctly, the planning guide pointed out, "a skier can have the feeling of isolation and freedom of congestion."[13] Designers thus consciously shaped ski trails to help skiers feel as if they were personally interacting with the mountain, encouraging the kind of experience that helped skiers forget they were in a planned, human-made space. While chairlifts invited skiers to look out at distant peaks, fostering a sense of freedom and movement going down mountains depended, ironically, on constricted sightlines.

Along with framing views or hiding crowds, popular ski trails attracted skiers with their terrain. "Variety is key," the designer of Purgatory explained. Good trails needed steep and shallow pitches, room for cruising, and transitions between types of terrain. "That," he said, "is what can make it sensual." One famous instructor agreed, comparing such terrain to the human body and encouraging students to "caress the mountain, as you would a lover." With mountains as their medium, good trail designers thus shared with artists the goal of creating a work that would elicit a flash of emotions, a work that people could return to again and again, experiencing it differently each time. A few of them became acknowledged masters. Pfeifer's design of Aspen Mountain "had a rhythm you would feel," remembered racer Steve Knowlton. Another man described Aspen Mountain as "really a very romantic mountain." Big resorts like Snowmass and Vail have more space, he continued, but, he said, "you don't feel like your

[12] Stephen Bradley, "What's the Ideal Ski Hill?" *Skiing Area News* 2 (April 1967): 36–38.

[13] Friedl Pfeifer and Morten Lund, *Nice Goin': My Life on Skis* (Missoula, Mont.: Pictorial Histories Publishing Company, 1993),140; U.S. Department of Agriculture, *Planning Considerations*, 19.

blood is stirring up" there.[14] The ultimate goal for ski area designers, then, was to craft a trail on which skiers could feel an explicitly sensual kind of exhilaration.[15]

Snow conditions influenced how skiers interpreted their movement downhill, and represented yet another means by which area managers altered mountain landscapes to create a certain skiing experience. Before the advent of large ski areas, people skied on whatever snow was available. On good days, they enjoyed fresh powder. On bad days, soft, heavy snow, perhaps rutted from earlier skiers, presented obstacles that skiers accepted as part of the sport. Once the general public began to frequent ski areas in larger numbers, the slopes began to show more wear and tear. "Sitzmarks"—roughly equivalent to divots on the golf course and caused by skiers' less fortunate full-body contact with the mountain landscape—became a common problem. With the introduction of better equipment and shorter skis in the 1960s, and the continual increase in traffic on the slopes, "moguls" overtook sitzmarks as the meanest snow hazard. These fields of snow mounds, created by skiers repeatedly turning in the same places, tripped up those with less command over their turns. Through the 1950s it became increasingly apparent that masses of skiers could not be turned loose on the slopes without causing the snow conditions to deteriorate.

As with other problems caused by increased participation in the sport, ski area operators discovered a way to mitigate, mediate, and manage bad snow conditions. When lifts and lodges reduced the "natural" feel of the immediate landscape, developers pointed skiers toward breathtaking views of the neighboring mountains instead. When crowds of skiers left holes and moguls behind them, the ski industry took up "snow grooming." Steve Bradley, manager of Winter Park after the war, invented the country's first snow grooming tool and became known as the "Father of Slope Maintenance."[16] The "Bradley Packer," which he designed in 1951 and continued to modify for many years afterward, smoothed the snow as skiing employees pulled the contraption behind them. Other area owners and managers adopted

---

[14] Chet Anderson, interview by the author, June 7, 1994, Durango, Colorado; Peter Miller, "Make Love to the Mountain," *Ski*, November 1979, 157; Steve Knowlton, quoted in the documentary film by Beth and George Gage, *Fire on the Mountain* (Telluride, Colo.: Gage and Gage Productions, 1995); Charles Paterson, interview by the author, June 28, 1994, tape recording and transcript, AHS, 10.

[15] It is problematic to declare this kind of exhilaration gendered in any specific way. While male skiers made reference to the mountain landscape as female and sometimes wrote about their alpine experiences in terms suggestive of sex, they also described themselves in more passive terms. Woman skiers, moreover, often enjoyed aggressive skiing and the contradictions of the gendered relationship that accompanied it.

[16] Abbott Fay, *Ski Tracks in the Rockies: A Century of Colorado Skiing* (Evergreen, Colo.: Cordillera Press, 1984), 43; Grand County Historical Association, *Winter Park: Colorado's Favorite for Fifty Years, 1940–1990* (Denver: Winter Park Recreation Association, 1989), 72.

Bradley's packing method or developed their own, thus finding themselves in the business of smoothing trails as well as cutting and designing them.

Eventually the snowfall itself became a manageable resource. By the late 1950s ski areas had so much invested in providing a good experience for their customers that they faced huge financial losses should the snow refuse to fall. So ski area operators turned to making snow themselves.[17] The growth of snowmaking in Colorado represented yet another ski industry investment designed to ensure its continued popularity and growth. It also added another layer to the built environment of ski areas, now visible in snow guns, hoses, and the piles of snow they spewed (which they then had to groom). Finally, manmade snow altered human relationships to the environment. Ski area operators could manufacture a "natural" resource upon which they depended; and skiers could scratch one more worry off their vacation-planning list. While this technology primarily helped ski areas in the East and Midwest, even Colorado resorts occasionally needed a few more inches than the weather provided. Magic Mountain outside Denver installed a snowmaking system in the late 1950s, followed by Ski Broadmoor, a small area that catered to skiers in Colorado Springs. In addition to boosting ski areas' snow cover, snowmaking could lengthen the season. By 1968 Loveland Basin was using manmade snow to open in mid-October, a month before other areas.[18] Corporate competition and increasingly available technology eventually kicked off a race among ski areas to open first. After the devastatingly lean 1976–77 snow season, most other big Colorado areas invested in snowmaking technology, also. They had too much at stake, by that point, to do otherwise.

Scenic views, a perception of solitude, and snowy, smooth, sensual terrain created an exhilarating experience. For many, so did the feeling of adventure and risk. While most prewar skiers imagined avalanches and serious injury as potential risks for everyone but themselves, they had to accept personal responsibility in the case of an accident—there was simply no one else to blame. Part of the sport's early rugged reputation—its very meaning for especially masculine types—was based on the idea that skiers pitted their skills, speed, and daring against an untamed natural landscape. Danger, in this case, was not just acceptable—it was desirable. Yet the dangers posed by crowds of skiers overestimating the limits of their skills

[17] "Guaranteed snow! Think of it!" *Ski* magazine declared in 1957. An engineering firm in Massachusetts, originally involved in irrigation equipment, had developed a snowmaking system that one eastern ski area used profitably that year. "Snow-making promises to take the weather risk out of skiing," the article claimed. It would remove (or at least reduce) "your risk, when you plan your ski vacation or weekend, the operator's risk, and consequently the risk that everyone with a recreational or commercial interest in the sport must take." See "New Future," *Ski*, December 1957, 68–72.

[18] "Ski Areas," *Historic Georgetown Centennial Gazette 1868/1968*, 23, Colorado Tourism file, Routt County Collection, Buddy Werner Memorial Library, Steamboat Springs, Colorado.

proved to be quite an unappealing postwar alternative to untamed mountain landscapes. Enhancing a feeling of adventure and at the same time providing a safe skiing vacation for a broad range of customers proved to be yet another landscape conundrum the ski industry had to confront.

Limiting beginner skiers to beginner slopes was not an option. Designating where certain skiers could and could not ski—even in the interest of safety—would threaten the feelings of freedom and exhilaration on which the whole industry was based. Faced with the reality of increasingly crowded slopes, ski areas relied instead upon the National Ski Patrol. Members of this organization marked dangerous terrain, helped injured skiers, and made sure everyone was off the mountain safely at the end of the day, usually in return for free skiing and sometimes for pay.[19] They represented yet another tier of control and management in postwar ski resorts. Their presence on constructed ski area landscapes, moreover, helped alter the meaning of those landscapes and even of the sport itself. The advent of beginner "bunny slopes," snow grooming, and the ski patrol signified the redefinition of skiing as a safe, fun, family activity, one whose meanings hinged upon a designed, constructed, and patrolled landscape.

Resort Landscapes

Once incorporated into destination resorts, the Rocky Mountains became "wild" landscapes neatly packaged for tourist consumption. Destination resorts, while highlighting their skiing terrain, also featured restaurants, hotels, condominiums, nightclubs, and retail stores gathered at the mountain's base. These businesses posted invitations to consume goods associated with status and leisure throughout the resort landscape. Skiers thus came to understand their sport as more than a sensual physical experience; it became part of a vacation, only one aspect of a trip that also included shopping, dining, and socializing. As such, skiers expected that landscape to be constructed for their own and their families' enjoyment. Tourists' expectations ultimately proved powerful enough to transform the image of a resort and the resort itself.[20] Indeed, the success of the ski industry economy has come to depend upon the degree to which resort landscapes could define the

---

[19] Established in 1938 by Minot Dole and his colleagues in the Amateur Ski Club of New York, the National Ski Patrol System (NSPS) grew along with the ski industry after World War II. It originated as an organization of volunteers and eventually incorporated professional ski patrollers. While patrollers may seem like agents of the state to some renegade skiers and snowboarders, they have no connections to government. See Minot Dole, *Adventures in Skiing* (New York: Franklin Watts, 1965) for the founder's account of how the NSPS developed.

[20] See Colin Michael Hall, *Tourism and Politics*, 178.

local community as mythic and hide the relations of class, labor, and environmental impact that would mar tourists' vacations.[21]

A particular ski culture permeated destination resorts and promoted a certain understanding of that space—one that glossed over the constructed nature of the landscape and focused instead on the images that appealed to skier-tourists. Resort ski culture's emphasis on appearance, for example, allowed skiers to change their class identities while on vacation. Buying the right clothes, going to the right bars, and drinking the right scotch transformed businessmen and housewives into members of the jet set. Just as resort culture dressed up skier-tourists in images of European savoir-faire and status, it also dressed up the landscape. Tourists' nostalgia for rural images, furthermore, encouraged them to accept destination resort landscapes that would have otherwise stretched the limits of credibility. Hotels, condominiums, and restaurants that would have scarred the town with their quantity and form became, instead, architectural tools to help Rocky Mountain visitors transport themselves to quaint Victorian mining towns, the Wild West, or even the Alps. Breckenridge restored its Victorian buildings and houses on Main Street, for instance, to emphasize the town's mining past. Restaurants, shops, motels, and ice cream stands thus evoked images of nineteenth-century mining rather than the tourist economy that supported them. Even Vail's parking garage, hidden below ground for the most part, carefully nudges people from its depths into the heart of the area's "European" walking village. Developments on the mountains accomplished this feat as well. Huge high-speed lifts fit almost seamlessly into resort settings once their towers and engines were christened the "Vista Bahn" (at Vail) or the "Silver Queen" (at Aspen).

The names of ski trails also incorporated physical development into the resort culture and allowed skiers to focus on images rather than reality. Telluride recalled the town's mining days with its Mine Shaft, Apex, and Silver Glade trails, and its summit, Gold Hill. Steamboat Springs pushed its "Old West" ranching image when it named a midmountain lodge Rendezvous Saddle, a lift Rough Rider, and various ski trails Chute One, High Noon, Flintlock, Buckshot, and Quick Draw.[22] Nor did these names languish quietly on trail maps. Skier-tourists animated resort images when they made

[21] This reality has important consequences for those who work at ski resorts, because their labor must remain hidden from view. With the exception of visible experts including ski instructors, members of the ski patrol, and chefs, ski resort workers have little power. After World War II the figure of the "ski bum" idolized ski resort workers by virtue of their generally upper-class status, athleticism, and youthful sexuality. More recently, out-of-sight housing prices and cost of living have effectively hidden a growing class of immigrant laborers—along with middle-class professionals—miles and miles away from the resorts.

[22] Vail exercised a self-conscious sense of humor in this naming process—its famous Riva Ridge trail connected to a trail called Tourist Trap.

plans to meet friends on the mountain, described to each other where they had skied, and flaunted their athletic exploits later on in the bar.

Images conjured up by resort architecture and trail names did much more than create an atmosphere of the Alps or the Wild West: they helped erase the work and development that went into creating those images. Every landscape, geographers Donald Meinig and Peirce Lewis remind us, "is at once a panorama, a composition, a palimpsest, a microcosm," both an accumulation and a code through which we can decipher cultural and social meaning. Rocky Mountain ski resorts are physical, material places, built by working-class laborers, but they are also representations for sale—commodifications of western and rural mythic images and images of wilderness. As such, they are inextricably entwined in the social relations and politics that created and marketed them. Landscapes have the power to both reflect and influence social relations, and rural landscapes often do so by appearing unworked, or natural. They become, as Raymond Williams characterized them, both a work and an erasure of work.[23] Tourist landscapes have embraced this contradiction to an especially high degree, since visitors purchase and participate in representations of the landscape more consciously than they do the material environment. Vail's parking garage, for instance, represents the physical labor of those who built it, an expensive parking garage, and an entrance into the elite, European, shopping district of Vail Village. It is the latter image that skier-tourists focus on and pay to experience, just as they interpret their runs down the mountain as exhilarating moments in the wilderness of the West rather than in a highly planned and constructed fantasy land.

A hidden relationship between the state and corporate interests helped refine this sleight of hand. During the 1970s the environmental movement prompted skier-tourists to become increasingly concerned with the overdevelopment of their resorts. The industry's response to this new mind-set was to construct mountain landscapes even more self-consciously than before. The U.S. Forest Service supported this choice and declared that area developers should "make the ski area look more like natural terrain." "Failing to produce this visual effect," one planner argued, "is the crux of much criticism of ski developments." Indeed, by the 1990s the Forest Service was employing computer technology to assess the visual impact of area expansion and stressing the need to paint lift towers an appropriate color.[24] Their

[23] See Perice F. Lewis, "Axioms for Reading the Landscape," and D. W. Meinig, "Introduction," in *The Interpretation of Ordinary Landscapes: Geographical Essays*, ed. D. W. Meinig (New York: Oxford University Press, 1979); Don Mitchell, *The Lie of the Land: Migrant Workers and the California Landscape* (Minneapolis: University of Minnesota Press, 1996), introduction; Hall, *Tourism and Politics;* and Raymond Williams, *The Country and the City* (New York: Oxford University Press, 1973), 32–34.

[24] Mike Maginn, "The Problem with Doing Business in the Woods," *Skiing Area News* 5 (summer 1970): 42; U.S. Department of Agriculture, *Planning Considerations*, 30; H. Peter Wingle,

efforts, unconsciously appreciated by thousands of skiers, accompanied the industry's continued growth through the 1970s.

A special challenge rose in the 1990s from skiers who tired of the managed environment. For skiers who had been drawn to the sport by the serene mountain landscape and the chance to feel alone in the wilderness, Rocky Mountain destination resorts had lost much of their appeal. Some skiers abandoned downhill recreational skiing in the 1970s for a sport more akin to its nineteenth-century roots: cross-country skiing. Foregoing the convenience of mechanized lifts renewed the possibility of skiing silently and alone in the woods. This trend was a direct response, in part, to the increasing development of alpine resort areas.[25] Back-country skiing and extreme skiing have been more recent manifestations of this desire to get away from the crowds and construction of resorts. Searching for an experience unmediated by lifts, lodges, and human-made trails, these skiers trek between mountain huts or climb rugged peaks for the thrill of skiing steep, narrow, and rocky terrain. Both the wilderness and the extreme descents that these skiers respectively seek exist only where development and management do not. This fact describes both an attractive and frightening situation. For where there are no crowds, lifts, or signs funneling skiers to the "easiest way down," there are also no signs to mark cliffs, no avalanche control, and no ski patrol. The unmitigated danger that has drawn skiers from resort areas to the scenic adventure candyland called "the back country" has also brought them to the emergency room. Avalanches claimed forty-one lives in the seven years before 1995; exposure and frostbite left their marks on many others. Despite—and often because of—these real dangers, back-country skiing and extreme skiing continue to attract followers.[26]

Resorts met the challenge by responding to the views of critics. Unwilling to concede the independent success of cross-country and extreme skiing, destination resorts have managed, largely, to incorporate both sports within their own constructed landscapes. As early as 1978 one reporter

---

Considerations for Winter Sports Resort Development (USDA Washington, D.C.: Forest Service, Rocky Mountain Region, 1994), 28–31.

[25] U.S. Department of Agriculture, Forest Service, *Growth Potential of the Skier Market in the National Forests,* Research Paper WO-36 (Washington, D.C.: Government Printing Office, 1979), 6. See also "Highlights from the 1987 Guide to Cross Country Skiing Survey," *Cross Country Skiing,* April 1978, 1–2.

[26] The vast majority of skiers, however, continue to flock to resorts. They, too, have become increasingly aware of their surroundings since the 1970s. Rather than opt for a "real wilderness experience," complete with discomfort and danger, they have come to appreciate and expect a certain degree of development. The frightening irony of this construction is that it has created so many obstacles for skiers that, between the 1988–89 season and the 1994–95 season, as many people died from collisions within ski area boundaries as from avalanches in the backcountry. Howard Pankratz and Chance Conner, "Liability Ruling Assessed," *Denver Post,* December 20, 1995, 4B.

noticed that most ski areas offer organized touring centers with miles of maintained trails. Most cross-country skiers, moreover, despite their desire to "get into the country," preferred to ski on a groomed track and have come to depend upon snowmaking to ensure the trail's quality.[27] While rejecting downhill ski resort landscapes, these skiers came to accept similarly constructed ones often owned and operated by the very same developers.

More recently, the ski industry has enveloped the sport of extreme skiing. Once the province of mountaineer-alpinist daredevils, extreme skiing acquired a wide following in America during the 1980s and boasted its first World Extreme Ski Championships in 1991. Rather than ignore the implicit criticism of resort landscapes that these thrill-seeking people acted out on the steeps, ski area managers sought to attract them into their resorts. Trail designers reversed their 1960s decision to focus on easy terrain and opened steep, narrow chutes for skier-tourists who wanted to test their skill and nerve. As of 1996 Breckenridge, Copper, Crested Butte, Telluride, Snowmass, A-Basin, and Loveland all offered (and patrolled) areas of "extreme" terrain within ski area boundaries. Ski area managers thus attracted those disillusioned with the typical resort ski slopes, ironically, to equally constructed spaces. Resort marketers could advertise exhilaration in a wild and dangerous landscape at the same time as they promised a plush, comfortable, pampered vacation experience. One 1995 advertisement for the Beaver Creek Hyatt Regency featured a photo of an extreme skier and the text "the rugged outdoors—where men are men and their boots are buckled for them." Visitors could simultaneously explore the wild, manly wilderness of the mountains and enjoy extreme pampering below, this ad implied, with absolutely no conflict. James Bond and any skier who wanted to emulate him would be right at home. Ads like this abound and they seem to be working; the ski industry has negotiated this contradictory terrain to a remarkably successful degree.[28]

Presented with the initial problem of providing a scenic and exhilarating skiing experience for as many people as possible, ski resort designers, developers, and managers have successfully built more than scenic and exhilarating mountain landscapes. They have constructed, managed, and patrolled places defined largely by sensuality, wilderness, and danger. They

[27] Meyers, "It Will Be 'Hotter,'" 15; "Highlights from the 1978 Guide to Cross Country Skiing Survey"; Jonathan B. Wiesel, "Cross Country Snowmaking: Where It's Been ... Where It's Going," *Ski Area Management* (March 1982), 64, 67–68.

[28] Michael Romano, "Going to Extremes," *Rocky Mountain News*, March 16, 1994, 1B; Charlie Meyers, "Taking the Risk Out of Extreme," *Denver Post*, February 16, 1996, 12D. Even back-country skiing, while impossible to do in-bounds by definition, entered the ski industry through its high-tech fashion and equipment-oriented culture. James Brooke, "The Business of Skiing Gets Bigger," *New York Times*, September 9, 1996, B8. For another perspective on the industry's growth from 1976 to 1993, see Charles R. Goeldner, "We've Come A Long Way," *Ski Area Management* 33 (July 1994): 41.

have built mythically western and rural towns with the latest amenities. More than simply altering the mountain landscape, in other words, these people have infused that landscape with specific meanings and sold those meanings through the ski industry. Skier-tourists thus consumed not only a physical resort environment, but a representation of that landscape and of the act of skiing itself. Destination ski resorts, beyond merely altering the environment, have come to represent wilderness, sensuality, and danger precisely because of their degree of development. By successfully offering both safety and danger, comfort and wilderness, destination resorts allow skier-tourists to mix the mild with the wild.

The Politics of Resort Communities

The tension between these contradictions supported the ski industry's consumer culture, and they have created a new, contested, kind of rural community in the Rocky Mountains since the 1950s. In adopting a destination resort economy, western towns essentially commodified their own communities and the "wild" mountains and national forest land near them. Meanwhile, the problem was that selling rural communities and a wild, unsettled landscape necessarily placed those very things in danger. The politics of Colorado ski resort towns have come to reflect this realization, and contestations over what is wild and rural have moved to center stage.

On one level, the ski industry has altered western communities demographically, introducing a never-ending succession of visitors to once small and isolated rural towns. One author defined tourism as "a principal means by which modern people define for themselves a sense of identity."[29] Becoming even a temporary participant in a town's local culture served as part of the attraction for city dwellers and suburbanites who took up skiing. The sense of community in resort towns like Aspen—a result of their geographic isolation and their small, "colorful" populations of old-timers—drew city folk to the country for their vacations. The fact that many of them bought second homes so they could participate in that community from the inside rather than as visitors, however, fundamentally changed the community's nature. Walter and Elizabeth Paepcke told their friends in the late 1940s that they should come out to Aspen, that "we love it and want to start something big and make it well known." They convinced photographer Ferenc Berko and Bauhaus designer Herbert Bayer to move there, when "it was a beautiful place but all the town was 300 miners." June Hodges told her husband, who was a prominent Denver lawyer and

---

[29] John A. Jakle, *The Tourist: Travel in Twentieth-Century North America* (Lincoln: University of Nebraska Press, 1985), 22.

president of the city's elite Arlberg skiing club, "we have just got to have a little place in Aspen—it is the most wonderful little town, beautiful mountains, and the locals all were wonderful." As skier John Litchfield remembered it, "pretty soon [after Paepcke spread the word about Aspen] people came out of the woods and took the place over."[30] Like those in Aspen, resort town residents across the state noticed higher-brow residents and business people moving in and calling the town home, at once celebrating and altering the population of "wonderful" locals.

This demographic layering made discerning who was a local, or insider, increasingly problematic.[31] And it made for a particular version of resort town politics, since newer residents often used their political voices to define themselves as local. Old-timers and longtime local families who chose not to participate in the new tourist economy, or who could not keep up with its snowballing momentum, either left or found themselves on the margins. "The people who started [Aspen skiing] and who were enthusiastic in the beginning have mostly sold their homes and moved," Dick Durrance explained in 1993. "The new ones have come in and it's become a community, of, well you might say, outsiders." This process began in Aspen as early as 1946 and continues to this day. In Telluride, newcomers came into conflict with old-timers in their effort to shape local growth and define themselves as locals. "The new finally took over the politics and they liked to make a big to-do about it," one miner remembered of the 1960s. "They got rid of the old cronies in Telluride, guys like me."[32] With the continuous movement of people to resort towns, however, their dominance could not last. Achieving political status as "locals" placed these people in the same position as those they had worked so hard to oust upon their arrival. Newer residents, in turn, worked to claim political power and insider status as their own.

With new residents came different opinions about resort development. At the moment when towns adopted tourism to supplement their rural economies, most residents accepted the change as necessary if not ideal. But people who moved to resort towns for their scenic views, sport, and

[30] Ferenc Berko, Music Associates of Aspen "High Notes" talk, June 29, 1994, Aspen, Colorado, transcript, AHS; June Hodges, interview by the author, June 19, 1994, Denver, Colorado, tape recording and transcript, AHS, 1; John Litchfield, interview by the author, September 29, 1994, Denver, tape recording and transcript, AHS, 4. The people Litchfield remembered coming to Aspen included Harold Ross, editor of the *New Yorker*, Bill Douglass and his father, who was chairman of Quaker Oats, a Mr. Bingham who ran the *Louisville Courier*, and Henry Stein from Chicago.

[31] Rothman uses the term "neo-native" to describe locals' changing identities. I am reluctant to create a separate category for transplanted locals. So many people have defined themselves as locals in different ways and at different times that it is virtually impossible to distinguish natives from newcomers, insiders from outsiders.

[32] Dick Durrance, interview by Jeanette Darnauer, August 18, 1993, Aspen, video recording and transcript, AHS, 15; Bill Mahoney, interview by the author, June 6, 1994, Telluride, tape recording and transcript, 5.

quaint ruralness recognized the impact that continued development would have on their "wonderful little town." A whole generation of Aspen residents who moved to town in the late 1940s and early 1950s bemoaned the changes the town underwent later, and out of their ranks came organizations such as the Aspen Wilderness Workshop, established in 1966.[33] Even these residents lived at odds with the old-timers who had supported the resort's initial development. Remnants of the older rural community came to be represented increasingly by groups like historical societies, which stressed the cultural significance of older locals by packaging their "old-timer" identity for tourist consumption and downplaying their willingness to develop the town for tourists.

Contradictions built into ski industry consumer culture manifested themselves through physical development as well as through conflicts among different layers of locals. Skiing tourists demanded highly constructed landscapes that made them feel both pampered and on the edge of the wilderness. Maintaining a balance between development and access to nature proved increasingly difficult as the ski industry grew. Booming real estate prices lured older residents into selling their homes and altered the physical landscape. In 1966 one (exceptional) Aspen woman reportedly rejected a $90,000 offer for her "hillside shack" and homestead land, originally valued at $950. New buildings and retail establishments rose up right along with prices. In 1961 alone, the town issued licenses to twenty-nine hotels with 1,139 beds; the next year the condominium craze began. To accommodate such growth the city authorized a new electric system and decided to pave fourteen of its downtown blocks. The boom of the 1960s affected resorts across the country and did not slow for over a decade. Between building vacation homes, lodges, and condominiums, real estate threatened even to overtake skiing as a catalyst for growth and tip the balance toward overdevelopment. "Some small towns are changing," one Coloradan noted in 1970, "sacrificing their singularity to become plush look-alike playgrounds for urbanites."[34]

Successful playgrounds came at a high price—one that endangered the resort town itself. With the rise of recreational tourism around the globe, destination resort towns and their resident populations have changed. Commodifying resort communities, in other words, put not just the physical environment at stake but also the culture and identity of the town. Ski resort communities such as Aspen found themselves in the 1960s and 1970s facing inadequate municipal water and sewage service, a rising crime

[33] Joy Caudill, interview with the author, July 26, 1994, Aspen, Colorado, tape recording and transcript, AHS, 6–8.

[34] Al Nakkula, "Aspen, Where Everyone Skis," *Rocky Mountain News,* January 9, 1966, 52, clipping, AHS; Peggy Clifford and John Macauly Smith, "The Distressing Rebirth of Aspen," *Denver Post Empire Magazine,* August 16, 1970, 9, 8.

rate, traffic jams, parking problems, and unprecedented pollution. Residents struggled with the environmental, social, and political ramifications of providing for skiing tourists' contradictory demands. They found that the tension between wild landscapes and a service economy, so beautifully negotiated in resort advertisements, proved much more treacherous in the local political arena. In the late 1960s Aspenites formed groups including Citizens for Community Action and the "Aspen Liberation Front" to protect their town from overdevelopment.[35] At issue in 1969 was an initiative to expand Highway 82 west of the city from two to four lanes, a debate that remains unresolved and equally contentious in the late 1990s.

In the mountains, where skiers could enjoy views of fourteen-thousand-foot peaks and wilderness areas while sipping Chardonnay, development proved to be a similarly thorny issue. The National Environmental Policy Act of 1970 required that every government agency prepare an Environmental Impact Statement (EIS) for any future project on public lands "significantly affecting the quality of the human environment," including ski area development and expansion.[36] This law reflected Americans' growing concern with environmental issues and forced the ski industry (among others) to pay attention to the consequences of its built landscapes. Through the EIS review process, in which federal, state, and local agencies as well as the public had opportunities to voice concerns over the proposed action and the EIS itself, such concerns became a characteristic part of Rocky Mountain politics. More than regulate ski area development itself, the federal government provided bureaucratic channels and a public forum for discussion. In identifying issues of environmental concern and providing an arena for their debate, the state helped bring the development behind the ski industry to light and made it a political issue.

Resort developers created the image of wilderness for their skiers, and in the process they attracted the attention of groups determined to preserve that wilderness. Vail's development of Beaver Creek—originally planned for use in the 1976 Olympics which Colorado voters declined to host—became the focus of a Herculean struggle between development proponents and opposing factions. Begun in 1970, Vail Associates' planning and negotiations for Beaver Creek had cost it $6 million by 1974 when the Forest Service filed its draft EIS. Without the Winter Olympics to help justify their project, Vail Associates entered a bureaucratic black hole. "The state's 13-agency review of the EIS was so critical," ranger Paul Hauk wrote, "that even development-oriented Governor John Vanderhoof requested the Forest Service to delay issuing a permit to Vail Associates."

[35] Jennifer J. Hammond, "Growth Management in Aspen, Colorado, 1960–1977," unpublished manusript, AHS, 19, 21.
[36] Kirkpatrick Sale, *The Green Revolution: The American Environmental Movement, 1962–1992* (New York: Hill and Wang, 1993), 26–27.

After a long debate between the Forest Service and Governor Lamm (who opposed the site's development and worked to reverse outgoing Governor Vanderhoof's last-minute approval of the project), the Sierra Club filed an appeal to block the development. Finally, after more studies, plans, and compromises, Vail Associates got its special use permit for Beaver Creek in March of 1976. Still, two more appeals, from the Environmental Defense Fund and from an individual from Gunnison, delayed groundbreaking ceremonies until July of 1977. The resort finally opened in 1980, a decade after the project began.[37]

Even planning an expansion could raise political problems. Proposed expansions at Colorado destination resorts raised a variety of environmental issues that stirred up local communities, generated regional and (usually unfavorable) national press coverage, and galvanized opposition from environmental groups toward ski resort developers. In the early 1990s Snowmass planned to build ski lifts and trails on Burnt Mountain, thereby extending the resort to the edge of the Maroon Bells–Snowmass Wilderness Area and endangering the local elk habitat. Plans for increased snowmaking, which would divert water from local streams during the brown trout spawning season, prompted the Aspen Wilderness Workshop to bring the case before the Colorado Supreme Court. A *New York Times* reporter picked up the story (as had regional reporters) and introduced the environmental issues surrounding snowmaking to the national public. The local population divided when it had to judge the relative importance of protecting the local elk herd, the integrity of the wilderness area, and brown trout spawning habitat against additional jobs and business for the town.[38] These issues raised tempers across the state and placed the environmental consequences of resort development in the public forum.

Such controversies arose directly out of the contradictions inherent in the ski industry—that combination of rural communities graced with luxury hotels, restaurants, and mythic images; of high-speed chairlifts,

---

[37] Paul Hauk, *Beaver Creek Ski Area Chronology* (Glenwood Springs, Colo.: Forest Service, White River National Forest, 1979), 5; for more on the Beaver Creek development see ibid., 3–10, and Fay, *Ski Tracks in the Rockies*, 59–61. Few ski corporations dared propose new resorts after Beaver Creek, lest they be subject to the same costly delays and controversies; no new ski area has been developed since.

[38] Dirk Johnson, "On Ski Slopes of Colorado, A Battle of Snow vs. Water," *New York Times*, November, 14, 1994, A1, A10; John Brinkley, "Snowmaking Imperils Snowmass Creek?" *Rocky Mountain News*, April 20, 1994, 8A; Hugh Dellios, "Ski Resorts, Environmentalists Battle Over Snowmaking," *Denver Post*, January 22, 1995, 4C; Mark Obmascik, "Fish Can Only Squirm over Race to Make Snow," ibid., October 14, 1995; Paul Anderson and Brighid Kelly, "Snowmass Power Struggle," *Aspen Times*, April 11, 1992, 1A; Cameron M. Burns, "Snowmass Unchained," ibid., March 12, 1994, 1A; Paul Larmer, "Does Aspen Need Thousands More Skiers?" *High Country News*, October 4, 1993, 4; and USDA, White River National Forest, Aspen Ranger District, *Record of Decision Snowmass Ski Area: Final Environmental Impact Statement* (Glenwood Springs, Colo.: March 1994).

groomed trails, and comfortable lodges amidst untouched wilderness. This group of characteristics has attracted millions of skiers to the Colorado destination resorts every year, and the politics associated with it have become characterized by the struggle to maintain its contradictions. Resort towns attracted skiing tourists by defining themselves as rural. But the sheer numbers of outsiders visiting mountain resort towns, with their cosmopolitan tastes and demand for amenities, constantly endanger the rural identity of many Colorado communities. Residents have found it much more difficult to sustain this image of their landscape than it has been for marketers to sell it. Ski town politics have become highly contentious because rural residents and developers at once need and threaten each other.

These are still rural communities, however, and they will find ways to remain so in the future, because their ski industry and tourist economies rely upon their ability to define themselves as such. Even if the local ranching economy has fallen off, for instance, tourists expect to see fields, rather than only subdivisions, surrounding resort towns. Living out their vacation in a mythically western community depends upon a degree of open space. About 90 percent of the respondents to a 1993 survey of summer visitors to Steamboat Springs said that ranch meadows with wildflowers, birds, and grazing cows and horses added to their enjoyment of their vacation, and almost half said they would not return if ranch land continued to be developed into golf courses and condominiums. Accordingly, ranchers and environmentalists have teamed up to protect agricultural land from developers by forming land trusts. Ranchers who donate the development rights for their land to such land trusts can cut future estate taxes in half and ensure that the land will be used in perpetuity for ranching. Developers and tourists, in turn, capitalize on the so-called "beachfront property" that borders protected farmland.[39] Counterintuitive alliances, such as this one between conservationists and ranchers, capture the contradictions that characterize the politics of tourism in rural towns.

Maintaining those contradictions has grown even more difficult in the mountains than in town. On October 19, 1998, a group of environmental activists called the Earth Liberation Front (ELF) set fire to several of Vail Resort's buildings and chairlifts, causing $12 million in damage to protect an animal that does not live in Colorado. The ELF issued a statement opposing Vail's expansion onto a ridge overlooking a national forest, saying that "putting profits ahead of Colorado's wildlife will not be tolerated," and

---

[39] James Brooke, "Rare Alliance in the Rockies Strives to Save Open Spaces," *New York Times*, August 14, 1998, A16. Similarly, European governments have spent almost $2 billion to subsidize agri-tourism, paying farmers to create accommodations for guests and add "innkeeper" to their job description in order to protect the architectural heritage of farms and villages. John Tagliabue, "Preserving a Heritage via Bed and Barns," *New York Times*, August 13, 1998, C1.

Scenic views from one of Vail's hi-tech, highspeed chairlifts draw skiers and snowboarders to Blue Sky Basin, the site of violent protest over development, and of what one recent ad touted as "a backcountry experience...from skiing's more innocent past." Photo courtesy of Jack Affleck/Vail Resorts.

justifying their arson as "on behalf of the lynx."[40] There are no lynx, however, to be seen. The ELF sought to protect potential habitat for lynx reintroduction, fiercely insisting that part of the Rockies remain "wild" in the face of an ever-expanding tourist and ski industry. More significantly, their arson testifies to Vail's success in maintaining the tensions inherent in destination resort landscapes. Vail is one of the biggest and most highly developed ski resorts in the world. In claiming the national forest land where Vail was planning to expand for the lynx, the ELF essentially defined that landscape as wild. Because of the ELF, then, tourists will be able to ski Vail's new Blue Sky Basin and shop in the village below, confident in the knowledge that they are indeed on the edge of untouched wilderness.

Vail Resorts and the ELF, like the ranchers and environmentalists in Steamboat Springs, need each other as much as they hate each other. Their battles and unexpected alliances have redefined the rural identity of Colorado's ski towns and come to characterize the politics of the ski industry. Beyond that,

[40] James Brooke, "Group Claims Responsibility for Blazes at Vail Resort," *New York Times*, October 22, 1998, A14; David Johnson, "Vail Fires Were Probably Arson, U.S. Agents Say," ibid., October 23, 1998, A16.

they exemplify the problems and promise of rural tourism in general. Commodifying rural communities and "wild" landscapes demands a Herculean effort to hide the development that tourism generates. Since World War II tourism has created a kind of politics rooted less in institutions of the state than in the land and rural communities, a politics based on maintaining the image of the rural and simultaneously calling that image into question. At the close of the twentieth century, the politics of rural tourism had come to celebrate the call of the mild.

From the Heartland to Seattle

The Family Farm Movement of the 1980s and the Legacy of Agrarian State Building

MARY SUMMERS

This essay is dedicated to Rachel Anne Gaschott Ritchie
(12/7/1979–11/27/2000), her family and friends, and the
power of their love, work, faith, memory, politics, and imagination.

We believe that the power of government—in other words of the people—
should be expanded (as in the case of the postal service) as rapidly and
as far as the good sense of an intelligent people and the teachings of
experience shall justify, to the end that oppression, injustice and poverty
shall eventually cease in the land.

—People's Party of America, Omaha Platform (July 1892)

Looking for effective progressive political movements in the United States in the 1980s, I was intrigued by the response of organizations of family farmers in the Midwest and politicians like Jim Hightower and Tom Harkin to the farm crisis. Farm activists organized advocacy and support networks, militant demonstrations, and highly effective lobbying and get-out-the-vote efforts. They raised issues ranging from stopping aid to the Contras in Nicaragua to

Research for this article has been funded in part by grants from the Agrarian Studies Program at Yale University, a Yale University Dissertation Fellowship, a Robert M. Leylan Fellowship from Yale University, and a fellowship in the History of Home Economics and Nutrition from the New York State College of Human Ecology and Mann Library at Cornell University. Many thanks to Robert Johnston, Rogers Smith, Stephen Skowronek, James Scott, Jess Gilbert, Nancy Cott, Neil Basen, Robert Weise, and Mark Ritchie for their readings and comments.

the protection of groundwater, from drought relief in the Midwest to famine relief in Africa, relating all these concerns to the government's failure to adopt economically and environmentally sustainable agriculture and trade policies.[1]

The movement formed many somewhat surprising alliances. The Black Congressional Caucus endorsed its call for cutting farm subsidies and increasing spending on food stamps. The United Auto Workers and International Machinists helped highlight the dependence of a large sector of the American workforce on a healthy farm economy. Environmentalists joined campaigns against the heavy use of pesticides and the soil erosion associated with capital-intensive production techniques. Church groups supported efforts to raise issues of hunger and rural development around the world. Country music and rock stars who found their themes in small-town America provided much of the movement's financial support with the Farm Aid concerts.[2]

While deeply rooted in their members' view of their material interests, the organizing efforts of these farm groups were not confined to narrow economic demands, but spoke to broader visions of political economy, built new coalitions, and worked for concrete goals both inside and outside the party system and the government. Their example suggested that people who care deeply about particular issues and constituencies can sometimes represent one of the best sources of hope for broader democratic politics. Because these farm groups contradicted so much of the conventional wisdom about the limits of twentieth-century American interest group politics, I was drawn to a study of the historical roots of their program, ideas, and claims upon the government.[3] This essay seeks to explore the implications

---

[1] The following essay draws in part on my experience as a speech writer for Jesse Jackson in his 1984 presidential campaign and for Harriett Woods in her 1986 campaign for the Senate in Missouri. I owe much of my understanding of the family farm movement to conversations with Mark Ritchie, then president of the League of Rural Voters, and the journalist Jim Ridgeway. For examples of literature produced by Mark Ritchie and the League of Rural Voters, see: Kevin Ristau and Mark Ritchie, "The Farm Crisis: History and Analysis," *Shmate: A Journal of Progressive Jewish Thought* 16 (1986): 10–20; Mark Ritchie and Kevin Ristau, *Crisis by Design: A Brief Review of U.S. Farm Policy* (Minneapolis: League of Rural Voters Education Project, 1987) (pamphlet in the possession of the author); Mark Ritchie and Kevin Ristau, "Politics and Farm Policy: New Directions for the Democratic Party," unpublished paper presented to the Democratic Policy Commission, January 1986, in the possession of the author. For examples of Jim Ridgeway's work, see "Heartland Heartbreak," *Village Voice*, October 2, 1984, 22–24; "Organizing the Farm Belt," *Texas Observer*, October 10, 1986. Neil Basen, Jess Gilbert, and Jon Lauck referred me to two excellent academic sources on the progressive farm groups of the 1980s: William C. Pratt, "Using History to Make History? Progressive Farm Organizing During the Farm Revolt of the 1980s," *Annals of Iowa* 55 (1996): 24–45, and Patrick H. Mooney and Theo J. Majka, *Farmers' and Farm Workers' Movements: Social Protest in American Agriculture* (New York: Twayne, 1995), 97–119.

[2] Pratt, "Using History to Make History?"

[3] For critiques of conventional postwar views of interest group politics, see Peter Schuck, "Against (and For) Madison: An Essay in Praise of Factions," *Yale Law and Policy Review* 15 (1997): 553; Mary Summers, "Putting Populism Back In," *Agricultural History* 70 (spring

of this movement for our understanding of American politics: first by looking at its impact on the 1985 farm bill debates; second by looking at its
program; and third by looking at the roots of this program in the history
of American agricultural politics.

The Family Farm Movement and the 1985 Farm Bill

The "permanent" Agricultural Adjustment Act of 1938 continues to structure farm policy debate in the United States with its mandate that Congress
pass a new farm bill every five years. Were Congress to fail to pass a bill, the
original terms of the 1938 act would be reinstituted. In this context Senator Tom Harkin's 1985 Farm Policy Reform Act, resurrected in 1986 as the
Harkin/Gephardt Save the Family Farm Act, represented much of the central thrust of the family farm movement's efforts to transform the nation's
agriculture. Harkin's bill called for a referendum on a "supply management program" to be held among the producers of all the major commodities. If a majority of a producer group voted to participate, its members would be required to set aside a portion of their tillable crop acres to
balance supply with demand. The bill mandated locally approved conservation practices on all set-aside land; it also contained prohibitions against
"sod-busting" and draining wetlands. With a program for the control of
"surplus production" thus established, the bill eliminated farm subsidies
(government payments to farmers when the price of the commodities they
produce falls below a certain level). A commodity price-support loan program would instead set a floor under commodity prices at around the cost
of production. Farmers would, for example, receive a loan of about $3.71
a bushel for the corn they produced. If market prices fell below that cost,
they could store the corn until prices rose again. When prices rose, they
would sell the corn and pay back the loan with interest.[4]

Most agricultural policy experts thought these proposals represented
nothing new. Political scientist William Browne, in his extensive study of
the 1985 farm bill process, described the protesters' platform as a "form of
better-funded commodity programs rather than... comprehensive reform." Indeed, Browne saw the family farm movement as sabotaging what

---

1996): 395–414; Mary Summers, "Conflicting Visions: Farmers Movements and the Making
of the United States Department of Agriculture" (Ph.D. diss. in progress, Political Science
Department, Yale University).

[4] William P. Browne, *Private Interests, Public Policy, and American Agriculture,* (Lawrence: University Press of Kansas, 1988), 221; Tom Harkin, "The Save The Family Farm Act," in *Is There
a Moral Obligation to Save the Family Farm?* ed. Gary Comstock (Ames: Iowa State University
Press, 1987), 388–96.

he and many other policy experts, both liberal and conservative, regarded as the potential for "real reform" in the 1985 farm bill. Rather than the Harkin-Gephardt approach to maintaining commodity prices, these academic reformers urged the need to dismantle all price supports and production controls as well as farm subsidies, as the only way of achieving less expensive, more market-oriented farm programs in accordance with "basic business values."[5]

At the beginning of the farm bill process, these experts had high hopes for seeing conventional farm programs phased out. Their reform agenda had the support of a popular president, a mobilized business community, and the largest of the nation's farm groups, the American Farm Bureau Federation. Even the farm groups that had traditionally fought for higher commodity price supports (the National Farmers' Union and the National Farmers Organization) seemed reluctant to do so in the face of Congressional concern with rising budget deficits.[6]

In the course of the farm bill debates, however, the academic reformers found themselves increasingly isolated. The farm protesters' dramatization of worsening farm conditions upstaged the policy experts' carefully written position papers and lobbying efforts. Many members of the American Farm Bureau Federation, "the long-time leader of the free-market philosophy in agriculture," joined farm protest groups and agitated for state organizations to endorse the family farm movement's program. The Alabama Farm Bureau actually withdrew from the national organization and hired its own national lobbyists. Similar actions were taken by some commodity groups, like the Nebraska Wheat Board. In response to such pressures, the leaders of the Farm Bureau emerged from a series of meetings with leaders of commodity groups with a proposal in favor of basic price supports.[7]

Except for the Fertilizer Institute, few business leaders wanted to devote time or money to a political process whose outcome seemed more and more uncertain. Twenty-two Republicans were up for election in the Senate, over half of them from important farm states, and most distanced

---

[5] Browne, *Private Interests*, 35, 107, 218–22, 227–28. Despite his somewhat jaundiced view of the family farm movement, this article will draw frequently on Browne's work, since Browne provides some fairly clear measures of the protesters' impact and influence. I am grateful to Shoon Murray for calling this invaluable resource to my attention. Two key texts that reflect the experts' consensus in the 1980s are William A. Galston, *A Tough Row to Hoe: The 1985 Farm Bill and Beyond* (Washington, D.C.: Hamilton Press, 1985) and Bruce Gardner, ed., *U.S. Agricultural Policy: The 1985 Farm Legislation* (Washington, D.C.: American Enterprise Institute for Public Policy Research, 1985).

[6] Browne, *Private Interests*, 35, 218–22, 227–28.

[7] Ibid., 93–94, 107–8, 223–24. For the almost messianic terms in which the Farm Bureau leadership had traditionally denounced price supports, see Charles B. Shurman's Presidential Message (1961) in George McGovern, ed., *Agricultural Thought in the Twentieth Century* (Indianapolis: Bobbs-Merrill, 1967), 472–85.

themselves as much as possible from David Stockman's calls for further cuts in farm subsidies. Harkin's Farm Policy Reform Act received thirty-six votes in the Senate; it was defeated by only forty-two votes in the House. Browne's interviews with farm state legislators revealed that those who opposed the Harkin bill "found it personally unpalatable but politically impossible" to do anything but vote for higher farm subsidies, the only obvious "pro-farmer" alternative to the Harkin bill's plan to abolish subsidies by raising commodity prices with production controls. As a result of such dynamics, a "widely circulated comment from a USDA source...stated that the protest movement added $10 billion dollars in costs to the initially estimated $52 billion three year (1986–1988) commodity program package."[8]

The protest movement also shaped the final 1985 farm bill's other most prominent feature besides its cost: its relatively strong environmental program. In other years many farm group lobbyists and legislators had routinely denounced proposals for conservation compliance requirements for participation in farm programs as unwarranted meddling with the freedom to farm. However, the family farm movement's fight for production controls as a way of promoting a more environmentally sound agriculture, as well as saving the taxpayers' money by reducing price-depressing surpluses and deficiency payments, created the context for new alliances. Suddenly conservation provisions became a relatively easy, "agreeable" basis for building the coalitions necessary to pass a farm bill. In short, the influence of the family farm movement on farm bill negotiations provided a fairly dramatic example of the ways in which broader political struggles can change conventionally accepted definitions of group interests, coalitions, and patterns of bargaining.[9]

Nor did the family farm movement's influence end with the passage of the 1985 farm bill. At the beginning of the 1988 presidential campaign season, the Iowa League of Rural Voters' *Presidential Report* took reasonable pride in the "surprising degree of unity" in the Democratic candidates' positions on farm policy. Michael Dukakis, for example, who had formerly been known as a critic of the Harkin-Gephardt farm bill, emerged from a private interview with Dixon Terry, one of the founders of the Iowa Farm Unity coalition, as a man committed to the principles of production controls and higher prices for farm products. Senators Joseph Biden and Paul Simon underwent similar conversion experiences. Members of the Iowa Farm Unity Coalition also helped to arrange some of Jesse Jackson's most dramatic campaign appearances, with large crowds applauding his ringing

[8] Browne, *Private Interests*, 125–28, 218–28, 108, 222.
[9] Browne compares the significance of the inclusion of these conservation measures for environmentalists to that of the food stamp program in the farm bills of the early 1970s for labor and urban interests, but fails to note any connection with the family farm movement's program. Ibid., 132–38, 230–33.

calls for parity not charity, farm aid not Contra aid, and support for the Harkin-Gephardt approach to raising farm income.[10]

No matter how familiar it might seem to experts like Browne, the family farm movement's program—and the excitement and support it generated—were an extraordinary phenomenon in the 1980s. In almost every other political arena, free marketeers were in the saddle. The air rang with calls for privatization, and most Democratic politicians were busily disassociating themselves from "the old New Deal liberalism," much less economic planning and production controls. Where, then, did the family farm movement's program come from? Why was the logic of its support so compelling to so many politicians, even in the 1980s? In order to come to terms with these questions, we need to know more about the roots and growth of the family farm movement.

The Roots of the Family Farm Movement

The person who best explained the family farm movement's program to me was Mark Ritchie. When I met him in 1986, Ritchie was working as an assistant to Minnesota Agriculture Commissioner Jim Nichols. Mark was also the president of the League of Rural Voters, an organization dedicated to increasing rural voter turnout and political participation. Born in Georgia, where his grandparents were farmers, Ritchie grew up in Iowa, where his father worked for the Department of Agriculture. Active in student and urban politics in the 1960s, he became involved in the politics of food, nutrition, and trade as an organizer of the International Baby Food Action Network's boycott of Nestlé in the mid-1970s. In the late seventies Ritchie was one of many young activists with farm backgrounds who were becoming increasingly interested in the politics of agriculture, as they watched or participated in the mass mobilizations of the American Agriculture Movement (AAM).[11]

In January of 1978 AAM had mobilized forty to fifty thousand farmers and their supporters to lobby for a farm bill sponsored by Congressmen George Brown and Richard Nolan, which like Harkin-Gephardt would have established higher commodity prices and supply management and environmental protection programs and abolished subsidies. Congress's

[10] Iowa League of Rural Voters, *Presidential Report* (August 21, 1987), pages not numbered (pamphlet in the possession of the author); Jesse L. Jackson, "Save the Family Farm and the Farm Family," in *Straight from the Heart*, ed. Roger D. Hatch and Frank E. Watkins (Philadelphia: Fortress Press, 1987), 282–88; Pratt, "Using History to Make History?" 36–37.

[11] Much of the following section draws on my conversations with Mark Ritchie. Some of his extensive files on the history of the family farm movement are available on the Institute for Agriculture and Trade Policy's web site: http://www.iatp.org. For references to other contemporary farm leaders and activists, see Pratt, "Using History to Make History?" 27–36, 40–41.

response was to pass a bill that raised farm subsidies 11 percent, but failed to raise the floor under commodity prices. In the winter of 1979, AAM brought five tractorcades to Washington, but the result of these demonstrations was only widespread denunciations for tying up traffic. It looked as if AAM's militant mobilizations were not enough to change the nation's farm policies.[12]

Feeling betrayed by Carter, who had as a candidate called for cost-of-production commodity prices, and disgusted with his embargo on wheat sales to the Soviet Union, some of AAM's leaders campaigned for Ronald Reagan in 1980. Activists like Ritchie however, with broader commitments to progressive politics, saw such a course as disastrous. They were eager to find ways to build on AAM's mass-organizing efforts among farmers, while appealing to broader constituencies than could ever be reached by AAM's archaic-sounding calls for "One Hundred Percent of Parity."[13]

In March of 1980 Ritchie organized a conference entitled "Strong Winds Across the Land: The Historical Roots of Agrarian Protest" for the U.S. Farmers Association (USFA) at Iowa State University. Initiated as an effort to honor veterans of an increasingly isolated progressive Left in American farm politics, the conference served to bring younger activists together with "old-timers" like Fred Stover, the president of the USFA. An Iowa farmer who had played an enthusiastic leadership role in the New Deal farm programs, Stover had joined the Iowa Farmers' Union (the base of the Farm Holiday Association leader, Milo Reno, in the 1930s) in 1943. Within a year, he was elected vice president and then president of the state organization. Stover worked with James Patton, the liberal president of the National Farmers' Union (NFU), to support New Deal domestic reform programs and an internationalist foreign policy against the increasing conservatism of the Truman administration. In 1948, however, Patton supported Truman, while Stover made the nominating speech for Henry Wallace at the Progressive party convention. An open split occurred in 1950 over Stover's public opposition to the Korean War. In 1956 the leadership of the NFU obtained a

---

[12] This discussion of the history of AAM draws on Lowell K. Dyson, *Farmers' Organizations* (New York: Greenwood Press, 1986), 8–14; William P. Browne and Allan J. Cigler, *U.S. Agricultural Groups: Institutional Profiles* (New York: Greenwood Press, 1990), 8–12; Allan J. Cigler and John Mark Hansen, "Group Formation Through Protest: The American Agriculture Movement," in *Interest Group Politics*, ed. Allan J. Cigler and Burdett A. Loomis (Washington, D.C.: Congressional Quarterly Press, 1983), 84–109; Allan J. Cigler, "From Protest Group to Interest Group: The Making of the American Agriculture Movement, Inc.," in Cigler and Loomis, *Interest Group Politics*, 2d ed. (Washington, D.C.: Congressional Quarterly Press, 1986), 46–69; Browne, *Private Interests*, 66–72; William Browne, "Challenging Industrialization: The Rekindling of Agrarian Protest in a Modern Agriculture, 1977–1987," *Studies in American Political Development* 7 (1993): 11–14.

[13] "Parity prices," a recurrent demand of farm groups since these indices were first calculated by USDA economists in the 1920s, would guarantee farmers the purchasing power that they would have received from selling the same commodities in the "golden age of agriculture" from 1910 to 1914. Dyson, *Farmers' Organizations*, 8–10.

federal injunction to forbid Stover and the Iowa chapter from using the Farmers' Union name. Stover, however, continued to lead the "small but remarkably loyal" Iowa-based organization that eventually adopted the name of the United States Farmers Association.[14]

Decade after decade, Stover had remained a cheerfully formidable figure in American farm politics, always ready to encourage resurgent farmers' organizing efforts, as well as to support the causes of international peace and civil rights. In the 1960s he had added "and Power to the People" to the group's logo of "Peace and Parity." In the 1970s when the National Farmers' Union had failed to back the American Agriculture Movement's demands for "parity price legislation," the USFA gave the new movement its full support.[15]

At Ritchie's conference younger activists listened to Stover and his friends explain the parallels they saw between the current farm situation and the crash in commodity prices and land values that had followed the boom of World War I. As the only way out of what they were sure would be a deepening farm crisis, the old-timers urged the rationale for the early New Deal farm programs. Given the unequal relationship between thousands of farmers and a handful of grain traders, their argument ran, and the seemingly unlimited increases in production made possible by science and technology, farmers who grow basic commodity crops have no effective market mechanisms for balancing supply and demand for their products. The more farmers produce, the more prices fall—and the more they expand production to make up in volume for falling prices. The harder they work, the more they invest, the more prices fall, and the more money they ultimately lose.[16]

The early New Deal farm programs sought to solve these problems by giving farmers a vote on whether or not to participate in production control programs that would seek to balance supply and demand. Participating farmers would receive government-backed loans based on their expected output and the estimated cost of production. Backed by these loans, they could then hold their crops off the market, until they received prices that would allow them to pay their loans back with interest. The old-timers cited the nation's farm programs from the New Deal through the early 1950s as evidence that such an approach could stabilize farm prices and income with-

[14] Membership may have expanded somewhat from the organization's original base of about seventeen hundred members, "but it is difficult to know the proportion of farmers to peace movement sympathizers." The following discussion of Stover and the USFA draws on Dyson, *Farmers' Organizations*, 345–48; Pratt, "Using History to Make History?"; and Mooney and Majka, "Farmers' and Farm Workers' Movements," 97–119. I am also grateful to Patrick Mooney for sharing transcripts of his interviews with Fred Stover.

[15] Dyson, *Farmers' Organizations*, 270; Browne, *Private Interests*, 92–93.

[16] Browne, "Challenging Industrialization," 1–2; Willard Cochrane, *Farm Prices: Myth and Reality* (Minneapolis: University of Minnesota Press, 1958).

out being a burden to the taxpayers, since there were no government payments involved.[17]

The older activists portrayed attacks on such policies as driven by business interests like fertilizer companies, grain traders, and commodity speculators, who would make greater profits from expanded production and falling prices. The policies these interests pushed in the name of "free trade" had been disastrous, the activists declared, for both farm families and the taxpayers. After Eisenhower's secretary of agriculture, Ezra Taft Benson, persuaded Congress to lower price supports and loosen acreage controls in 1955, for example, government costs for storage programs soared, as farmers tried to make up for lower commodity prices with increased production.[18]

The Kennedy administration, with the support of the Farmers' Union and the National Farmers' Organization, fought hard to restore farm programs based on higher commodity prices and production controls. Agriculture Secretary Orville Freeman toured the country, juxtaposing the administration's goal of keeping family farmers on the land with those in a proposal from the business-sponsored Committee for Economic Development (CED) that called for allowing commodity prices to fall and moving one-third of the nation's farmers off the land in a five-year period. Members of the National Farmers Organization built bonfires of Sears catalogues and protested at their local Ford dealers, until both companies disassociated themselves from the CED report, which became for generations of farm organizers proof of an organized conspiracy of corporate America to drive family farmers off the land.[19]

The leaders of the American Farm Bureau Federation, however, eagerly carried on Benson's anticommunist, pro–free market crusade against planning and production controls. Appealing to a potent mix of self-interest and ideology, they argued that production controls interfered with both individual profits and freedom. In the end the Farm Bureau's allies succeeded in defeating the Kennedy farm programs in Congress by a narrow margin, and without more stringent production controls, the cost of government commodity storage programs continued to grow.[20]

In 1973, however, a year of world crop shortages and a falling dollar, Agriculture Department Secretary Earl Butz declared "an historic turning point"

[17] McGovern, *Agricultural Thought*, xxvi–xxviii.

[18] Wesley McCune, *Who's Behind Our Farm Policy?* (New York: Praeger, 1956); McGovern, *Agricultural Thought*, xxix–xxx.

[19] Don Hadwiger and Ross Talbot, *Pressures and Protests: The Kennedy Farm Program and the Wheat Referendum of 1963* (San Francisco: Chandler, 1965), 218–22 and passim; Willard Cochrane, "The Case for Production Control," in McGovern, *Agricultural Thought*, 427–37; Richard A. Levins, *Willard Cochrane and the American Family Farm* (Lincoln: University of Nebraska Press, 2000).

[20] Individual state Farm Bureau campaigns included slide shows with bayonets and nooses wrapped around shocks of wheat (Illinois) and suggestions that "the original farm price support programs were communist inspired" (Mississippi). Hadwiger and Talbot, *Pressures and Protests*, 250–53; Shuman, "Presidential Message," in McGovern, *Agricultural Thought*, 472–85.

in the nation's farm programs, as he urged farmers to plant from "hedgerow to hedgerow" to respond to the "ever-growing worldwide demand for food and fiber." "Get big or get out" was his message to the nation's farmers, reinforced by extension agents and bankers, who urged farmers to take out big loans, backed by rising land values, to expand production. But as harvests around the world improved, glutted markets resulted in a sharp decline in commodity prices by 1977 and the lowest net farm income since 1936. It was these conditions that inspired a handful of farmers in Campo, Colorado to found the American Agriculture Movement in September, 1977.[21]

The Crisis of the 1980s

Under the Reagan administration, every prediction the old-timers had made about the worsening crisis in America's heartland came true. Rising interest rates and a sharp decrease in exports, due largely to the increasing strength of the American dollar, proved disastrous for overcapitalized farm operations that had become more and more dependent on export markets. Farmland values started to fall in 1980 and declined for more than six consecutive years—the sharpest decline since the Depression. Net farm income was cut in half between 1981 and 1983. Bankruptcies soared, and it was overwhelmingly the operators of large and middle-sized farms— the "progressive farmers"—who were going broke.[22]

As sales abroad dropped, surpluses at home soared, and commodity prices plummeted. The Reagan administration's farm programs, intended to cushion a temporary transition to a market-driven economy through subsidies or "deficiency payments" to farmers when prices fell below a set "target price," cost more than all previous farm programs combined. In 1983, in an attempt to reduce the cost of storage for price-depressing surpluses, the government instituted a payment-in-kind program, which paid farmers with stored crops to idle their land. Farmers took more than one-third of the land normally planted in program crops out of production.[23]

By 1982 the increasingly frustrated leadership of the American Agriculture Movement had split into at least two factions. Declaring that farmers

[21] Douglas Bowers, Wayne Rasmussen, and Gladys Baker, *History of Agricultural Price-Support and Adjustment Programs, 1933–1984* (Washington, D.C.: Economic Research Service, U.S. Department of Agriculture, December, 1984), 29; Dyson, *Farmers' Organizations*, 8–10; Diana Hunter, *Breaking Hard Ground: Stories of the Minnesota Farm Advocates* (Duluth, Minn.: Holy Cow! Press, 1990); Kathryn Marie Dudley, *Debt and Dispossession: Farm Loss in America's Heartland* (Chicago: University of Chicago Press, 2000), 21–36.
[22] Neil E. Harl, *The Farm Debt Crisis of the 1980s* (Ames: Iowa State University Press, 1990); Browne, *Private Interests*, 217–18; Galston, *Tough Row*, 12.
[23] Browne, *Private Interests*, 35; Kristen Allen and Barbara J. Elliott, "The Current Debate and Economic Rationale for U.S. Agricultural Policy," in *U.S. Agriculture in a Global Setting: An*

needed "an inside track" in Washington, the leadership of the larger group, AAM Inc., established a PAC and mounted ongoing lobbying efforts in support of higher minimum commodity prices, inventory controls, and supply management. Some farmers who resented AAM Inc.'s abandonment of the uncompromising demands and looser organizational style of the earlier movement formed another organization, Grassroots AAM. This group's calls for a national farm strike, however, never resulted in any mass actions.[24]

In what was essentially a vacuum of any national mobilization in response to the growing farm crisis, close to fifty formal local, state, and regional farm groups formed around the country, often building on contacts made during earlier AAM actions and meetings like Ritchie's conference. Farm groups organized rallies and penny auctions to stop evictions and farm sales. In state after state they filed lawsuits and occupied the offices of the Farmers Home Administration to block foreclosures and force extensions of credit. They set up suicide hot lines, food banks, and advocacy networks. Texas Agriculture Commissioner Jim Hightower, a longtime critic of the nation's farm policies, and Mark Ritchie's boss Jim Nichols, the Minnesota state agriculture commissioner, worked closely with the leaders of state crisis committees both to promote ongoing grassroots protest and to develop a national focus for what was rapidly turning into the family farm movement.[25] Hightower and Nichols sponsored a series of hearings around the country in 1983 and 1984 "to get farmers' views" on the principles that they wanted written into the 1985 farm bill. Out of these hearings, these organizers then drafted the legislation that became Tom Harkin's Farm Policy Reform Act.[26]

Much of the agitation for this legislation reflected the logic that younger activists had learned from the old-timers. The Reagan administration's "35 billion dollar program to drive farmers off the land" proved, they argued, that expanding markets abroad would never serve to "get the government out of farming." "Free markets" inevitably forced commodity prices down below the cost of production. While American exporters had captured larger and larger shares of world markets, American farmers had become increasingly dependent on deficiency payments whenever there was a

---

Agenda for the Future, ed. M. Ann Tutwiler (Washington, D.C.: National Center for Food and Agricultural Policy, 1988), 26.

[24] Dyson, *Farmers' Organizations,* 13.

[25] As head of the Agribusiness Accountability Project, founded in 1970, Hightower had with Susan DeMarco published *Hard Tomatoes, Hard Times* (Cambridge, Mass.: Schenkman Publishing, 1973); Browne, *Private Interests,* 130–31, 136–37, 139–40; William Pratt cites an estimate of 100 to 150 new farm groups in the first half-decade of the 1980s in Keith Schneider, "Farm Groups Seen Affecting 1986 Elections," *New York Times,* January 5, 1986; Pratt, "Using History to Make History?" 25, 30–36.

[26] Browne, *Private Interests,* 222–25; Browne, *Challenging Industrialization,* 15; Mark Lundgren, "National Family Farm Coalition," in Browne and Cigler, *U.S. Agricultural Groups,* 163–67.

bumper crop or world demand dropped for any reason. Such subsidies amounted to a massive gift from the taxpayers to grain traders, corporate feedlots, and foreign buyers, who did not have to pay farmers the full costs of production. Price wars and wildly fluctuating markets were driving all but the biggest producers out of business.[27]

Just as policymakers in the days of the Dust Bowl had turned increasingly to the issue of soil conservation to justify the New Deal farm programs, so the farm organizers of the 1980s spoke again and again to the grave environmental consequences of high-production/low-price agriculture. Low prices meant that farmers could only hope to make a profit by squeezing every bushel of grain out of their land. They were driven to employing farming methods that destroyed topsoil, dried up the water table, and poisoned rivers, streams, lakes, and wells. If properly implemented, production controls could serve to maintain higher commodity prices and a decent standard of living, while promoting farming techniques that preserved the earth's resources. Such arguments both promoted and reflected new alliances, where before there had often been mutual suspicion and hostility. At the movement's Farmers' and Ranchers' Congress in St. Louis in 1986, for example, owners of multimillion-dollar corn and soybeans operations listened patiently to speeches about the virtues of organic farming.[28]

At the opening session of the World Food Assembly in Rome in 1984, Mark Ritchie pointed to the connection between world hunger and the falling commodity prices that were driving Third World farmers off their land into overcrowded cities with rising unemployment rates.[29] With regard to world trade talks, the leaders of the family farm movement, like many representatives of the European Community, argued for negotiated trade agreements that respected individual nations' commitments to maintaining farmers on their land. They urged that as a "price maker" supplying 60 percent of the world's feed grains and 40 percent of its wheat, the United States could and should act to stabilize world markets.[30]

In short, the political movement that responded to widespread farm bankruptcies in the United States in the 1980s had a program that called for a more planned agricultural economy, a more environmentally sound agri-

[27] Ritchie and Ristau, "Crisis by Design."

[28] I owe this last observation to Jim Ridgeway; Toxic Action Project, Citizens Action Coalition, National Campaign Against Toxic Hazards, *Pesticide Use and Chemical Dependency: The Need for Comprehensive FIFRA Reform and Agricultural Economic Restructuring* (n.d.[1987?]); "Agriculture and the Environment," handout from Mark Ritchie (n.d. [1987?]); both in the possession of the author.

[29] League of Rural Voters pamphlet, *U.S. Farm Policy and World Hunger: The Deadly Connection* (1985); Mark Ritchie, "Disappearance of Family Farm Agriculture in the U.S.: Implications for World Hunger," presentation to the opening plenary of the World Food Assembly, Rome, November 12, 1984, in the possession of the author.

[30] Michel Petit et al, "International Agricultural Negotiations: The United States and the European Community Square Off," in *U.S. Agriculture in a Global Setting*, ed. M. Ann Tutwiler

culture, and an end to trade wars. As surprising as its substance was the bold-ness with which family farm movement activists fought for this program within the mainstream of American politics. Both old and young, farmers and peace-and-justice activists seemed to draw a sense of power and re-sponsibility as well as urgency from their participation in a mass movement of men and women who were fighting both for their own survival and for a better world. A clear determination to produce real-world results inspired wide-ranging and imaginative efforts to influence public opinion, make new allies, and influence election campaigns and debates in Congress.

Out-Organizing the Right Wing

Catherine McNicol Stock has written persuasively about rural Americans' at-traction to extremist movements that combine a populist rage against elites with various forms of violent racism and anti-Semitism, patriarchal religi-osity, and intense anticommunism. She notes, for example, that in the 1980s, Posse Comitatus, the Aryan Nation, the Order, Christian Identity, and Lyndon LaRouche affiliates all made bankrupt farmers a target of their or-ganizing efforts. She cites the fact that "even the peace-and-justice activists of the Iowa Family Farm Coalition tried to work with right-wing groups" as telling evidence of the resonance of their appeals in farm communities.[31]

Stock is undoubtedly right about the dark side of agrarian politics. There is, however, no evidence that attraction to such ideologies is limited to the American countryside. Racist, patriarchal, and anticommunist appeals have emanated from our nation's capital as well as its frontiers; from its labor, re-ligious, intellectual, and, with some variation, even its women's movements, as well as those among farmers.[32]

Indeed, what makes farm politics in the 1980s so remarkable is not the fact that right-wing groups were trying to organize in rural communities, but that their efforts were so relatively unsuccessful. After interviewing hun-dreds of informants over more than a decade, political scientist William Browne concluded that despite the efforts of groups like Posse Comitatus

(Washington, D.C.: National Center for Food and Agriculture Policy, 1988), 93–94; Mark Ritchie, "U.S. Farm Politics and the Common Agricultural Policy," *Le Monde Diplomatique*, May 1987, 9; Harkin, "The Save the Family Farm Act," 393; Ritchie and Ristau, "Politics and Farm Policy: New Directions for the Democratic Party," 14.

[31] Catherine McNicol Stock, *Rural Radicals: Righteous Rage in the American Grain* (Ithaca: Cornell University Press, 1996), 162–63, 171–74, and passim; Jim Ridgeway, "Heartland Heartbreak"; Fact-Finding Department of the Civil Rights Division of the Anti-Defamation League of B'nai B'rith, *The American Farmer and the Extremists, An ADL Special Report* (New York, 1986), pamphlet in the possession of the author; Browne, "Challenging Industrialization," 14–15; Pratt, "Using History to Make History?" 27; Bethany Moreton, "Native Stock: The Agrarian Strain in the Radical Right," seminar paper, 1999, in the possession of the author.

[32] Rogers M. Smith, *Civic Ideals: Conflicting Visions of Citizenship in U.S. History* (New Haven, Conn.: Yale University Press, 1997).

to take advantage of the disintegration of AAM in the early 1980s, "leftists rather than right wingers went on to set the public-policy reform agenda of farm protest."[33] It was, after all, the family farm movement—not the Order, nor for that matter, even the Farm Bureau—that was organizing the mass demonstrations and coalitions, and setting the terms of the debates over farm policy in the 1980s. It may well have been members of Posse Comitatus who brought resolutions to abolish the Federal Reserve to the Farmers' and Ranchers' Congress in St. Louis in 1986, for example, but it was family farm movement activists who initiated the call and did the organizing that made this congress a significant event. And it was these progressive organizers who took the lead in arguing against and fairly easily defeating such resolutions.[34] What the outreach efforts of the family farm movement suggest, then, is that the countryside was in fact one of the few places in the 1980s where progressive activists seriously engaged and combated right-wing ideologies.

In short, the politics of the farm crisis of the 1980's presents several puzzling questions. Given what most scholars think they know about the American people's—especially farmers'—hatred of big government, why *wasn't* something like the demand of the Posse Comitatus to abolish the Federal Reserve the galvanizing response to the farm crisis? How was it that the biggest, best-organized grass-roots movement had a program calling for production controls, a more environmentally sound agriculture, and negotiated trade agreements aimed at upholding every nation's right to protect its farmers' security on the land? How could the family farm movement have had such an impact in a period that was certainly not known for its receptivity to left/liberal ideas and organizers?

As with any puzzle, these pieces are easier to put together when you can see the picture of which they are a part. The bigger picture that helps to explain both the program and the vibrant organizing efforts of the family farm movement is a strong tradition of agrarian state building: a tradition with roots that run from the Granger and Populist agitation of the nineteenth century, through the programs of the New Deal Agriculture Department, into what to most observers has become the increasingly arcane world of farm politics in the postwar period. The strength of the family farm movement activists lay in their ability to tap ideas, memories, even the conspiracy theories associated with years of farmers' organizing efforts with a program that also provided the foundations for broader coalitions. Accordingly, this essay will turn now to explore some of the historical evidence for this tradition, as well as some of the events—and the scholarship—that have obscured its vitality in recent decades.

[33] Browne, *Challenging Industrialization*, 15.
[34] I remember one young organizer as somewhat bemused at finding himself in the position of defending the Federal Reserve: "What am I supposed to say?...Viva Volcker?"

MARY SUMMERS

Making the Invisible Visible:
Notes toward a Theory of Agrarian State Building

Despite the fact that many New Dealers eagerly credited generations of agrarian protesters with laying the foundations for the nation's farm programs, the idea of populists as state builders has largely disappeared from postwar historiography.[35] In his recent survey of the impact of "the populist persuasion" on American politics, for example, Michael Kazin treats populism only as a vocabulary that appeals to popular hatred of elites. Our national historical forgetting of agrarian movements' platforms and efforts at institution building has both reflected and facilitated the efforts of right-wing ideologues, like Pat Buchanan, to identify with the Jeffersonian yeoman as a primal link between their contemporary attacks on "big government" and the farmers' movements of the past. A persistent image of true farmers' politics as resentful resistance to state authority has provided militia groups with an aura of populist authenticity while rendering the political program and accomplishments of the family farm movement virtually invisible.[36]

In fact, generations of rural people have fought for an American state that would enhance their ability to make a living from the land. Farmers' as well as free soil/free labor agitation for "peoples' universities" and a "farmer's department" resulted in the founding of the Department of Agriculture and land-grant funding for state colleges after the South left the Union in 1862. After the war the Grangers, Greenbackers, Farmers' Alliances, and Populists fought for a state that would abolish economic monopolies and ensure that farm families benefited as much from the great changes of the new age as railway men, industrialists, and Wall Street. The Populists advocated the nationalization of the railroads; their subtreasury plan was a proposal for a powerful new federal institution to meet the financial needs of farmers who had to borrow seed and fertilizer money in the spring and sell their products in the fall.[37]

Any effort to establish some connections between nineteenth- and twentieth-century agrarian politics and state building must, however, account for the dichotomy between the two in so much postwar scholarship. Schol-

---

[35] M. L. Wilson, *Democracy Has Roots* (New York: Carrick & Evans, 1939); Henry C. and Anne Dewees Taylor, *The Story of Agricultural Economics in the United States, 1840–1932* (Ames: Iowa State College Press, 1952), 3–28 and passim; Carl Taylor, *The Farmers' Movement 1620–1920* (New York: American Book Company, 1953); John D. Hicks, *The Populist Revolt* (1931; reprint ed., Lincoln: University of Nebraska Press, 1959), 404–23 and passim; Theodore Saloutos and John D. Hicks, *Twentieth-Century Populism* (Lincoln: University of Nebraska Press, 1951). For an exceptional contemporary study of the Populists' legacy in the progressive expansion of the American state, see Elizabeth Sanders, *The Roots of Reform: Farmers, Workers, and the State, 1877–1917* (Chicago: University of Chicago Press, 1999).

[36] Michael Kazin, *The Populist Persuasion: An American History* (New York: Basic Books, 1995).

[37] Summers, "Conflicting Visions."

318

ars like the political scientist Grant McConnell and the historian Lawrence Goodwyn taught us to treat the Populists' organizing efforts with respect as critical challenges to the developing hegemony of industrial capital. They also, however, taught us to dismiss as instances of a co-opted interest group politics the long history of twentieth-century farm organizations' efforts to organize cooperatives and fight for state agricultural institutions that would better serve farm families' needs.[38] Any effort to reconnect twentieth-century agricultural politics to the mass movements of the nineteenth century raises, then, the question of whether we can see any ongoing challenges to the goals and values of corporate capitalism.

A keenly critical view of the New Deal Agriculture Department as having turned over the making of agricultural policy to selfish commercial farmers at the expense of consumers, the rural poor, and the public treasury lies at the heart of many postwar scholars' conceptions of a co-opted twentieth-century farm politics. The main legacy of the New Deal Agriculture Department is, in such accounts, the development of agribusiness.[39]

Such interpretations, however, obscure the political base and the institutional history that made the New Deal's significant reform efforts possible: the Farm Security Administration's (FSA) programs for the rural poor, for example, and the grassroots planning programs of the Bureau of Agricultural Economics (BAE), focused on making full employment, land use planning, and good nutrition for all Americans the broader goals of the nation's farm programs. Spurred to confront some of the limitations and contradictions in the department's programs in part by contemporary farmers', farmworkers', and sharecroppers' organizing efforts and in part by their own political and intellectual agendas, the leaders of these agencies both built on the Agriculture Department's heritage and brought to a head many of the underlying conflicts of race and class that had often been ignored or overridden in earlier drives for "equality for agriculture."[40]

[38] McConnell, *Decline of Agrarian Democracy;* Lawrence Goodwyn, *The Democratic Promise* (New York: Oxford University Press, 1976).

[39] Grant McConnell, *The Decline of Agrarian Democracy* (Berkeley: University of California Press, 1963); Grant McConnell, *Private Power and American Democracy* (New York: Alfred A. Knopf, 1968); Theodore Lowi, *The End of Liberalism,* 2d ed. (New York: W. W. Norton, 1979); Pete Daniel, *Breaking the Land* (Urbana: University of Illinois Press, 1985); William A. Galston, *A Tough Row to Hoe: The 1985 Farm Bill and Beyond* (Washington, D.C.: Hamilton Press, 1985); Catherine McNicol Stock, *Main Street in Crisis: The Great Depression and the Old Middle Class on the Northern Plains* (Chapel Hill: University of North Carolina Press, 1992); Roger Biles, *The South and the New Deal* (Lexington: University Press of Kentucky, 1994); Mary Neth, *Preserving the Family Farm: Women, Community, and the Foundations of Agribusiness in the Midwest, 1900–1940* (Baltimore: Johns Hopkins University Press, 1995); Victoria Saker Woeste, *The Farmer's Benevolent Trust: Law and Agricultural Cooperation in Industrial America, 1865–1945* (Chapel Hill: University of North Carolina Press, 1998); Don Paarlberg and Robert Paarlberg, "Agricultural Policy in the Twentieth Century," *Agricultural History* 74 (spring 2000): 136–61.

[40] Sidney Baldwin, *Poverty and Politics: The Rise and Decline of the Farm Security Administration* (Chapel Hill: University Press of North Carolina, 1968); Donald Holley, *Uncle Sam's Farmers:*

Much of the leadership of the American Farm Bureau Federation, for example, whose own organization had in large part been built by the Extension Service's programs to promote the education, mobilization, and economic well-being of farmers, went on the offensive against efforts to extend similar services to sharecroppers and farmworkers. Cotton planters, organized into the newly forged Cotton Council, were outraged by what they correctly perceived as the desire of many of the leaders of the FSA and the BAE to dismantle the structures of racial and economic exploitation associated with plantation agriculture. Working in alliance with southern and western conservative congressmen, these groups used the annual hearings of the House Agricultural Appropriations Committee in the mid-1940's to accuse these agencies of such crimes as paying clients' poll taxes, allying with the CIO, the NAACP, and consumers, and insisting that imported Mexican labor be paid a minimum of thirty cents an hour. In the context of this relentless attack, the Truman administration finally agreed to abolish the FSA and to stop most of the BAE's sociological research in 1946; its economists were to be confined to statistical and fact-finding work, aimed only at improving the accuracy of crop and livestock reports.[41]

Jamie Whitten, a Mississippi congressman and cotton planter who helped to lead the attacks on the BAE in 1946, became chairman of the House Agricultural Appropriations subcommittee in 1949; he remained in this position for more than forty years until 1994 (excepting only the few years of Republican control of the House in the mid-1950s). Whitten used the power of the purse to act, according to the *Almanac of American Politics,* as "a kind of permanent Secretary of Agriculture." It was Whitten and his allies, not the leaders of the New Deal Agriculture Department but their triumphant opponents, who institutionalized the narrowly framed, conservative, class-based politics that came to define what we now think of as agricultural interest group politics.[42]

The New Deal Communities in the Lower Mississippi Valley (Urbana: University of Illinois Press, 1975); Richard Kirkendall, *Social Scientists and Farm Politics in the Age of Roosevelt* (1966; reprint ed., Ames: Iowa State University Press, 1982); Jess Gilbert, "Democratic Planning in Agricultural Policy: The Federal-County Land-Use Planning Program, 1938–1942," *Agricultural History* 70 (spring 1996): 233–50; Jess Gilbert, "Eastern Urban Liberals and Midwestern Agrarian Intellectuals: Two Group Portraits in the New Deal Department of Agriculture," *Agricultural History* (spring 2000): 162–80; Mary Summers, "The New Deal Farm Programs: Looking for Reconstruction in American Agriculture," *Agricultural History* (spring 2000): 241–71.

[41] Christiana Campbell, *The Farm Bureau and the New Deal* (Urbana: University of Illinois Press, 1962); Baldwin, *Poverty and Politics,* 350–51; Kirkendall, *Social Scientists and Farm Politics,* 195–254; McConnell, *Decline of Agrarian Democracy,* 97–111.

[42] See USDA historian Wayne Rasmussen's reminiscences regarding Whitten's efforts to get the names of the "communist" Henry Wallace and BAE chief Henry Tolley removed from the centenary history of the department; Arnita A. Jones and Wayne D. Rasmussen, "Wayne Rasmussen and the Development of Policy History at the United States Department of Agriculture," *Public Historian* 14 (1992): 19–21.

After the Congressional Democratic Caucus began electing leadership positions by secret ballot in 1974, Whitten, a supremely astute politician, began to regularly lead fights against cutbacks in food stamps—a program that he had not previously supported. He also began to call himself a New Dealer because he favored programs that protected commercial farmers from drops in commodity prices and catastrophic crop failures. He supported soil conservation program payments to farmers at the same time that he ensured that environmentally costly cotton crops remained the most expensive of all federal subsidy programs, and published his own passionate defense of DDT in response to Rachel Carson's *Silent Spring*.[43]

Whitten's methods of operating, therefore, reinforced scholars' increasingly cynical views of programs like food stamps and soil conservation as pawns in a log-rolling game designed chiefly to preserve government handouts to agribusiness. As time went on, many conservative scholars embraced liberals' critiques of interest group politics as a means of attacking *any* efforts whatever to intervene in the economy; and policymakers were left with little but abstract notions of market efficiency as the sole principle on which to construct any conception of the public welfare.[44]

Whitten's and his fellow conservatives' successful attacks on the New Deal Agriculture Department's commitments to broader goals and constituencies pushed liberal farm groups, however, in quite a different direction. The leadership of the Farmers' Union, for example, had supported the BAE's proposals for the Cotton South and the Truman administration's Brannan plan, both of which would have allowed commodity prices to fall, while guaranteeing farmers' incomes in the context of broader efforts to promote mass consumption and expand international trade: strategies that the leaders of the New Deal Department regarded as a *means* of guaranteeing a full-employment economy and a better, more stable living on the land. In the wake of the defeat of these programs, however, policymakers increasingly pursued such strategies as ends in themselves, divorced from any commitment to meeting the needs of farmers and workers, much less the rural and urban poor.[45] In this context, it became increasingly difficult

[43] Whitten's *New York Times* obituary described his book, *That We May Live*, as "conceived and subsidized by pesticide industry officials," defending pesticides generally as "an absolute necessity to our way of life." Jamie L. Whitten, *That We May Live* (Princeton, N.J.: D. Van Nostrand, 1966); David Binder, "Jamie Whitten, Who Served 53 Years in House, Dies at 85," *New York Times*, September 11, 1995, D13. Michael Barone and Grant Ujifusa, *The Almanac of American Politics 1988* (Washington, D.C.: National Journal, 1987), 652–53.

[44] Michael Crozier et al., *The Crisis of Democracy: Report on the Governability of Democracies to the Trilateral Commission* (New York: New York University Press, 1975); Mancur Olson, *The Rise and Decline of Nations* (New Haven, Conn.: Yale University Press, 1982); James T. Bennett and Thomas J. DiLorenzo, *Destroying Democracy* (Washington, D.C.: Cato Institute, 1985).

[45] Kirkendall, *Social Scientists and Farm Policy*, 252–53; Virgil W. Dean, "Why Not the Brannan Plan?" *Agricultural History* 70 (spring 1996): 268–82; Alan Brinkley, *The End of Reform: New Deal Liberalism in Recession and War* (New York: Alfred A Knopf, 1995). Brinkley seems to blame the liberals for most of the consequences of their lost battles.

for progressive farm organizers to conceive of an American state capable of guaranteeing farmers a fair return for their labor by any means other than maintaining commodity prices.[46] The final result of these trajectories was what we saw in the 1980s: an increasingly sharp division between farm experts and protest groups. Few scholars even seemed to recognize that it was the policy prescriptions of economists under Roosevelt and Kennedy that had become a cry from the grass roots under Reagan and Bush.

In large part what the family farm movement sought to resurrect was not the more far-reaching goals of the Farm Security Administration and the BAE, but the more makeshift, jerry-rigged commitments of the Agricultural Adjustment Acts to a more economically and environmentally sustainable commercial agriculture: the subject of so many subsequent attacks from both the Left and the Right. As we have seen, the family farm movements' efforts succeeded in once again forging some connections between the concerns of environmentalists and farm groups. The argument here is that their example also suggests the need for a more complex, more dialectical view of the historical roots and future possibilities of American agricultural politics.

With all its conflicts and shortcomings, the New Deal Agriculture Department represents the most significant outcome of the nation's long history of agrarian state building. Like all other large-scale attempts to use the state to address vast social problems, it has been the subject of passionate critiques made both by participants and by subsequent historians. Its programs frequently demonstrated the race, class, and gender prejudices of many reformers; they involved many compromises with powerful forces of opposition. Far too often, however, critiques of these programs' failures to do enough were co-opted into arguments that they should never have been undertaken in the first place.

The New Dealers made many mistakes; but the ferocious opposition they encountered was far more for what they did right. Blaming the New Deal Agriculture Department for the flourishing of agribusiness comes close to blaming the authors of Reconstruction for the imposition of Jim Crow. It leaves us without the tools and understanding with which to address the consequences of the reformers' defeat.

In order to understand the contribution of agrarian perspectives to the conflicted ideological heritage of the American state, it is crucially important not to read history backward. The scholar who looks only for the an-

---

[46] Richard Levins has developed a sympathetic but sharp critique of farm liberals' failure in putting forward such policy proposals to recognize the increasing power and profits of the agribusinesses that supply farm inputs. Higher commodity prices only increase farmers' gross intake, *not their net incomes;* thus, without a far-reaching restructuring of farm production methods, the profits from higher commodity prices are more likely to be captured by Monsanto, Novartis, and ConAgra than by farm families. Levins, *Willard Cochrane and the Family Farm;* Levins, "The Food System: A Holistic Policy Approach," http://agecon.lib.umn.edu/mn.html.

tecedents of the worst features of our contemporary landscapes disempowers the heirs of generations of agitators and reformers with the idea that every earlier step in agricultural state development, science, and technology was imposed by elites and inevitably led toward agribusiness-dominated monocropping and the industrialization of American agriculture. If we choose instead to explore reformers' often conflicting visions for agricultural labor, families, and communities, we may well uncover potential groundwork for the construction of more humane and environmentally sound systems of agricultural production.

For scholars like Grant McConnell and Theodore Lowi, the national Farm Bureau's political influence in the 1940s and 1950s became proof of the inherent evils of "interest group liberalism." The example of the family farm movement suggests, however, that America's farm programs have been constructed and reconstructed in political battles *that have not yet ended.* There have been farm groups, academics and professionals, politicians and bureaucrats on both sides of every important conflict about whom these programs should serve and how. The victors in the battles of the 1940s succeeded in making institutional changes with immense consequences. But if scholars today allow their victories to erase the ideas, the organizing efforts, and the achievements of their opponents from the historical record, we will lose sight of political dynamics that may yet again transform American agriculture: the programmatic, political, personal, and intellectual ties, for example, that link at least some New Deal agrarians backward to farmers' struggles in the nineteenth century, and forward to the civil rights movement of the 1960s, the family farm movement of the 1980s, the black land loss movement of the 1990s, and the movement against economic globalization that has ushered in the new millennium.[47]

Memory and Defeat; Forgetting and Survival

The family farm movement proved that it was possible—even in the 1980s—to organize a serious challenge to the status quo. Its leaders succeeded in out-organizing right-wingers, established farm groups, and ex-

[47] Lester M. Salamon, "The Time Dimension in Policy Evaluation: The Case of the New Deal Land-Reform Experiments," *Public Policy* 27 (1979): 129–83. I am grateful to Richard Valelly for this reference and to Jess Gilbert, who introduced me to Gary Grant, one of the leaders of the contemporary black land loss movement, who embodies some of these intergenerational dynamics. Grant's parents were founding members of the New Deal Resettlement community in Tillery, North Carolina, where his mother succeeded in registering to vote. As a teenager, Grant participated with other Tillery community members in the civil rights movements. As the director of Concerned Citizens of Tillery, Grant leads efforts to restore the New Deal community and resurrect its history, as well as ongoing local and statewide protests against the environmental consequences of giant hog farms. Conversations with Gary

perts and academics, in part because they mobilized desperate farmers around an analysis and a program that spoke to deeply felt historical understandings of their problems. Equally important, however, their vision of a more economically and environmentally sustainable agriculture provided the basis for building the broader coalitions critical to any reconstruction of the nation's farm programs. Their organizing efforts, therefore, not only evoked the struggles of the past, but offered farmers and their allies some real hope for the future. If left-progressives had organized as successfully—and fought right-wingers as directly—in the nation's cities, suburbs, churches, and media, as they did among bankrupt farmers in the 1980s, the nation's politics would have looked very different indeed.

The family farm movement's breadth and impact does not, however, argue for any easy optimism about the future possibilities for American politics. Despite their success in shaping broader debates and the 1985 farm bill, the movement's organizers ultimately failed in their efforts to establish a farm program that would ensure greater security on the land. When commodity prices began to briefly rise again, the movement's leaders found it increasingly difficult to sustain their organizing efforts. When no longer faced by a mobilized opposition, Newt Gingrich and his Republican revolution succeeded in enacting the experts' dream of dismantling many of the nation's farm programs with the passage of the 1996 "Freedom to Farm" Act. The result for many farmers in recent years has been disastrous. "Hog and corn prices go down and down and down," Mark Ritchie wrote me in February, 1999. "In relative terms, things in the countryside are worse than they were in 1985, but the organizing is very different...."[48]

It now seems that February 1999 may have represented the darkness before the dawn of many resurgent organizing efforts. Ritchie and other organizers of the family farm movement succeeded in keeping alive elements of their coalitions in the increasingly volatile politics of trade. A 1992 *Wall Street Journal* article, for example, credited Ritchie in his role as president of the Minneapolis-based Institute for Agriculture and Trade Policy (IATP) with playing a key role in bringing farm, environmental, and labor activists together in a campaign against NAFTA. The opening speaker at a 1996 forum at Columbia University called Ritchie "the Paul Revere" of a developing movement against the economic and environmental consequences of globalization: a movement that burst into national and international consciousness with the demonstrations against the World Trade Organization in Seattle in November, 1999. Going into the new millennium, the Institute

Grant; Black Farmers & Agriculturists Association: http://www.coax.net/people/lwf/bfaa pp.htm. For links between the family farm movement and the movement against globalization, see the IATP Web site: http://www.iatp.org.

[48] Correspondence, February 4, 1999, in the possession of the author.

for Agriculture and Trade Policy has a million-dollar budget and is working hard with many different allies to dramatize the arguments and mobilize the coalitions that oppose an increasingly monopolized, industrialized agriculture around the world. Independent stock farmers, anti–factory farm and community food activists, environmentalists, antitrust lawyers, and academics have joined projects sponsored by such groups as IATP and the Organization for Competitive Markets as well as state-sponsored task forces on agriculture in Iowa and Nebraska to attack such targets as giant hog farms, chicken factories, concentrated animal feeding operations, the widespread adoption of genetically modified crops, the sharp escalation in contract farming, and the mergers and consolidation in the agribusinesses that supply farm inputs and market farm products.[49]

It is possible, then, that organizers like Mark Ritchie will succeed in inspiring new groups and movements with the commitment of older generations of agrarian state builders to the construction of political economies that served their understanding of the broader needs, goals, and values of their constituents. The fate of the New Dealers' efforts to build a farmer/labor alliance capable of winning national commitments to full employment and healthy diets for all Americans reminds us, however, that some battles have been lost for as far as we can now see. It is quite possible that within the next ten years, the idea of state policies with a goal of keeping farmers on the land will seem as remote and unreal as does, today, the idea that every American has the right to a decent job.

Whether or not the family farm movement of the 1980s represented the last gasp of the agrarian state-building tradition, or a step toward the development of broader movements against the impact of economic globalization on human welfare and the environment, remains to be seen. The future will depend in part on whether we raise up scholars who help us to remember past dreams and visions, as well as leaders and organizers who seek to build on them.

---

[49] Pratt, "Using History to Make History?" 45; *Wall Street Journal*, December 23, 1992, 1; Jay Walljaper, "The Price of Thinking Globally," *Minneapolis Star Tribune*, November 30, 1995; Institute for Agriculture and Trade Policy, *1998–1999 Annual Report* (Minneapolis, 1999). For examples of the arguments made by the coalitions in which IATP participates, see the series of full-page ads in the *New York Times* on "Industrial Agriculture," sponsored by the Turning Point Project, 2000: www.turnpoint.org; http://www.iatp.org; www.competitivemarkets.com. For some of the political strategies suggested by this new movement's attention to the vastly increasing power of agribusiness, see Levins, "The Food System: A Holistic Policy Approach," 10–13.

Notes on Contributors

ANNIE GILBERT COLEMAN is Assistant Professor of History at Indiana University—Purdue University at Indianapolis. She has written "The Unbearable Whiteness of Skiing" in the *Pacific Historical Review* (1996) and is working on her first book, a cultural and environmental history of the Colorado ski industry.

DEBORAH FITZGERALD is Associate Professor of the History of Technology in MIT's Program in Science, Technology, and Society. She is the author of *The Business of Breeding: Hybrid Corn in Illinois, 1890–1940* (1990) and *Yeomen No More: The Industrialization of American Agriculture* (in press). She is currently working on the Green Revolution.

JESS GILBERT is a Professor of Rural Sociology at the University of Wisconsin, Madison. He is also Codirector of the new Center for Minority Land and Community Security, which is based at Tuskegee University in Alabama. Gilbert has published many articles on U.S. land tenure, family versus industrial farming, and agricultural policy, and he is currently writing a book on democratic planning and the agrarian intellectuals in the U.S. Department of Agriculture during the late New Deal.

CINDY HAHAMOVITCH is Associate Professor of History at the College of William & Mary and one of the founders of the Tidewater Labor Support Coalition in Williamsburg, Virginia. She is the author of *The Fruits of Their Labor: Atlantic Coast Farmworkers and the Making of Migrant Poverty, 1870–1945* (1997). She is studying the history of guest workers and is writing a book about Jamaican workers and the H2 program.

KARL JACOBY is Assistant Professor of History at Brown University and the author of *Crimes Against Nature: Squatters, Poachers, Thieves, and the Hidden History of American Conservation* (2001).

KATHERINE JELLISON is Associate Professor of History at Ohio University and the author of *Entitled to Power: Farm Women and Technology, 1913–1963* (1993). She is working on a book about the commercialization of American weddings.

BENJAMIN HEBER JOHNSON is Assistant Professor of History at the University of Texas at San Antonio. His dissertation, "Sedition and Citizenship in South Texas, 1900–1930," won Yale University's Beinecke Prize for the best dissertation in western American history. His writings on class conflict over environmentalism and graduate student unionization have appeared in *Environmental History, Social Policy,* and *Thought and Action.*

ROBERT D. JOHNSTON is Associate Professor of History and American Studies at Yale University. He received his bachelor's degree from Reed College and holds a doctorate from Rutgers. He is completing *The Radical Middle Class: Populist Democracy and the Question of Capitalism in Progressive Era Portland, Oregon,* and is co-editor, with Burton J. Bledstein, of *The Middling Sorts: Explorations in the History of the American Middle Class* (2001). He has also taught at Buena Vista College in Storm Lake, Iowa, where he was named 1994 Faculty Member of the Year after teaching courses on "The Family Farm in American History and Society" and "The History of the Midwest."

STEPHEN PITTI is Assistant Professor of History and American Studies at Yale University, where he teaches courses on Chicano and Latino history, Mexican immigration to the United States, and the twentieth-century American West. He has held Mellon and Ford Foundation Fellowships, as well as the President's Postdoctoral Fellowship at the University of California, San Diego. He is the author of a forthcoming book on the history of Mexicans and Mexican Americans in Silicon Valley.

DEBRA A. REID is Assistant Professor of History at Eastern Illinois University, Charleston, Illinois, upstate from her family's farm. She completed her Ph.D. in history at Texas A&M University, and her dissertation received the first Gilbert C. Fite Award, presented by the Agricultural History Society. Her publications include articles and book reviews in *Agricultural History, Rural History,* and, the *Bulletin of the Association for Living History, Farm and Agricultural Museums* (ALHFAM). She currently serves as the treasurer of the Rural

Women's Studies Association and as publications chair of ALHFAM, from which she received the 2000 John T. Schlebecker Award.

JOHANNA SCHOEN is Assistant Professor of History and Women's Studies at the University of Iowa. She is currently completing her book manuscript, "'A Great Thing for Poor Folks': Birth Control, Sterilization, and Abortion in Public Health and Welfare in the Twentieth Century."

JAMES C. SCOTT is the Sterling Professor of Political Science at Yale University. He is the Director of the Program in Agrarian Studies and a Southeast Asianist specializing in agrarian issues. Scott is the author of *The Moral Economy of the Peasant* (1976), *Weapons of the Weak; Everyday Forms of Peasant Resistance* (1985); *Domination and the Arts of Resistance* (1990); and *Seeing Like a State: How Certain Schemes to Improve the Human Condition Have Failed* (1998).

CATHERINE MCNICOL STOCK is Associate Professor of History and Director of the American Studies Program at Connecticut College. She received her B.A. and Ph.D. in American Studies from Yale University. She is the author of *Rural Radicals: Righteous Rage in the American Grain* (1996) and *Main Street in Crisis: The Great Depression and the Old Middle Class on the Northern Plains* (1992).

MARY SUMMERS is a Senior Lecturer in the University of Pennsylvania's Fox Leadership Program. She has worked for much of her life as a Physician Assistant. She has also been a speech writer, activist, graduate student in Political Science, and research fellow at Yale University. Her current projects include assisting in the development of an initiative on bioethics, food, and agriculture in the Agrarian Studies program at Yale, and preparing her dissertation, "Conflicting Visions: Farmers' Movements in the Making of the United States Department of Agriculture," for publication. She has published articles on farm politics in *Agricultural History*, on Jesse Jackson's 1984 presidential campaign in *The Nation*, and on John Daniels, the first African American mayor of New Haven, in *Urban Affairs Quarterly* and *PS: Political Science and Politics*.

ROBERT S. WEISE is Assistant Professor of History at Eastern Kentucky University, where he teaches American, southern, and Appalachian history. His book *Grasping at Independence: Debt, Male Authority, and Mineral Rights in Appalachian Kentucky, 1850–1915* was published in 2001. Currently, Weise is working on a study of the political economy of southern rural poverty in the twentieth century.

VICTORIA SAKER WOESTE is a Research Fellow at the American Bar Foundation in Chicago. She earned a B.A. from the University of Virginia and a Ph.D. from the University of California at Berkeley. She is the author of *The Farmer's Benevolent Trust: Law and Agricultural Cooperation in Industrial America, 1865–1945* (1998), which was awarded the 2000 J. Willard Hurst Prize by the Law and Society Association. Her current projects include a study of agriculture and anti-Semitism in the Henry Ford libel lawsuit of 1927 and a history of agriculture and antitrust since World War II.

Index

Federal Reserve System, 7
Federal Trade Commission, 7
Finegold, Kenneth, 213
Fish and Wildlife Service, 5
Ford, Jacob, 53
Fordism, 192, 194, 199–200, 208, 266
Ford Motor Company, 266–272
Forest and Stream magazine, 96–97,
    99–102
Freedom to Farm Act (1996), 1, 257
Friends of the Indian, 15

Galaraza, Ernesto, 161–185
Gamble, Clarence J., 113–114, 120–133
Game Protective Association, 109
Garden and Forest magazine, 92
Gender bias, 42, 45, 50–52, 54, 114–133
Globalization, x, 3, 11, 134–160, 304–325
Goodale, Elaine, 29
Good Neighbor Commission, 170
Good Neighbor policy, 165–166, 170, 177
Gordon, Linda, 123
Gray, L. C., 216–239
Great Depression, 67, 81–85, 138, 141,
    189–211, 240, 247–249, 258
Greenback Party, 21, 26–28, 318
Grinnell, George Bird, 99
Guestworker programs. *See* Bracero
    Program; H-2 program; Migrant labor

H-2 program, 136–138, 159–160
Hahn, Stephen, 36
Harkin, Tom, 304–309
Harris, J., 145, 150
Helping Hand, The, 48, 51
Hightower, Jim, 304
Hillard, Lena, 113, 126–129
Hofstadter, Richard, 36
Hollman Committee, 35
Homestead Act of 1862, 92
Hoover, Herbert, 203
Hough, Emerson, 99
Howell, Ed, 97–104
Hunter, Mary Evelyn V., 53–54
Hurt, R. Douglas, 17

Ideal farming methods, 197–199,
    201–202, 207–211
Immigrants, 66–68, 71, 81–88, 134–160,
    161–185
Immigration, 134–160, 161–185
    Jamaican, 138–160
    laws of, 134–160, 161–185
Immigration and Naturalization Service,
    152–154, 158–160, 183–185
Immigration Reform Act of 1986, 1

Indian assimilation, 17–21, 28–37
Indian policy, federal, 15–37
Indian Rights Association (IRA), 19,
    21–24, 28–34
Infant mortality, 117–119
Institute for Agriculture and Trade Policy,
    324–325
Internal Revenue Service (IRS), 5
International Monetary Fund (IMF), x
Interstate Commerce Commission, 7
Isaacs, Francis Isabela, 41, 50–51
Isaacs, William, 53

J. C. Penney–Gwinn Corporation Farms,
    202
Jamaican Democratic Party (JDP),
    142–144, 157
Jamaican Electives, 142
Jamaican immigration, 138–160
Jamaican Labor Party (JLP), 143–144, 157
Jefferson, Thomas, 17–18, 80, 139, 221,
    236, 245
Jim Crow laws, 43, 138, 150–154
Johnson Poultry Farm, 203

Kennedy, John F., 262–264
Kent, Alexander, 23
Kollmorgen, Walter M., 240–247,
    251, 256
Ku Klux Klan, 36

Labor, 161–185
Lacey Act of 1900, 110
Lake Mohonk Conference, 29–31
Land-grant colleges, 213
Langford, Nathaniel, 93
Lincoln, Abraham, 221, 236
Livingston Enterprise, 101–103, 109
Livingston Post, 100
Lynching, 47

MacDonald, Herbert, 145, 148, 152–156
MacLean, Nancy, 36
McCarren-Walter Act of 1952, 136
McDonald, Harry, 108
McGillycuddy, Valentine, 23–24
McNary-Haugen Bill, 192
McWilliams, Carey, 67, 71, 76, 165
Meacham, Alfred, 21
Mechanical agricultural labor, 190,
    207–211
Mexican labor, 140–141, 144, 161–185
Migrant labor, 66–67, 71, 81, 135–160,
    161–185, 202
Miller, Catherine, 72
Mitchell, H. L., 178